KODOCHA

SANA'S STAGE

KO NO
OMOCHA '94

I am
what
I am!

KODOCHA
SANA'S STAGE

Vol. 1

Written and Illustrated by Miho Obana
English Adaptation by Sarah Dyer

Los Angeles - Tokyo

Translator - Yukio Ichimura
Graphic Designers - Raseel El Djoundi and Monalisa J. de Asis
Production Specialist - Carol Conception
Editor - Paul Morrissey
Associate Editors - Robert Coyner, Trisha Kunimoto

Senior Editor - Jake Forbes
Production Manager - Fred Lui
Art Director - Matthew Alford
VP Production - Ron Klamert
Publisher - Stuart Levy

Email: editor@TOKYOPOP.com
Come visit us online at www.TOKYOPOP.com

A  book

TOKYOPOP® is an imprint of Mixx Entertainment, Inc.
5900 Wilshire Blvd. Ste 2000, Los Angeles, CA 90036

ISBN: 1-931514-50-X

First TOKYOPOP® printing: June 2002

10 9 8 7 6 5 4 3 2

Manufactured in Canada

KODOCHA
SANA'S STAGE

Vol. 1

CONTENTS

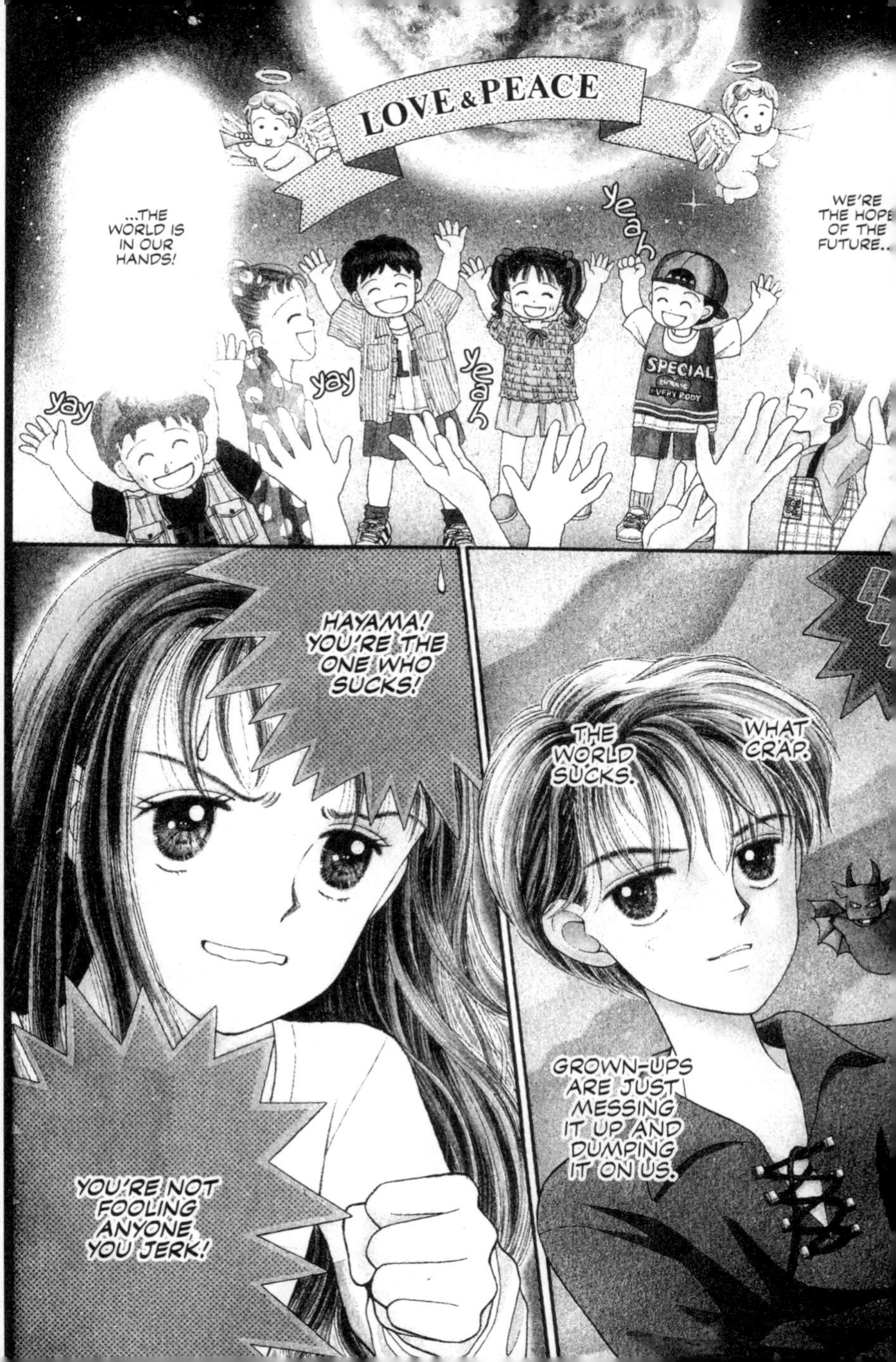
WE'RE THE HOPE OF THE FUTURE..
yeah
LOVE & PEACE
...THE WORLD IS IN OUR HANDS!
yeah
yay
yay
WHAT CRAP.
THE WORLD SUCKS.
GROWN-UPS ARE JUST MESSING IT UP AND DUMPING IT ON US.
HAYAMA! YOU'RE THE ONE WHO SUCKS!
YOU'RE NOT FOOLING ANYONE, YOU JERK!

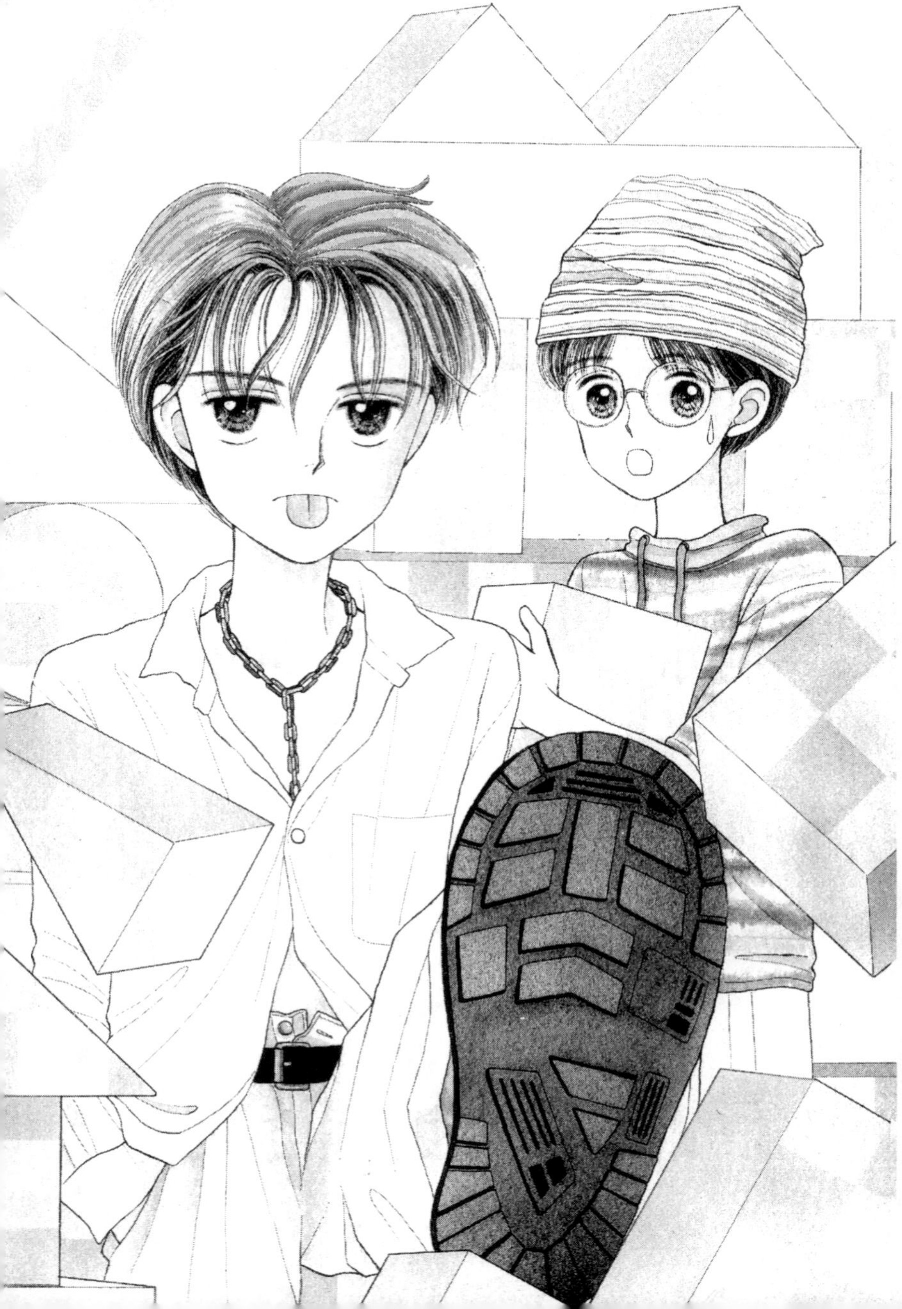

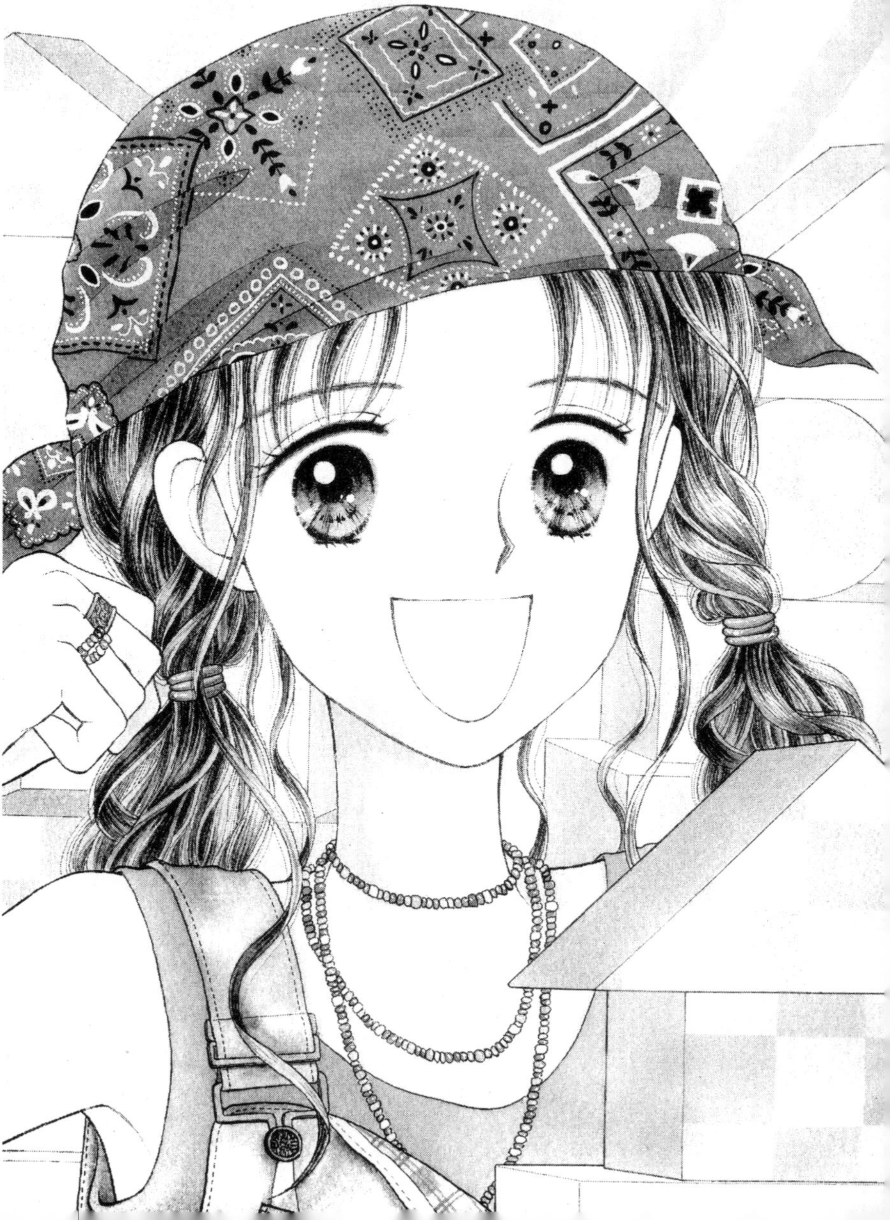

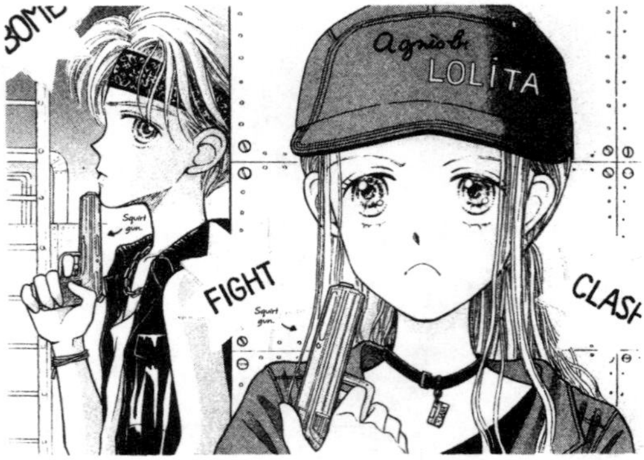
LOLITA
Squirt gun.
FIGHT
Squirt gun.

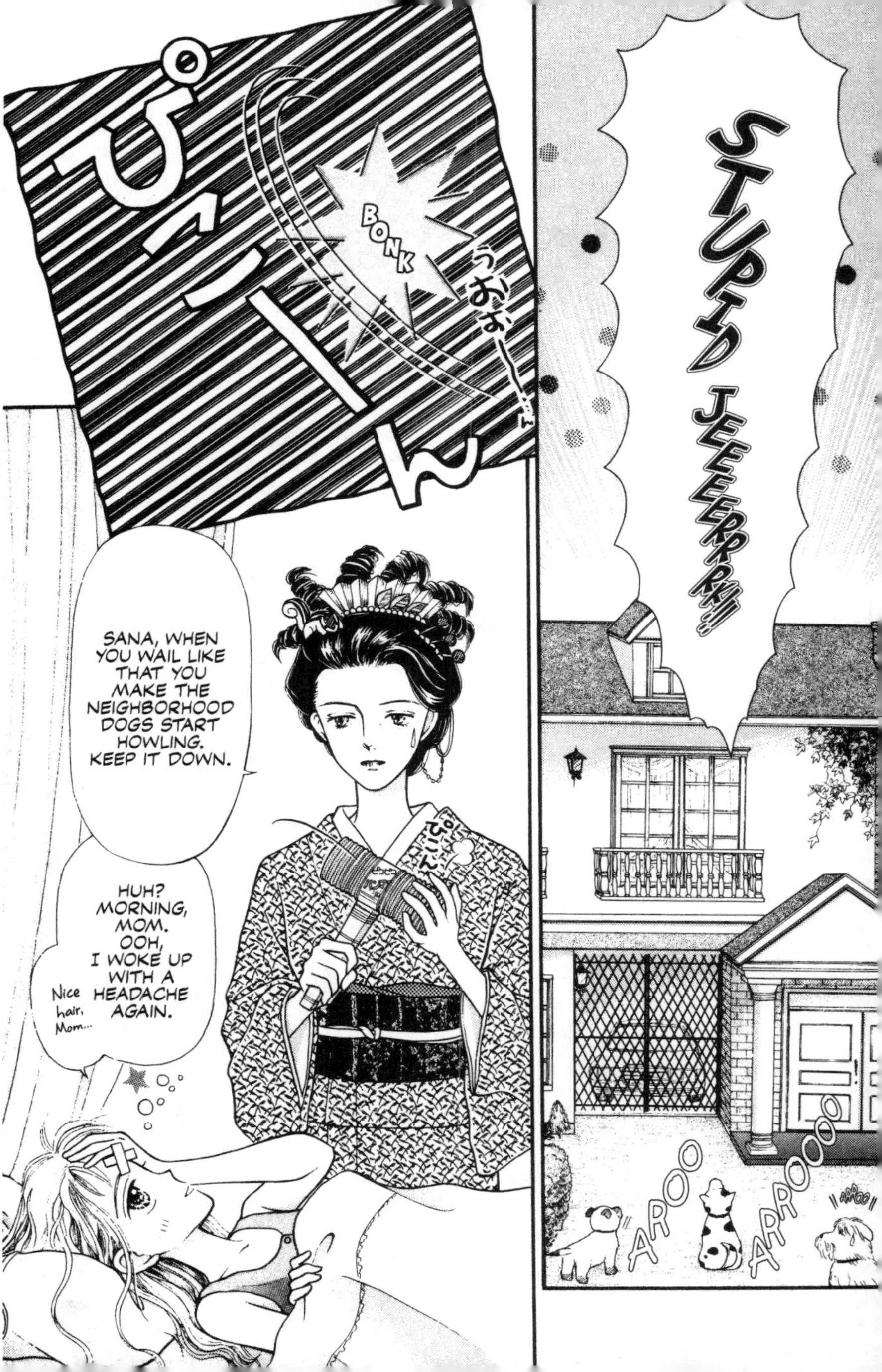
STUPID JEEEERRRK!!!
AROO
AROOOOO
ARROO
ぴこーん
BONK
うおぉ〜〜…ん
SANA, WHEN YOU WAIL LIKE THAT YOU MAKE THE NEIGHBORHOOD DOGS START HOWLING. KEEP IT DOWN.
ぴこん
HUH? MORNING, MOM. OOH, I WOKE UP WITH A HEADACHE AGAIN.
Nice hair, Mom...

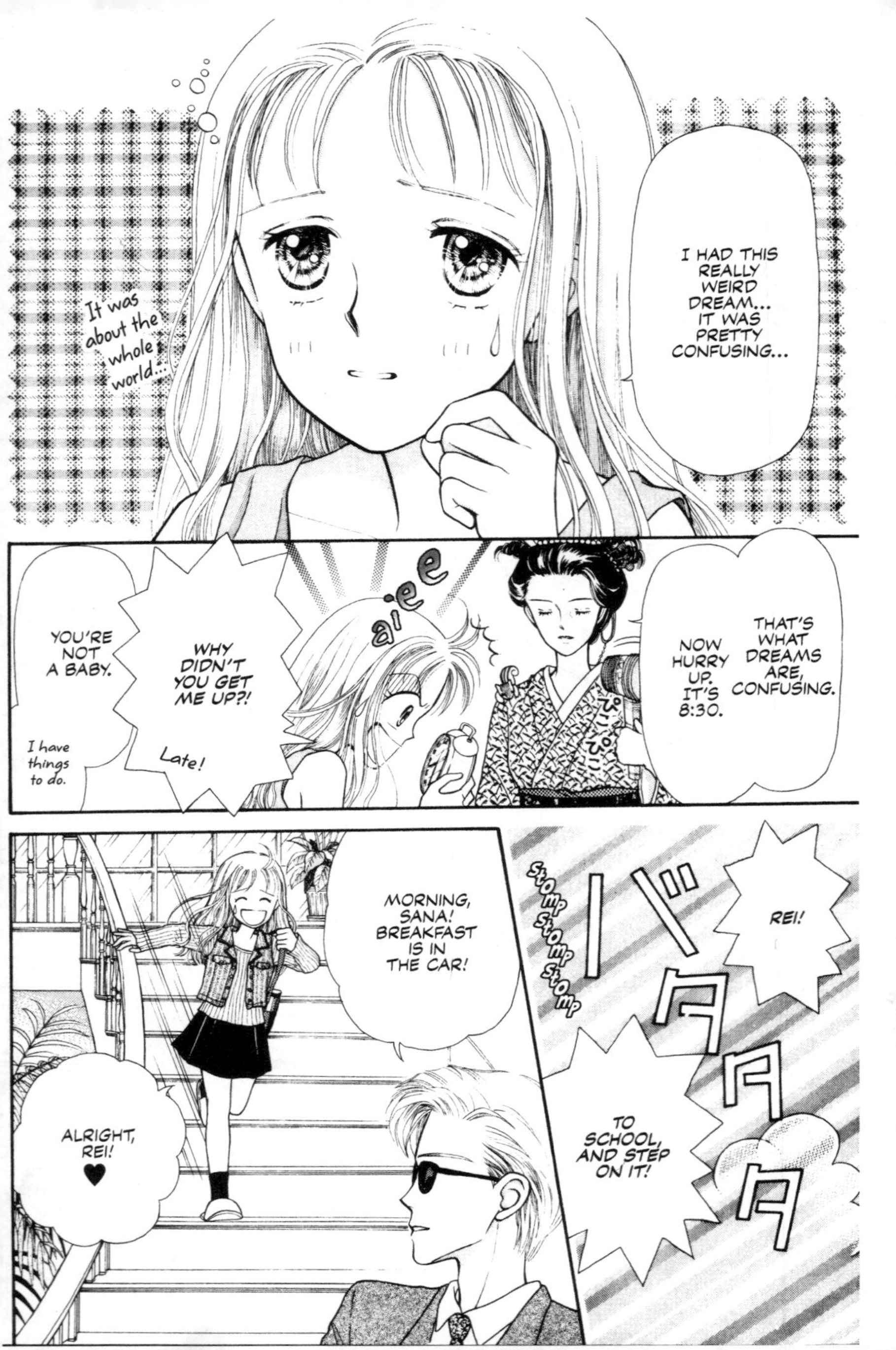
I HAD THIS REALLY WEIRD DREAM... IT WAS PRETTY CONFUSING...
It was about the whole world...
THAT'S WHAT DREAMS ARE, CONFUSING.
NOW HURRY UP. IT'S 8:30.
aiee
WHY DIDN'T YOU GET ME UP?!
Late!
YOU'RE NOT A BABY.
I have things to do.
REI!
Stomp Stomp Stomp
TO SCHOOL, AND STEP ON IT!
MORNING, SANA! BREAKFAST IS IN THE CAR!
ALRIGHT, REI! ♥

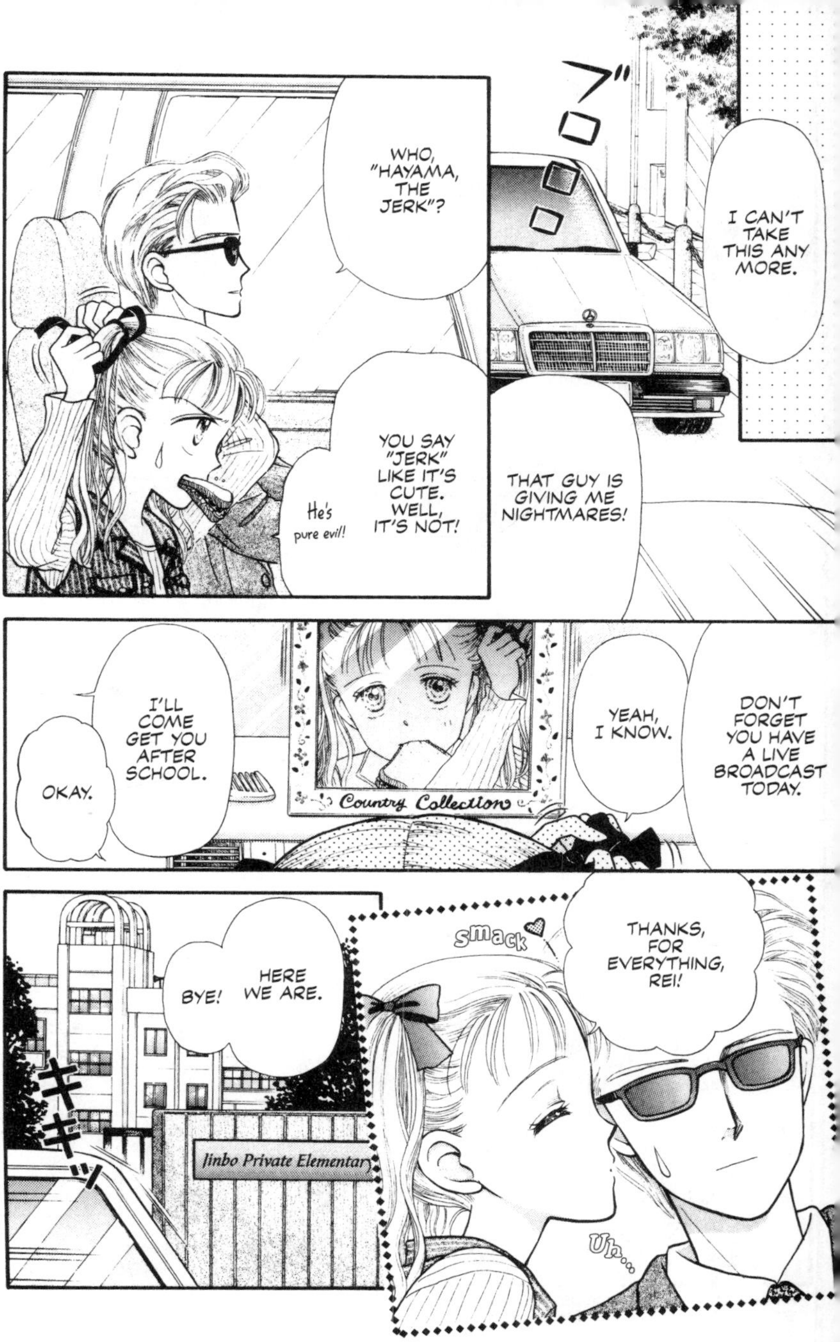
I CAN'T TAKE THIS ANY MORE.
ブロロ
THAT GUY IS GIVING ME NIGHTMARES!
WHO, "HAYAMA, THE JERK"?
YOU SAY "JERK" LIKE IT'S CUTE. WELL, IT'S NOT!
He's pure evil!
DON'T FORGET YOU HAVE A LIVE BROADCAST TODAY.
YEAH, I KNOW.
Country Collection
I'LL COME GET YOU AFTER SCHOOL.
OKAY.
THANKS, FOR EVERYTHING, REI!
smack
Uh...
HERE WE ARE.
BYE!
Jinbo Private Elementar
キキーッ

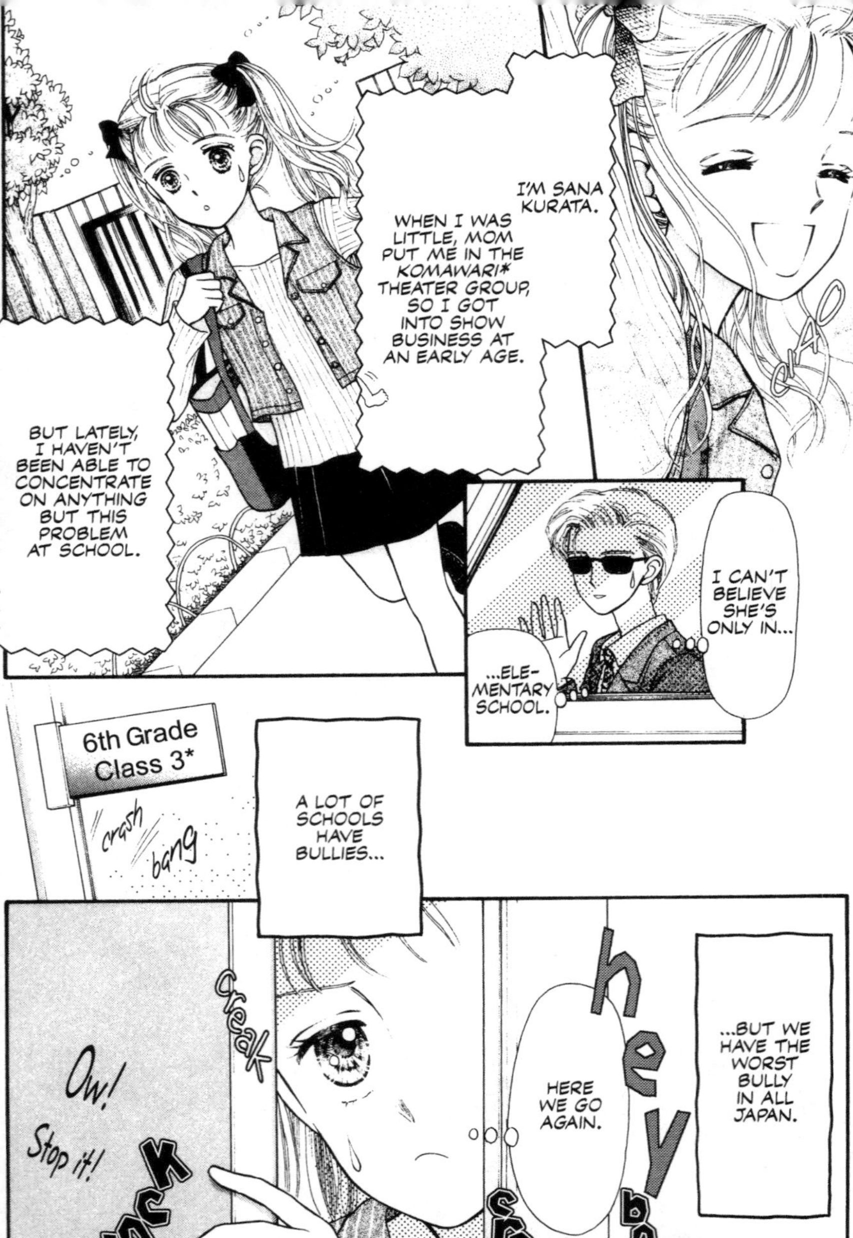
CIAO
I'M SANA KURATA.
WHEN I WAS LITTLE, MOM PUT ME IN THE KOMAWARI* THEATER GROUP, SO I GOT INTO SHOW BUSINESS AT AN EARLY AGE.
BUT LATELY, I HAVEN'T BEEN ABLE TO CONCENTRATE ON ANYTHING BUT THIS PROBLEM AT SCHOOL.
I CAN'T BELIEVE SHE'S ONLY IN...
...ELE-MENTARY SCHOOL.
A LOT OF SCHOOLS HAVE BULLIES...
6th Grade Class 3*
crash
bang
...BUT WE HAVE THE WORST BULLY IN ALL JAPAN.
hey
HERE WE GO AGAIN.
bang
crash
creak
Ow!
Stop it!
wack

*A PARODY OF THE FAMOUS HIMAWARI THEATER IN JAPAN.
*STUDENTS BELONG TO A HOMEROOM AND THE TEACHERS CHANGE CLASSES IN JAPANESE SCHOOL.

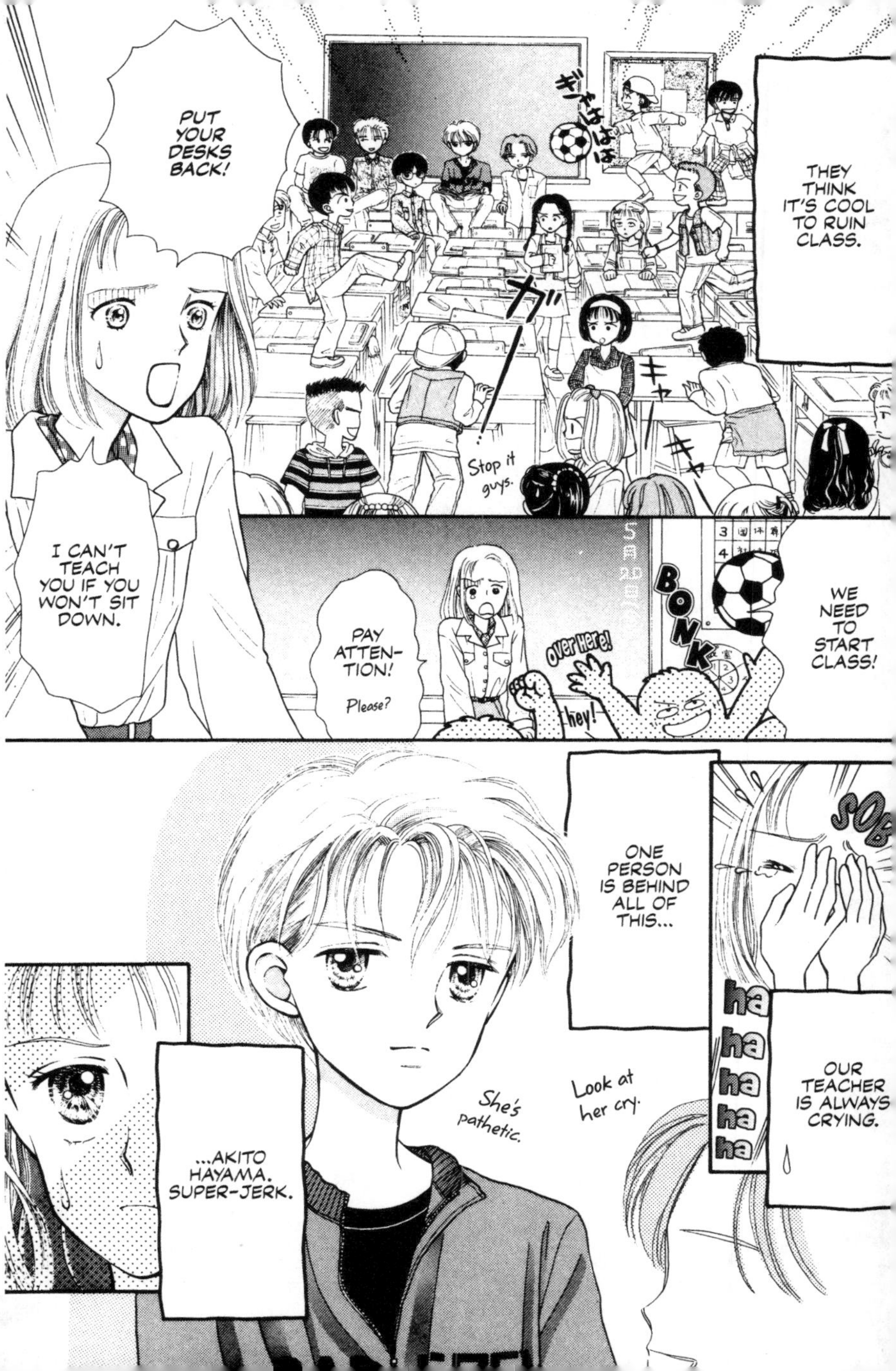
THEY THINK IT'S COOL TO RUIN CLASS.
ギャははは
ガ
キャ
キャ
Stop it guys.
WE NEED TO START CLASS!
BONK
over here!
hey!
PAY ATTENTION!
Please?
PUT YOUR DESKS BACK!
I CAN'T TEACH YOU IF YOU WON'T SIT DOWN.
SOB
ha ha ha ha ha
OUR TEACHER IS ALWAYS CRYING.
ONE PERSON IS BEHIND ALL OF THIS...
Look at her cry.
She's pathetic.
...AKITO HAYAMA. SUPER-JERK.

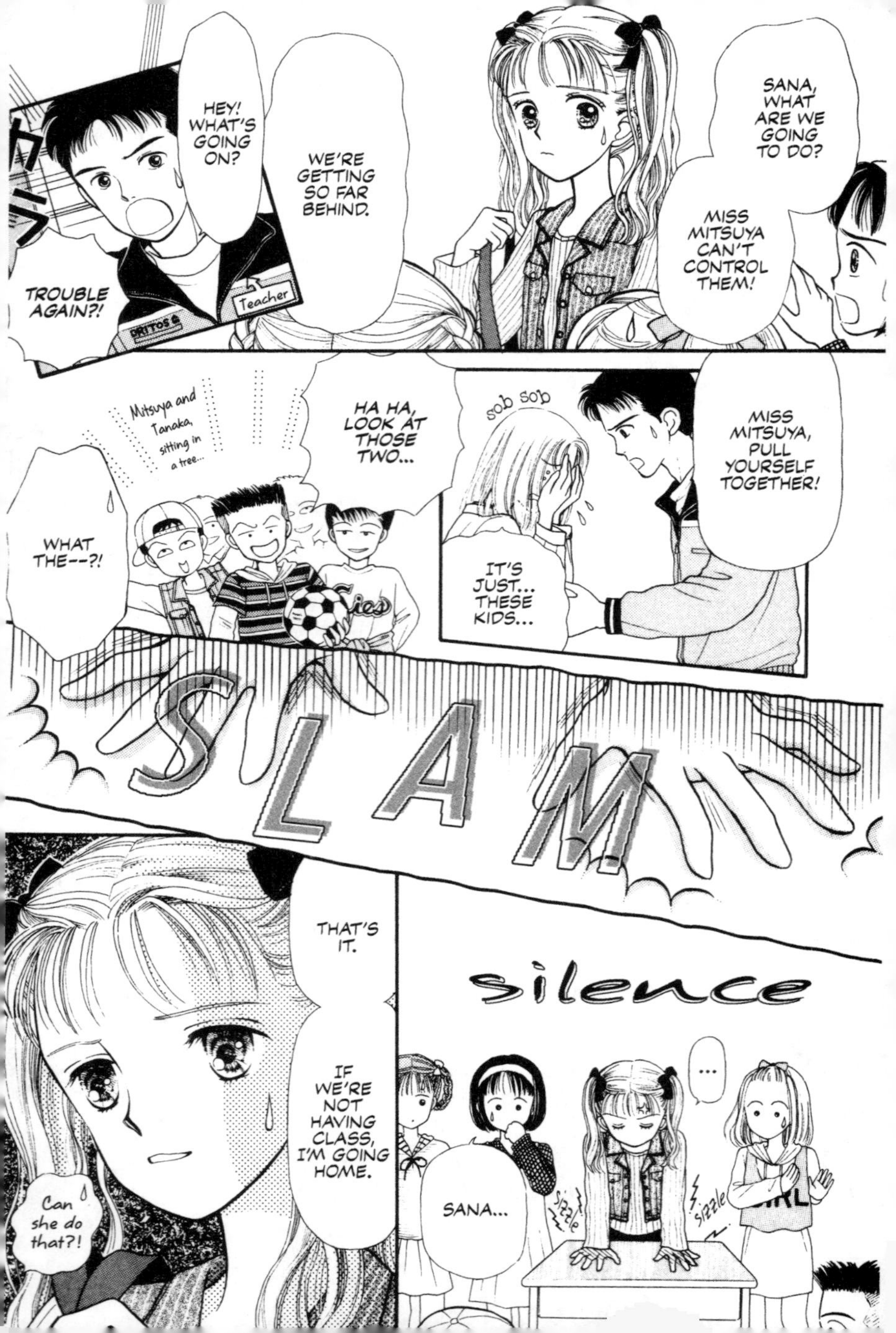
SANA, WHAT ARE WE GOING TO DO?
WE'RE GETTING SO FAR BEHIND.
MISS MITSUYA CAN'T CONTROL THEM!
HEY! WHAT'S GOING ON?
Teacher
TROUBLE AGAIN?!
MISS MITSUYA, PULL YOURSELF TOGETHER!
sob sob
IT'S JUST... THESE KIDS...
HA HA, LOOK AT THOSE TWO...
Mitsuya and Tanaka, sitting in a tree...
WHAT THE--?!
SLAM
silence
...
sizzle
sizzle
SANA...
THAT'S IT.
IF WE'RE NOT HAVING CLASS, I'M GOING HOME.
Can she do that?!

Obana's Incoherent Babbling

Hello. I'm a comic-book-drawing girl, Obana. Thanks for picking up Kodocha 1. This time around, I reversed the balance of the funny and serious from the last series I did. Thank you for following a story that walks such a thin line between funny and serious.♥ I know it can be confusing. Sometimes, I'm confused myself. (Ha!) I guess you're a reading expert, like I'm a drawing expert. I'm impressed...

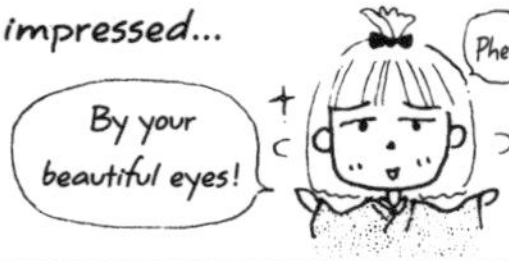

Phew.
By your beautiful eyes!

In these sections I'll be writing about whatever pops into my head. Feel free to skip them if you're in a hurry! Ciao♥

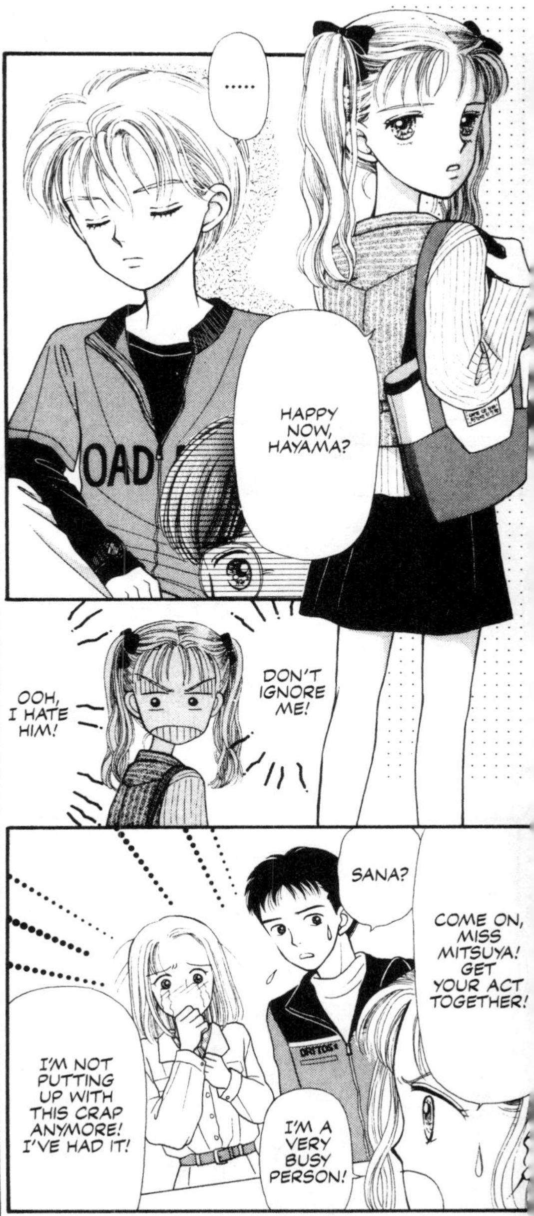

.....
HAPPY NOW, HAYAMA?
DON'T IGNORE ME!
OOH, I HATE HIM!
COME ON, MISS MITSUYA! GET YOUR ACT TOGETHER!
SANA?
I'M A VERY BUSY PERSON!
I'M NOT PUTTING UP WITH THIS CRAP ANYMORE! I'VE HAD IT!

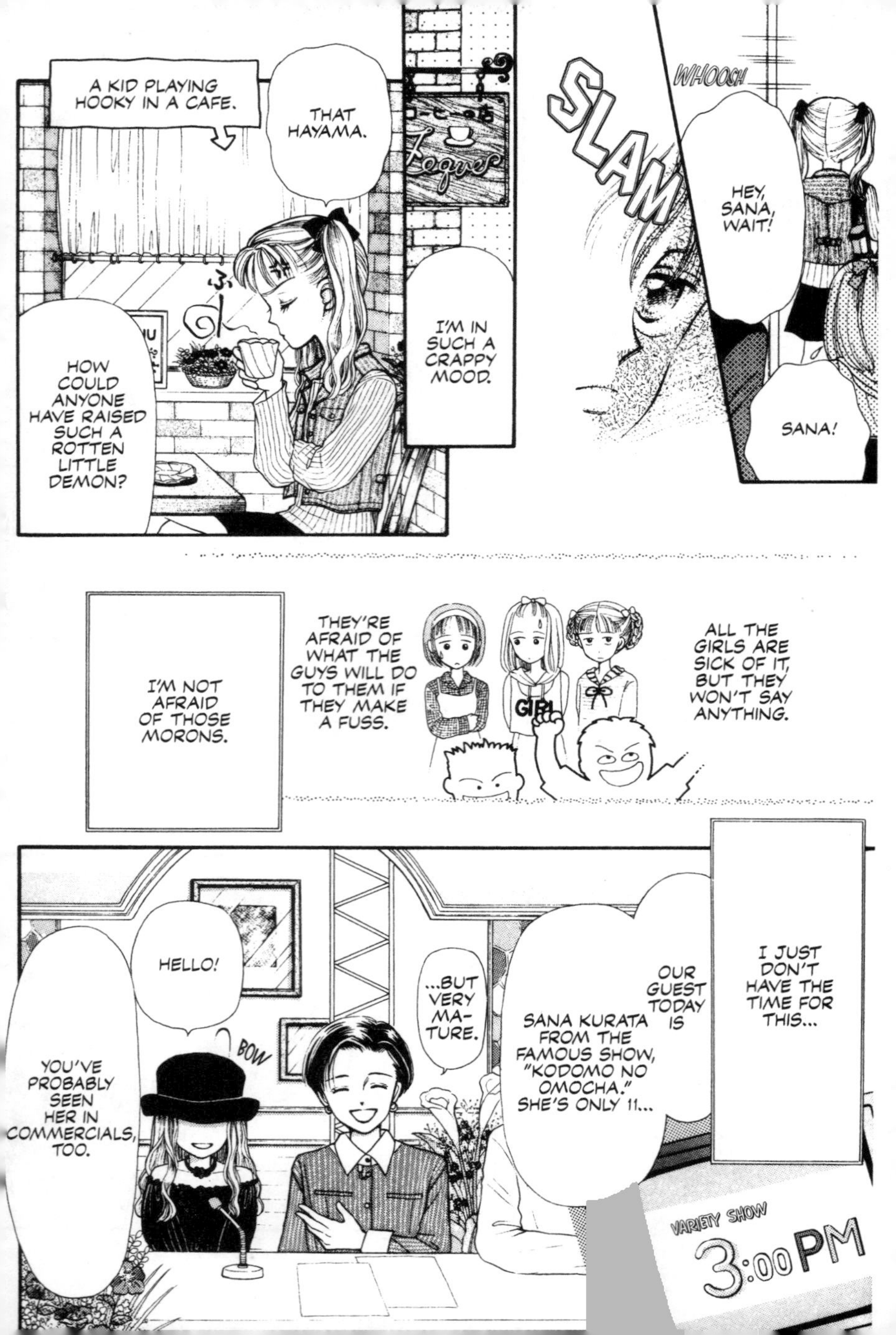
WHOOSH
SLAM
HEY, SANA, WAIT!
SANA!
THAT HAYAMA.
A KID PLAYING HOOKY IN A CAFE.
I'M IN SUCH A CRAPPY MOOD.
ふ
HOW COULD ANYONE HAVE RAISED SUCH A ROTTEN LITTLE DEMON?
ALL THE GIRLS ARE SICK OF IT, BUT THEY WON'T SAY ANYTHING.
THEY'RE AFRAID OF WHAT THE GUYS WILL DO TO THEM IF THEY MAKE A FUSS.
GIRL
I'M NOT AFRAID OF THOSE MORONS.
I JUST DON'T HAVE THE TIME FOR THIS...
VARIETY SHOW
3:00 PM
OUR GUEST TODAY IS
SANA KURATA FROM THE FAMOUS SHOW, "KODOMO NO OMOCHA." SHE'S ONLY 11...
...BUT VERY MA-TURE.
HELLO!
BOW
YOU'VE PROBABLY SEEN HER IN COMMERCIALS, TOO.

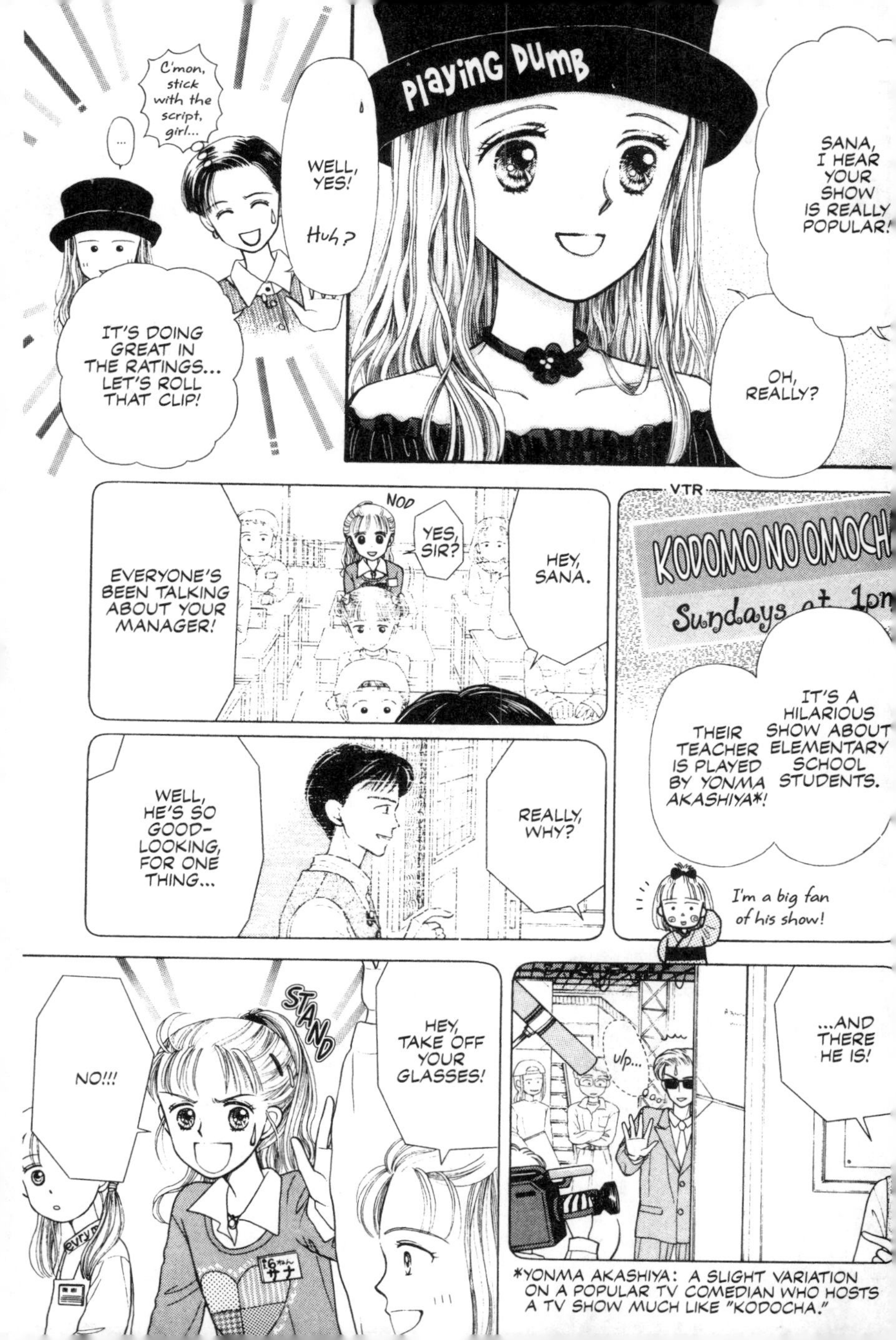
SANA, I HEAR YOUR SHOW IS REALLY POPULAR!
OH, REALLY?
PLAYING DUMB
WELL, YES!
Huh?
IT'S DOING GREAT IN THE RATINGS... LET'S ROLL THAT CLIP!
...
C'mon, stick with the script, girl...
VTR
KODOMO NO OMOCH
Sundays
IT'S A HILARIOUS SHOW ABOUT ELEMENTARY SCHOOL STUDENTS.
THEIR TEACHER IS PLAYED BY YONMA AKASHIYA*!
I'm a big fan of his show!
HEY, SANA.
NOD
YES, SIR?
EVERYONE'S BEEN TALKING ABOUT YOUR MANAGER!
REALLY, WHY?
WELL, HE'S SO GOOD-LOOKING, FOR ONE THING...
...AND THERE HE IS!
u/p...
HEY, TAKE OFF YOUR GLASSES!
STAND
NO!!!

*YONMA AKASHIYA: A SLIGHT VARIATION ON A POPULAR TV COMEDIAN WHO HOSTS A TV SHOW MUCH LIKE "KODOCHA."

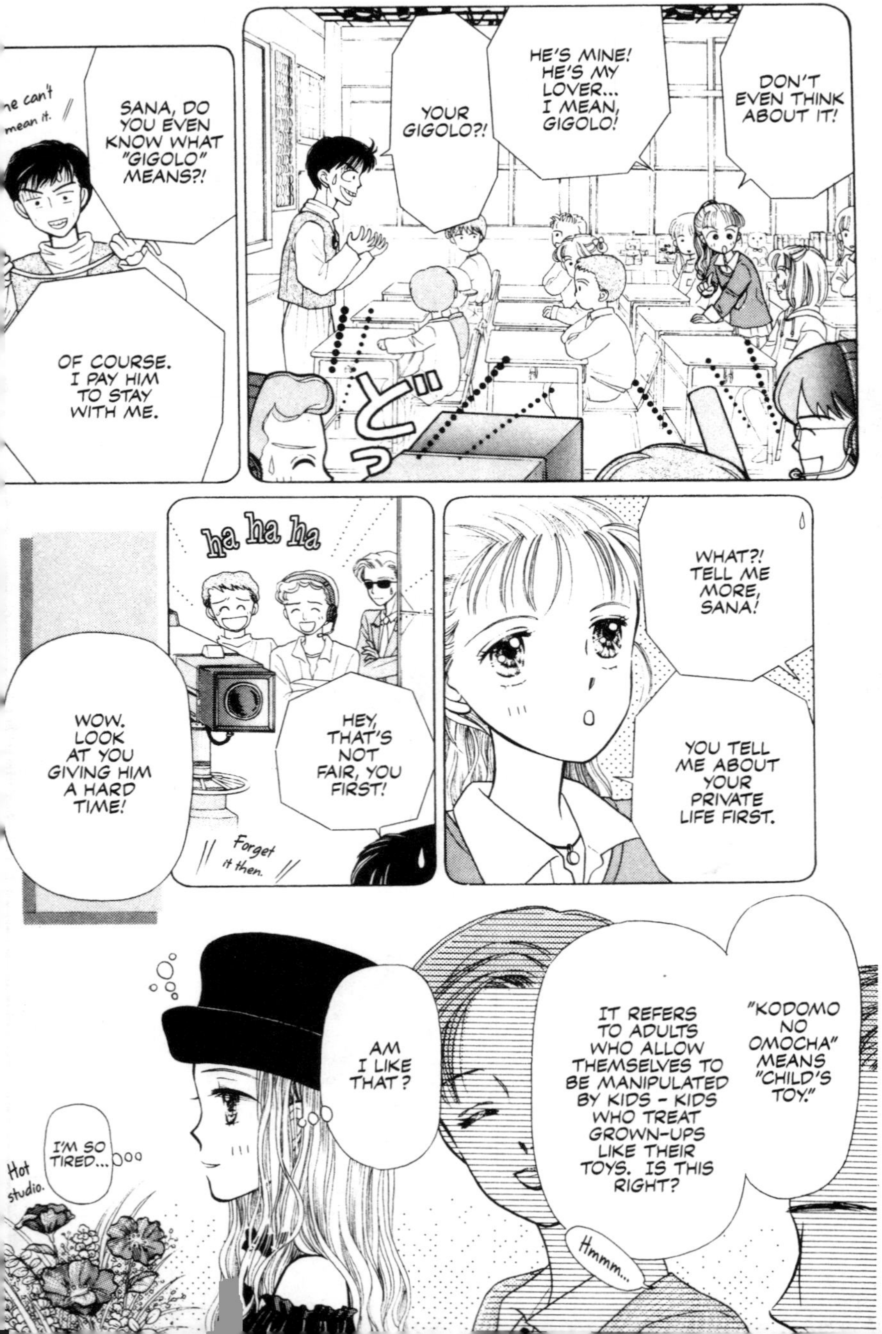
DON'T EVEN THINK ABOUT IT!
HE'S MINE! HE'S MY LOVER... I MEAN, GIGOLO!
YOUR GIGOLO?!
どっ
SANA, DO YOU EVEN KNOW WHAT "GIGOLO" MEANS?!
ne can't mean it.
OF COURSE. I PAY HIM TO STAY WITH ME.
WHAT?! TELL ME MORE, SANA!
YOU TELL ME ABOUT YOUR PRIVATE LIFE FIRST.
ha ha ha
HEY, THAT'S NOT FAIR, YOU FIRST!
Forget it then.
WOW. LOOK AT YOU GIVING HIM A HARD TIME!
"KODOMO NO OMOCHA" MEANS "CHILD'S TOY."
IT REFERS TO ADULTS WHO ALLOW THEMSELVES TO BE MANIPULATED BY KIDS - KIDS WHO TREAT GROWN-UPS LIKE THEIR TOYS. IS THIS RIGHT?
Hmmm...
AM I LIKE THAT?
I'M SO TIRED...
Hot studio.

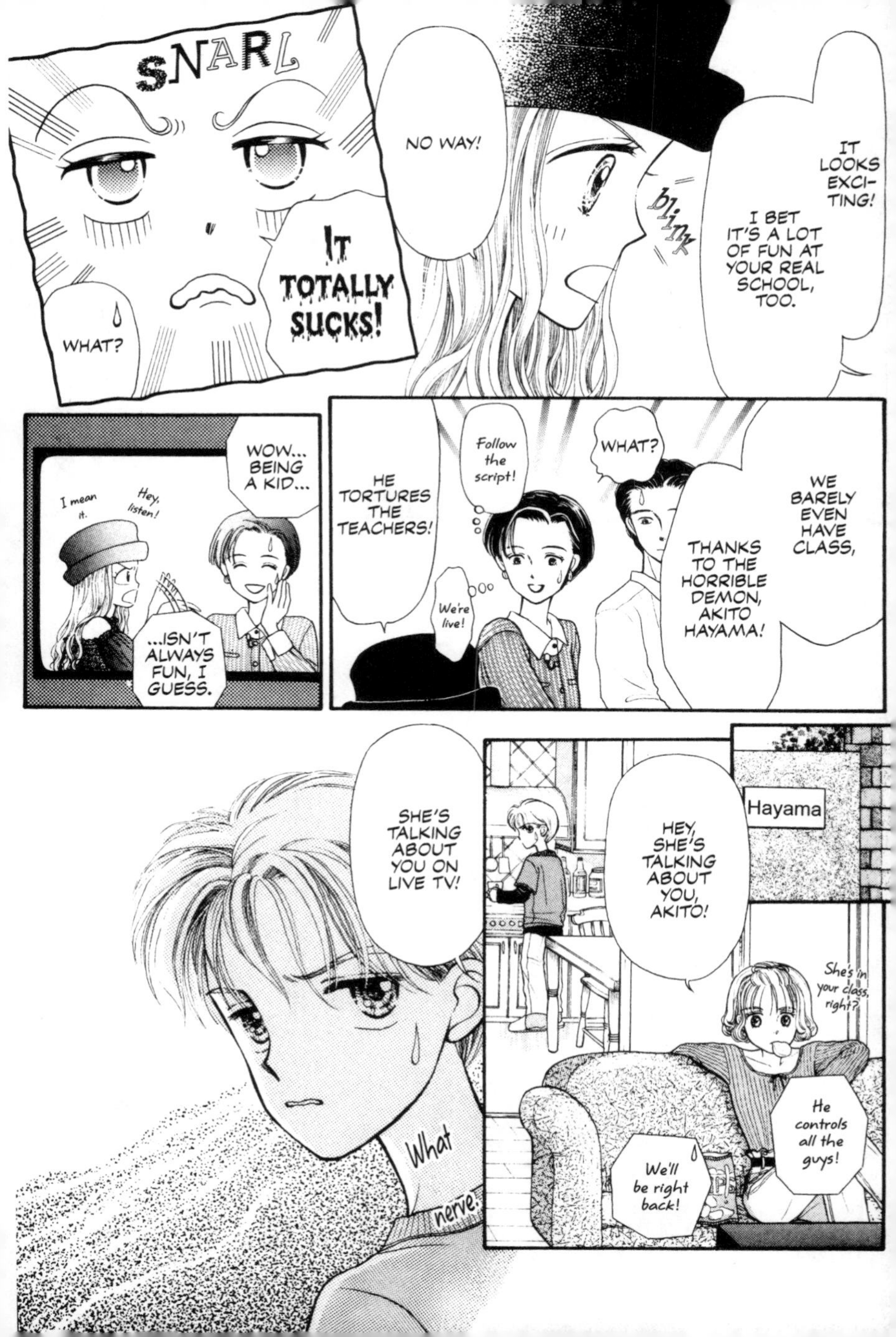
IT LOOKS EXCI-TING!
I BET IT'S A LOT OF FUN AT YOUR REAL SCHOOL, TOO.
blink
NO WAY!
SNARL
IT TOTALLY SUCKS!
WHAT?
WE BARELY EVEN HAVE CLASS,
THANKS TO THE HORRIBLE DEMON, AKITO HAYAMA!
WHAT?
Follow the script!
HE TORTURES THE TEACHERS!
We're live!
WOW... BEING A KID...
Hey, listen!
I mean it.
...ISN'T ALWAYS FUN, I GUESS.
Hayama
HEY, SHE'S TALKING ABOUT YOU, AKITO!
She's in your class, right?
He controls all the guys!
We'll be right back!
SHE'S TALKING ABOUT YOU ON LIVE TV!
What nerve.

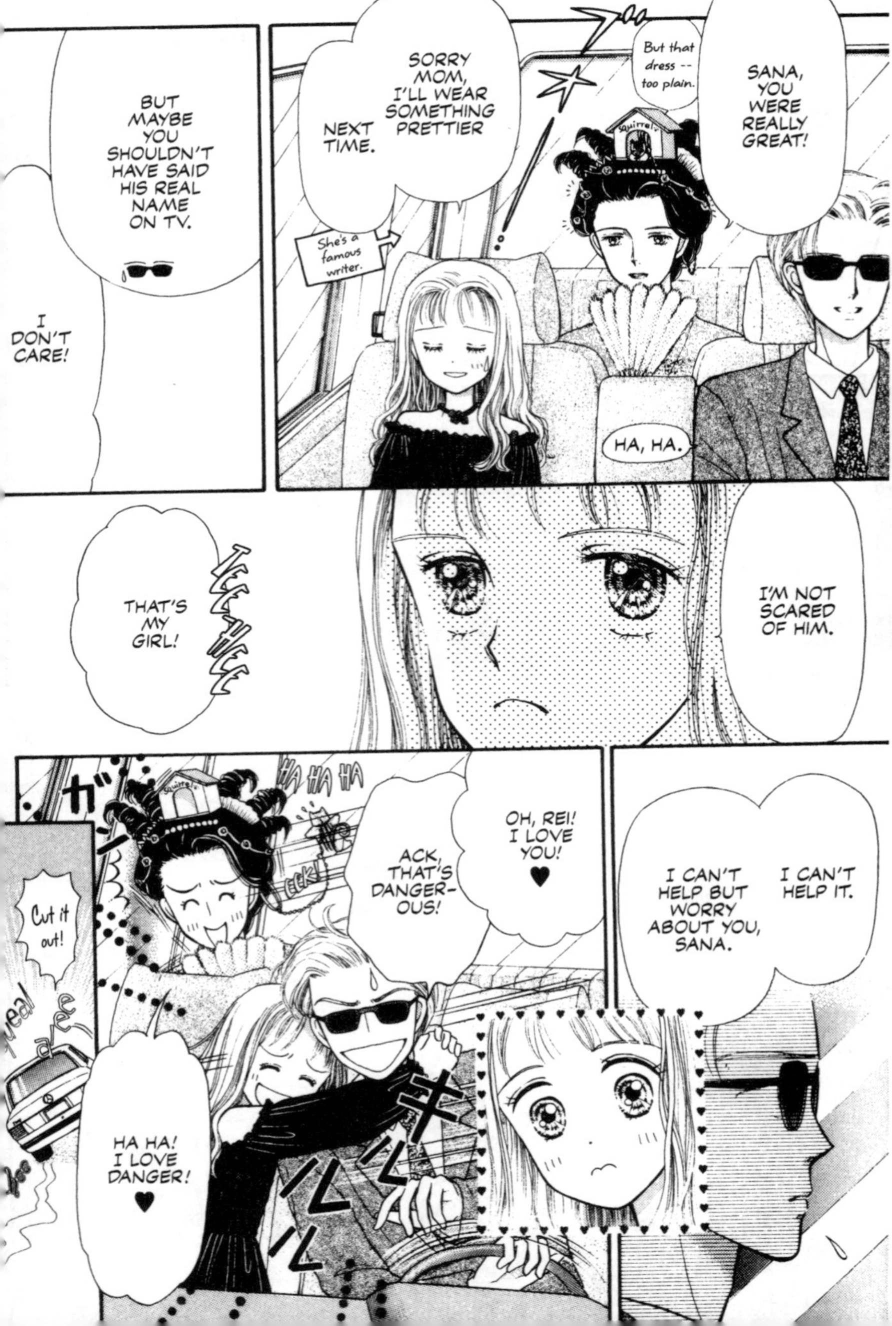
SANA, YOU WERE REALLY GREAT!
But that dress -- too plain.
SORRY MOM, I'LL WEAR SOMETHING PRETTIER NEXT TIME.
She's a famous writer.
HA, HA.
BUT MAYBE YOU SHOULDN'T HAVE SAID HIS REAL NAME ON TV.
I DON'T CARE!
I'M NOT SCARED OF HIM.
THAT'S MY GIRL!
I CAN'T HELP IT.
I CAN'T HELP BUT WORRY ABOUT YOU, SANA.
OH, REI! I LOVE YOU! ♥
ACK, THAT'S DANGER-OUS!
HA HA HA
Cut it out!
HA HA! I LOVE DANGER! ♥

On Assistants

I don't use an assistant very much - or help anyone else as an assistant. I get distracted too easily! When I have a friend over and we're supposed to work, I just want to play. So, I worked on my own for a long time. But for Book four of Kodocha, my schedule got out of control! I taught my sister, Kaori, how to add tones and got her to help me out. It took her an hour to do what I could do in minutes, so I was worried - but she's improved a lot. It's not a lot of work, but she's been a big help. Thanks, sis!♥ I'm trying to get her to do the same work as I do in the future.
How long will it take?

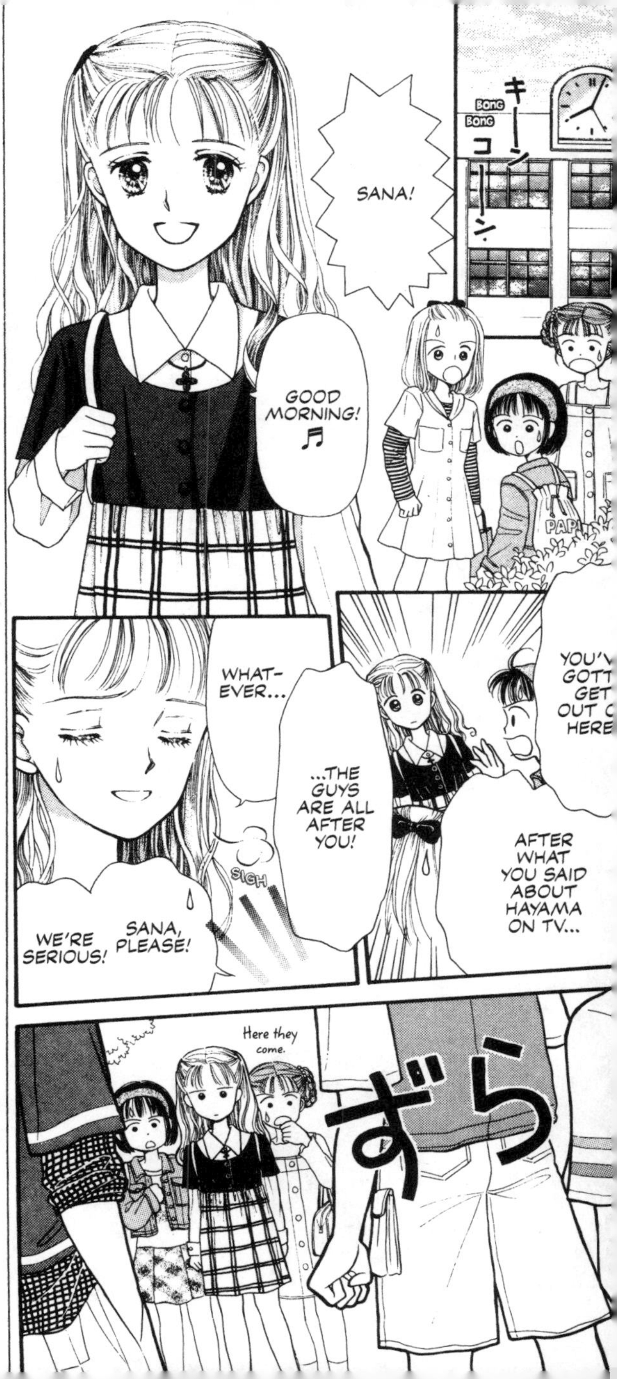

キーンコーン
BONG BONG
SANA!
GOOD MORNING! ♬
YOU'V GOTT GET OUT C HERE
AFTER WHAT YOU SAID ABOUT HAYAMA ON TV...
...THE GUYS ARE ALL AFTER YOU!
WHAT-EVER...
SIGH
SANA, PLEASE!
WE'RE SERIOUS!
ずら
Here they come.

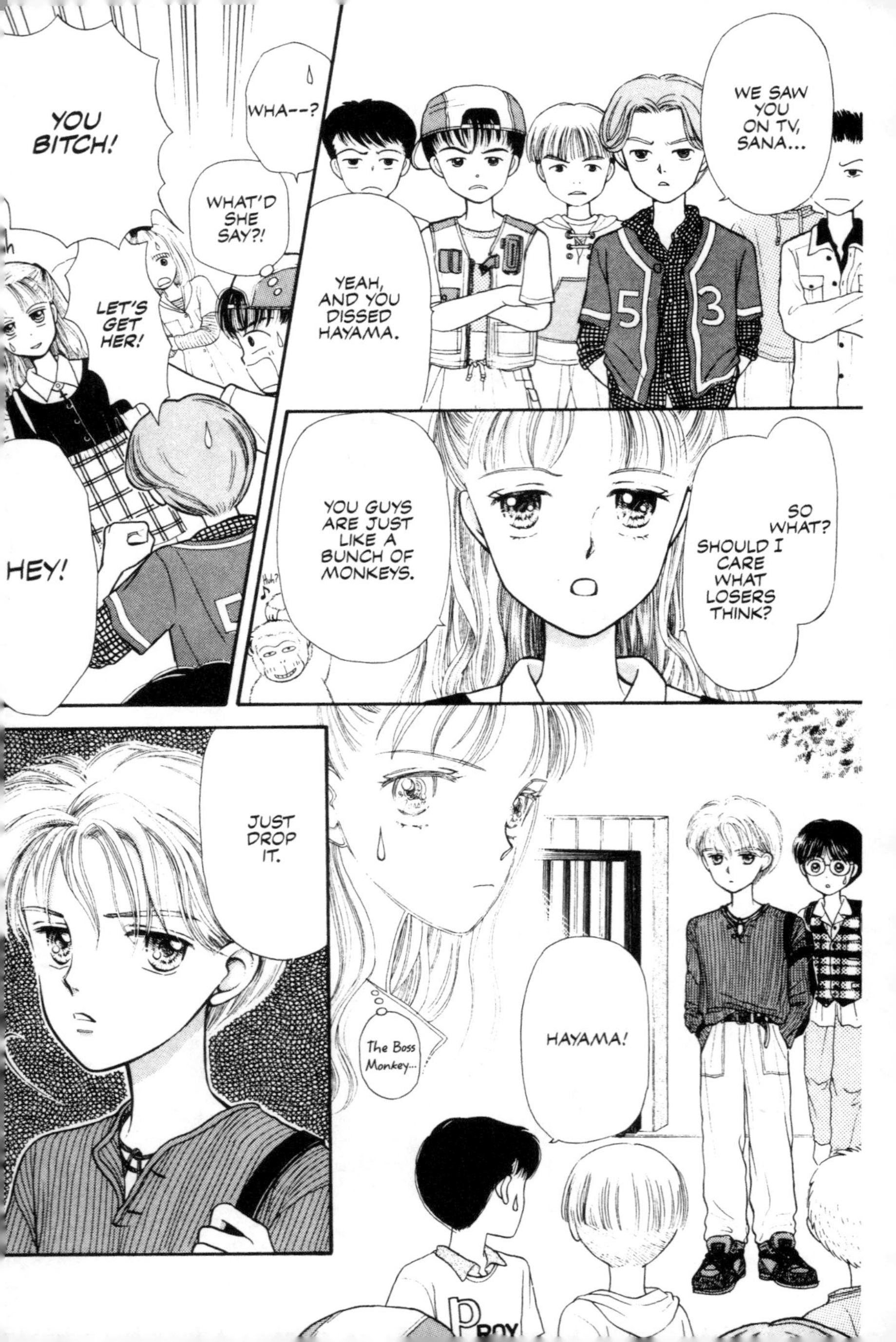
WE SAW YOU ON TV, SANA...
YEAH, AND YOU DISSED HAYAMA.
SO WHAT? SHOULD I CARE WHAT LOSERS THINK?
YOU GUYS ARE JUST LIKE A BUNCH OF MONKEYS.
Huh?
WHA--?
WHAT'D SHE SAY?!
YOU BITCH!
LET'S GET HER!
HEY!
HAYAMA!
The Boss Monkey...
JUST DROP IT.

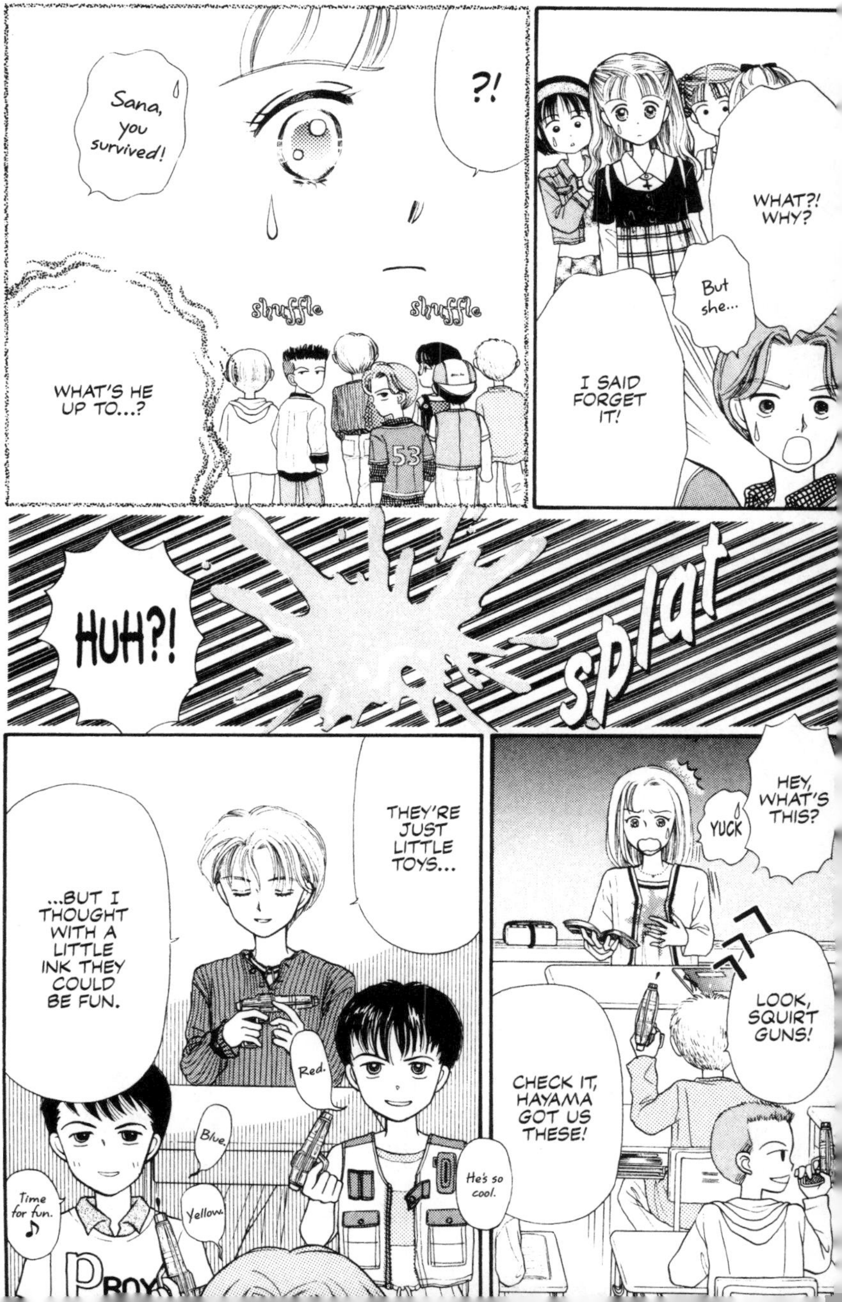
WHAT?! WHY?
But she...
I SAID FORGET IT!
?!
Sana, you survived!
shuffle
shuffle
WHAT'S HE UP TO...?
splat
HUH?!
HEY, WHAT'S THIS?
YUCK
LOOK, SQUIRT GUNS!
CHECK IT, HAYAMA GOT US THESE!
THEY'RE JUST LITTLE TOYS...
...BUT I THOUGHT WITH A LITTLE INK THEY COULD BE FUN.
Red.
He's so cool.
Blue.
Yellow.
Time for fun. ♪

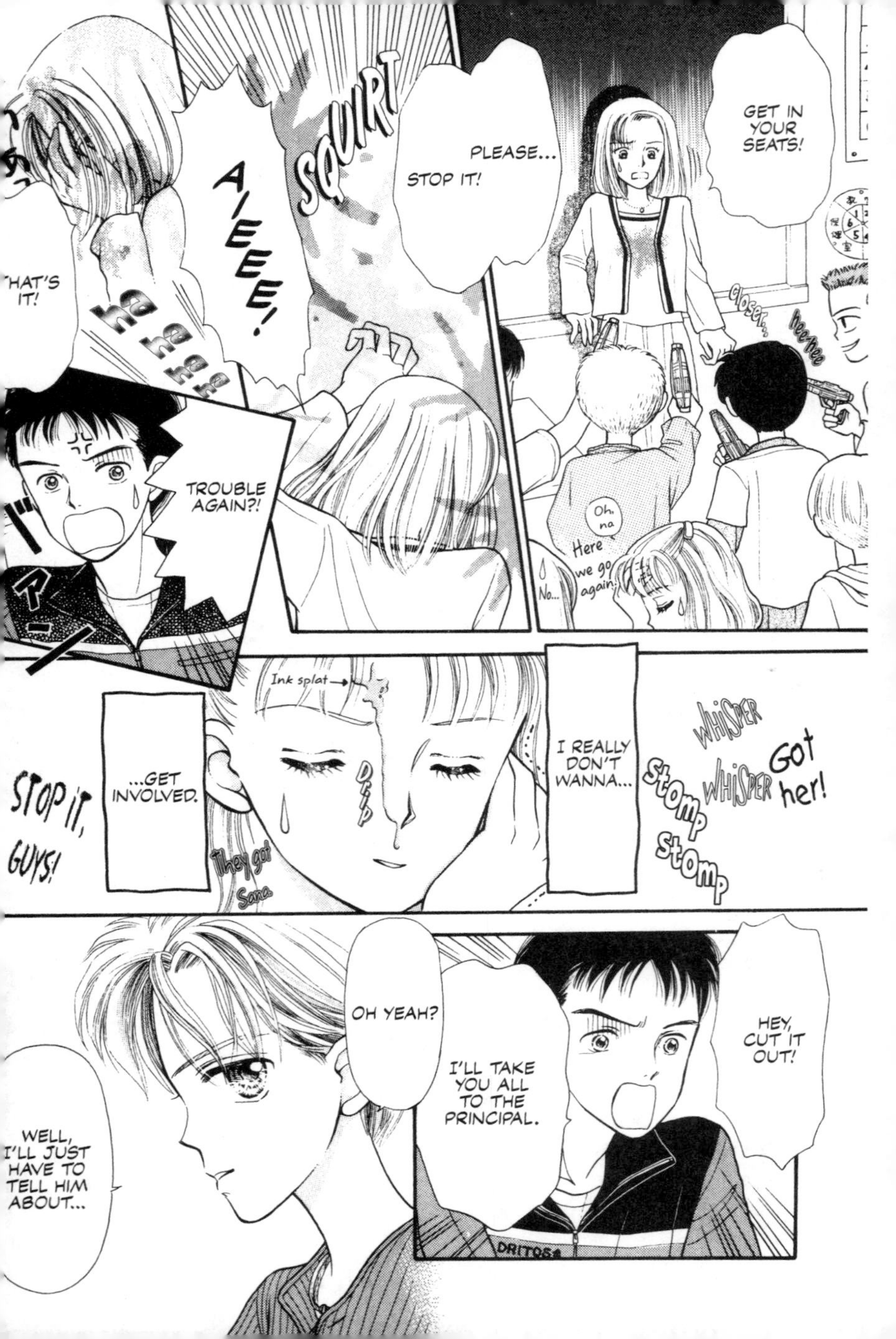
GET IN YOUR SEATS!
closer..
hee-hee
Oh, na
Here we go again.
No...
PLEASE...
STOP IT!
SQUIRT
A/EEE!
HAT'S IT!
ha ha ha ha
TROUBLE AGAIN?!
WHISPER
WHISPER
Got her!
Stomp
Stomp
Stomp
I REALLY DON'T WANNA...
Ink splat
Drip
...GET INVOLVED.
They got Sana
STOP IT, GUYS!
HEY, CUT IT OUT!
I'LL TAKE YOU ALL TO THE PRINCIPAL.
DRITOS
OH YEAH?
WELL, I'LL JUST HAVE TO TELL HIM ABOUT...

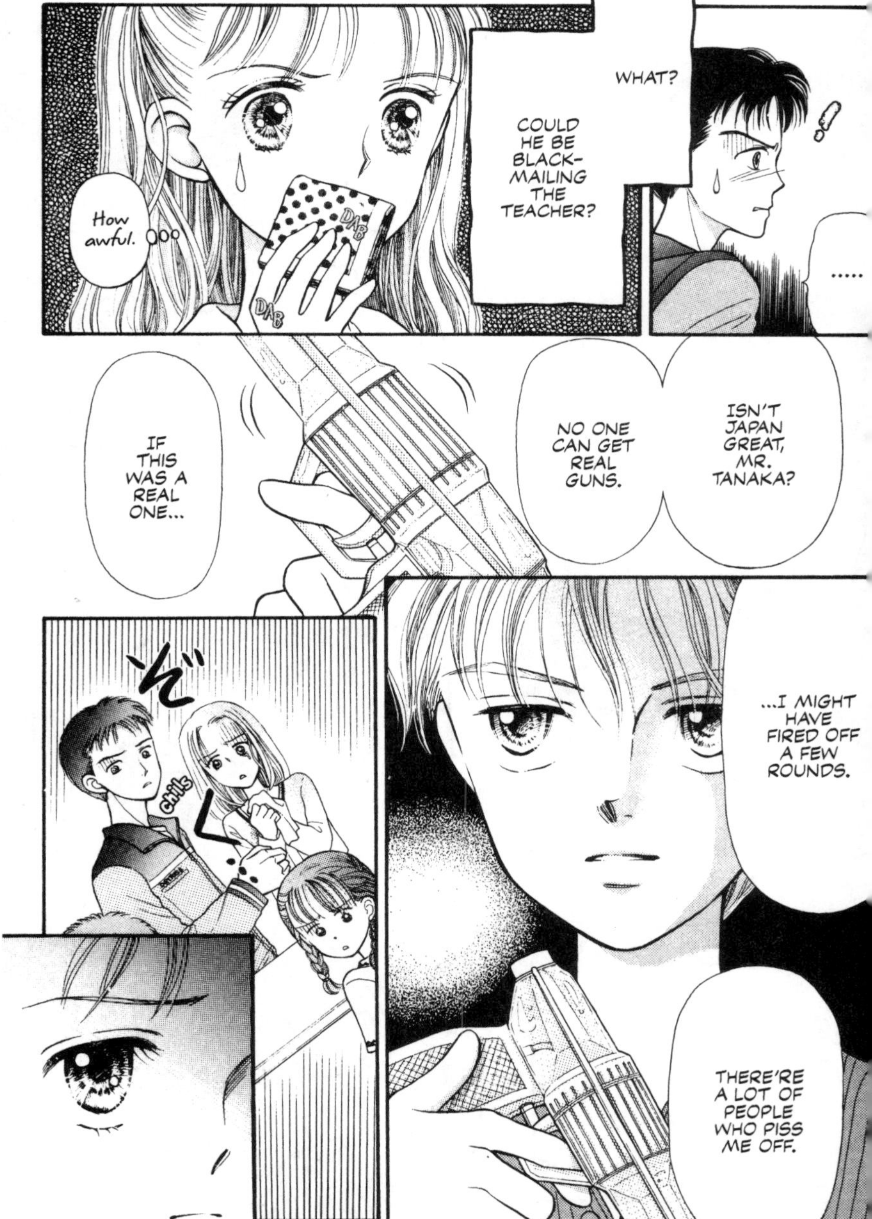
WHAT?
COULD HE BE BLACK-MAILING THE TEACHER?
.....
How awful.
DAB DAB
ISN'T JAPAN GREAT, MR. TANAKA?
NO ONE CAN GET REAL GUNS.
IF THIS WAS A REAL ONE...
...I MIGHT HAVE FIRED OFF A FEW ROUNDS.
THERE'RE A LOT OF PEOPLE WHO PISS ME OFF.
chills

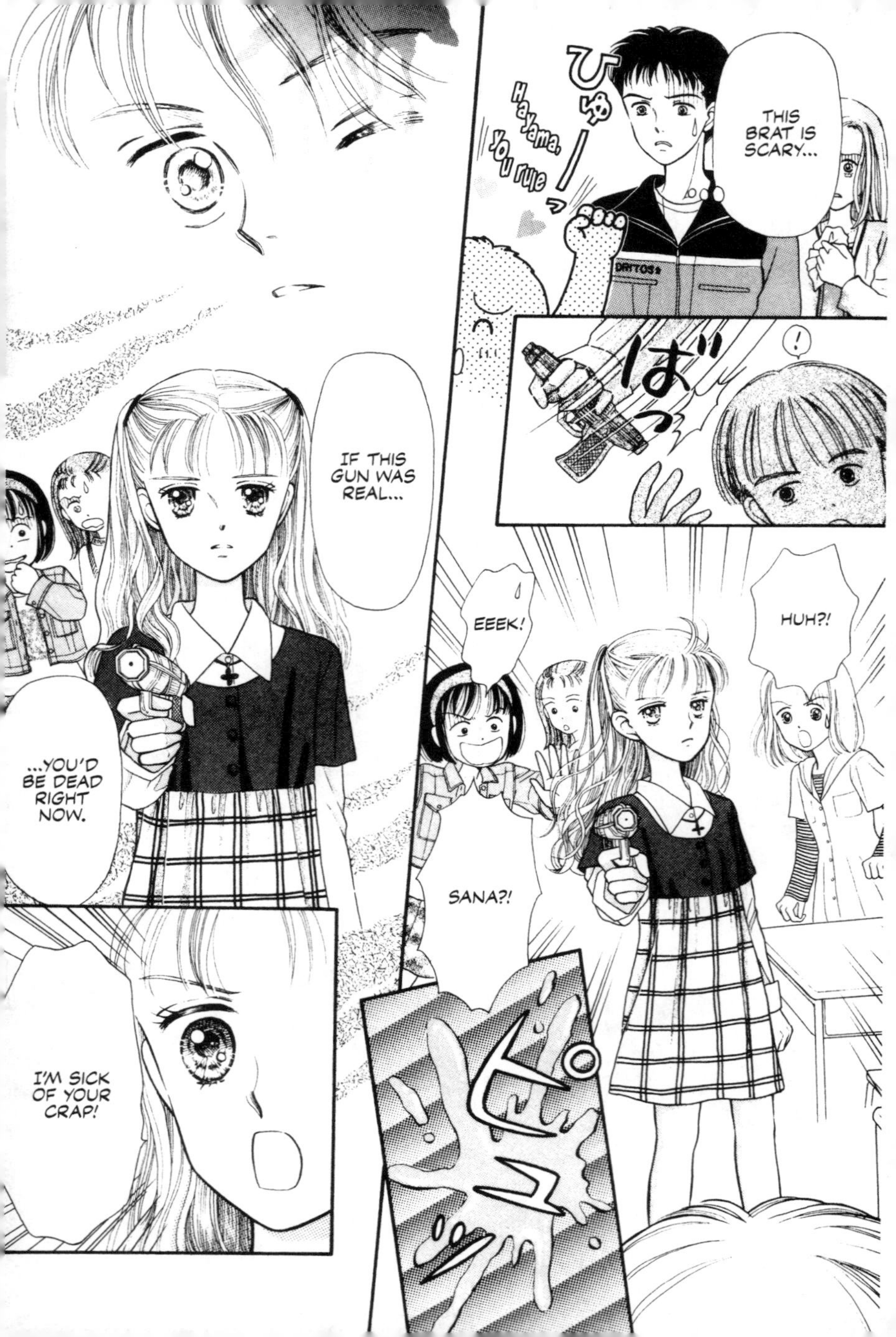

ひゅー
Hayama, you rule
THIS BRAT IS SCARY...
ばっ
!
HUH?!
EEEK!
SANA?!
IF THIS GUN WAS REAL...
...YOU'D BE DEAD RIGHT NOW.
I'M SICK OF YOUR CRAP!

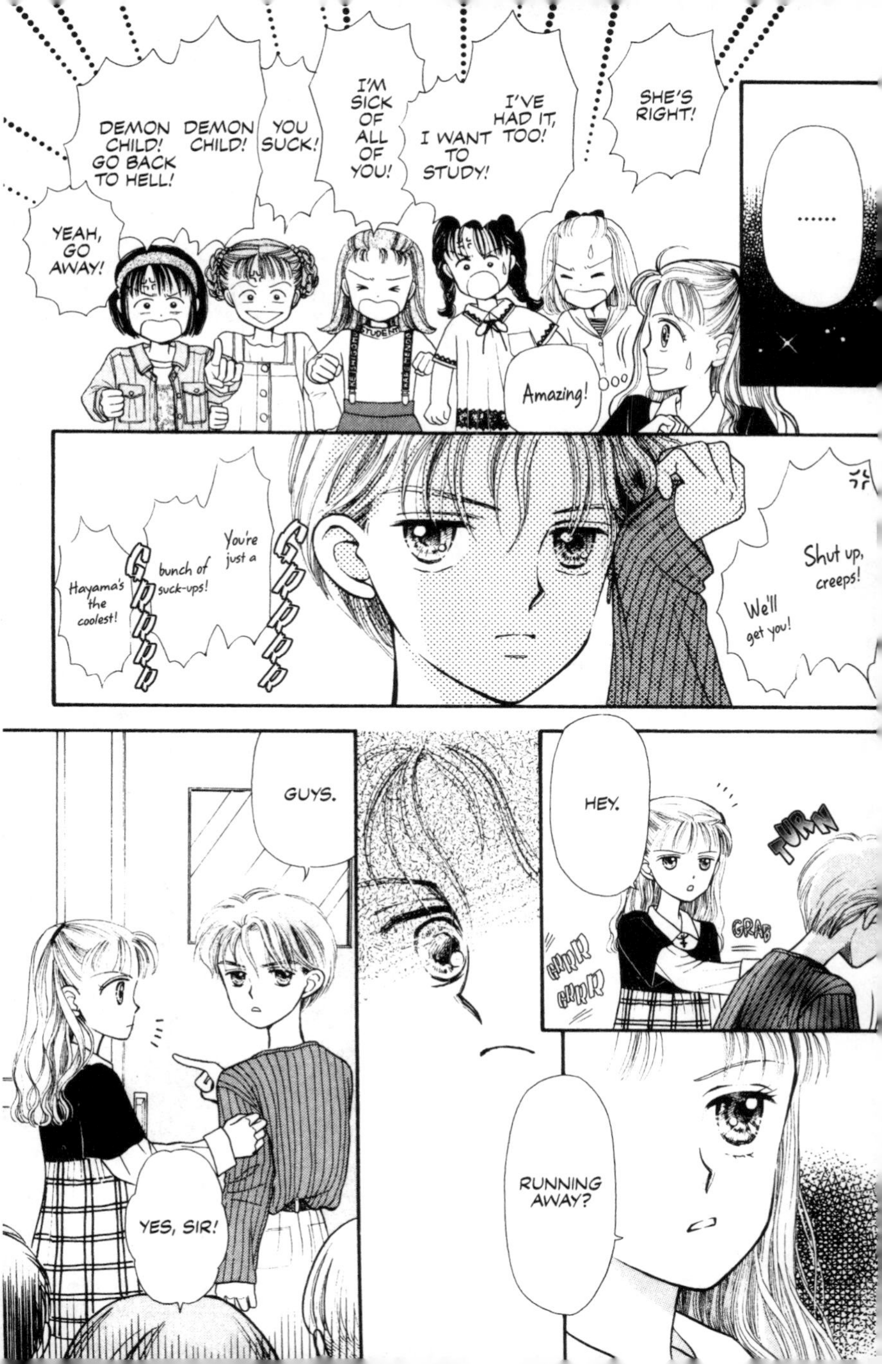
......
SHE'S RIGHT!
I'VE HAD IT, TOO!
I WANT TO STUDY!
I'M SICK OF ALL OF YOU!
YOU SUCK!
DEMON CHILD!
DEMON CHILD! GO BACK TO HELL!
YEAH, GO AWAY!
Amazing!
Shut up, creeps!
We'll get you!
GRRRR
You're just a bunch of suck-ups!
GRRRR
Hayama's the coolest!
HEY.
TURN
GRAB
GRRR
GRRR
RUNNING AWAY?
GUYS.
YES, SIR!

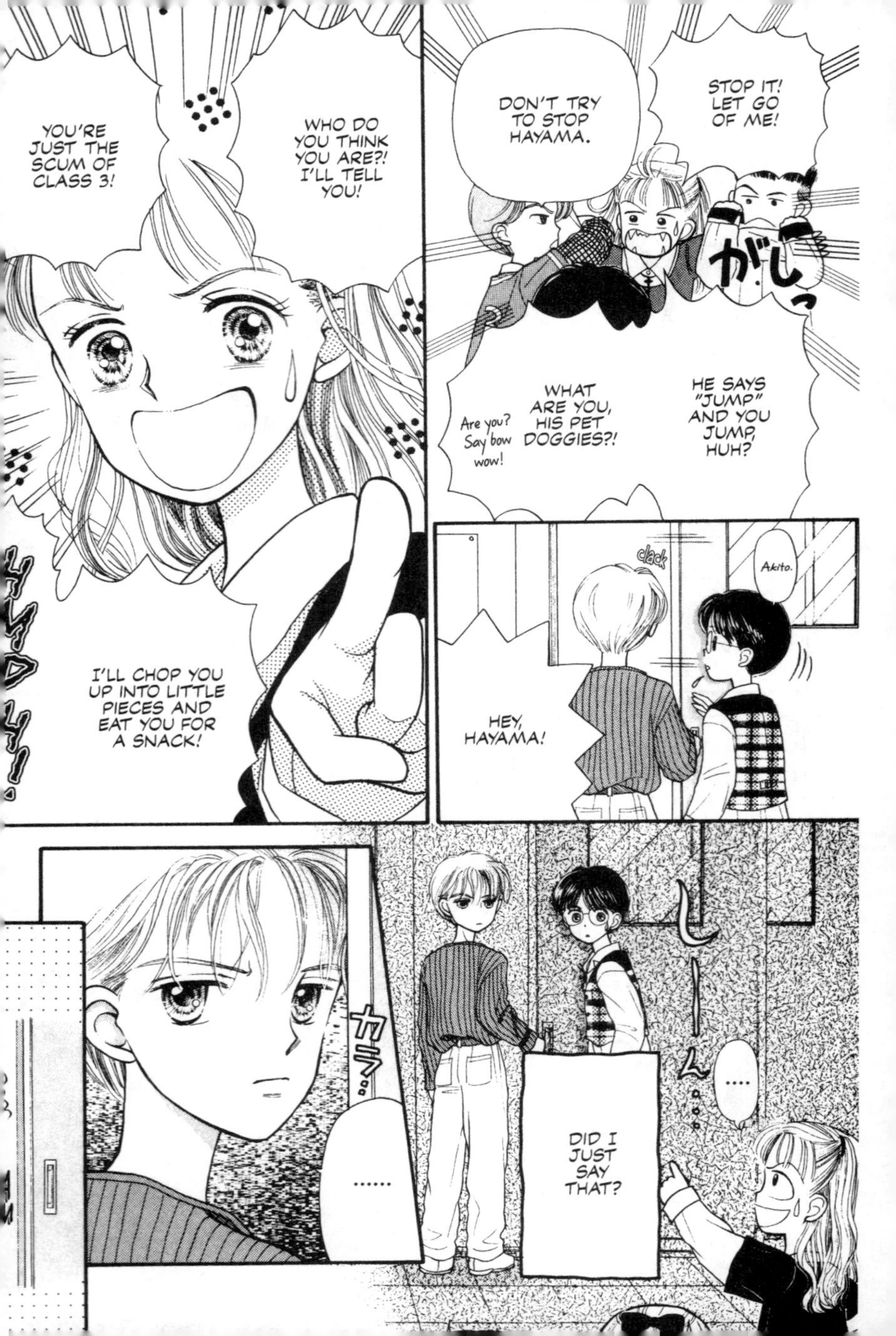
STOP IT! LET GO OF ME!
DON'T TRY TO STOP HAYAMA.
がしっ
HE SAYS "JUMP" AND YOU JUMP, HUH?
WHAT ARE YOU, HIS PET DOGGIES?!
Are you? Say bow wow!
Akito.
clack
HEY, HAYAMA!
WHO DO YOU THINK YOU ARE?! I'LL TELL YOU!
YOU'RE JUST THE SCUM OF CLASS 3!
I'LL CHOP YOU UP INTO LITTLE PIECES AND EAT YOU FOR A SNACK!
しーん...
....
DID I JUST SAY THAT?
カラ...
......

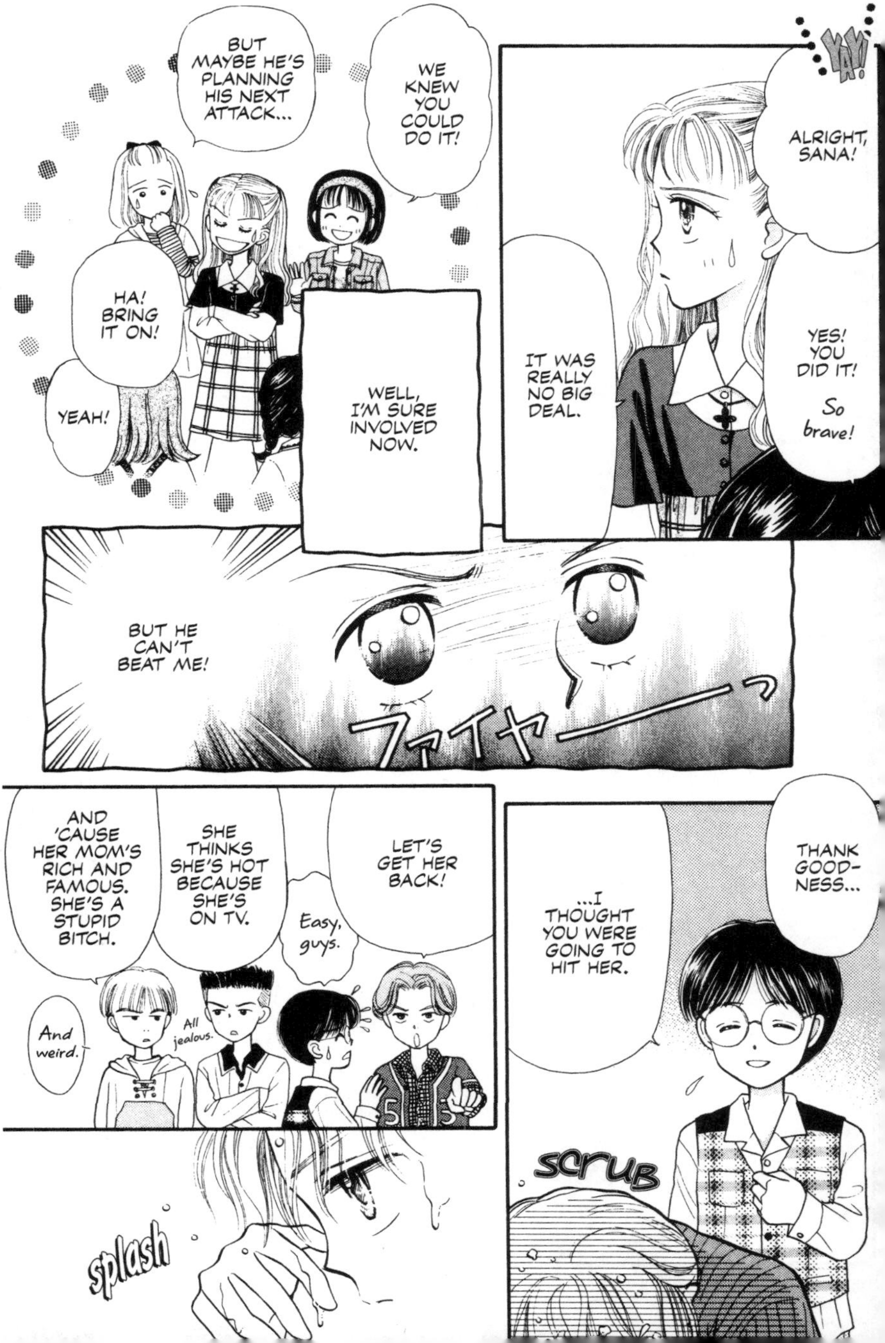
YAY!
ALRIGHT, SANA!
YES! YOU DID IT!
So brave!
IT WAS REALLY NO BIG DEAL.
WE KNEW YOU COULD DO IT!
BUT MAYBE HE'S PLANNING HIS NEXT ATTACK...
HA! BRING IT ON!
YEAH!
WELL, I'M SURE INVOLVED NOW.
BUT HE CAN'T BEAT ME!
ファイヤーーっ
THANK GOODNESS...
...I THOUGHT YOU WERE GOING TO HIT HER.
SCRUB
LET'S GET HER BACK!
Easy, guys.
SHE THINKS SHE'S HOT BECAUSE SHE'S ON TV.
AND 'CAUSE HER MOM'S RICH AND FAMOUS. SHE'S A STUPID BITCH.
All jealous.
And weird.
splash

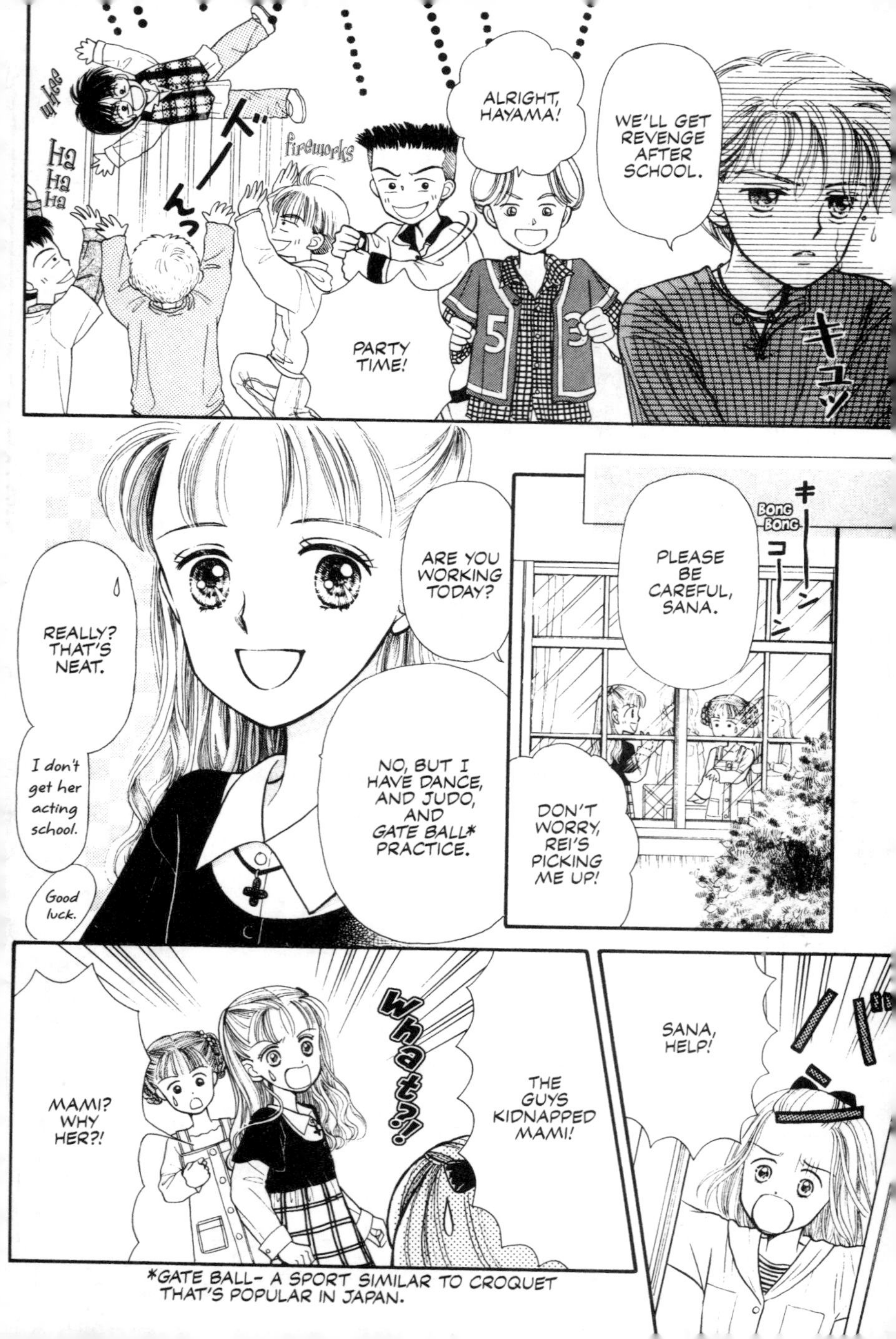
WE'LL GET REVENGE AFTER SCHOOL.
ALRIGHT, HAYAMA!
fireworks
PARTY TIME!
Ha Ha Ha
ukee
PLEASE BE CAREFUL, SANA.
BONG BONG
DON'T WORRY, REI'S PICKING ME UP!
ARE YOU WORKING TODAY?
NO, BUT I HAVE DANCE, AND JUDO, AND GATE BALL* PRACTICE.
REALLY? THAT'S NEAT.
I don't get her acting school.
Good luck.
SANA, HELP!
THE GUYS KIDNAPPED MAMI!
What?!
MAMI? WHY HER?!

*GATE BALL- A SPORT SIMILAR TO CROQUET THAT'S POPULAR IN JAPAN.

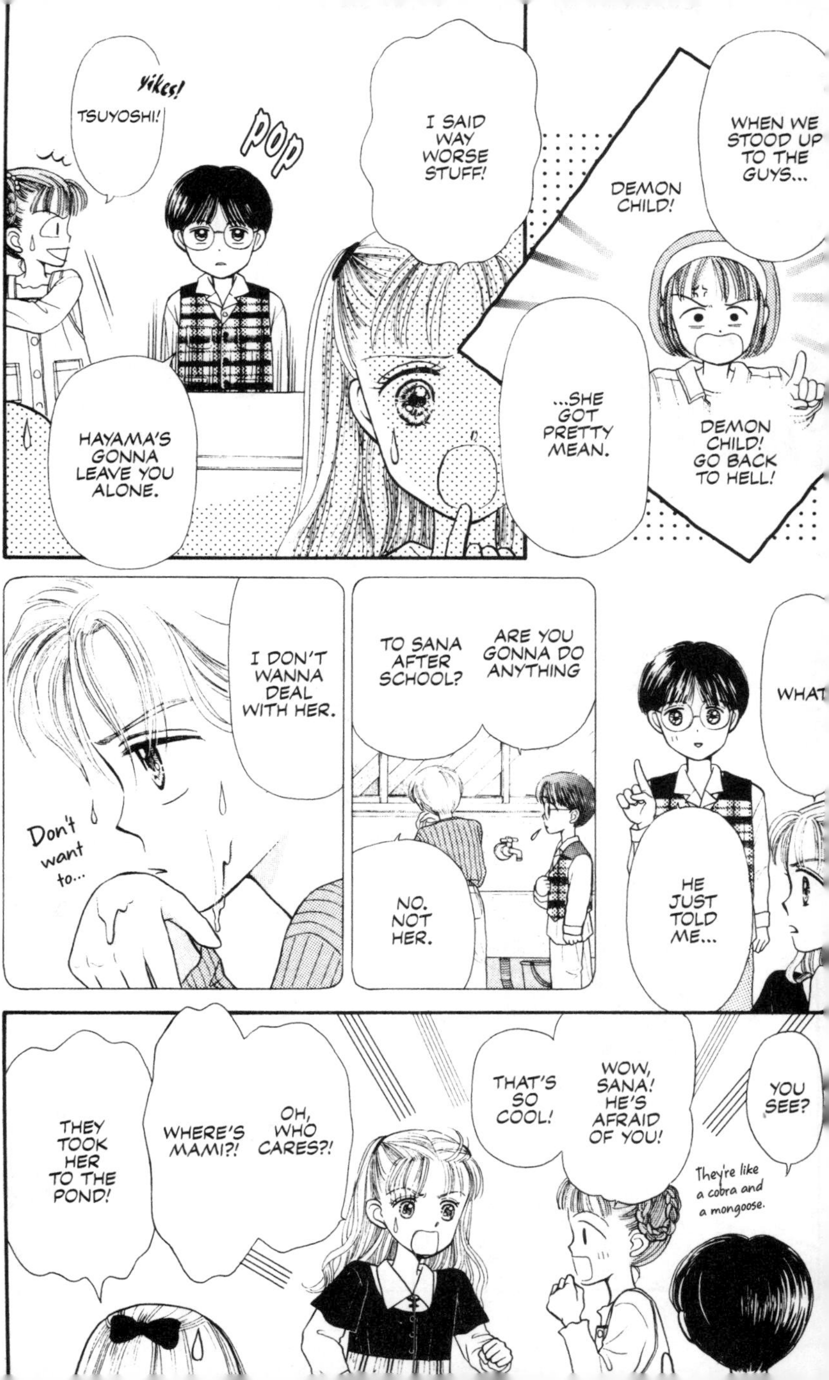
WHEN WE STOOD UP TO THE GUYS...
DEMON CHILD!
DEMON CHILD! GO BACK TO HELL!
...SHE GOT PRETTY MEAN.
I SAID WAY WORSE STUFF!
POP
yikes!
TSUYOSHI!
HAYAMA'S GONNA LEAVE YOU ALONE.
WHAT
HE JUST TOLD ME...
ARE YOU GONNA DO ANYTHING
TO SANA AFTER SCHOOL?
NO. NOT HER.
I DON'T WANNA DEAL WITH HER.
Don't want to...
YOU SEE?
They're like a cobra and a mongoose.
WOW, SANA! HE'S AFRAID OF YOU!
THAT'S SO COOL!
OH, WHO CARES?!
WHERE'S MAMI?!
THEY TOOK HER TO THE POND!

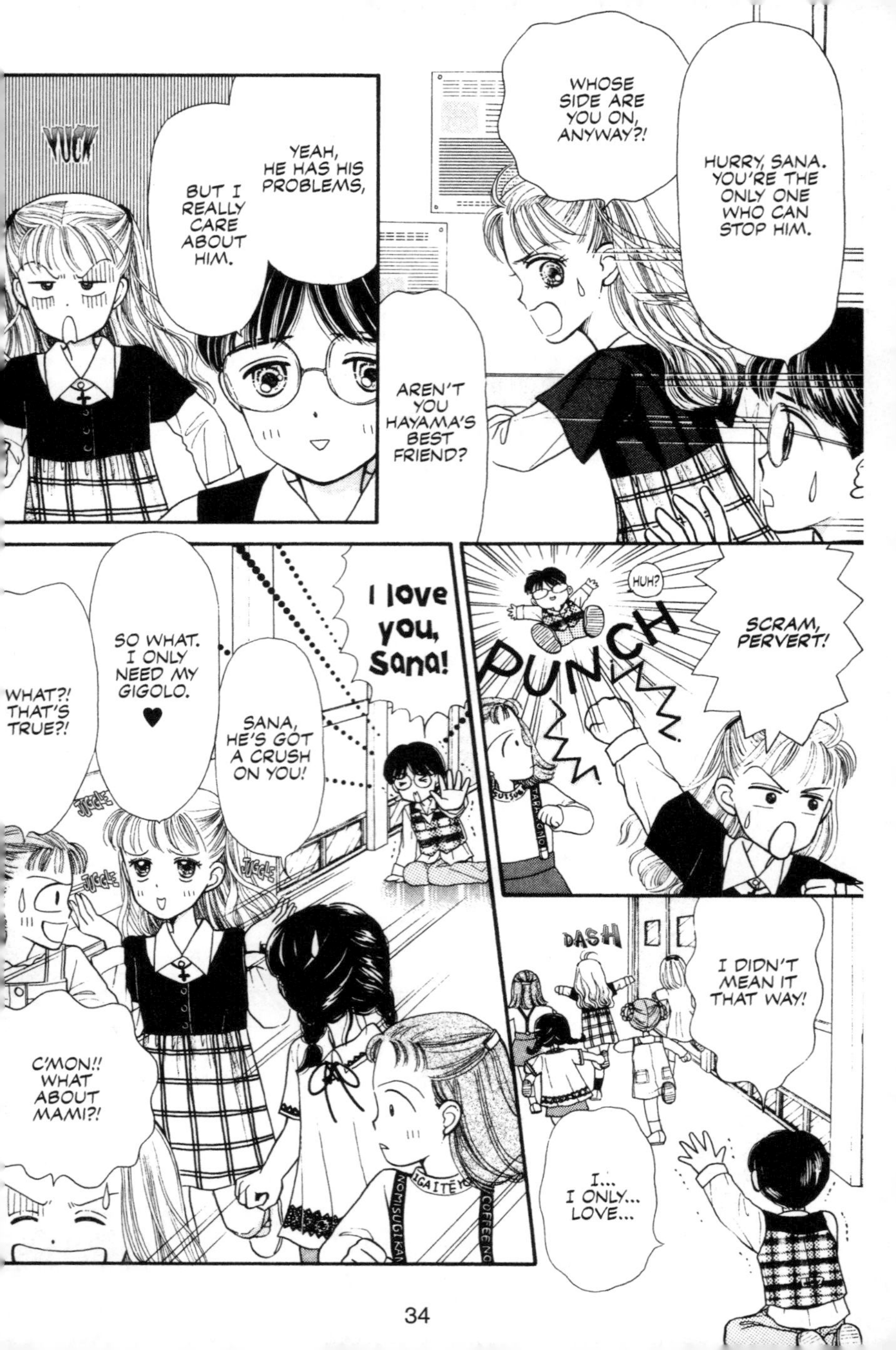
HURRY, SANA. YOU'RE THE ONLY ONE WHO CAN STOP HIM.
WHOSE SIDE ARE YOU ON, ANYWAY?!
AREN'T YOU HAYAMA'S BEST FRIEND?
YEAH, HE HAS HIS PROBLEMS,
BUT I REALLY CARE ABOUT HIM.
YUCK
SCRAM, PERVERT!
HUH?
PUNCH
I DIDN'T MEAN IT THAT WAY!
DASH
I... I ONLY... LOVE...
I love you, Sana!
SANA, HE'S GOT A CRUSH ON YOU!
SO WHAT. I ONLY NEED MY GIGOLO. ♥
WHAT?! THAT'S TRUE?!
JIGGLE
JIGGLE
JIGGLE
C'MON!! WHAT ABOUT MAMI?!

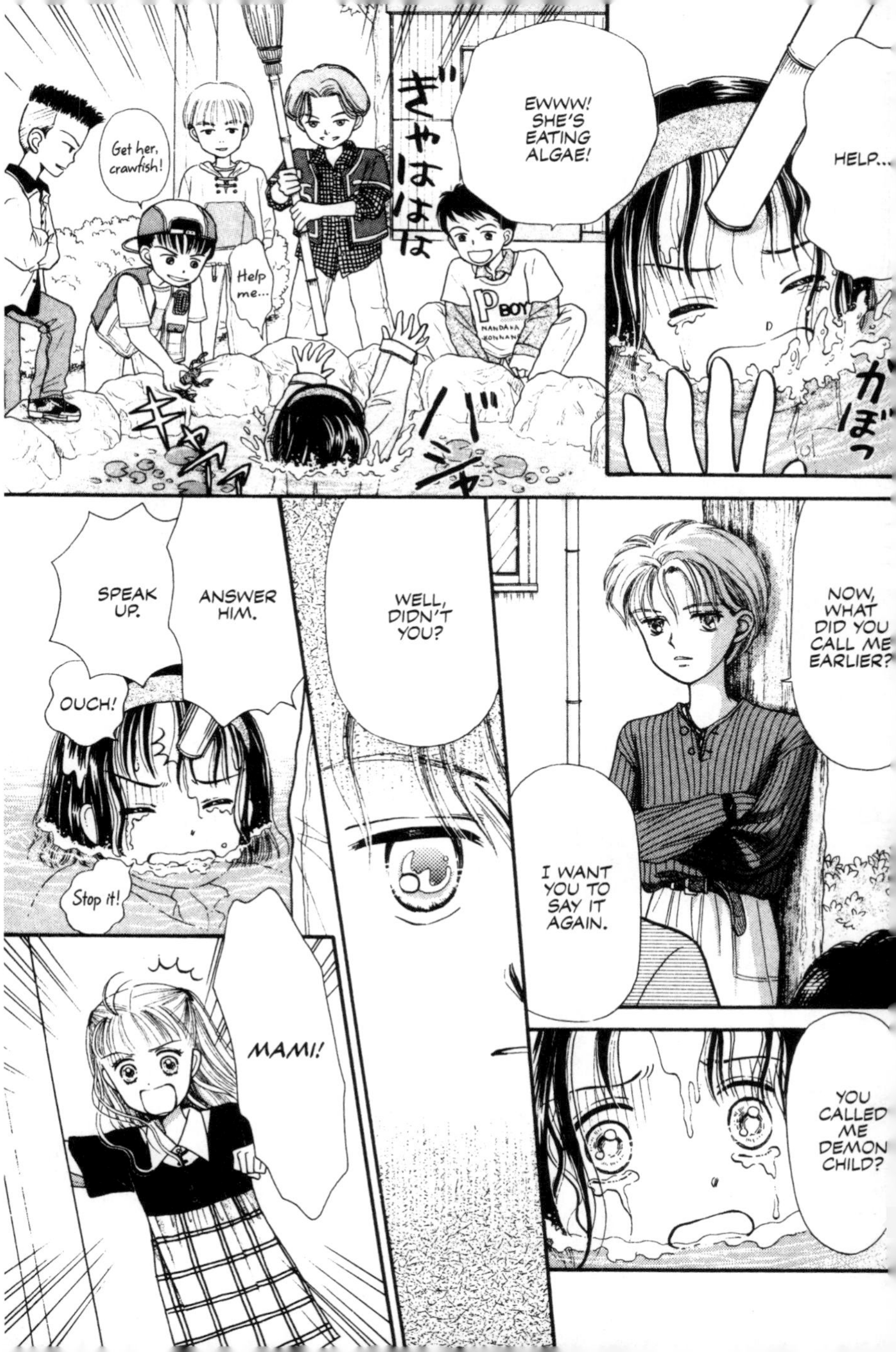
HELP...
がぼっ
EWWW! SHE'S EATING ALGAE!
ぎゃははは
Get her, crawfish!
Help me...
バシャ
NOW, WHAT DID YOU CALL ME EARLIER?
I WANT YOU TO SAY IT AGAIN.
YOU CALLED ME DEMON CHILD?
WELL, DIDN'T YOU?
ANSWER HIM.
SPEAK UP.
OUCH!
Stop it!
MAMI!

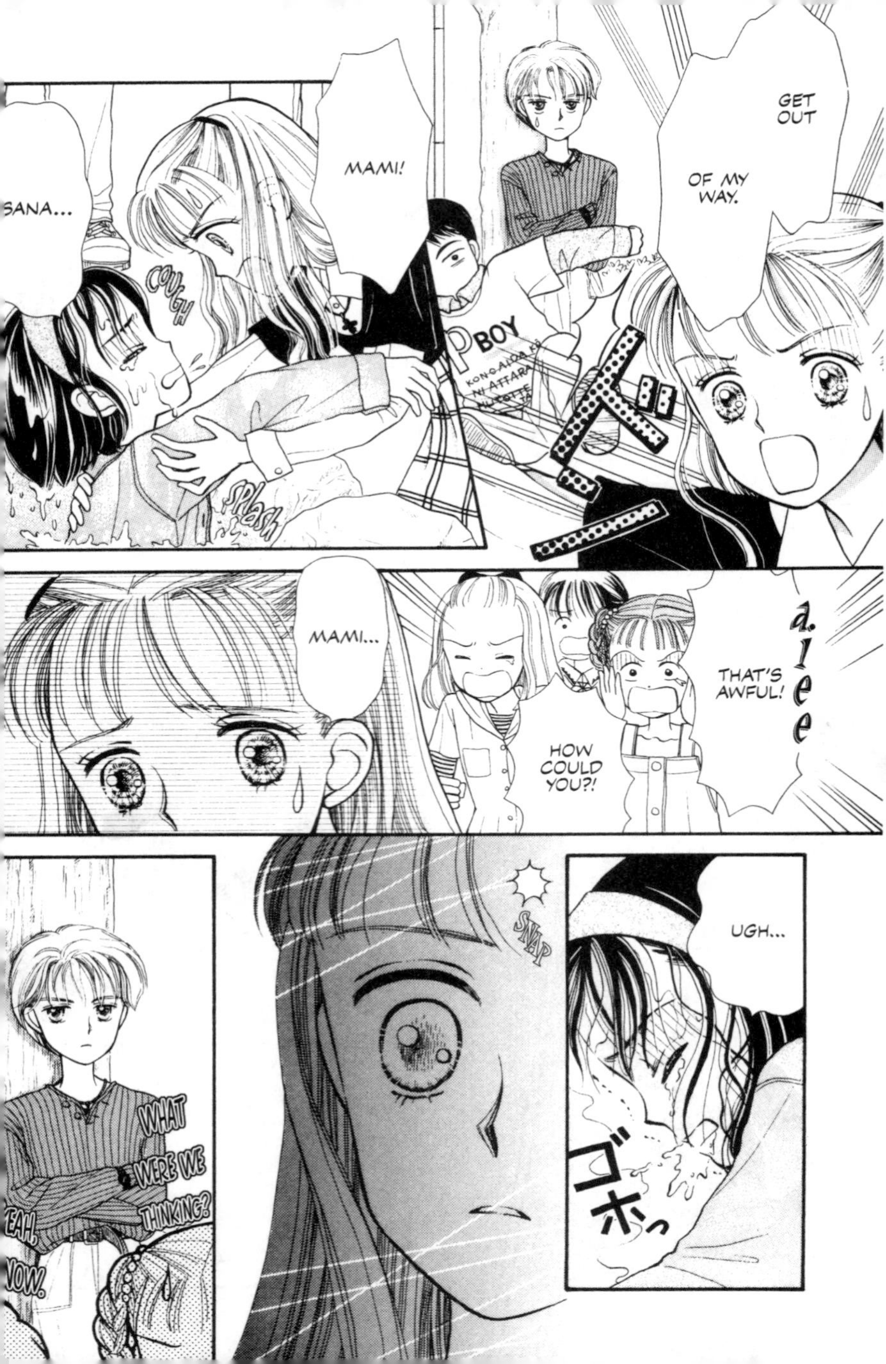
GET OUT
OF MY WAY.
MAMI!
SANA...
COUGH
SPLASH
aiee
THAT'S AWFUL!
HOW COULD YOU?!
MAMI...
UGH...
ゴホっ
SNAP
WHAT WERE WE THINKING?
EAH, NOW.

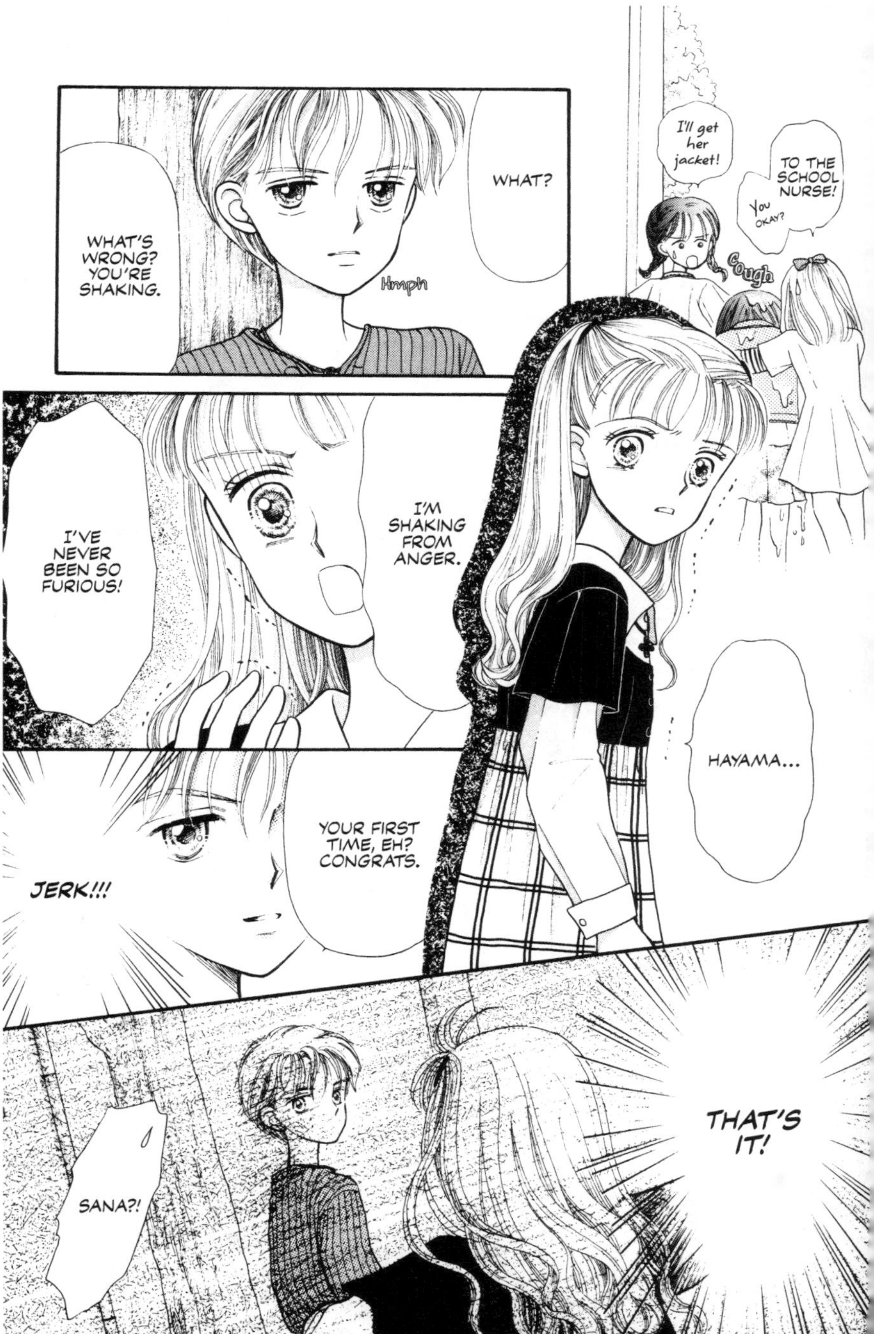
I'll get her jacket!
TO THE SCHOOL NURSE!
You OKAY?
Cough
HAYAMA...
WHAT?
WHAT'S WRONG? YOU'RE SHAKING.
Hmph
I'M SHAKING FROM ANGER.
I'VE NEVER BEEN SO FURIOUS!
YOUR FIRST TIME, EH? CONGRATS.
JERK!!!
THAT'S IT!
SANA?!

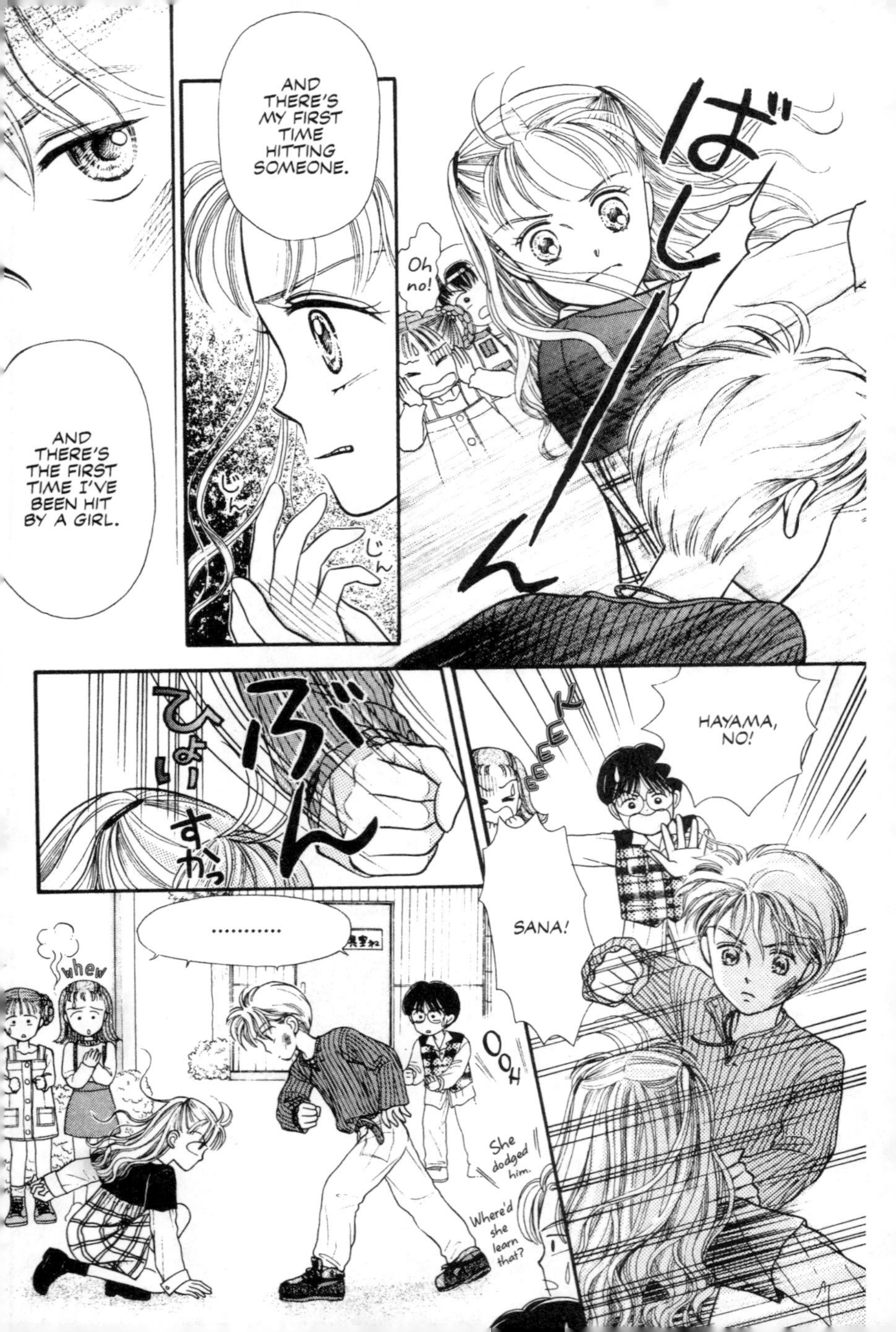
ばしん
Oh no!
AND THERE'S MY FIRST TIME HITTING SOMEONE.
じん
じん
AND THERE'S THE FIRST TIME I'VE BEEN HIT BY A GIRL.
HAYAMA, NO!
EEEEK
SANA!
ぶん
ひょい
すかっ
OOH
She dodged him.
Where'd she learn that?
....
whew

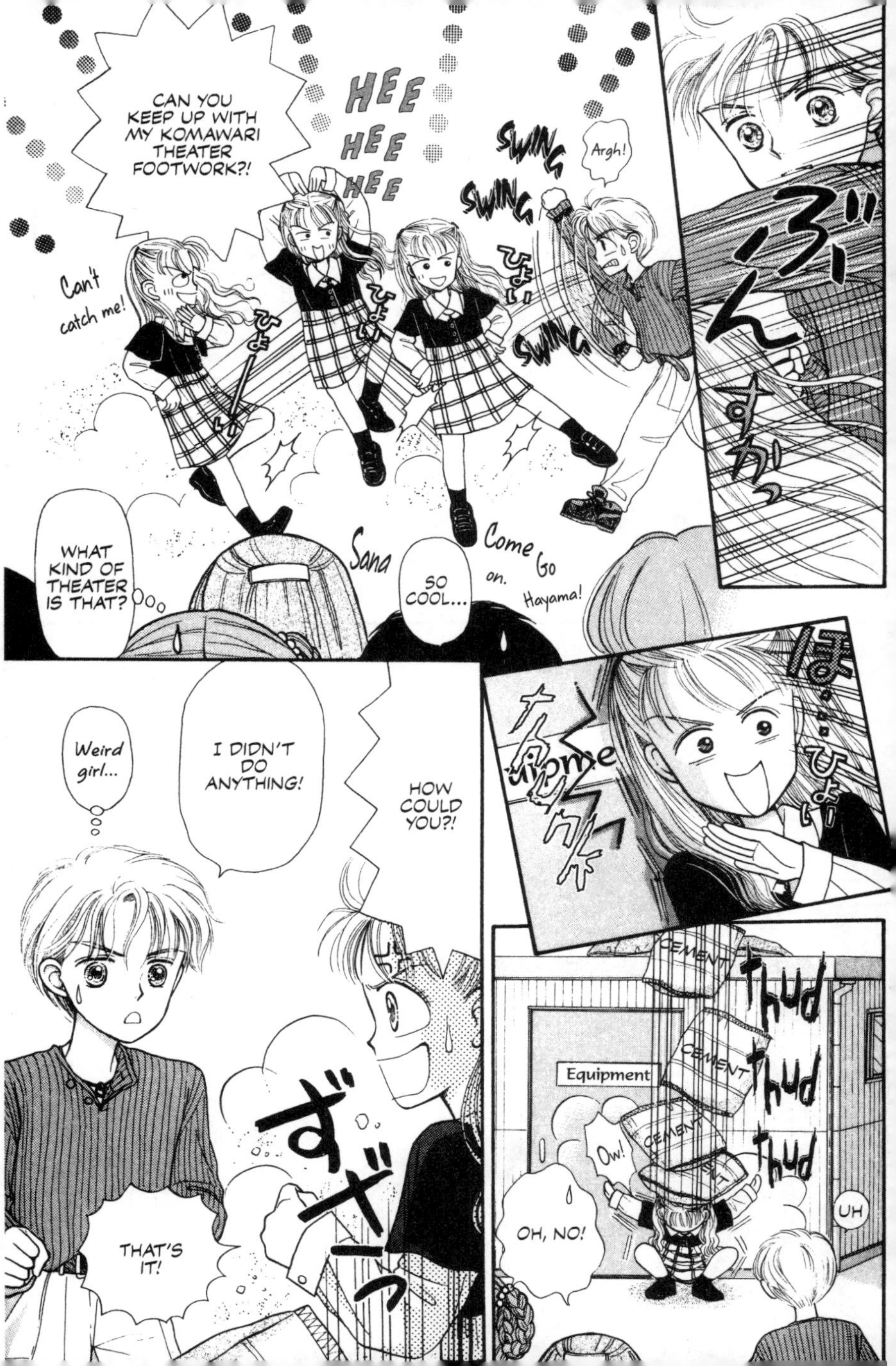
ぶん
すかっ
CAN YOU KEEP UP WITH MY KOMAWARI THEATER FOOTWORK?!
HEE HEE HEE
SWING SWING SWING
Argh!
ひょい
ひょい
ひょ
Can't catch me!
Go Hayama!
Come on.
SO COOL...
Sana
WHAT KIND OF THEATER IS THAT?
ほ
ひょい
thud thud thud
Equipment
CEMENT
CEMENT
CEMENT
Ow!
UH
OH, NO!
HOW COULD YOU?!
I DIDN'T DO ANYTHING!
Weird girl...
ずざーっ
THAT'S IT!

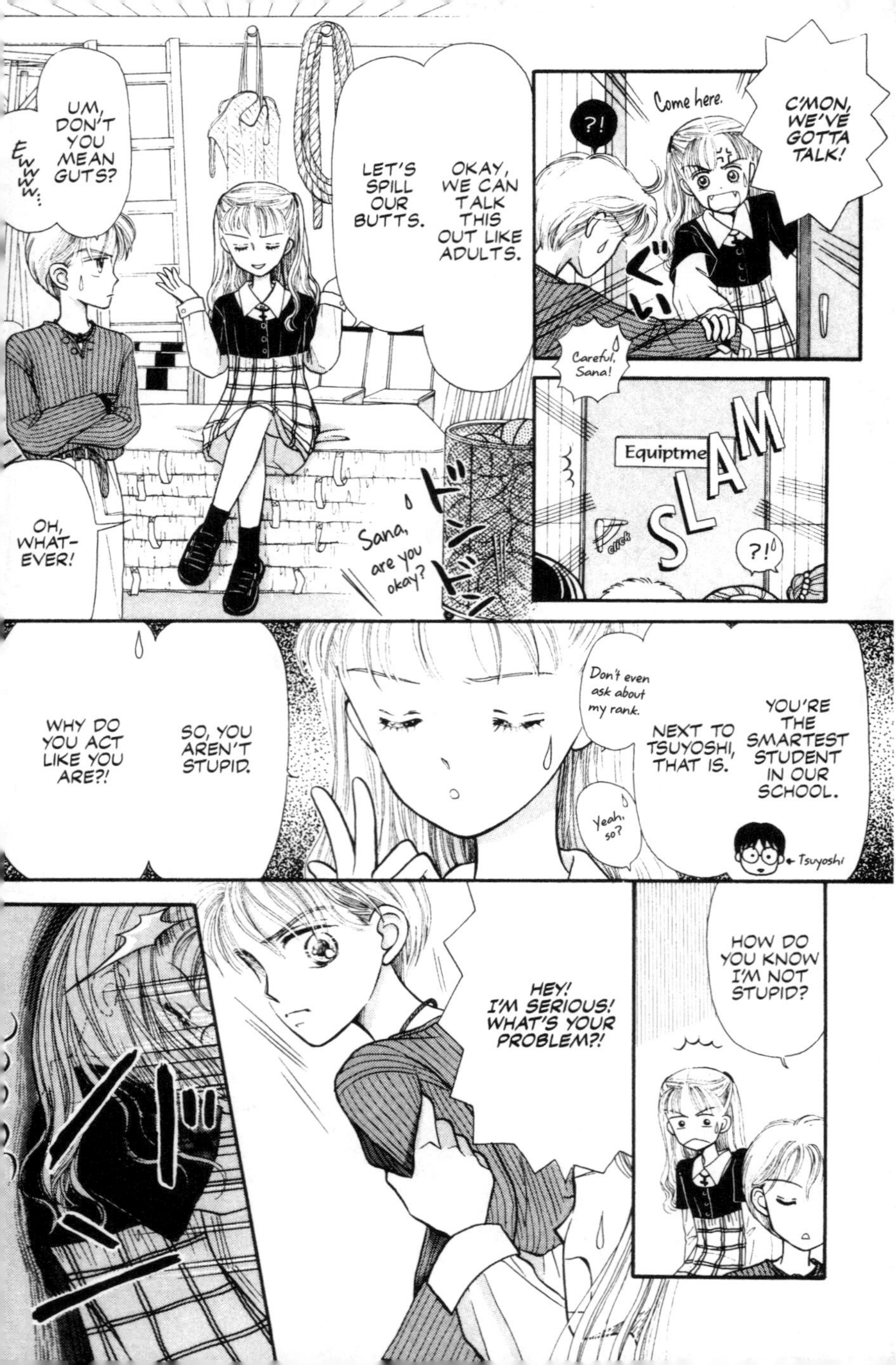
C'MON, WE'VE GOTTA TALK!
Come here.
?!
Careful, Sana!
Equiptme
SLAM
click
?!
OKAY, WE CAN TALK THIS OUT LIKE ADULTS.
LET'S SPILL OUR BUTTS.
UM, DON'T YOU MEAN GUTS?
Ewwww...
OH, WHAT-EVER!
Sana, are you okay?
YOU'RE THE SMARTEST STUDENT IN OUR SCHOOL.
NEXT TO TSUYOSHI, THAT IS.
Don't even ask about my rank.
Yeah, so?
Tsuyoshi
SO, YOU AREN'T STUPID.
WHY DO YOU ACT LIKE YOU ARE?!
HOW DO YOU KNOW I'M NOT STUPID?
HEY! I'M SERIOUS! WHAT'S YOUR PROBLEM?!

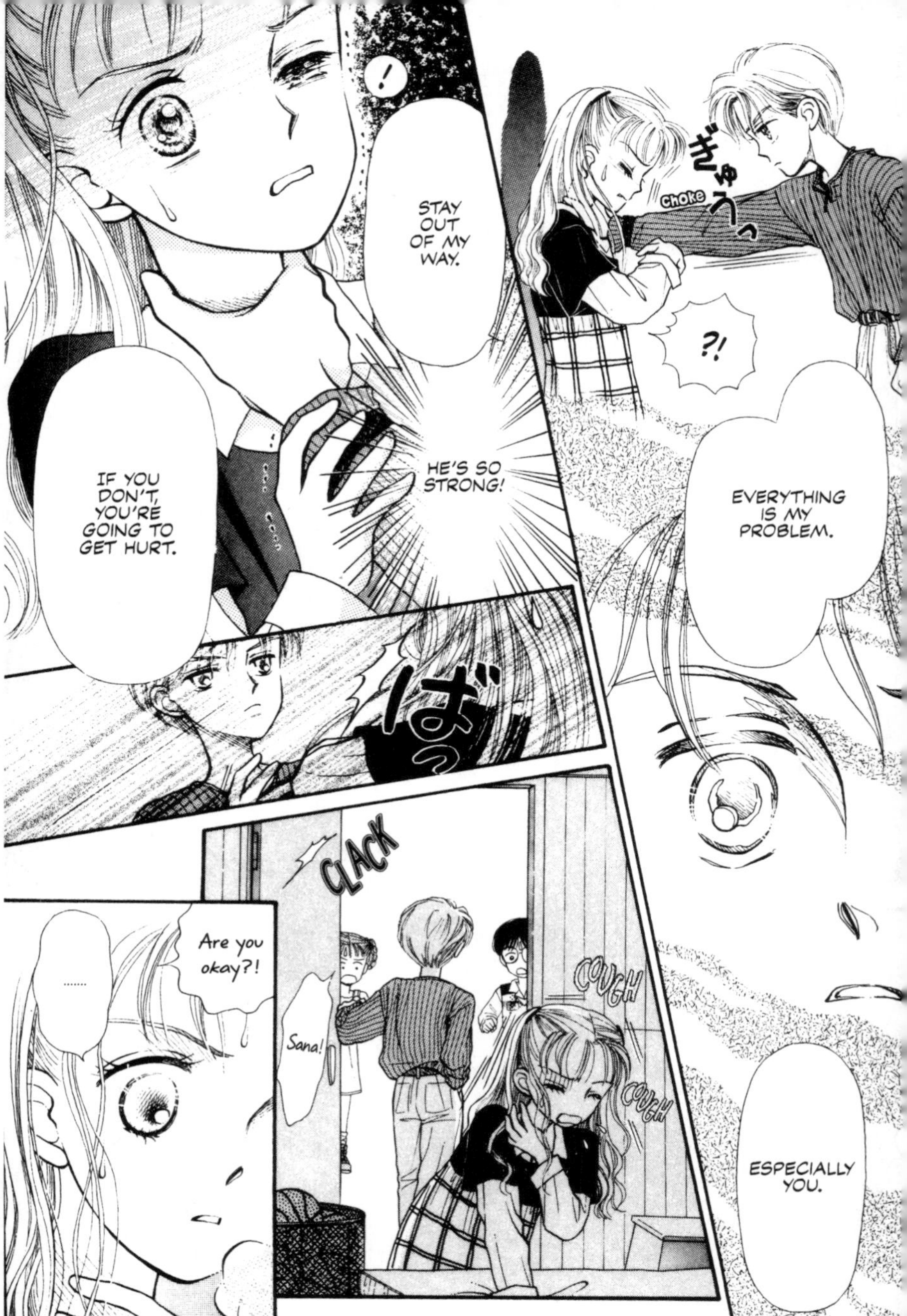
Choke
?!
!
STAY OUT OF MY WAY.
HE'S SO STRONG!
IF YOU DON'T, YOU'RE GOING TO GET HURT.
EVERYTHING IS MY PROBLEM.
ESPECIALLY YOU.
ばっ
CLACK
Sana!
COUGH
COUGH
Are you okay?!
......

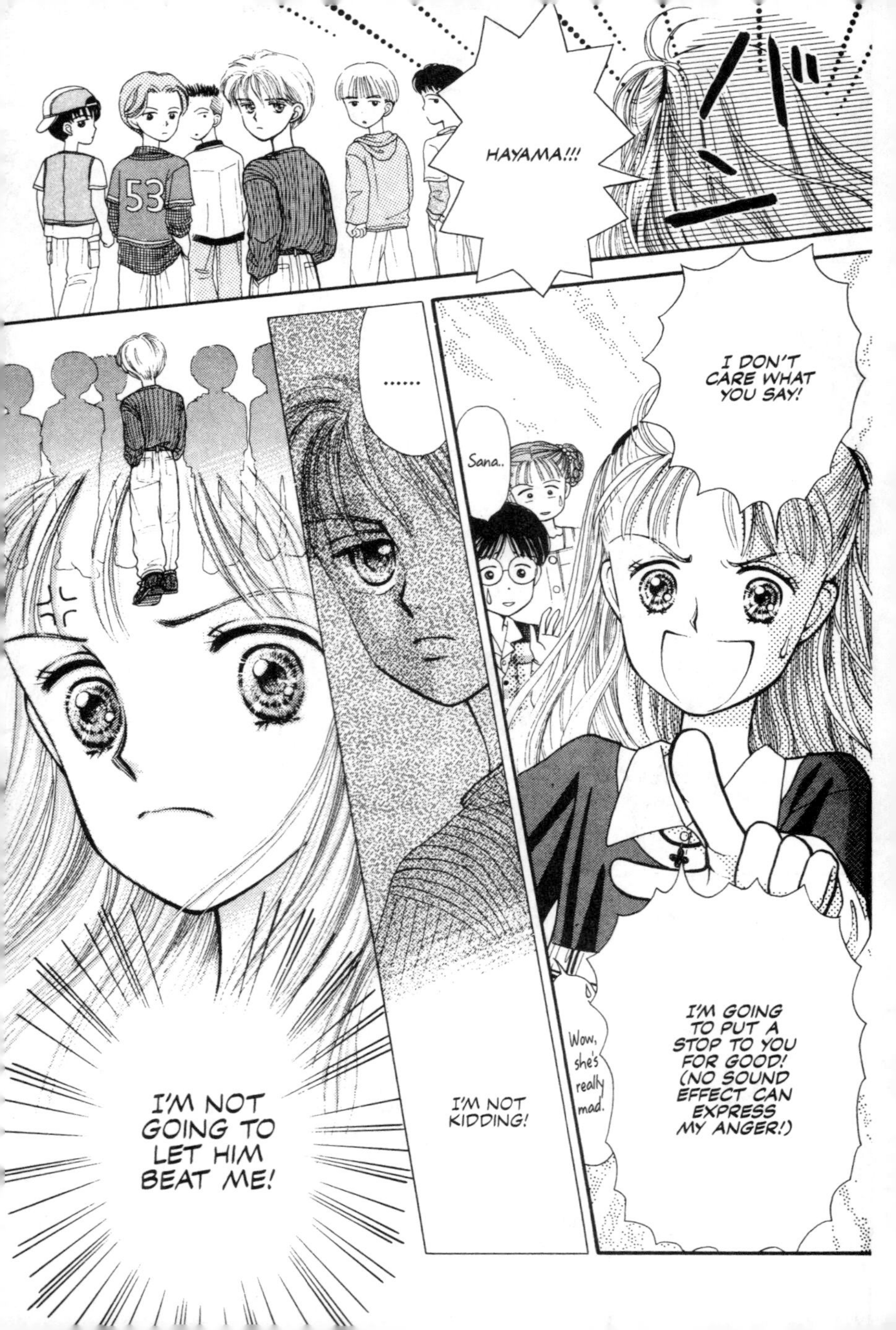
HAYAMA!!!
I DON'T CARE WHAT YOU SAY!
Sana..
I'M GOING TO PUT A STOP TO YOU FOR GOOD! (NO SOUND EFFECT CAN EXPRESS MY ANGER!)
Wow, she's really mad.
......
I'M NOT KIDDING!
I'M NOT GOING TO LET HIM BEAT ME!

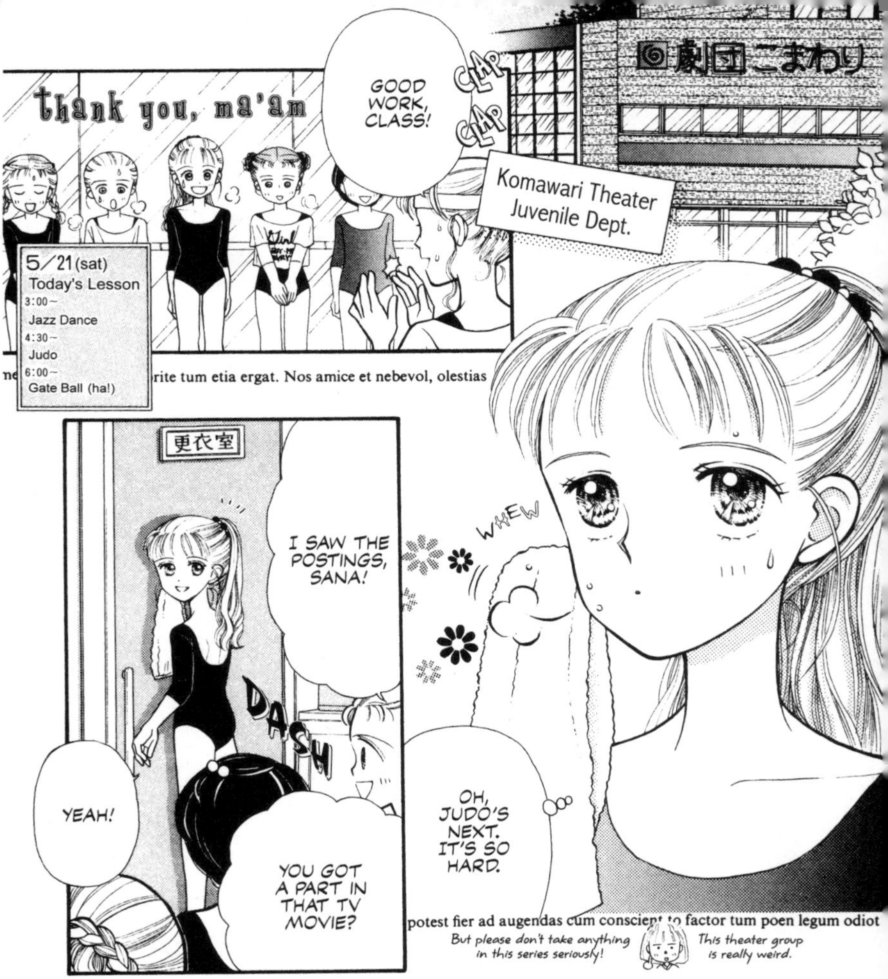
劇団こまわり
Komawari Theater Juvenile Dept.
GOOD WORK, CLASS!
CLAP CLAP
thank you, ma'am
5/21 (sat) Today's Lesson 3:00~ Jazz Dance 4:30~ Judo 6:00~ Gate Ball (ha!)
ne rite tum etia ergat. Nos amice et nebevol, olestias
WHEW
OH, JUDO'S NEXT. IT'S SO HARD.
更衣室
I SAW THE POSTINGS, SANA!
DASH
YEAH!
YOU GOT A PART IN THAT TV MOVIE?
potest fier ad augendas cum conscient to factor tum poen legum odiot
This theater group is really weird.
But please don't take anything in this series seriously!

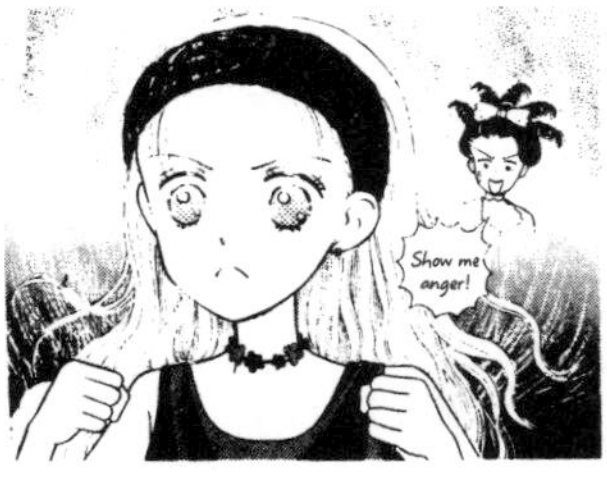
Show me anger!

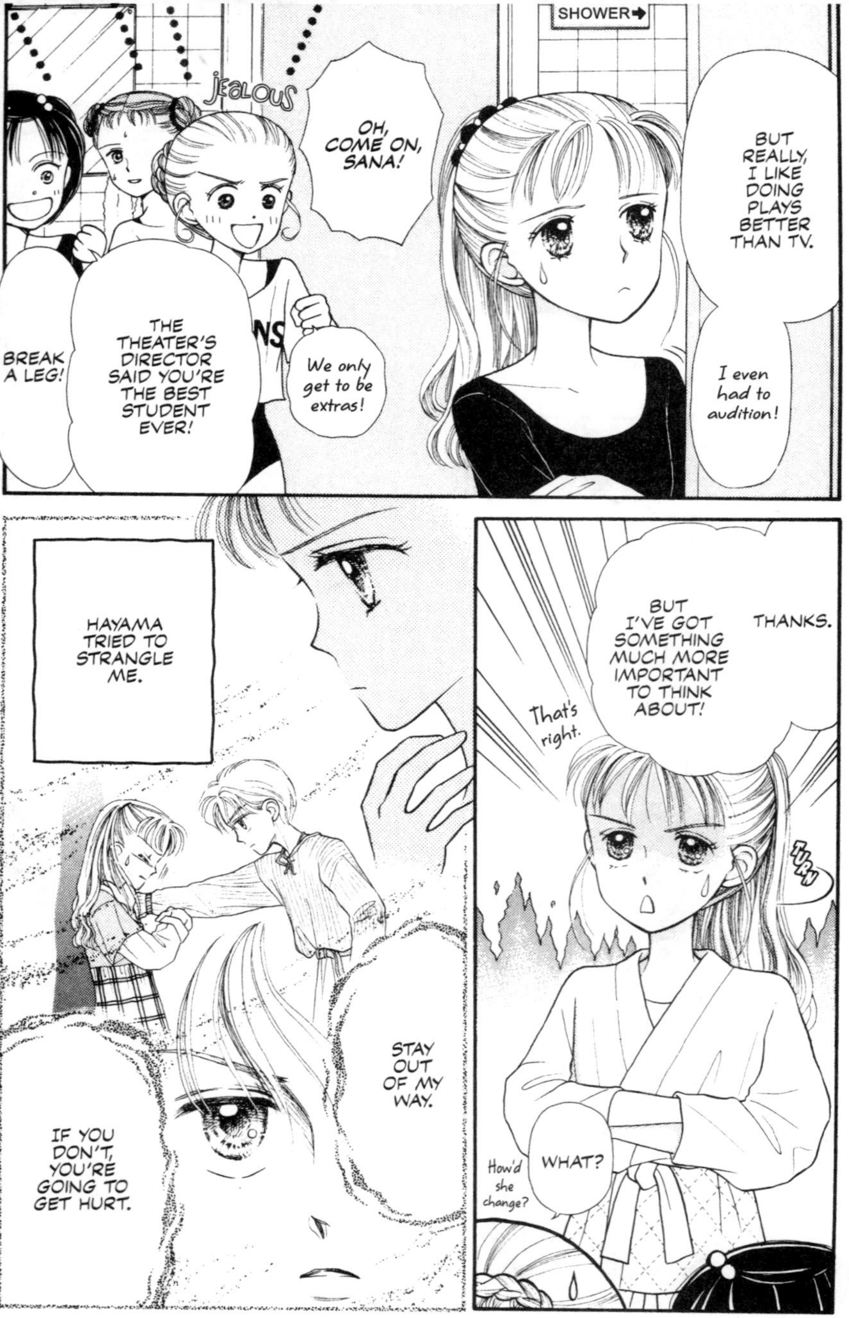
SHOWER
BUT REALLY, I LIKE DOING PLAYS BETTER THAN TV.
I even had to audition!
jealous
OH, COME ON, SANA!
We only get to be extras!
THE THEATER'S DIRECTOR SAID YOU'RE THE BEST STUDENT EVER!
BREAK A LEG!
THANKS.
BUT I'VE GOT SOMETHING MUCH MORE IMPORTANT TO THINK ABOUT!
That's right.
TURN
WHAT?
How'd she change?
HAYAMA TRIED TO STRANGLE ME.
STAY OUT OF MY WAY.
IF YOU DON'T, YOU'RE GOING TO GET HURT.

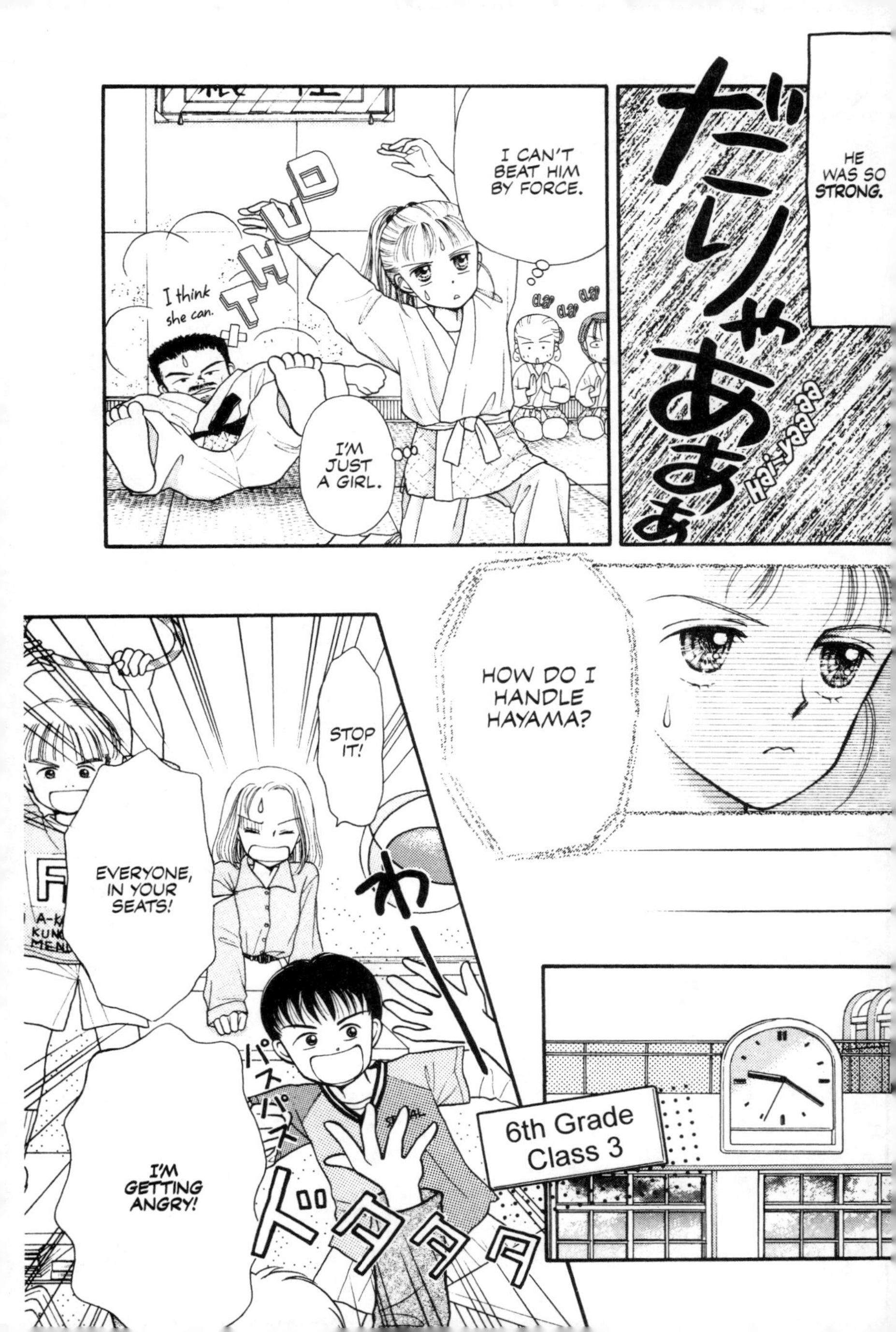
HE WAS SO STRONG.
だりゃあああ
HAI-YAAAA
I CAN'T BEAT HIM BY FORCE.
THUD
I think she can.
CLAP CLAP CLAP
I'M JUST A GIRL.
HOW DO I HANDLE HAYAMA?
6th Grade Class 3
わー
STOP IT!
EVERYONE, IN YOUR SEATS!
パスパス
ドタタタ
I'M GETTING ANGRY!

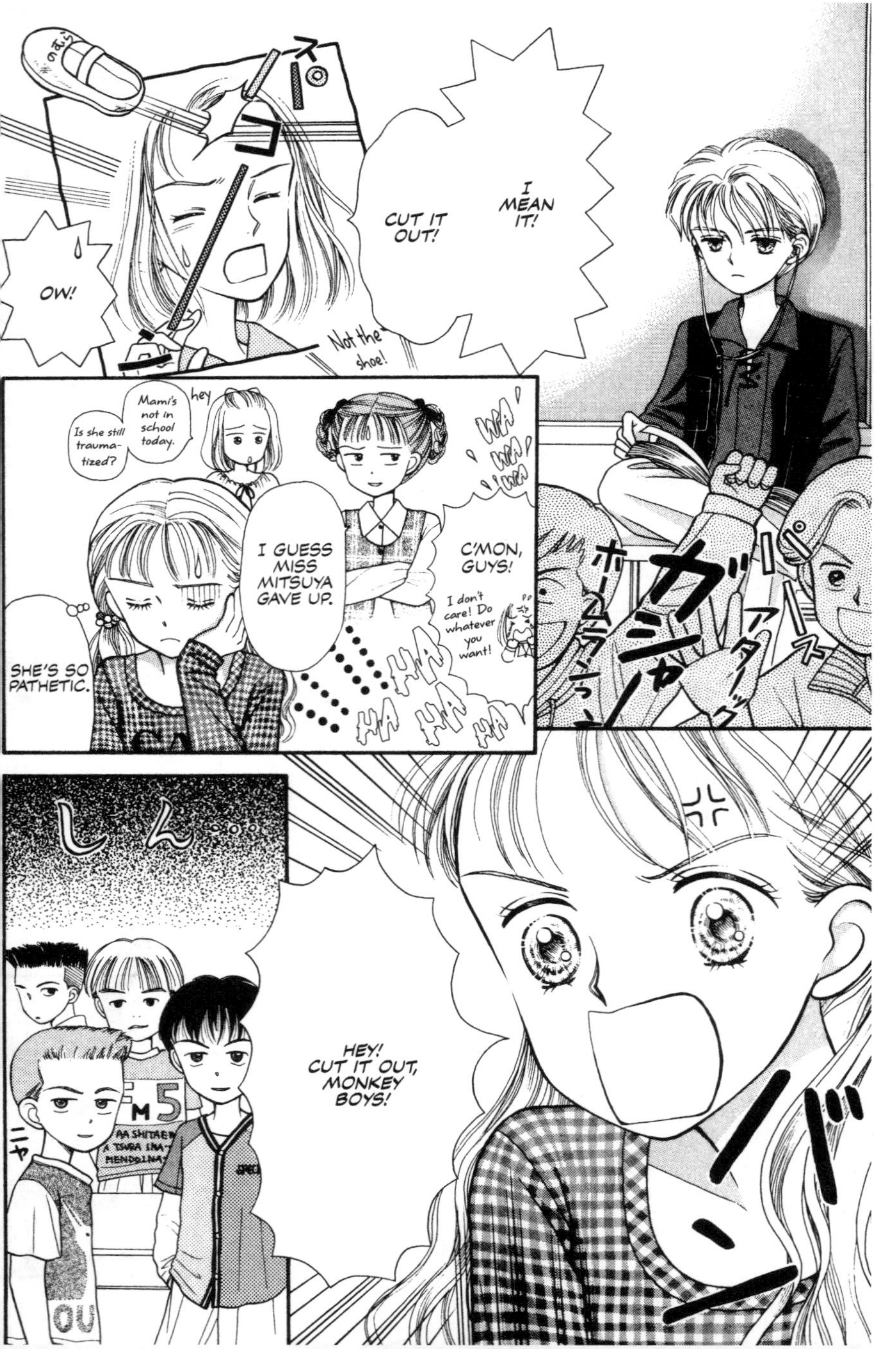
CUT IT OUT!
I MEAN IT!
OW!
Not the shoe!
WA WA WA
C'MON, GUYS!
I don't care! Do whatever you want!
hey
Mami's not in school today.
Is she still traumatized?
I GUESS MISS MITSUYA GAVE UP.
SHE'S SO PATHETIC.
HA HA HA HA
HEY! CUT IT OUT, MONKEY BOYS!

Story From My Elementary School.

How was (or is) your elementary school? My 5th & 6th grade years were pretty terrible because of all the kids who picked on the teachers and other students. Our teacher was always crying. She looked so happy on our graduation day--but we didn't really care. Unlike Sana, I didn't get involved at all -- because the teacher was a big part of the problem.

At one point, I was really harassed by the boys in my class! Yeah, for real! I was a good student 'til junior high. (Doesn't that sound stuck-up?) School work was easy for me, and I was given a few leadership positions, too. (Really stuck-up!) The kids in class got jealous because they thought the teacher favored me over them. I was like, "Well, why don't you just do better on the tests?!" Yup, they sure hated me.
To be continued... I think!

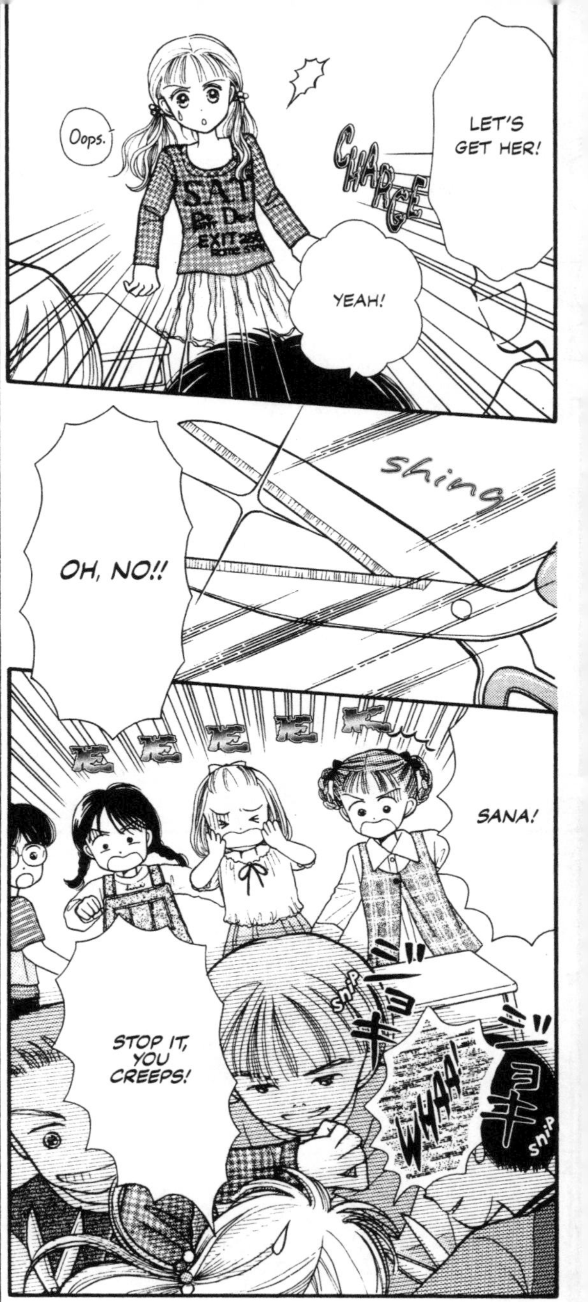
LET'S GET HER!
CHARGE
Oops.
YEAH!
shing
OH, NO!!
SANA!
SNIP
STOP IT, YOU CREEPS!
SNIP

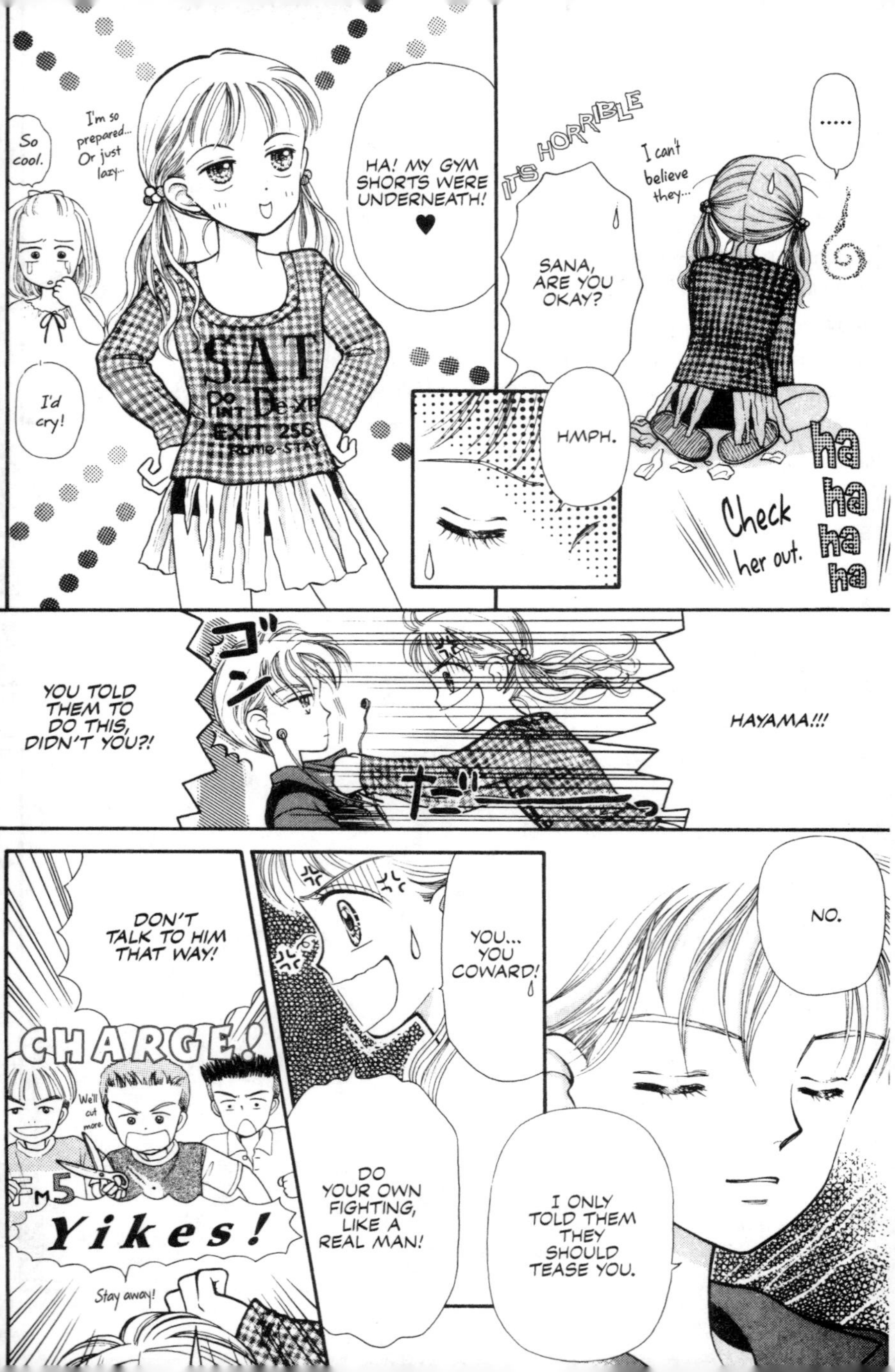
......
I can't believe they...
IT'S HORRIBLE
SANA, ARE YOU OKAY?
Check her out.
ha ha ha ha
HMPH.
HA! MY GYM SHORTS WERE UNDERNEATH! ♥
I'm so prepared... Or just lazy...
So cool.
I'd cry!
HAYAMA!!!
YOU TOLD THEM TO DO THIS, DIDN'T YOU?!
NO.
I ONLY TOLD THEM THEY SHOULD TEASE YOU.
YOU... YOU COWARD!
DO YOUR OWN FIGHTING, LIKE A REAL MAN!
DON'T TALK TO HIM THAT WAY!
CHARGE!
We'll cut more.
Yikes!
Stay away!

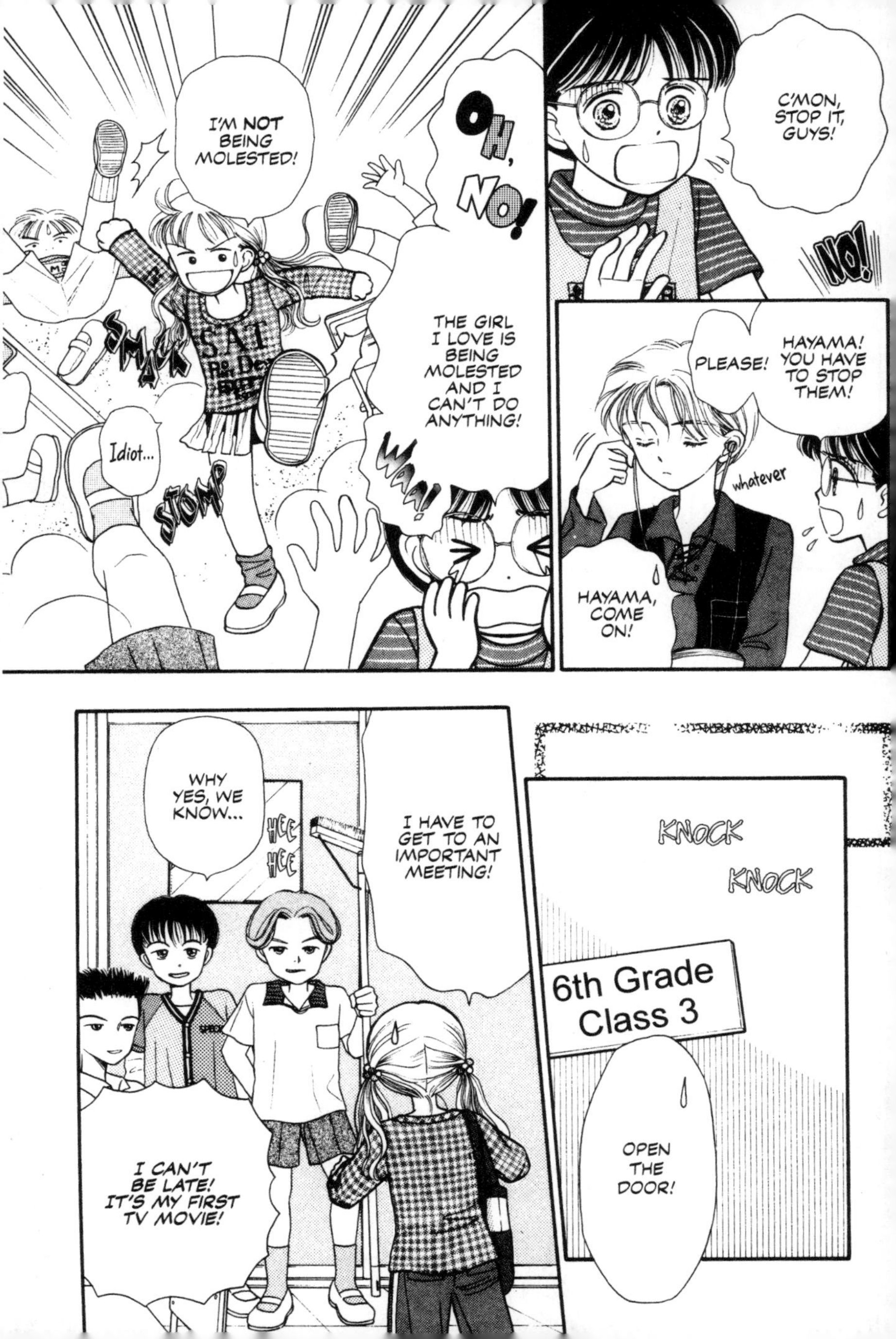
C'MON, STOP IT, GUYS!
NO!
HAYAMA! YOU HAVE TO STOP THEM!
PLEASE!
whatever
HAYAMA, COME ON!
OH, NO!
I'M NOT BEING MOLESTED!
THE GIRL I LOVE IS BEING MOLESTED AND I CAN'T DO ANYTHING!
WAAA!
SMACK
Idiot...
STOMP
KNOCK
KNOCK
6th Grade Class 3
OPEN THE DOOR!
I HAVE TO GET TO AN IMPORTANT MEETING!
WHY YES, WE KNOW...
HEE HEE
I CAN'T BE LATE! IT'S MY FIRST TV MOVIE!

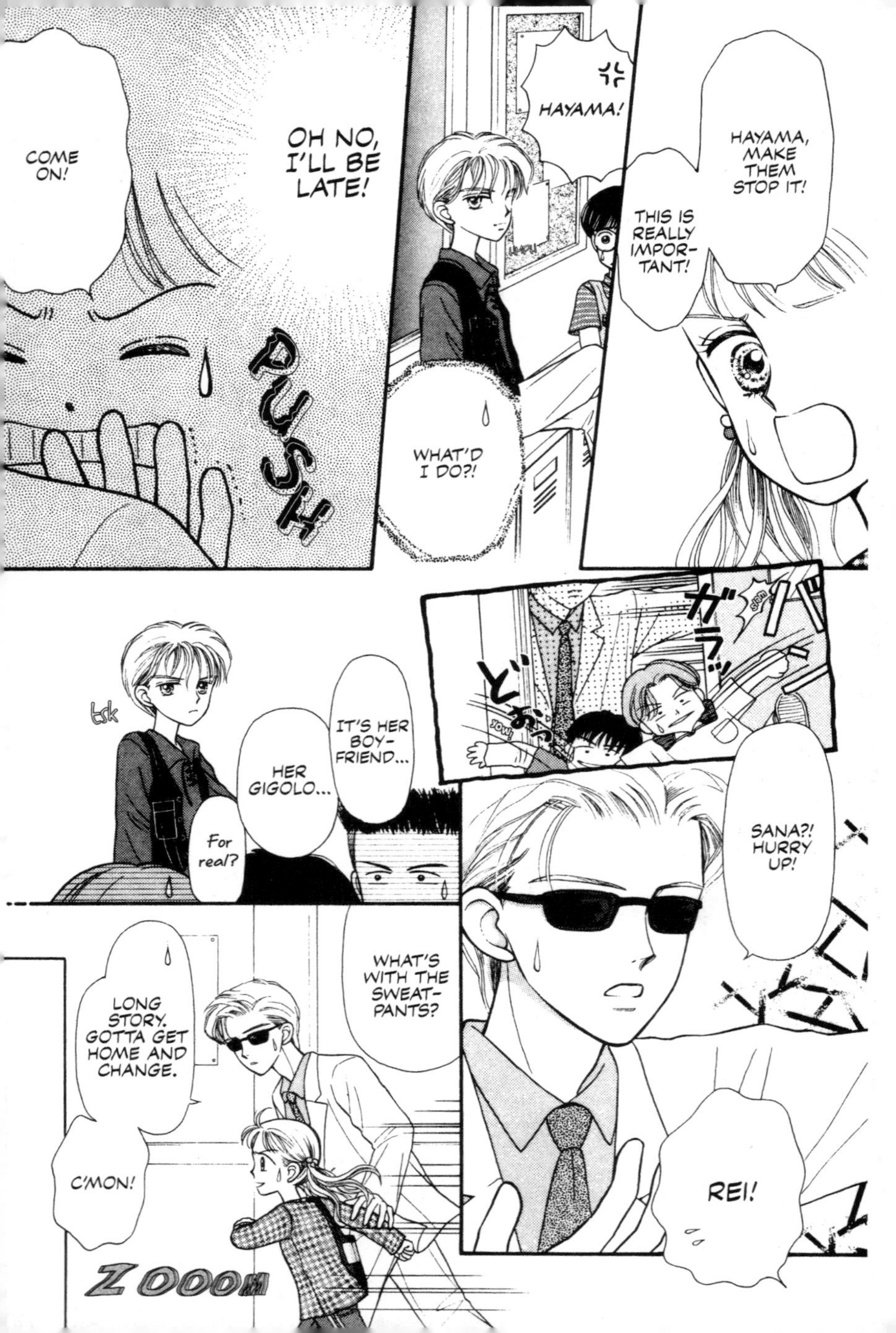
HAYAMA, MAKE THEM STOP IT!
THIS IS REALLY IMPORTANT!
HAYAMA!
WHAT'D I DO?!
OH NO, I'LL BE LATE!
COME ON!
PUSH
gom
YOW!
tsk
IT'S HER BOYFRIEND...
HER GIGOLO...
For real?
SANA?! HURRY UP!
REI!
WHAT'S WITH THE SWEATPANTS?
LONG STORY. GOTTA GET HOME AND CHANGE.
C'MON!
ZOOOM

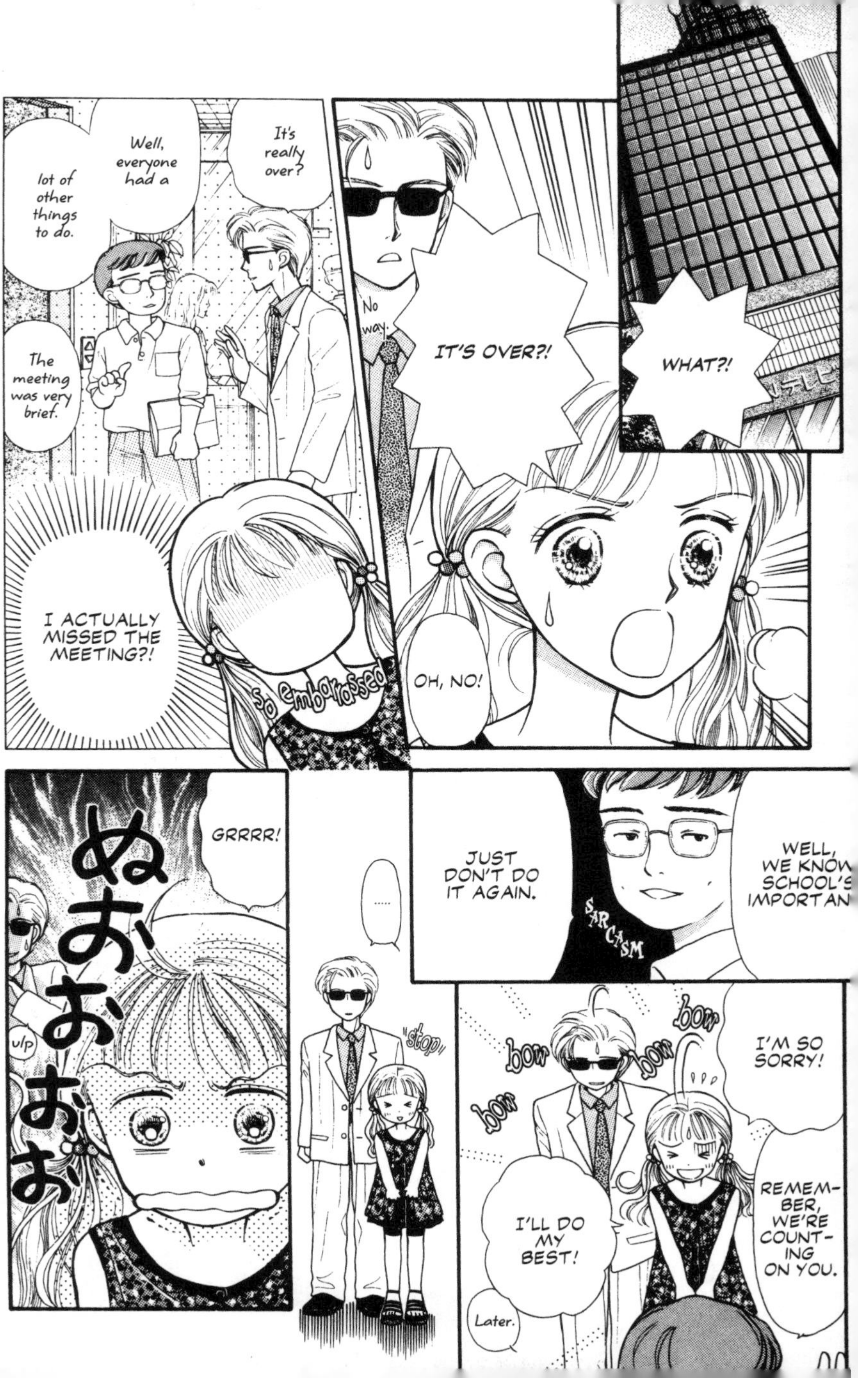
WHAT?!
IT'S OVER?!
No way.
OH, NO!
It's really over?
Well, everyone had a lot of other things to do.
The meeting was very brief.
I ACTUALLY MISSED THE MEETING?!
so embarrassed
WELL, WE KNOW SCHOOL'S IMPORTAN
SARCASM
JUST DON'T DO IT AGAIN.
bow bow bow bow
I'M SO SORRY!
REMEMBER, WE'RE COUNTING ON YOU.
I'LL DO MY BEST!
Later.
stop
.....
GRRRR!
ぬおおおお
u/p

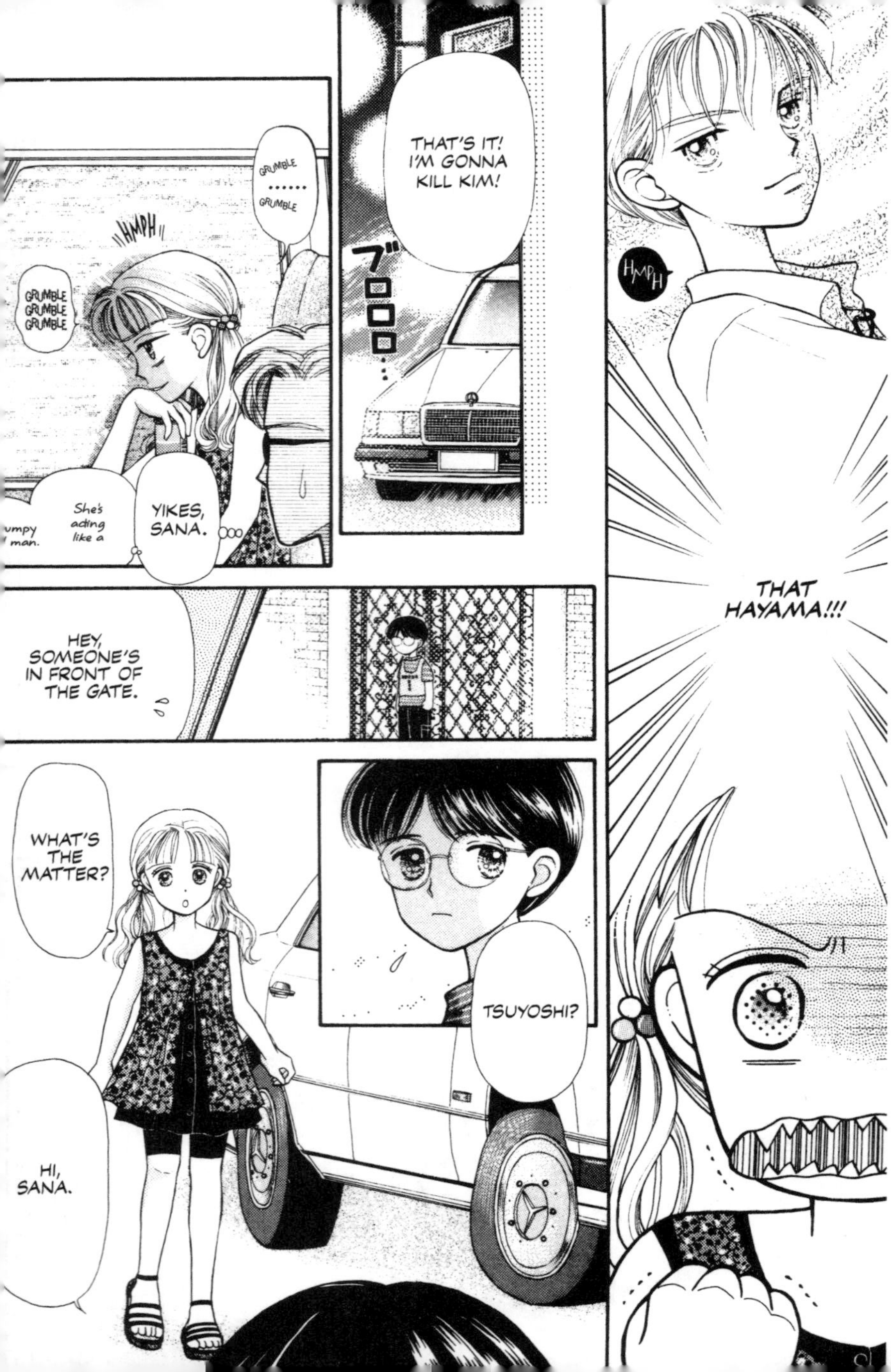
HMPH
THAT HAYAMA!!!
THAT'S IT! I'M GONNA KILL KIM!
ブロロロ...
GRUMBLE ...... GRUMBLE
HMPH
GRUMBLE GRUMBLE GRUMBLE
YIKES, SANA.
She's acting like a
umpy man.
HEY, SOMEONE'S IN FRONT OF THE GATE.
TSUYOSHI?
WHAT'S THE MATTER?
HI, SANA.

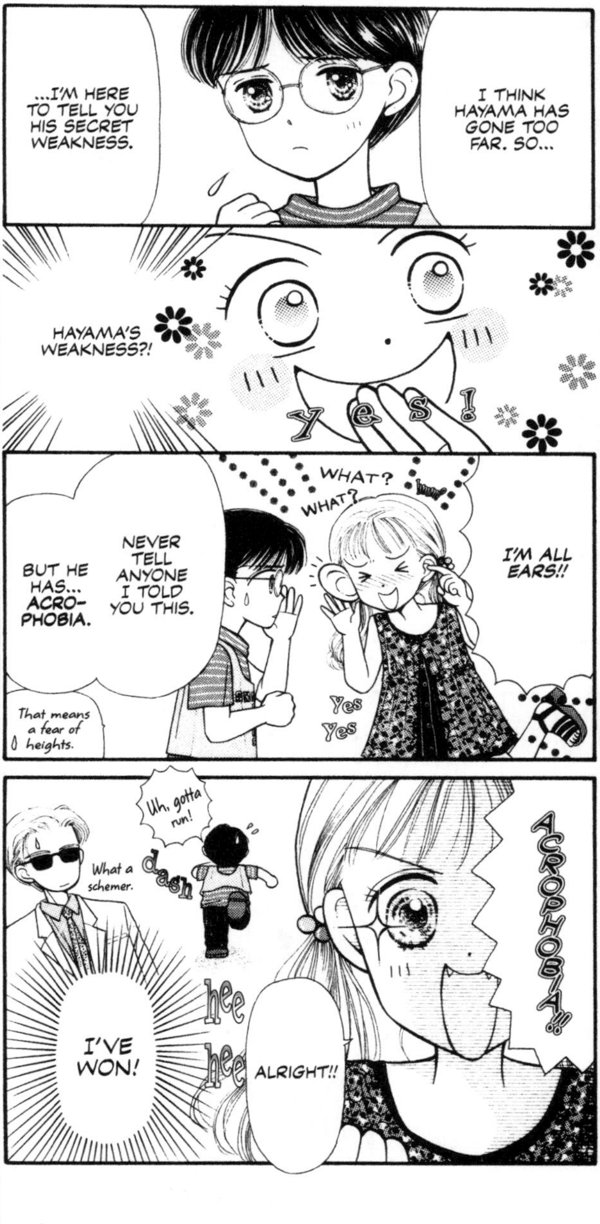
I THINK HAYAMA HAS GONE TOO FAR. SO...
...I'M HERE TO TELL YOU HIS SECRET WEAKNESS.
yes!
HAYAMA'S WEAKNESS?!
I'M ALL EARS!!
WHAT? WHAT?
Yes Yes
NEVER TELL ANYONE I TOLD YOU THIS.
BUT HE HAS... ACROPHOBIA.
That means a fear of heights.
ACROPHOBIA!!
ALRIGHT!!
hee hee
I'VE WON!
Uh, gotta run!
dash
What a schemer.

Part II (I think...)

So, the stupid boys attacked me and gave me a really hard time. Looking back on it, my few good friends really helped me to get through it. (Also, when they found out that I have relatives in the mob, things got peaceful fast! Ha!) I think good friends who really understand you are very important. And luckily, I could talk to my mom about anything. If you think I was some kind of smarty-pants, don't worry. I got really stupid around 9th grade. I've been stupid ever since, for 10 years now! I'm much happier now that I'm stupid. Ha, ha.

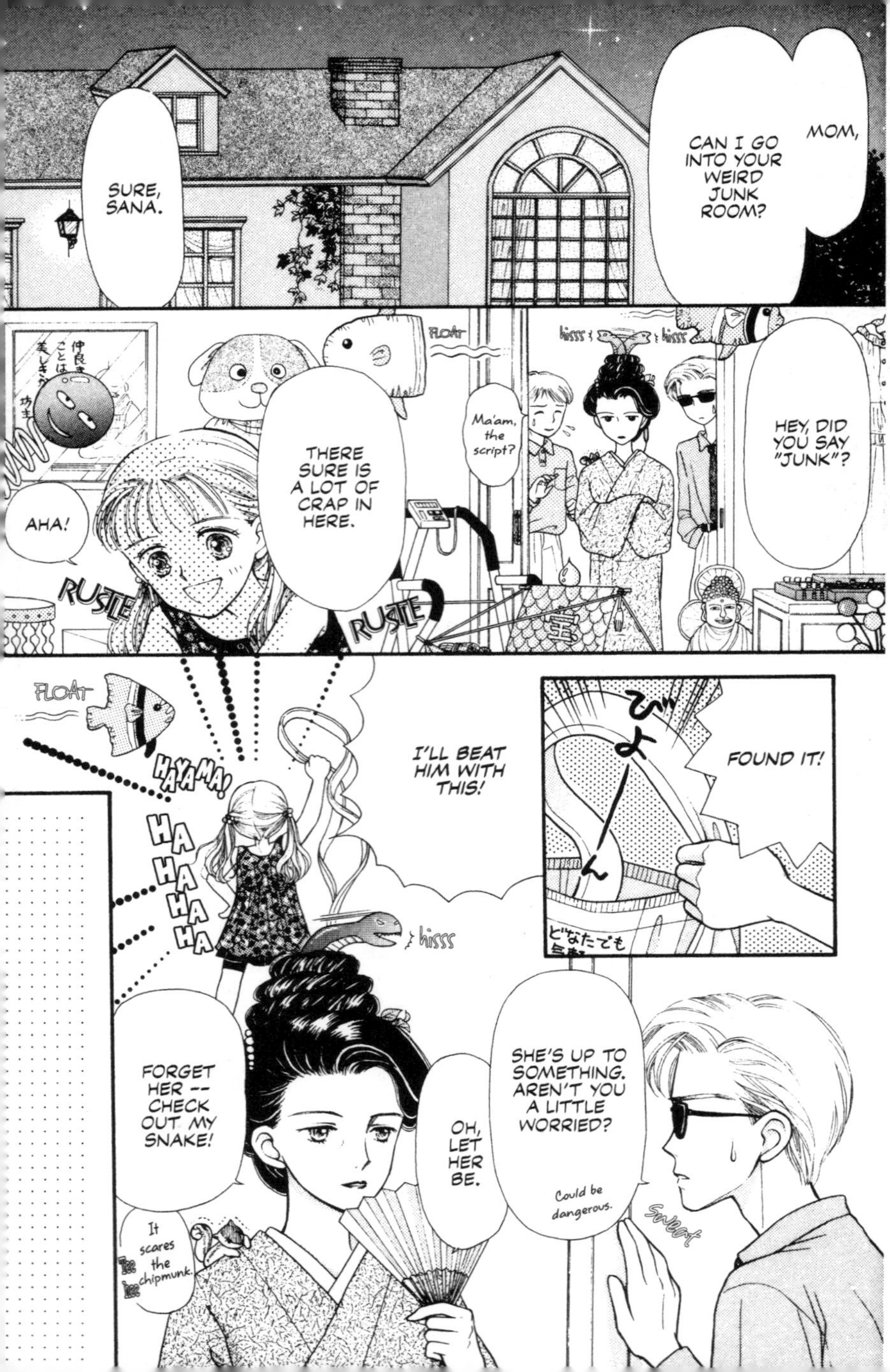

MOM,
CAN I GO INTO YOUR WEIRD JUNK ROOM?
SURE, SANA.
HEY, DID YOU SAY "JUNK"?
hisss hisss
Ma'am, the script?
FLOAT
THERE SURE IS A LOT OF CRAP IN HERE.
AHA!
RUSTLE
RUSTLE
FOUND IT!
ぴよーん
I'LL BEAT HIM WITH THIS!
HAYAMA!
HAHAHAHAHA
FLOAT
hisss
SHE'S UP TO SOMETHING. AREN'T YOU A LITTLE WORRIED?
Could be dangerous.
Sweat
OH, LET HER BE.
FORGET HER -- CHECK OUT MY SNAKE!
It scares the chipmunk.
Tee Tee

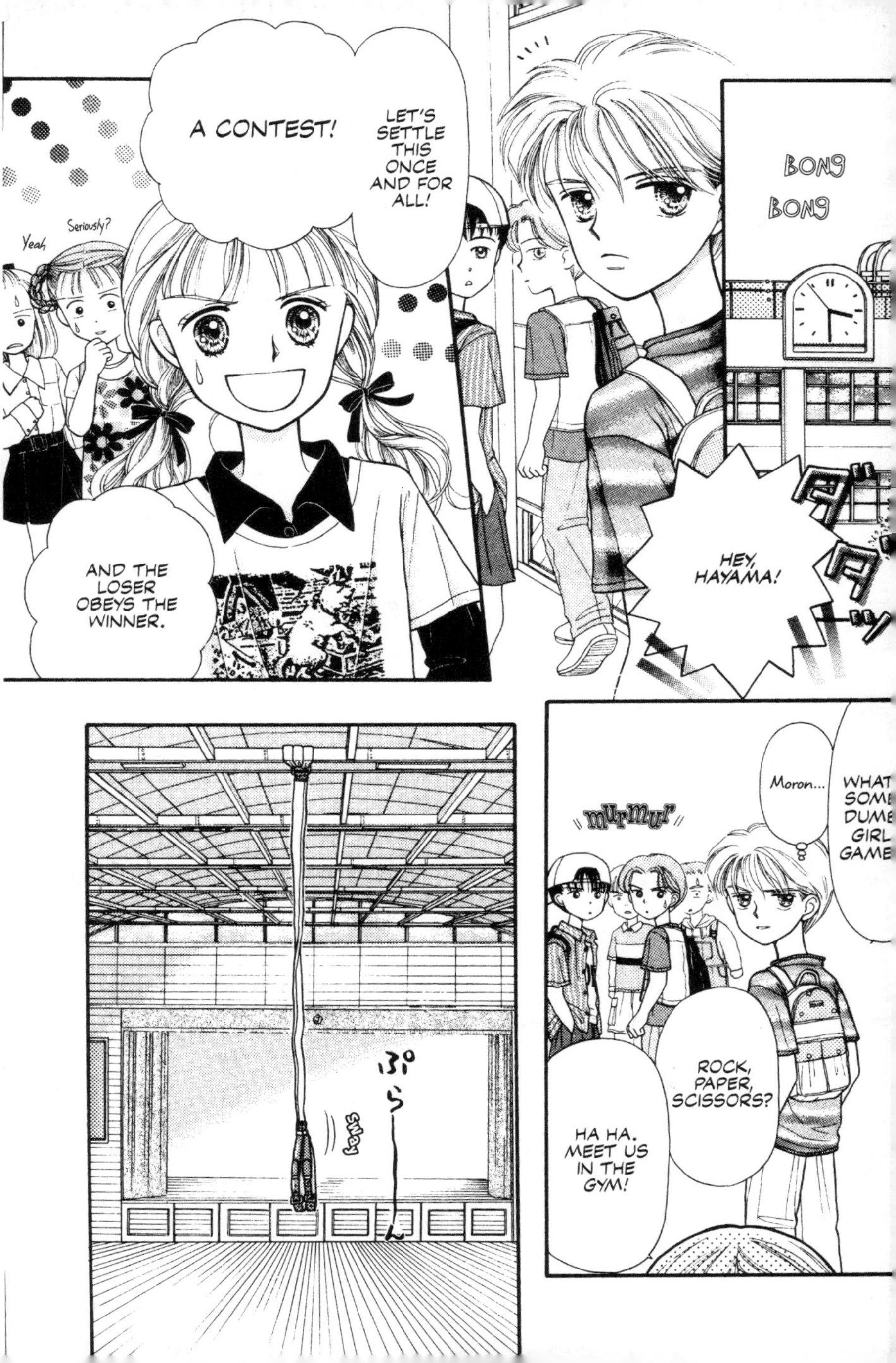
BONG
BONG
HEY, HAYAMA!
ダダッ
LET'S SETTLE THIS ONCE AND FOR ALL!
A CONTEST!
AND THE LOSER OBEYS THE WINNER.
Seriously?
Yeah
murmur
WHAT SOME DUMB GIRL GAME
Moron...
ROCK, PAPER, SCISSORS?
HA HA. MEET US IN THE GYM!
ぷらーん
sway

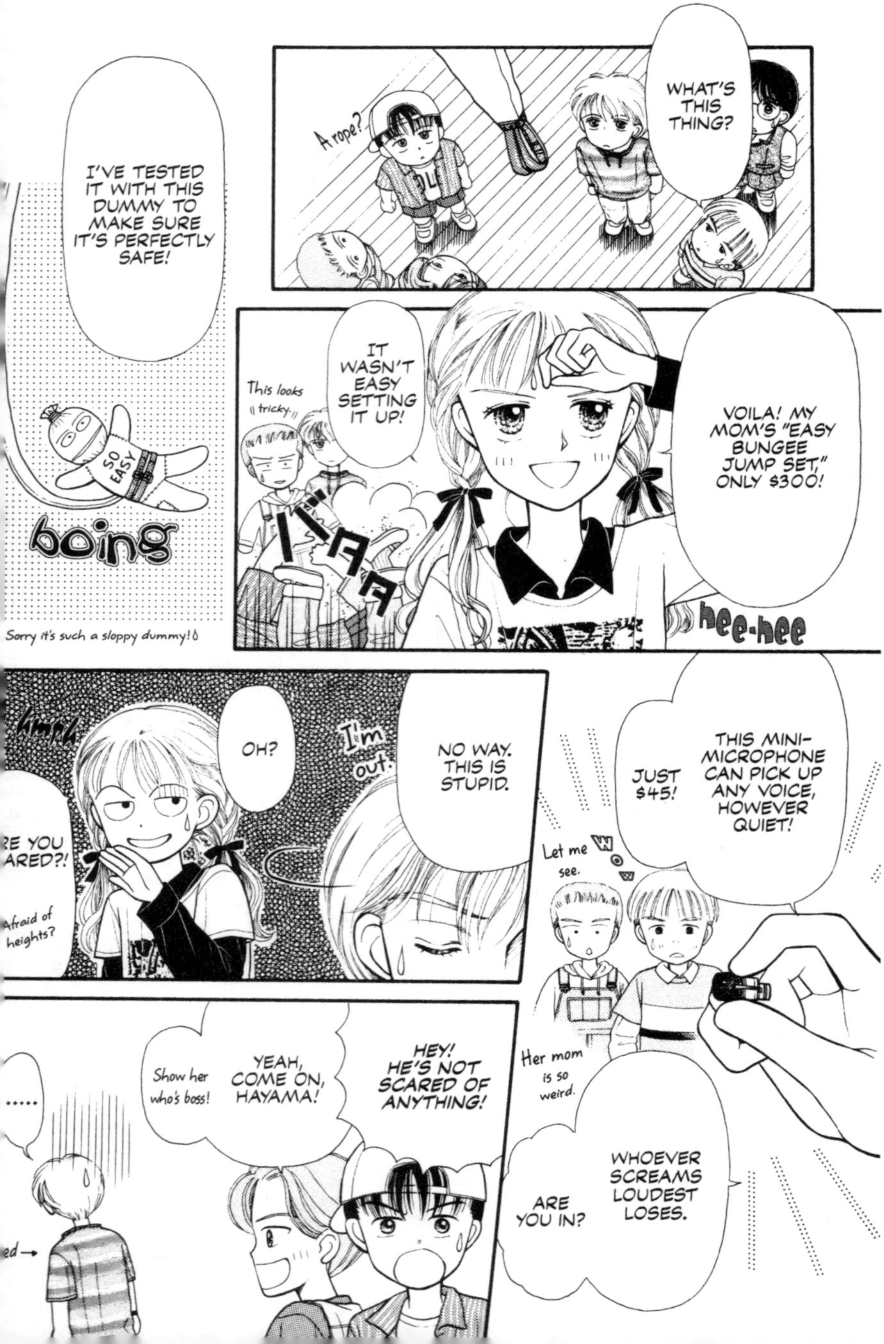
WHAT'S THIS THING?
A rope?
VOILA! MY MOM'S "EASY BUNGEE JUMP SET," ONLY $300!
hee-hee
IT WASN'T EASY SETTING IT UP!
This looks tricky.
バタタ
I'VE TESTED IT WITH THIS DUMMY TO MAKE SURE IT'S PERFECTLY SAFE!
SO EASY
boing
Sorry it's such a sloppy dummy!
THIS MINI-MICROPHONE CAN PICK UP ANY VOICE, HOWEVER QUIET!
JUST $45!
Let me see.
WOW
Her mom is so weird.
WHOEVER SCREAMS LOUDEST LOSES.
ARE YOU IN?
NO WAY. THIS IS STUPID.
I'm out.
OH?
hmph
RE YOU ARED?!
Afraid of heights?
HEY! HE'S NOT SCARED OF ANYTHING!
YEAH, COME ON, HAYAMA!
Show her who's boss!
......

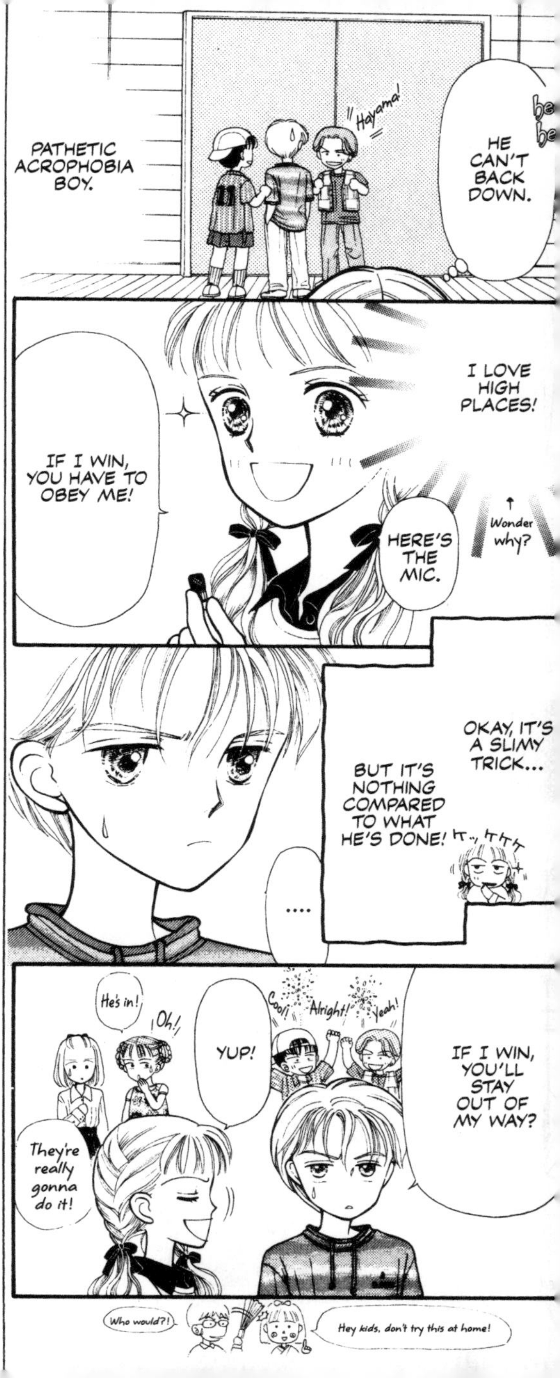
HE CAN'T BACK DOWN.
Hayama!
PATHETIC ACROPHOBIA BOY.
I LOVE HIGH PLACES!
Wonder why?
HERE'S THE MIC.
IF I WIN, YOU HAVE TO OBEY ME!
OKAY, IT'S A SLIMY TRICK...
BUT IT'S NOTHING COMPARED TO WHAT HE'S DONE!
....
IF I WIN, YOU'LL STAY OUT OF MY WAY?
Yeah!
Alright!
Cool!
YUP!
Oh!
He's in!
They're really gonna do it!
Hey kids, don't try this at home!
Who would?!

About "S"

"S" and I went to the same school from elementary all the way through high school. Sana is partially based on her. "S" was in the Himawari Theater and was on TV a lot. She sang in my band during high school. She even put me on her radio commercial! "S" was a cheerful and pretty girl, and had a lot of boyfriends. (Duh!) I mixed her cheerfulness, my stupidity, and the image of Kie-chan from the TV show, "Appare*" for Sana's character. (Kie's great. The way she plays dumb is unbelievable!) The name, Sana, comes from my sister's friend. I heard my sister say that name a lot on the phone and thought it was pretty. (Her name's spelled differently, though.) Speaking of names I stole... Hee-hee. The next section is About Gertie. Sorry for jumping from one subject to another.

* Appare - The TV show in this series, "Kodomo no Omocha," is based on this famous TV show.

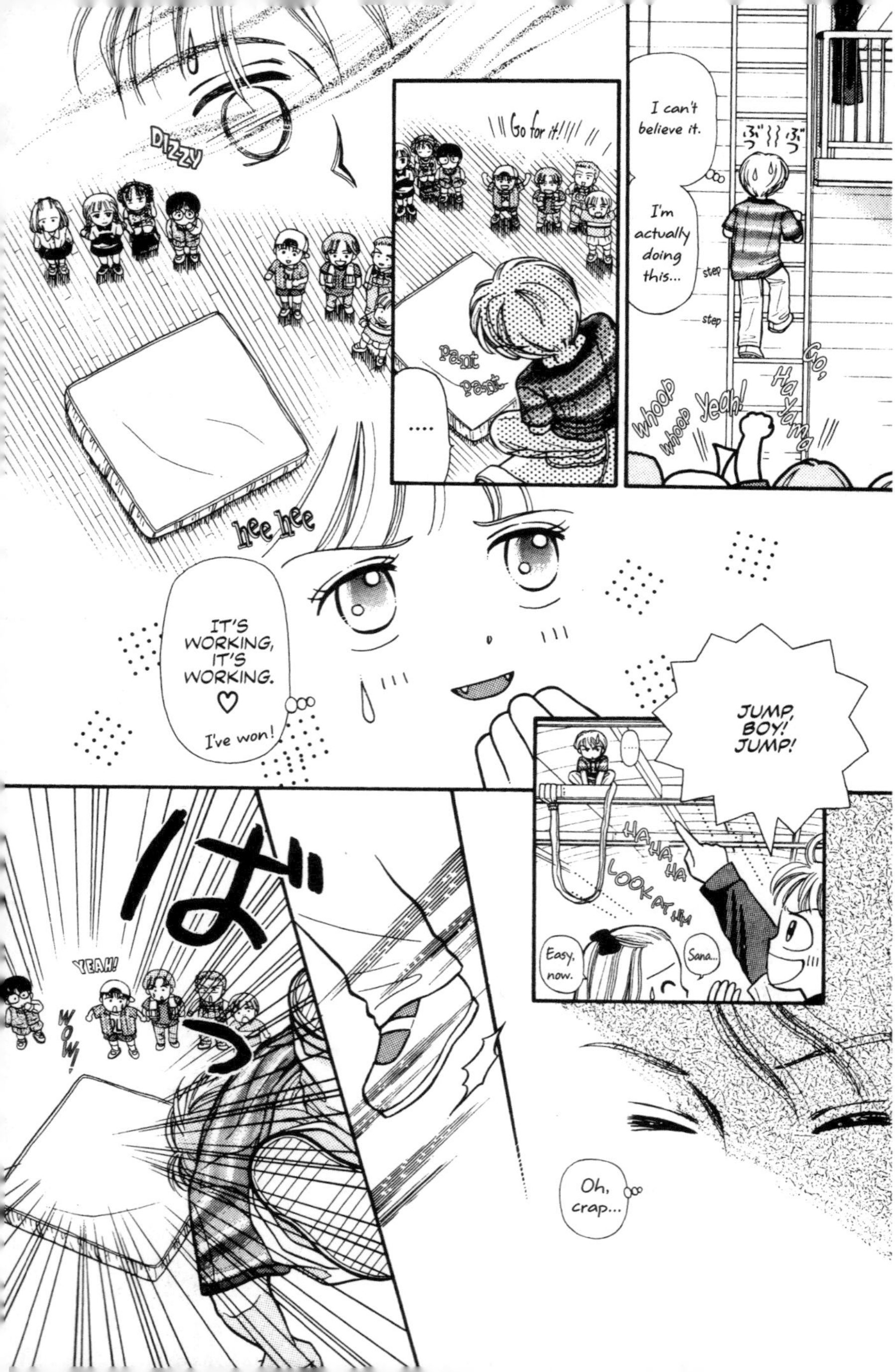
I can't believe it.
I'm actually doing this...
ぶ ぶ
step
step
Go, Hayama
whoop whoop Yeah!
Go for it!
pant pant
....
DIZZY
hee hee
IT'S WORKING, IT'S WORKING. ♡
I've won!
JUMP, BOY! JUMP!
....
HAHAHA LOOK AT HIM
Sana...
Easy, now.
Oh, crap...
ばっ
YEAH!
WOW!

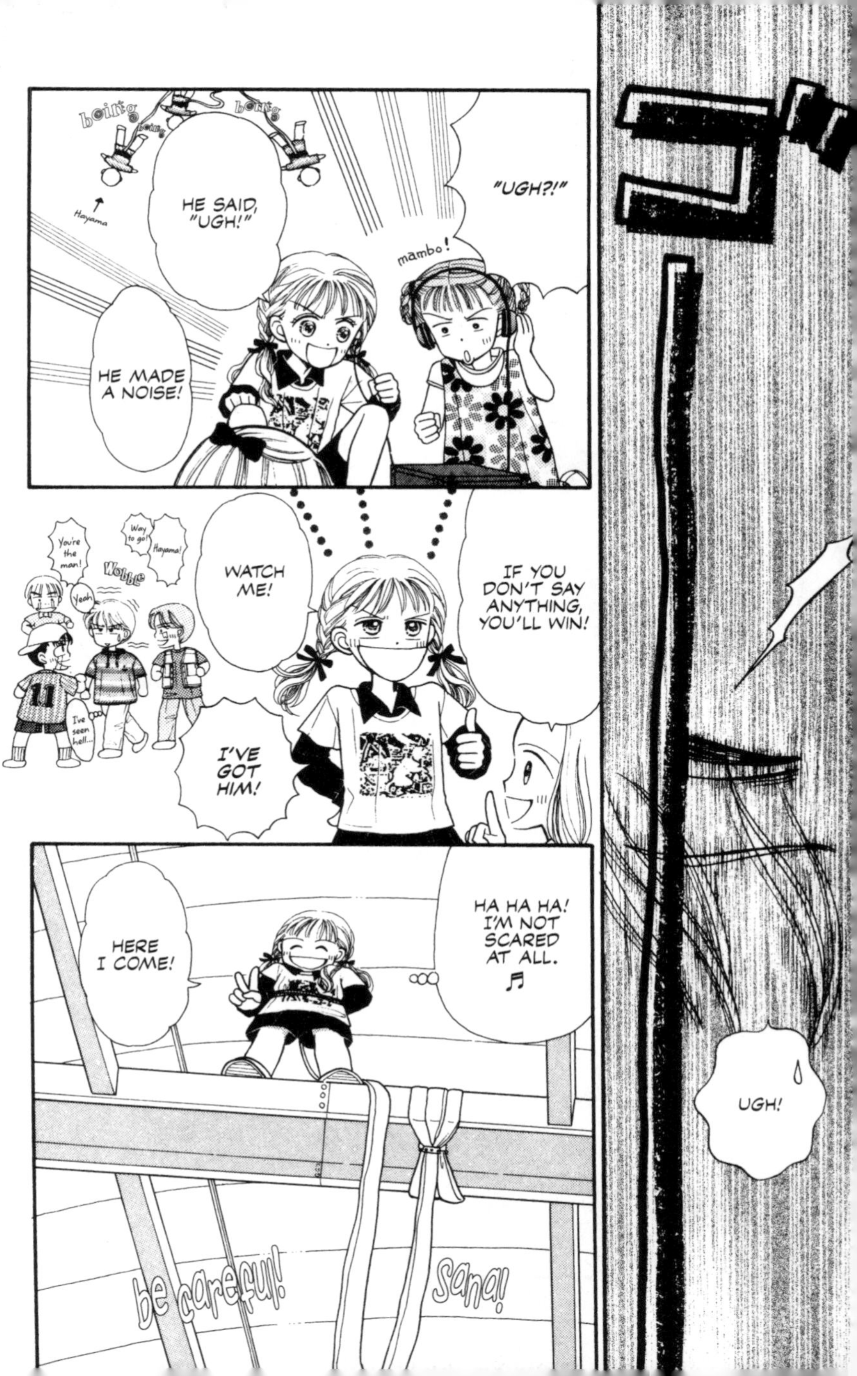
UGH!
"UGH?!"
mambo!
HE SAID, "UGH!"
boing boing boing
Hayama
HE MADE A NOISE!
IF YOU DON'T SAY ANYTHING, YOU'LL WIN!
WATCH ME!
I'VE GOT HIM!
Way to go!
Hayama!
You're the man!
Wobble
Yeah
I've seen hell...
HA HA HA! I'M NOT SCARED AT ALL. ♬
HERE I COME!
Sana!
be careful!

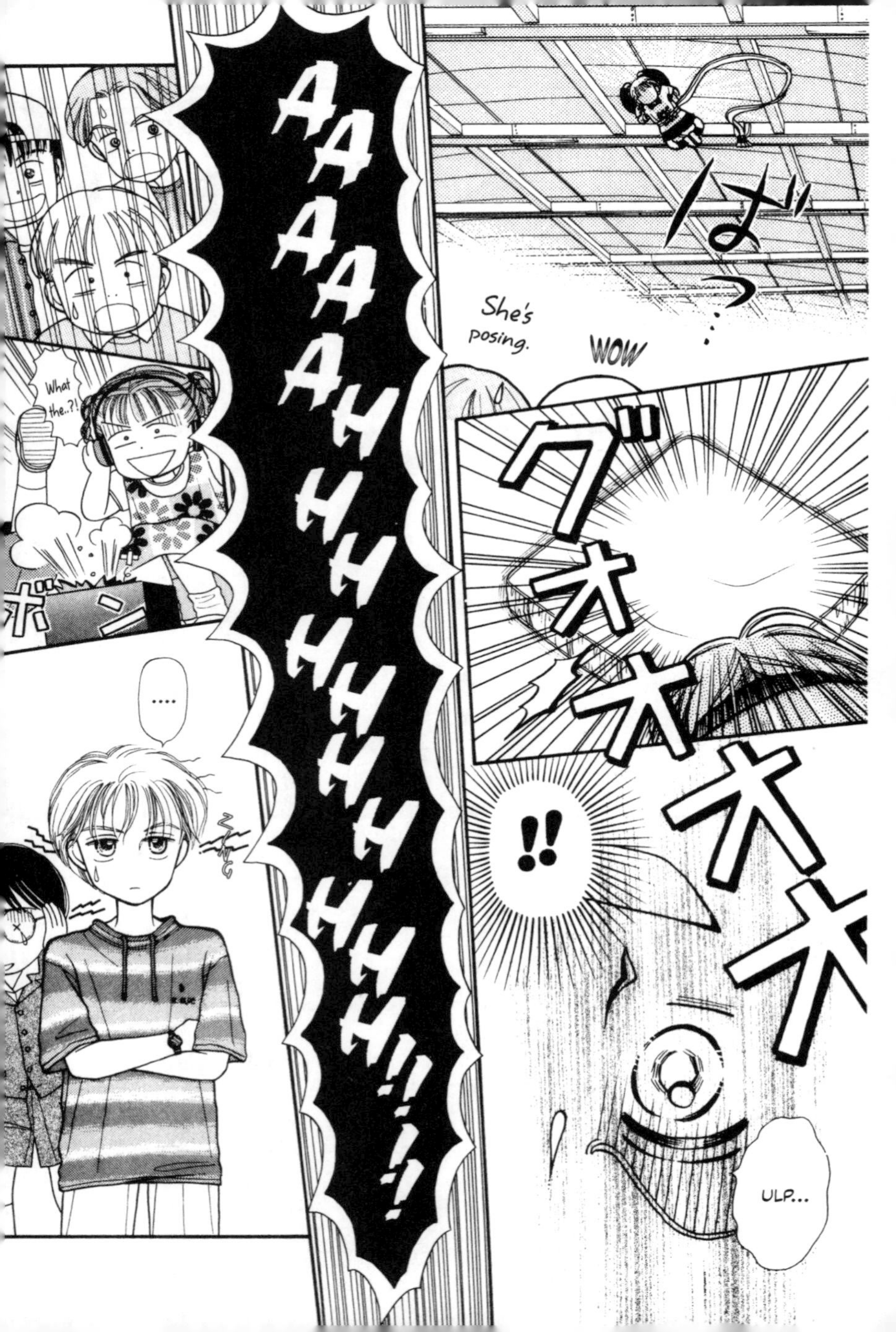
ぱっ
She's posing.
WOW
グオオオオ
!!
ULP...
AAAAAHHHHHHHHHHHHH!!!!
What the..?!
ボン
.....
ZING

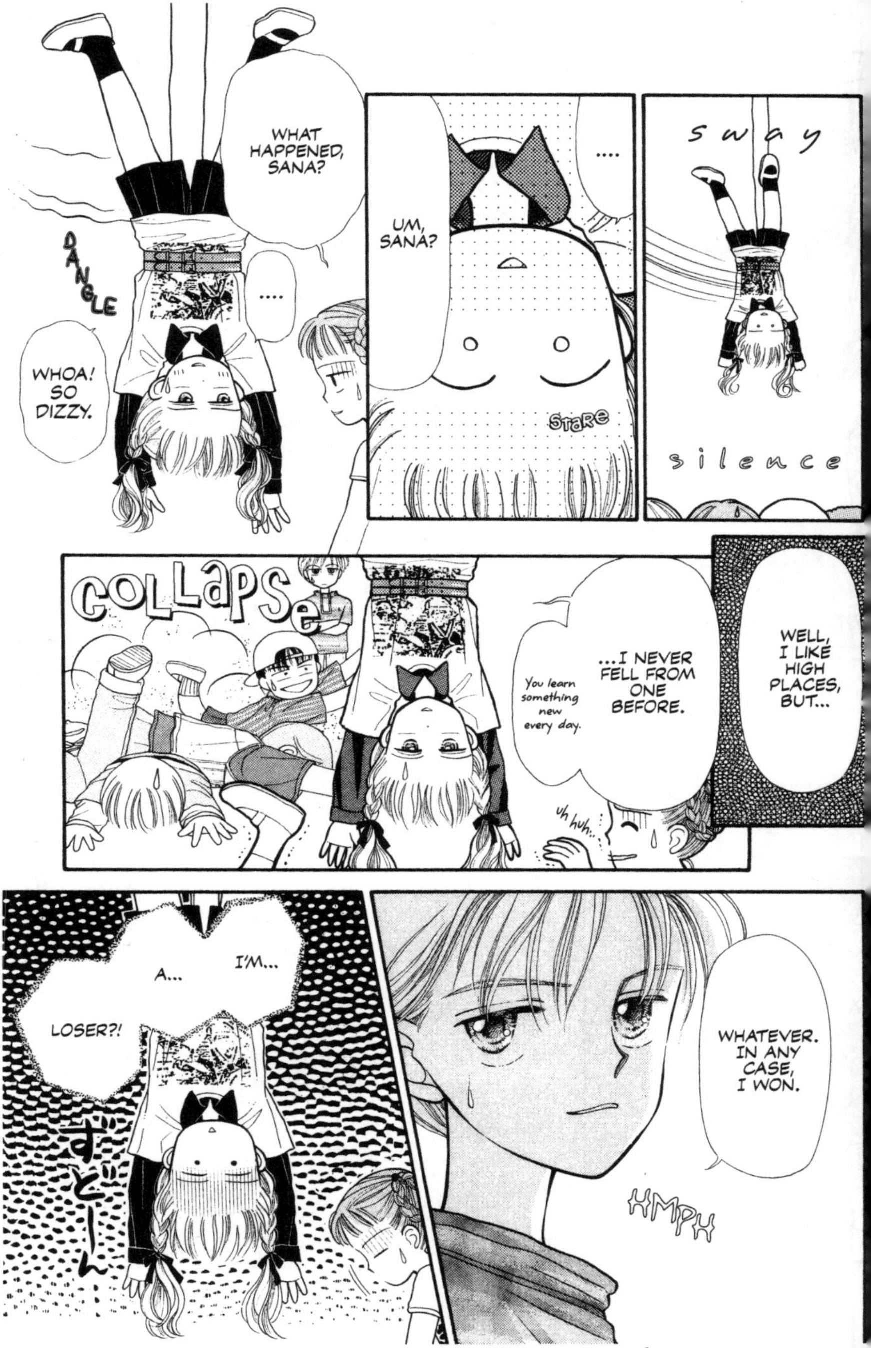
sway
silence
....
UM, SANA?
STARE
WHAT HAPPENED, SANA?
....
WHOA! SO DIZZY.
DANGLE
WELL, I LIKE HIGH PLACES, BUT...
...I NEVER FELL FROM ONE BEFORE.
You learn something new every day.
uh huh...
COLLAPSE
WHATEVER. IN ANY CASE, I WON.
HMPH
I'M...
A...
LOSER?!
ずどーん

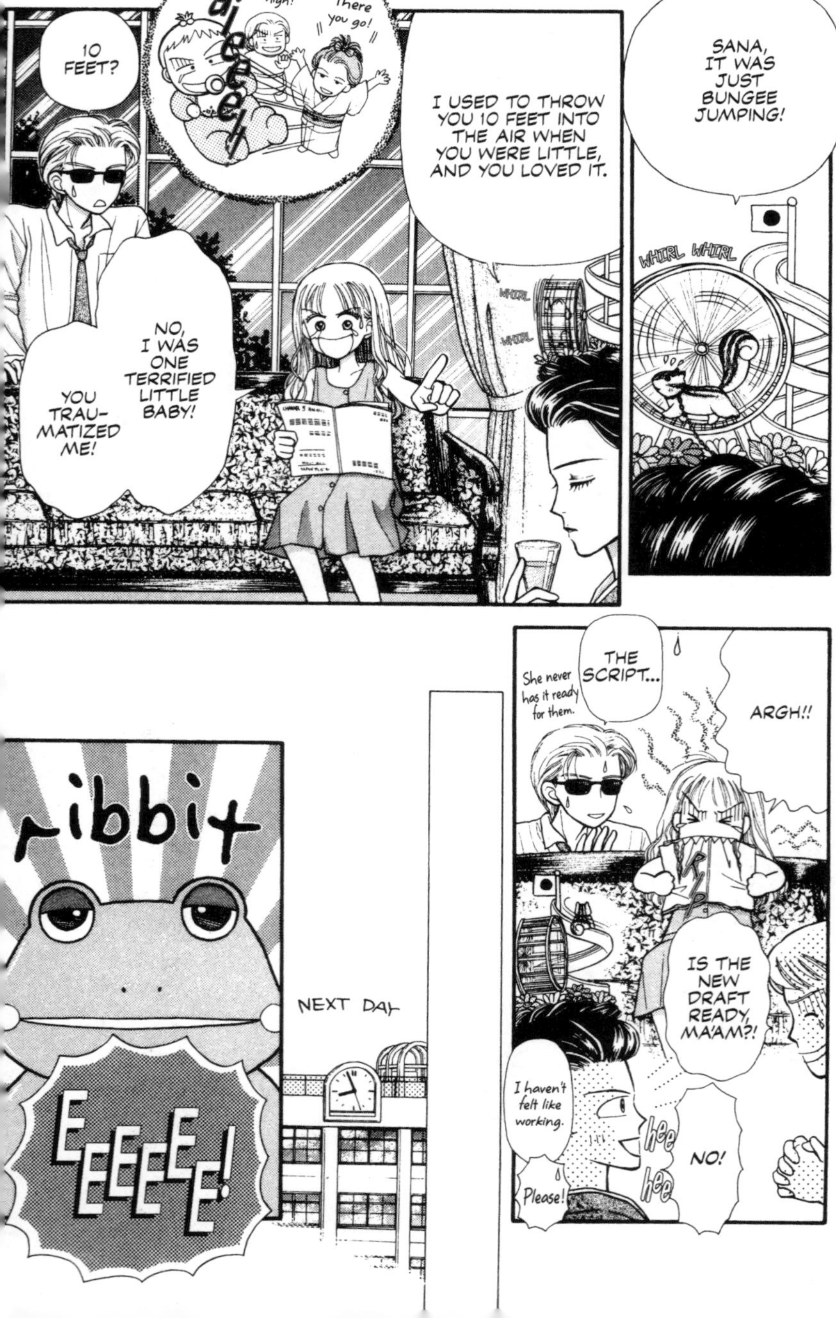
SANA, IT WAS JUST BUNGEE JUMPING!
WHIRL WHIRL
I USED TO THROW YOU 10 FEET INTO THE AIR WHEN YOU WERE LITTLE, AND YOU LOVED IT.
10 FEET?
There you go!
That's too high!
WHIRL
WHIRL
NO, I WAS ONE TERRIFIED LITTLE BABY!
YOU TRAUMA-MATIZED ME!
THE SCRIPT...
She never has it ready for them.
ARGH!!
IS THE NEW DRAFT READY, MA'AM?!
I haven't felt like working.
hee hee
NO!
Please!
NEXT DAY
ribbit
EEEEEEE!

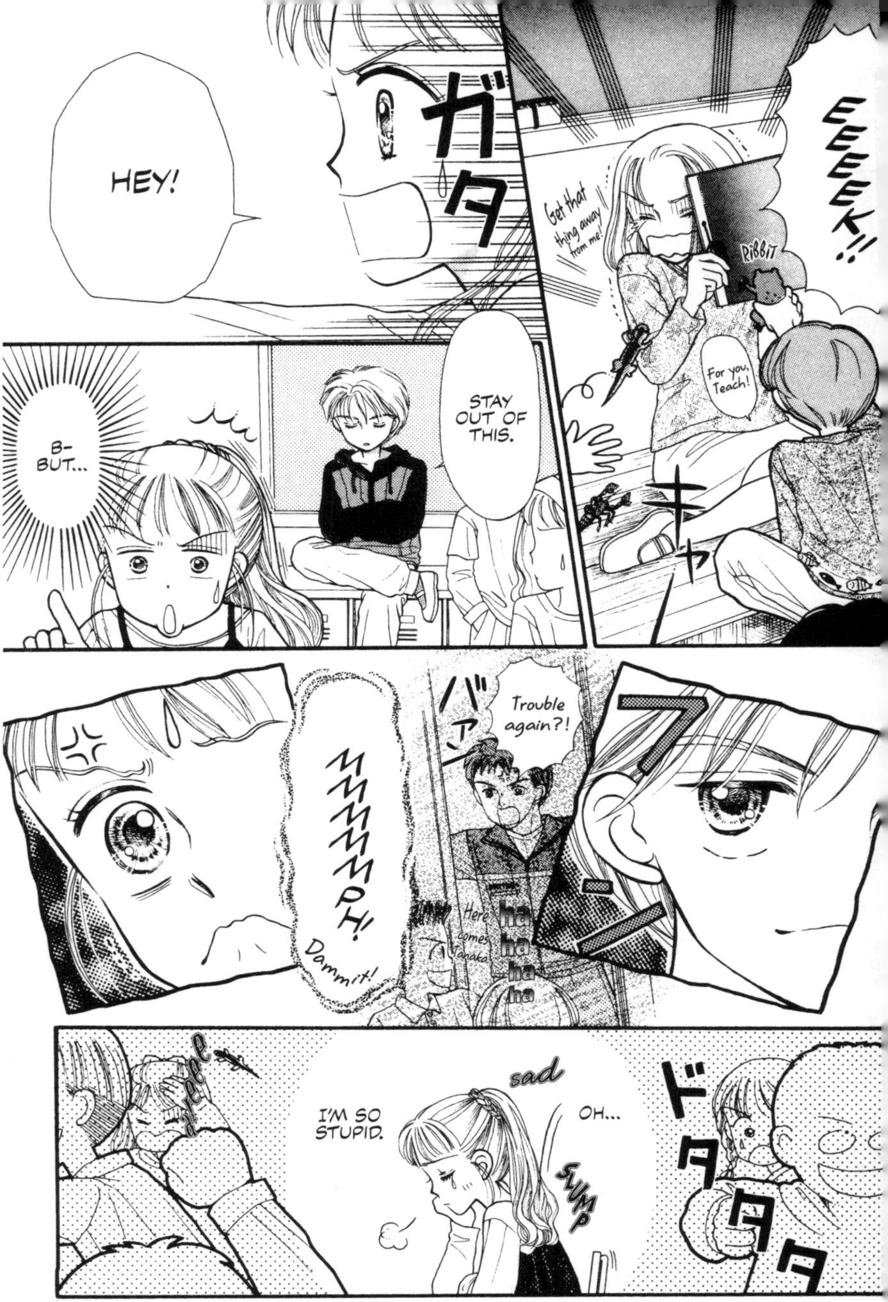
EEEEEK!!
Get that thing away from me!
RIBBIT
For you, Teach!
キャ
ガタ
HEY!
STAY OUT OF THIS.
B-BUT...
Trouble again?!
バァン
Here comes Tanaka
ha ha ha ha
MMMMMPH!
Dammit!
ドタタタ
OH...
sad
SLUMP
I'M SO STUPID.

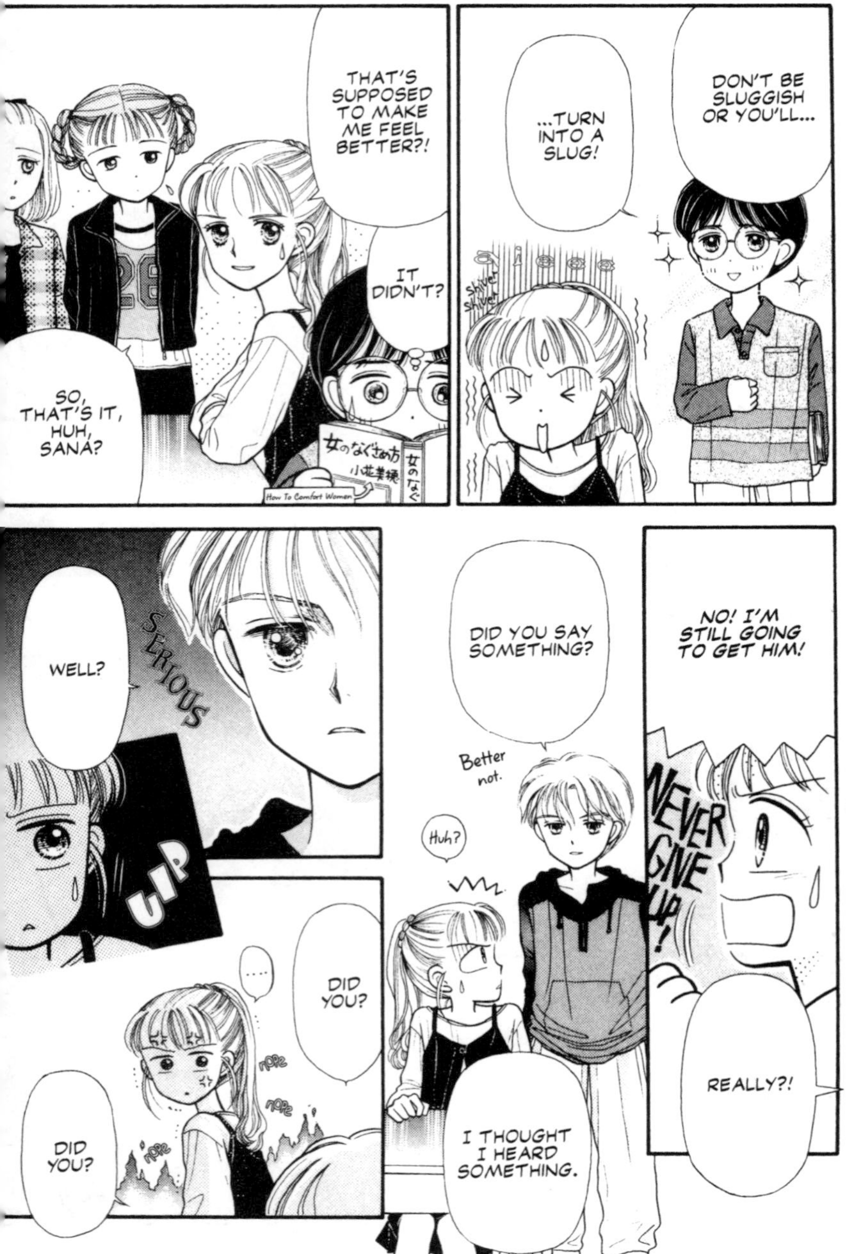
DON'T BE SLUGGISH OR YOU'LL...
...TURN INTO A SLUG!
shiver shiver
THAT'S SUPPOSED TO MAKE ME FEEL BETTER?!
IT DIDN'T?
SO, THAT'S IT, HUH, SANA?
女のなぐさめ方
小花美穂
女のなぐ
How To Comfort Women
NO! I'M STILL GOING TO GET HIM!
NEVER GIVE UP!
REALLY?!
DID YOU SAY SOMETHING?
Better not.
Huh?
I THOUGHT I HEARD SOMETHING.
WELL?
SERIOUS
UP
....
DID YOU?
nope
nope
nope
DID YOU?

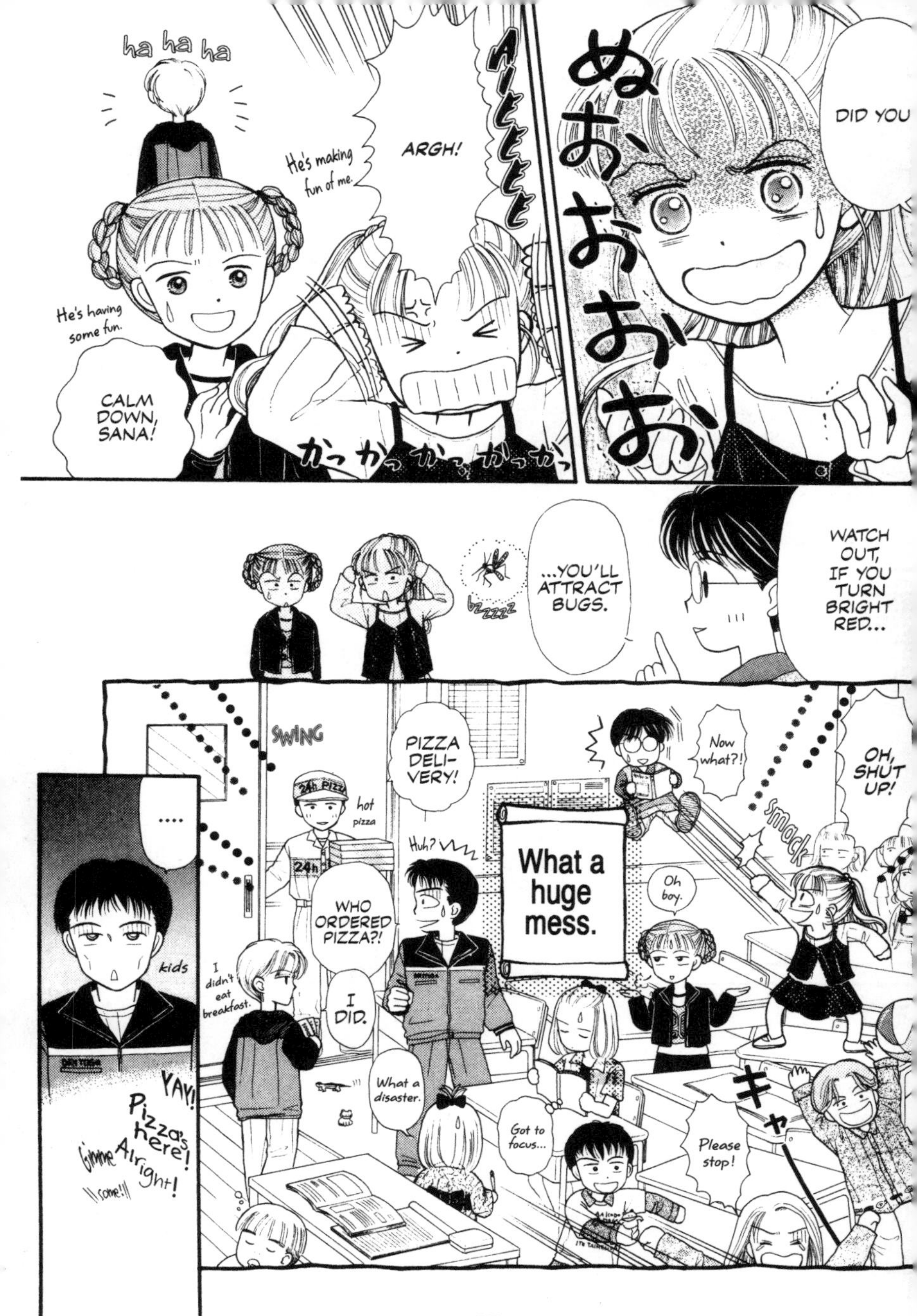
DID YOU
ぬおおおお
He's making fun of me.
ARGH!
ha ha ha
He's having some fun.
CALM DOWN, SANA!
かっかっかっかっかっ
WATCH OUT, IF YOU TURN BRIGHT RED...
...YOU'LL ATTRACT BUGS.
bzzzz
OH, SHUT UP!
smack
Now what?!
What a huge mess.
PIZZA DELIVERY!
SWING
hot pizza
Huh?
WHO ORDERED PIZZA?!
I DID.
I didn't eat breakfast.
Oh boy.
キャ
Please stop!
Got to focus...
What a disaster.
....
kids
YAY!
Pizza's here!
Alright!
Gimme some!!

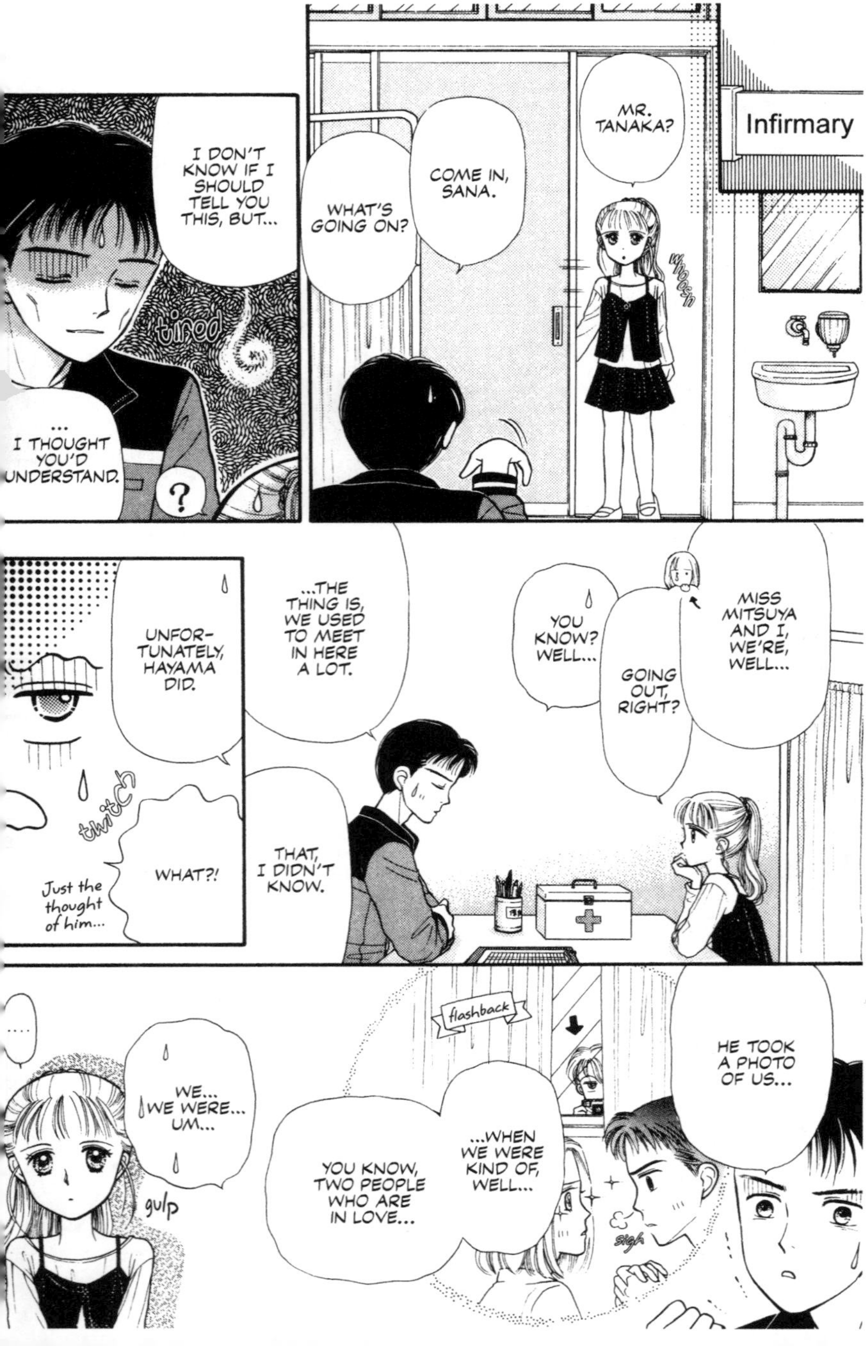
Infirmary
MR. TANAKA?
whoosh
COME IN, SANA.
WHAT'S GOING ON?
I DON'T KNOW IF I SHOULD TELL YOU THIS, BUT...
tired
...I THOUGHT YOU'D UNDERSTAND.
?
MISS MITSUYA AND I, WE'RE, WELL...
GOING OUT, RIGHT?
YOU KNOW? WELL...
...THE THING IS, WE USED TO MEET IN HERE A LOT.
THAT, I DIDN'T KNOW.
UNFORTUNATELY, HAYAMA DID.
twitch
WHAT?!
Just the thought of him...
HE TOOK A PHOTO OF US...
flashback
sigh
...WHEN WE WERE KIND OF, WELL...
YOU KNOW, TWO PEOPLE WHO ARE IN LOVE...
WE... WE WERE... UM...
gulp
....

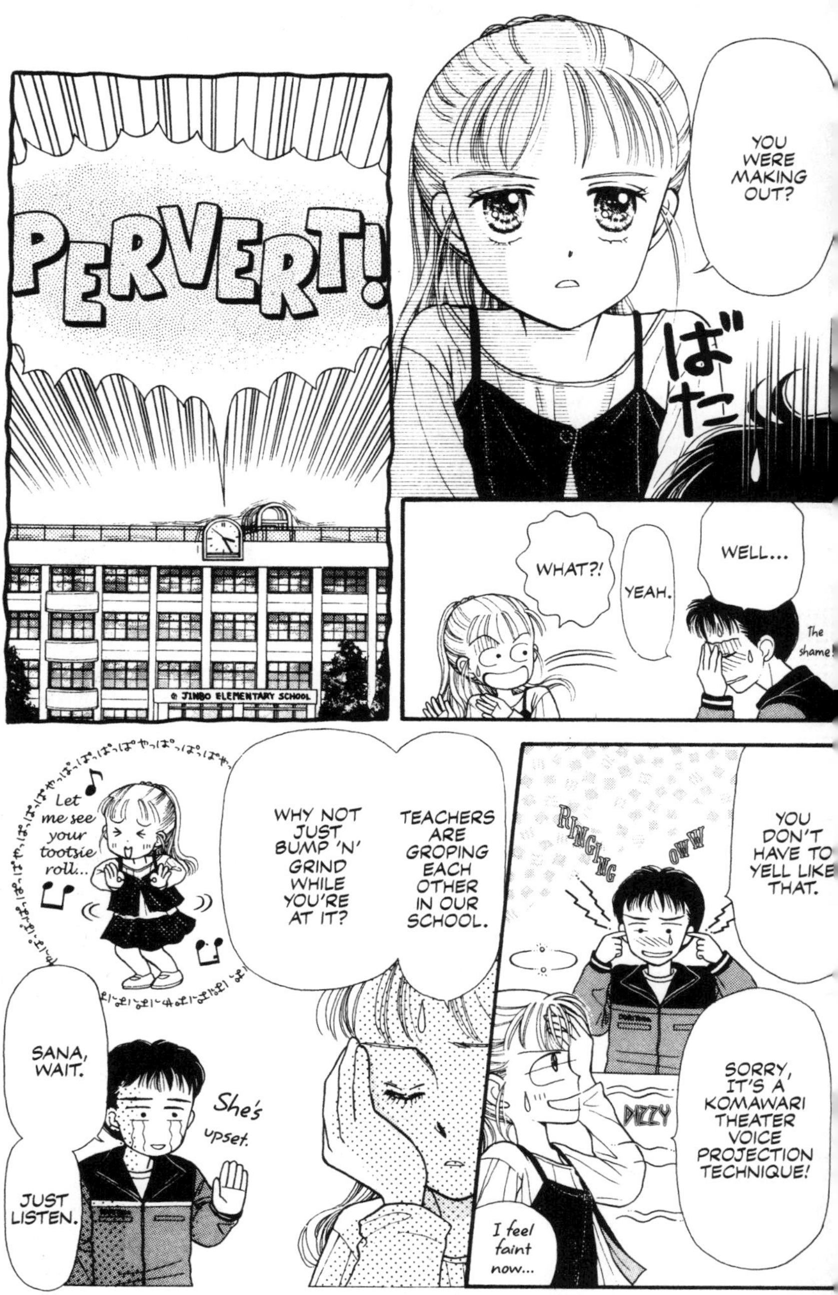
YOU WERE MAKING OUT?
ばた
WELL...
YEAH.
WHAT?!
The shame!
PERVERT!
JINBO ELEMENTARY SCHOOL
YOU DON'T HAVE TO YELL LIKE THAT.
RINGING
OWW
SORRY, IT'S A KOMAWARI THEATER VOICE PROJECTION TECHNIQUE!
DIZZY
I feel faint now...
TEACHERS ARE GROPING EACH OTHER IN OUR SCHOOL.
WHY NOT JUST BUMP 'N' GRIND WHILE YOU'RE AT IT?
Let me see your tootsie roll...
SANA, WAIT.
She's upset.
JUST LISTEN.

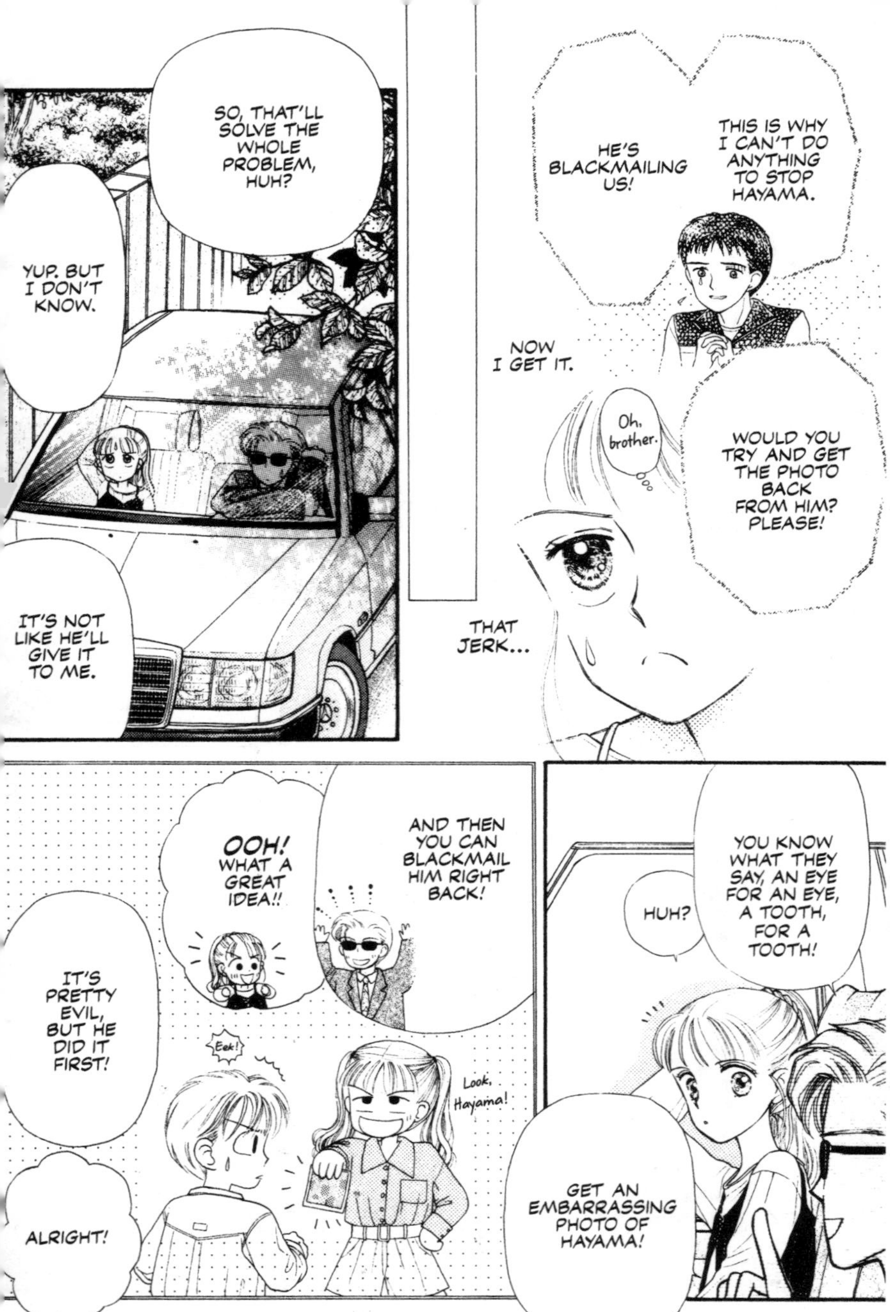
THIS IS WHY I CAN'T DO ANYTHING TO STOP HAYAMA.
HE'S BLACKMAILING US!
NOW I GET IT.
WOULD YOU TRY AND GET THE PHOTO BACK FROM HIM? PLEASE!
Oh, brother.
THAT JERK...
SO, THAT'LL SOLVE THE WHOLE PROBLEM, HUH?
YUP. BUT I DON'T KNOW.
IT'S NOT LIKE HE'LL GIVE IT TO ME.
YOU KNOW WHAT THEY SAY, AN EYE FOR AN EYE, A TOOTH, FOR A TOOTH!
HUH?
GET AN EMBARRASSING PHOTO OF HAYAMA!
AND THEN YOU CAN BLACKMAIL HIM RIGHT BACK!
OOH! WHAT A GREAT IDEA!!
IT'S PRETTY EVIL, BUT HE DID IT FIRST!
Look, Hayama!
Eek!
ALRIGHT!

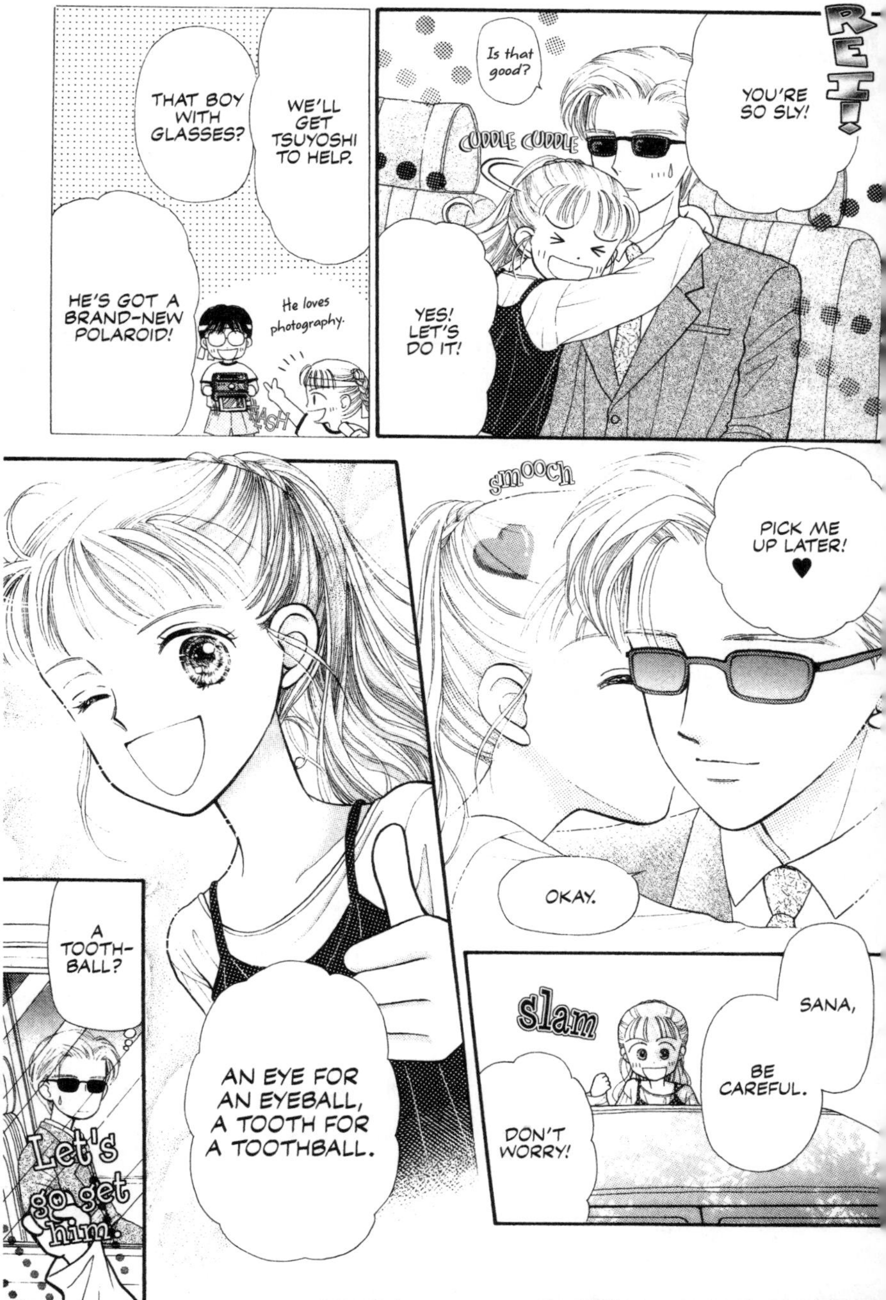
R-E-I!
YOU'RE SO SLY!
Is that good?
CUDDLE CUDDLE
YES! LET'S DO IT!
WE'LL GET TSUYOSHI TO HELP.
THAT BOY WITH GLASSES?
HE'S GOT A BRAND-NEW POLAROID!
He loves photography.
smooch
PICK ME UP LATER! ♥
OKAY.
SANA, BE CAREFUL.
slam
DON'T WORRY!
AN EYE FOR AN EYEBALL, A TOOTH FOR A TOOTHBALL.
A TOOTH-BALL?
Let's go get him.

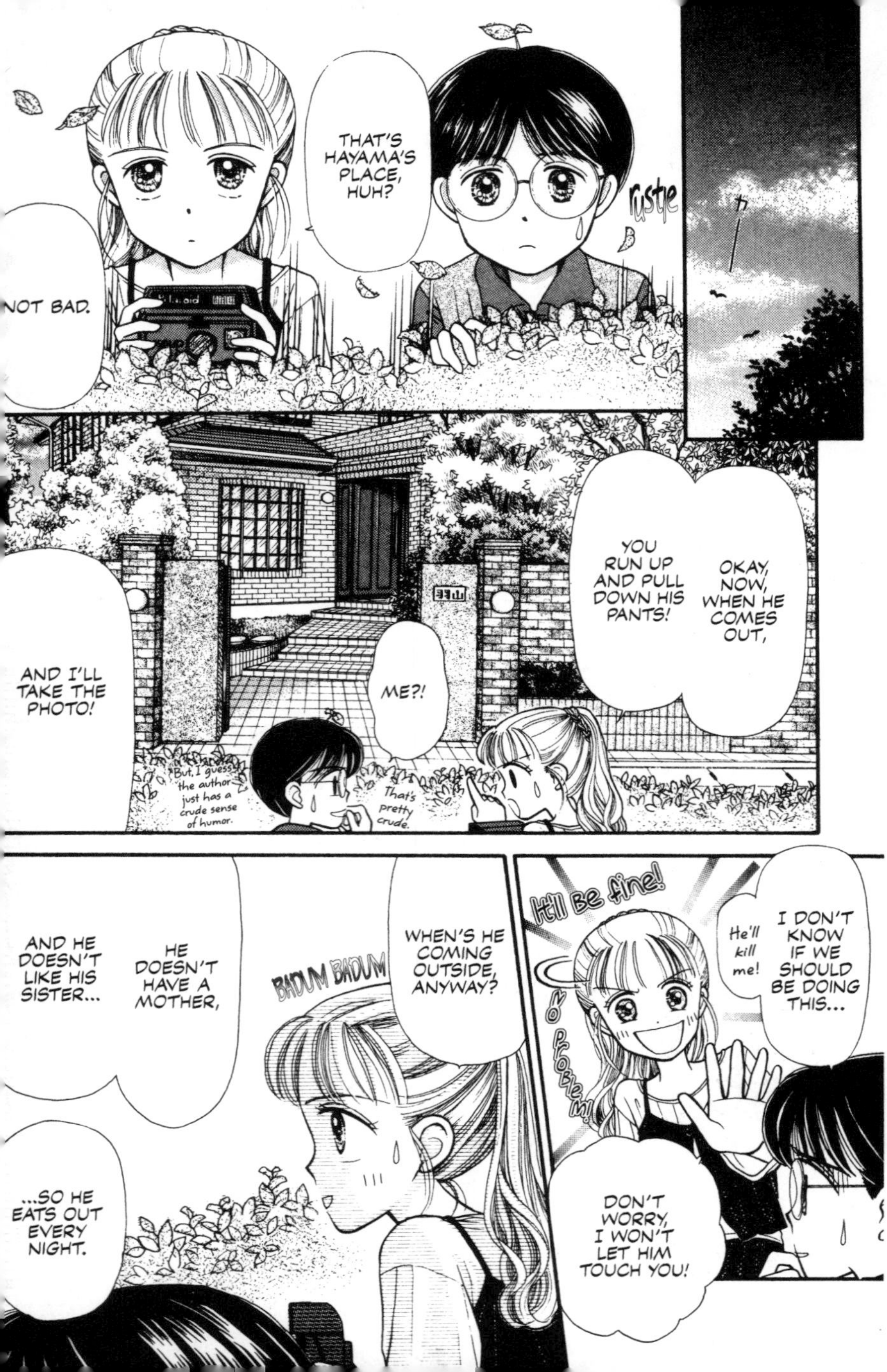
rustle
THAT'S HAYAMA'S PLACE, HUH?
NOT BAD.
OKAY, NOW, WHEN HE COMES OUT,
YOU RUN UP AND PULL DOWN HIS PANTS!
AND I'LL TAKE THE PHOTO!
ME?!
That's pretty crude.
But, I guess the author just has a crude sense of humor.
I DON'T KNOW IF WE SHOULD BE DOING THIS...
He'll kill me!
It'll be fine!
No problem!
DON'T WORRY, I WON'T LET HIM TOUCH YOU!
WHEN'S HE COMING OUTSIDE, ANYWAY?
BADUM BADUM
HE DOESN'T HAVE A MOTHER,
AND HE DOESN'T LIKE HIS SISTER...
...SO HE EATS OUT EVERY NIGHT.

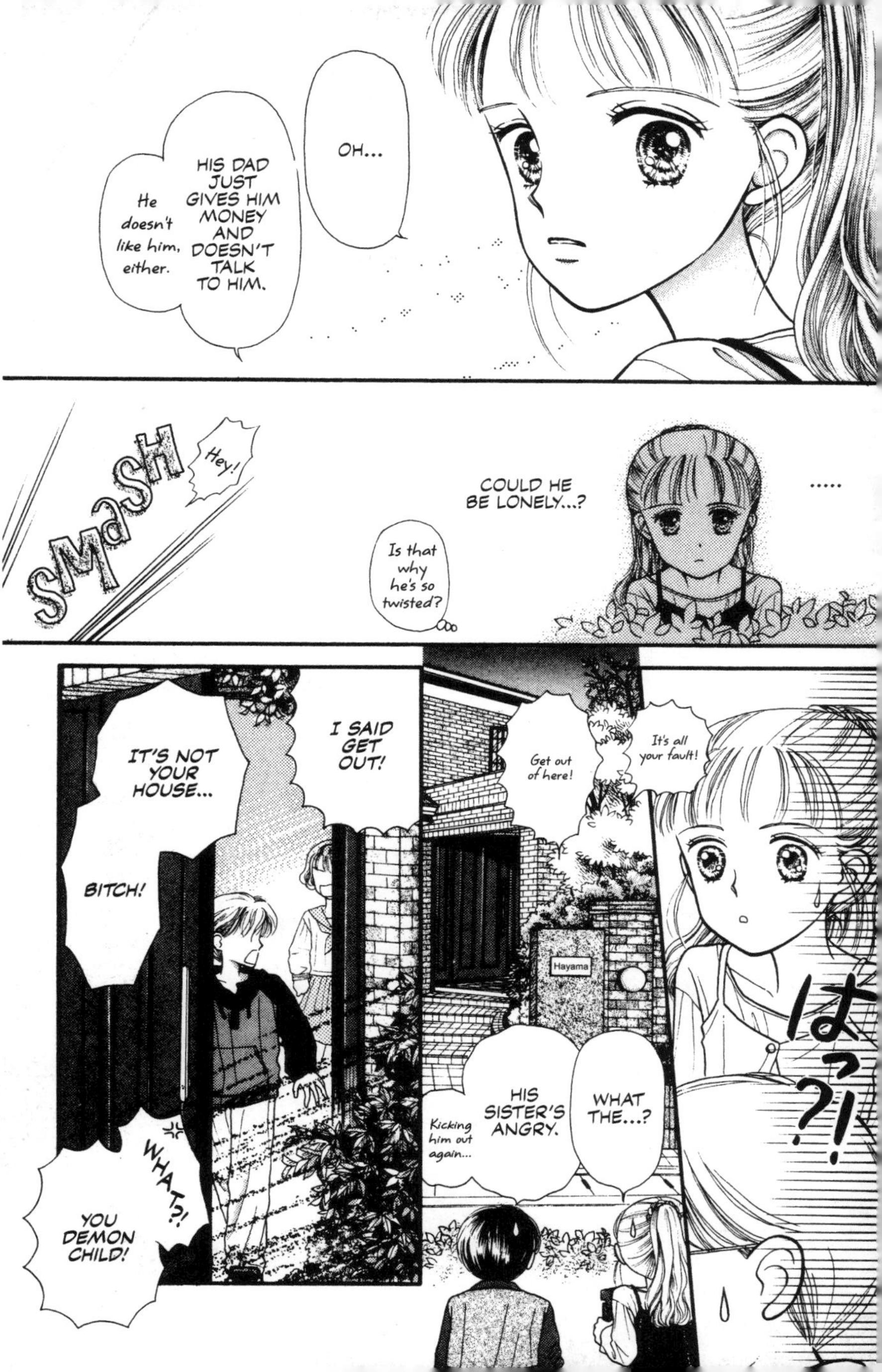
OH...
HIS DAD JUST GIVES HIM MONEY AND DOESN'T TALK TO HIM.
He doesn't like him, either.
.....
COULD HE BE LONELY...?
Is that why he's so twisted?
Hey!
SMASH
はっ?!
It's all your fault!
Get out of here!
Hayama
WHAT THE...?
HIS SISTER'S ANGRY.
Kicking him out again...
I SAID GET OUT!
IT'S NOT YOUR HOUSE...
BITCH!
WHAT?!
YOU DEMON CHILD!

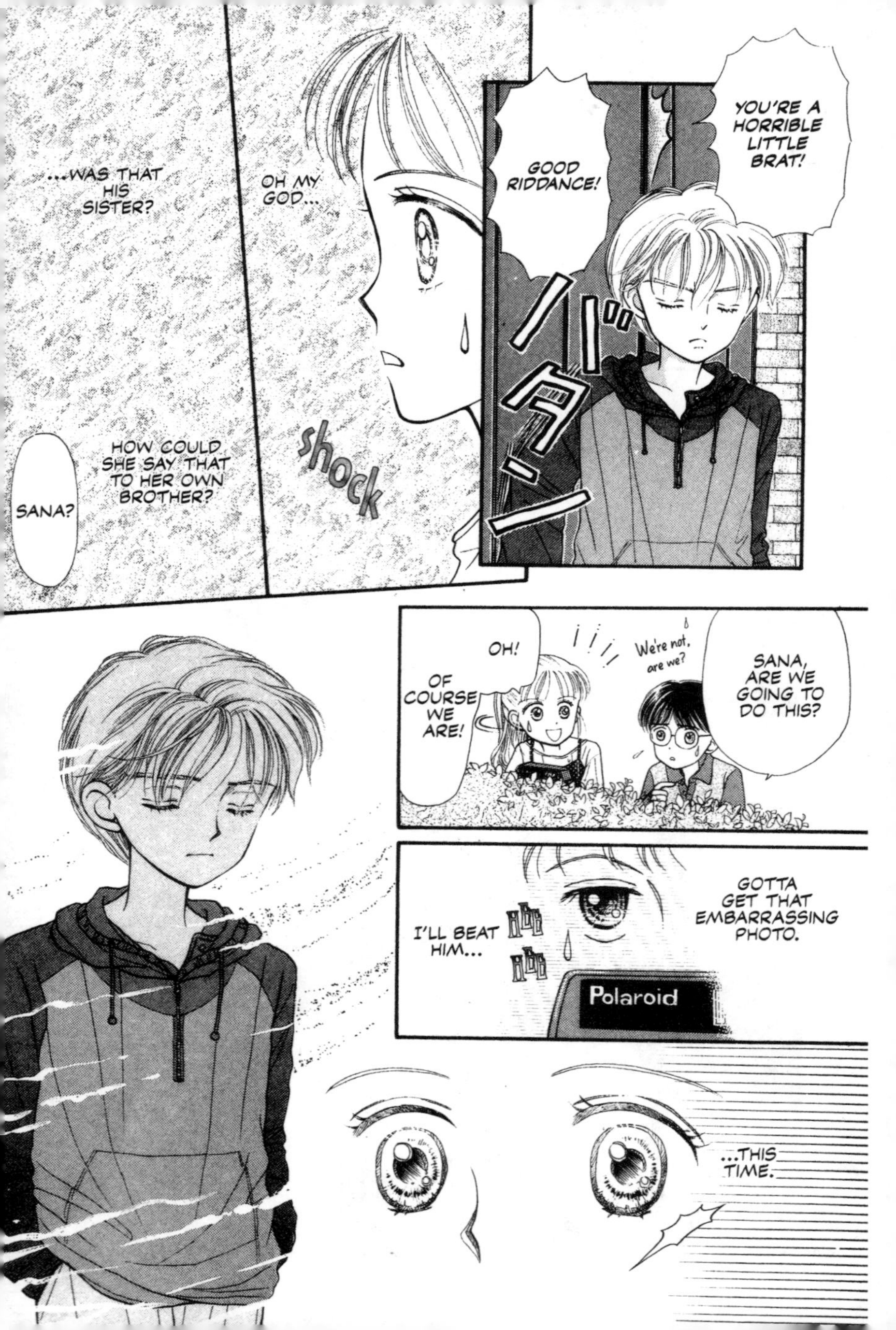
YOU'RE A HORRIBLE LITTLE BRAT!
GOOD RIDDANCE!
バタン
OH MY GOD...
shock
...WAS THAT HIS SISTER?
HOW COULD SHE SAY THAT TO HER OWN BROTHER?
SANA?
SANA, ARE WE GOING TO DO THIS?
We're not, are we?
OH!
OF COURSE WE ARE!
GOTTA GET THAT EMBARRASSING PHOTO.
I'LL BEAT HIM...
Polaroid
...THIS TIME.

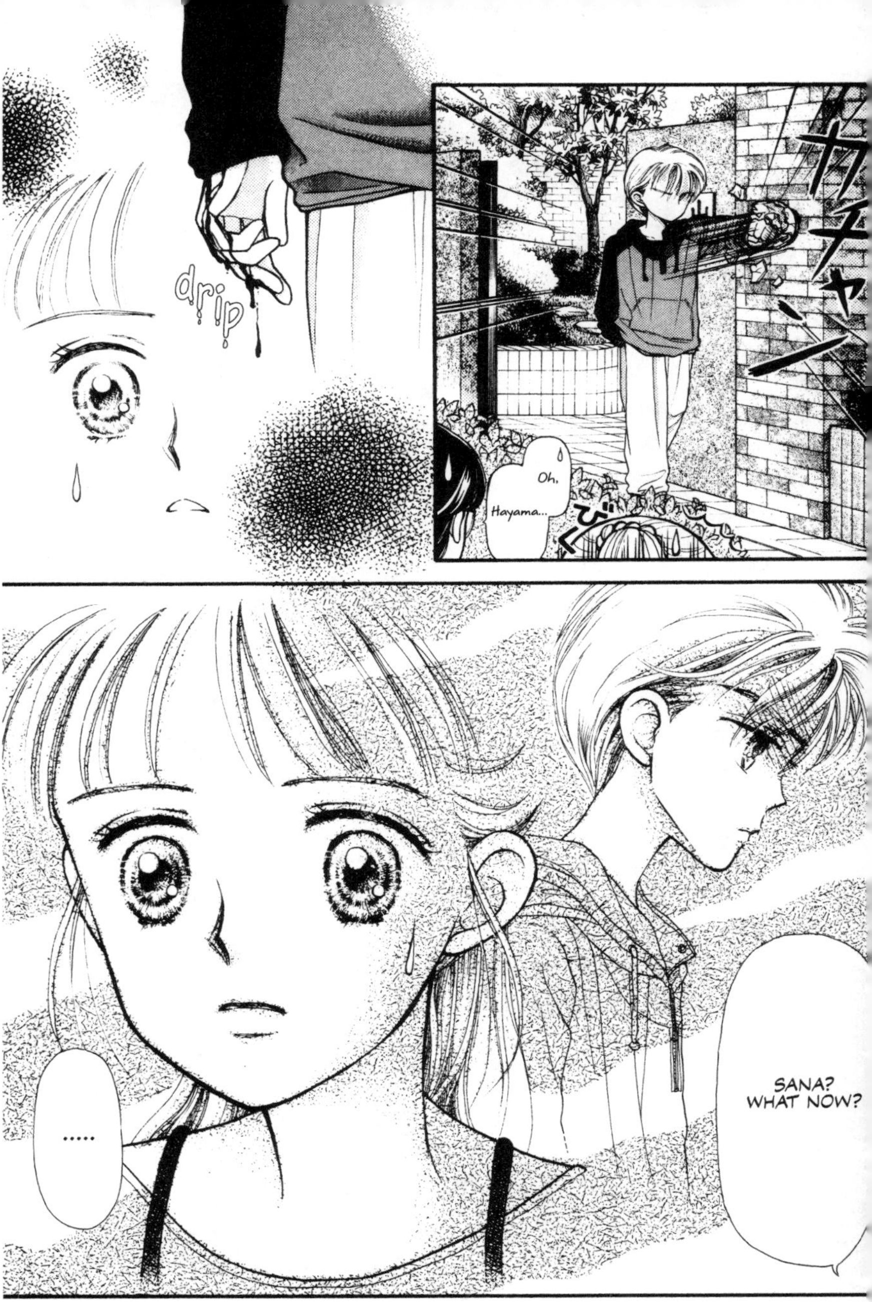
Oh, Hayama...
drip
SANA? WHAT NOW?
.....

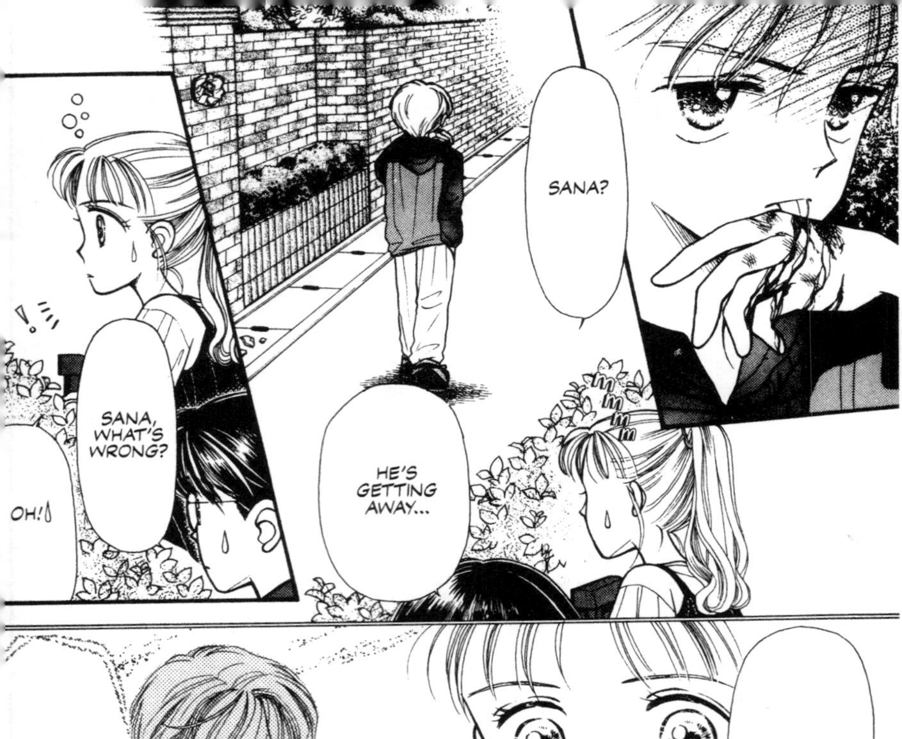
SANA?
mmmm
HE'S GETTING AWAY...
SANA, WHAT'S WRONG?
OH!
THIS IS SUCH A SHOCK.
HAYAMA LOOKED SO LONELY.
I'VE NEVER SEEN HIM LIKE THAT BEFORE.

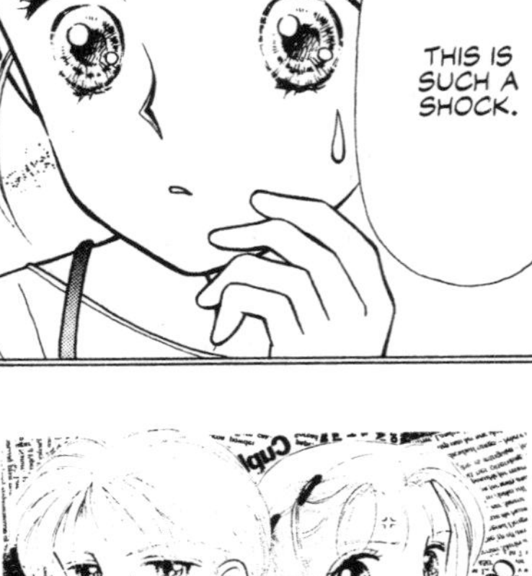

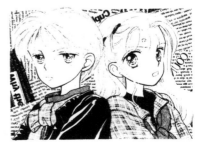

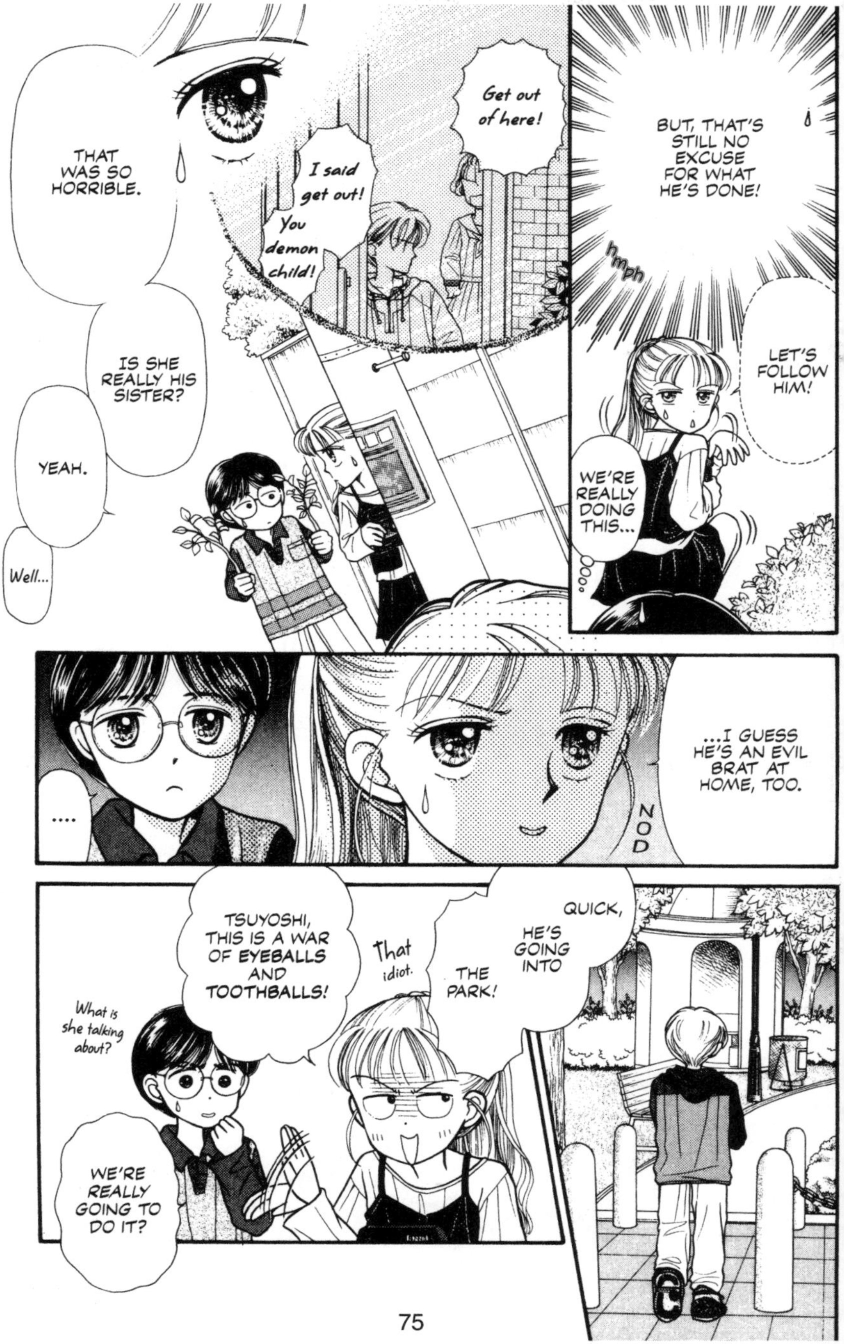
BUT, THAT'S STILL NO EXCUSE FOR WHAT HE'S DONE!
hmph
LET'S FOLLOW HIM!
WE'RE REALLY DOING THIS...
Get out of here!
I said get out!
You demon child!
THAT WAS SO HORRIBLE.
IS SHE REALLY HIS SISTER?
YEAH.
Well...
...I GUESS HE'S AN EVIL BRAT AT HOME, TOO.
NOD
....
QUICK, HE'S GOING INTO THE PARK!
That idiot.
TSUYOSHI, THIS IS A WAR OF EYEBALLS AND TOOTHBALLS!
What is she talking about?
WE'RE REALLY GOING TO DO IT?

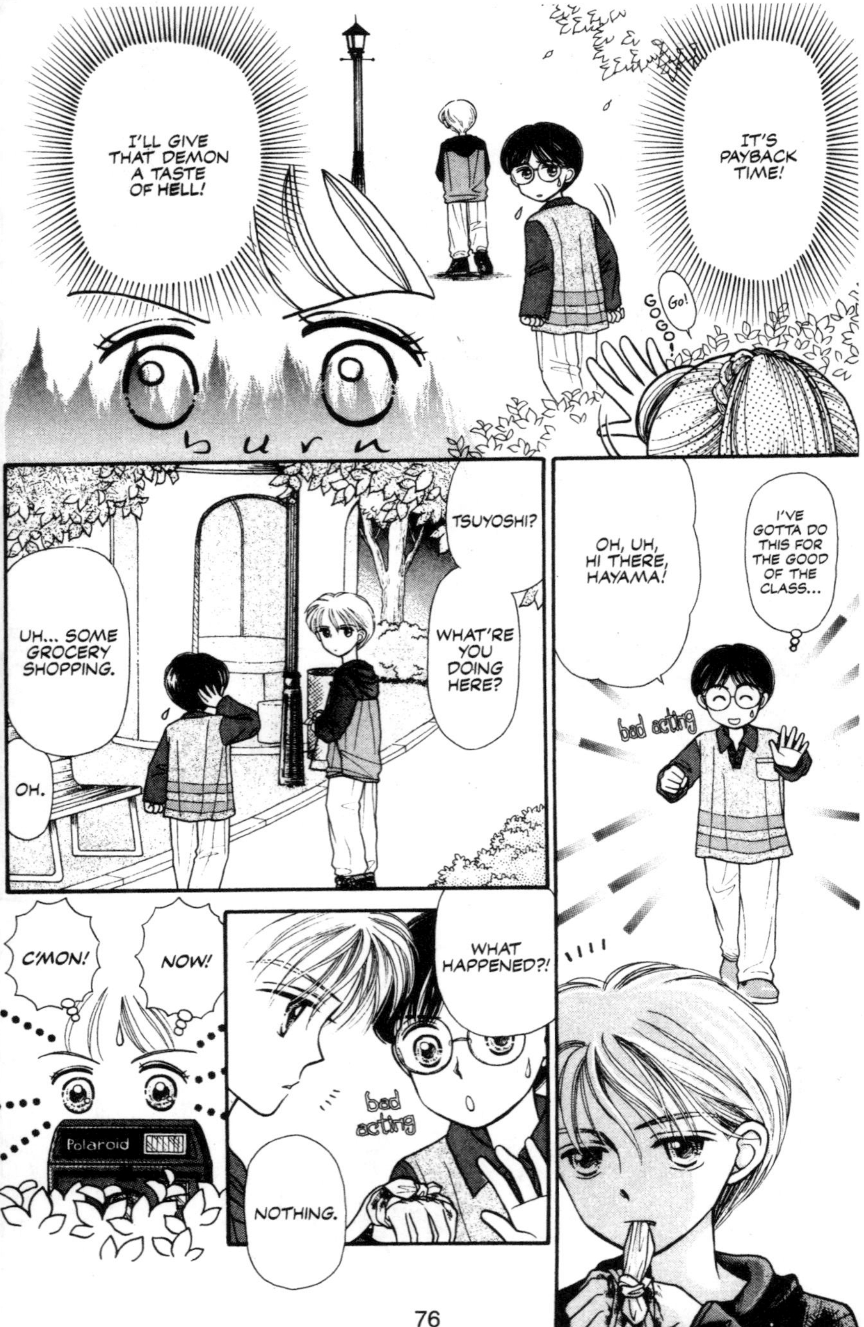
IT'S PAYBACK TIME!
GO!
GOGOGO!
I'LL GIVE THAT DEMON A TASTE OF HELL!
burn
I'VE GOTTA DO THIS FOR THE GOOD OF THE CLASS...
OH, UH, HI THERE, HAYAMA!
bad acting
TSUYOSHI?
WHAT'RE YOU DOING HERE?
UH... SOME GROCERY SHOPPING.
OH.
WHAT HAPPENED?!
bad acting
NOTHING.
NOW!
C'MON!
Polaroid

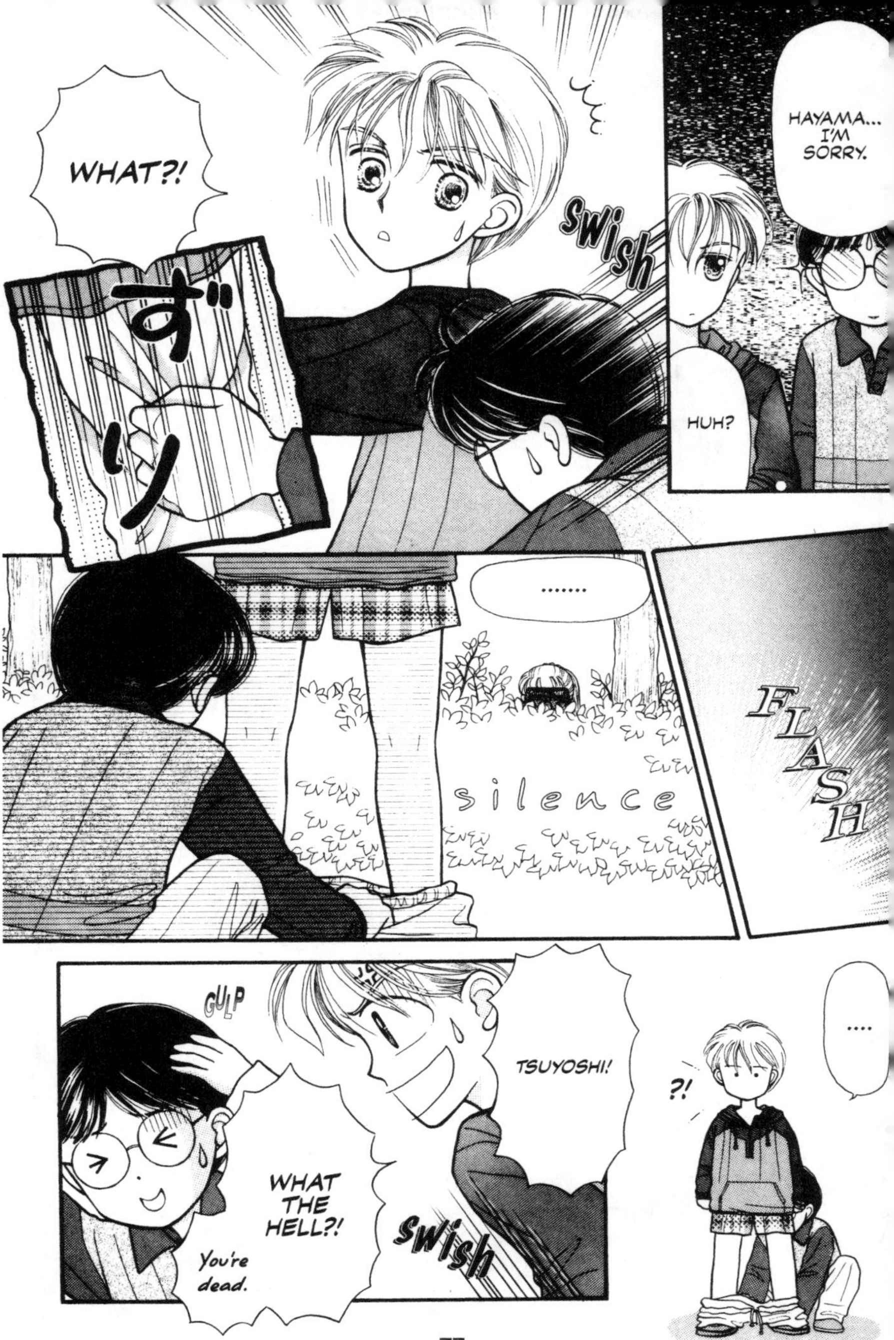

HAYAMA... I'M SORRY.
HUH?
WHAT?!
ずり
SWISH
FLASH
....
silence
....
?!
GULP
TSUYOSHI!
WHAT THE HELL?!
SWISH
You're dead.

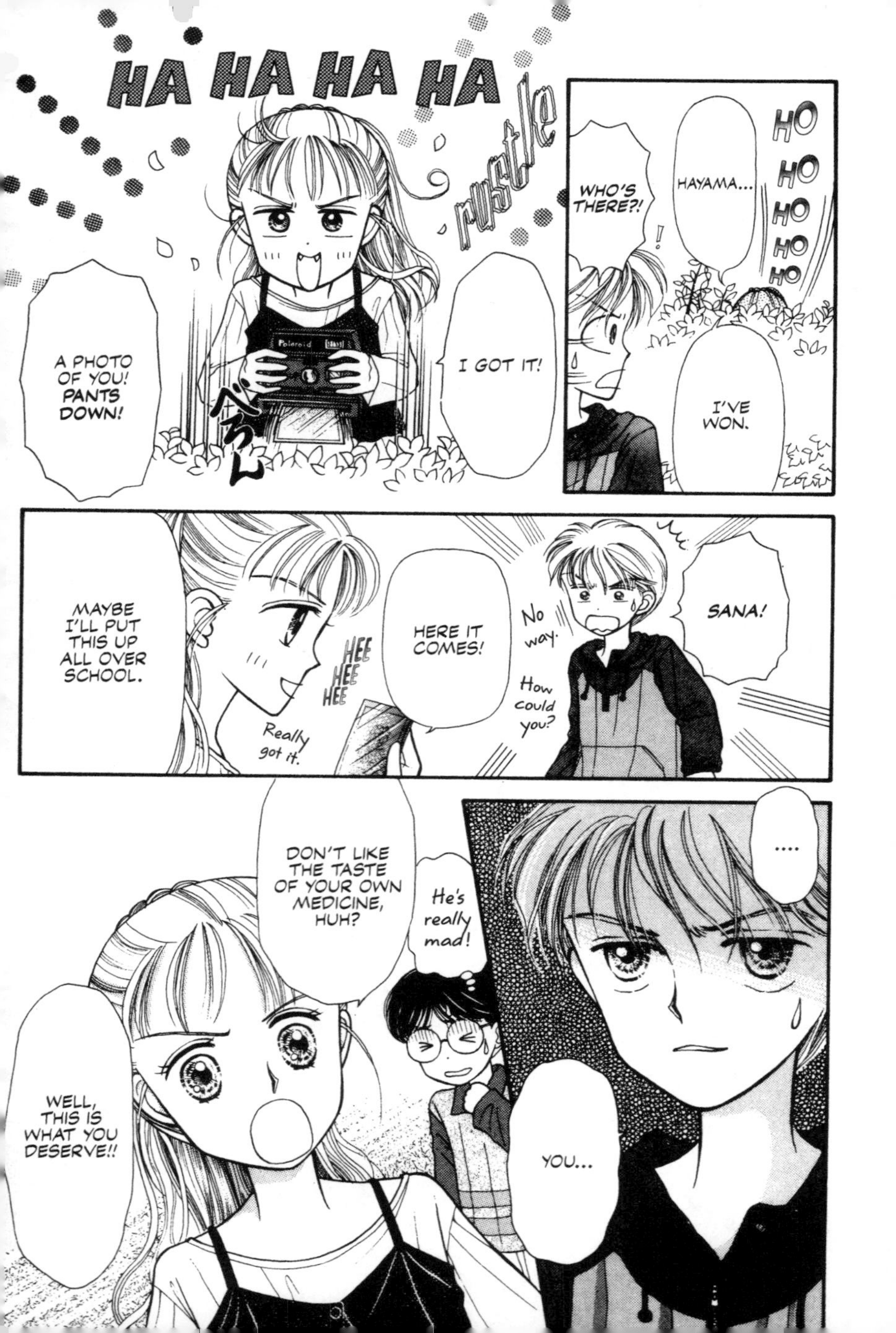
HO HO HO HO HO HO
HAYAMA...
WHO'S THERE?!
!
I'VE WON.
HA HA HA HA HA
rustle
I GOT IT!
A PHOTO OF YOU! PANTS DOWN!
SANA!
No way.
How could you?
HERE IT COMES!
HEE HEE HEE
Really got it.
MAYBE I'LL PUT THIS UP ALL OVER SCHOOL.
....
YOU...
He's really mad!
DON'T LIKE THE TASTE OF YOUR OWN MEDICINE, HUH?
WELL, THIS IS WHAT YOU DESERVE!!

About Gertie

I have a lot of plots filed away. I spent a lot of time working out the story for this series, which made it easy for me to actually sit down and write it. (But it still takes 17 days to finish each installment.)
Anyway, the main character's name in one of my favorite plots that I haven't worked on yet is Gertie. I think it's a pretty name and I like it. I don't watch too many movies, but when I saw E.T. in elementary school, I really liked the main character Elliot's sister, Gertie. She is what I remember when I think about E.T. I never liked my own name, so maybe I think too much about names. The story of Gertie is not gonna be as popular as Kodocha, so I'm not sure when I'm going to draw it -- sometime, somewhere... Hee-hee.

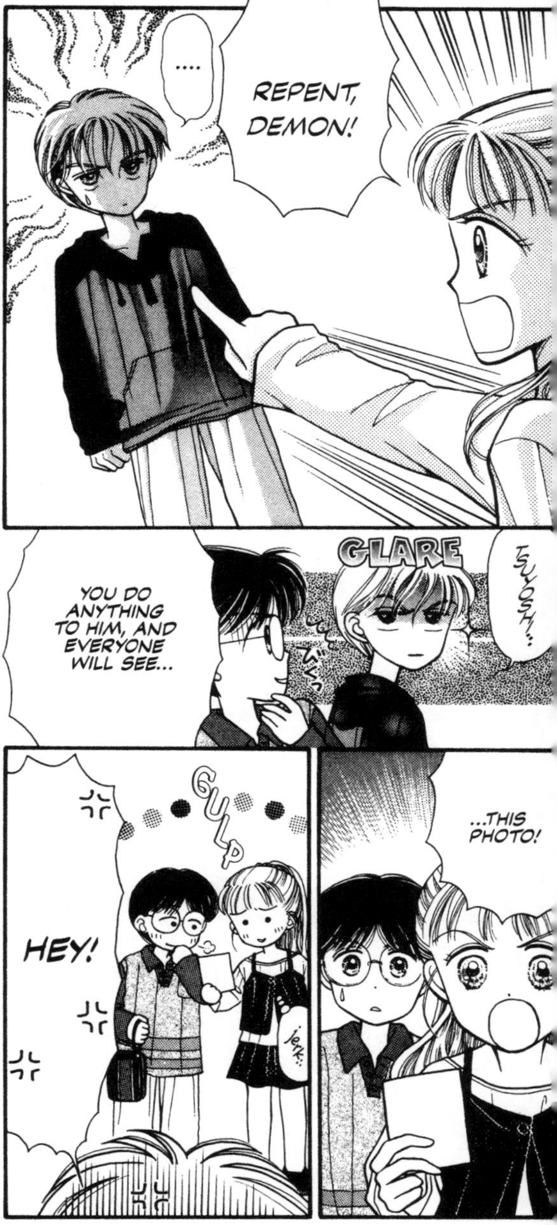
REPENT, DEMON!
....
TSUYOSHI...
GLARE
YOU DO ANYTHING TO HIM, AND EVERYONE WILL SEE...
...THIS PHOTO!
GULP
HEY!
jerk..

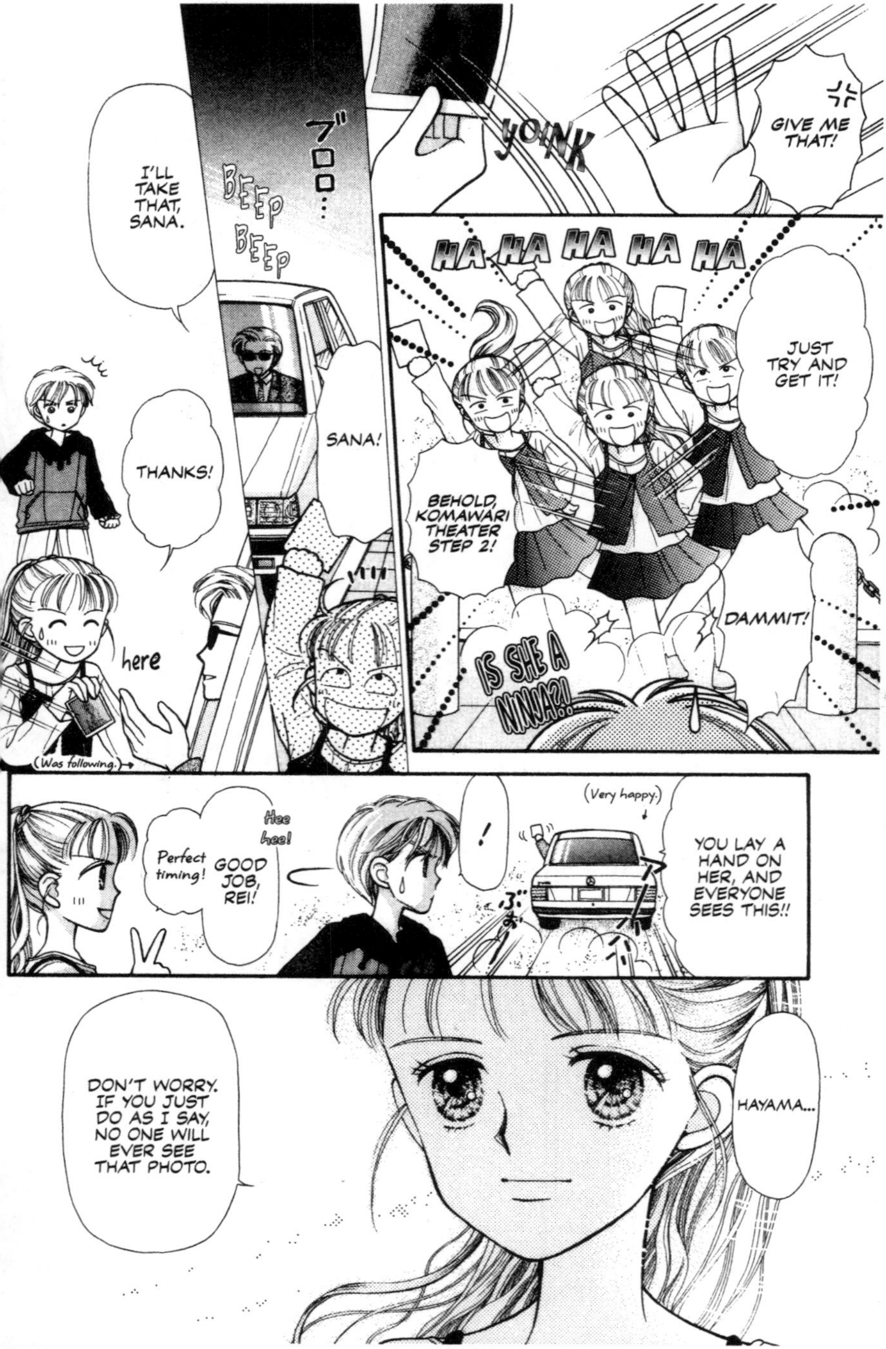
YOINK
GIVE ME THAT!
HA HA HA HA HA
JUST TRY AND GET IT!
BEHOLD, KOMAWARI THEATER STEP 2!
DAMMIT!
IS SHE A NINJA?!
ブロロ…
BEEP BEEP
SANA!
I'LL TAKE THAT, SANA.
THANKS!
here
(Was following.)
(Very happy.)
YOU LAY A HAND ON HER, AND EVERYONE SEES THIS!!
!
GOOD JOB, REI!
Hee hee!
Perfect timing!
HAYAMA...
DON'T WORRY. IF YOU JUST DO AS I SAY, NO ONE WILL EVER SEE THAT PHOTO.

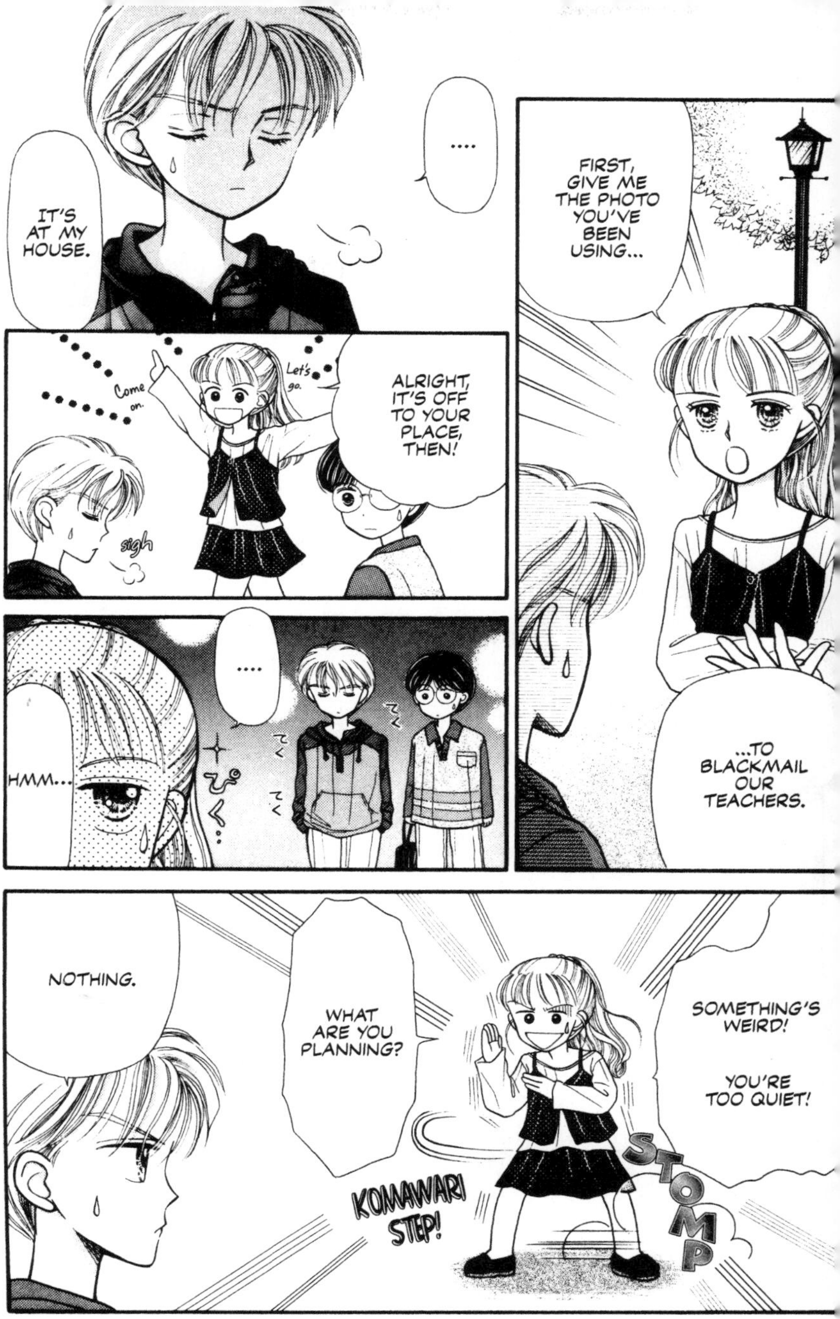
FIRST, GIVE ME THE PHOTO YOU'VE BEEN USING...
...TO BLACKMAIL OUR TEACHERS.
....
IT'S AT MY HOUSE.
ALRIGHT, IT'S OFF TO YOUR PLACE, THEN!
Let's go.
Come on.
sigh
....
HMM...
SOMETHING'S WEIRD!
YOU'RE TOO QUIET!
STOMP
KOMAWARI STEP!
WHAT ARE YOU PLANNING?
NOTHING.

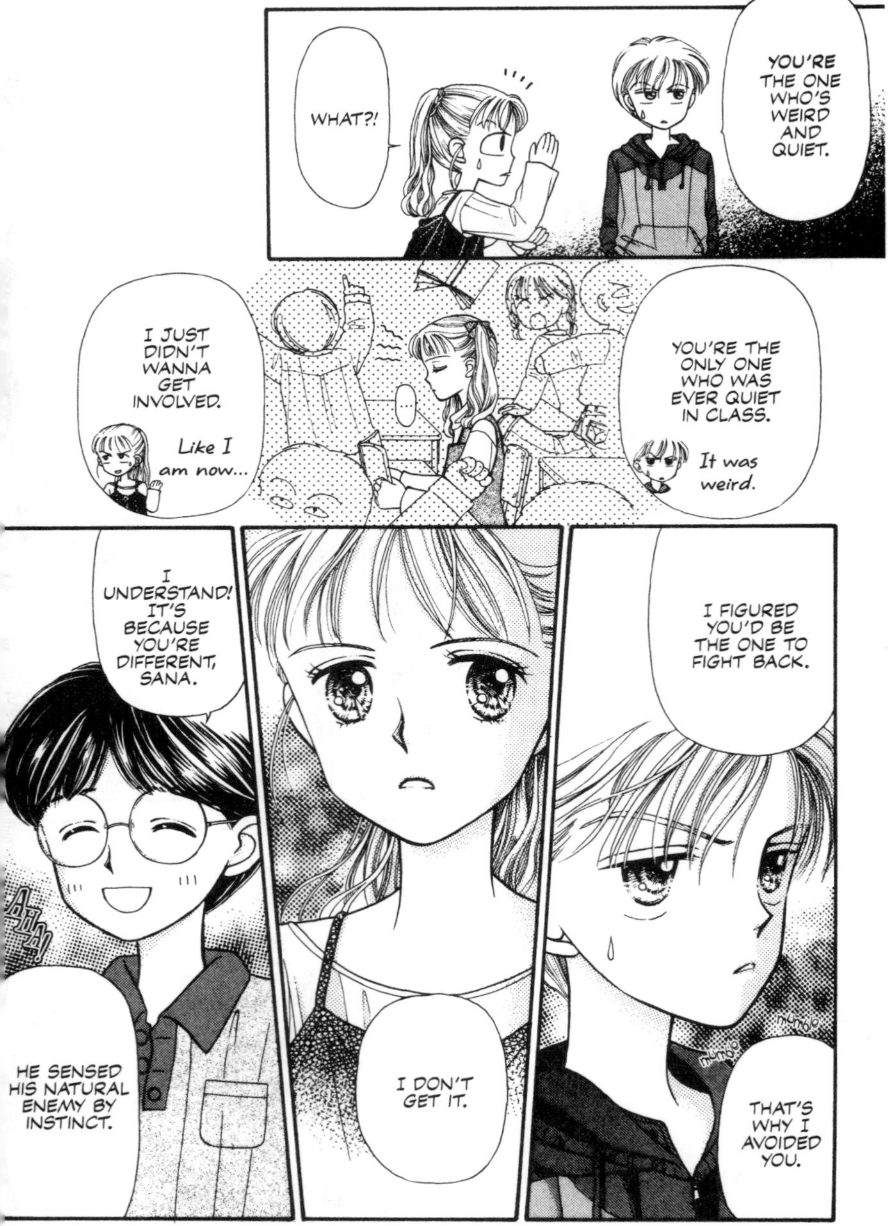

YOU'RE THE ONE WHO'S WEIRD AND QUIET.
WHAT?!
YOU'RE THE ONLY ONE WHO WAS EVER QUIET IN CLASS.
It was weird.
...
I JUST DIDN'T WANNA GET INVOLVED.
Like I am now...
I FIGURED YOU'D BE THE ONE TO FIGHT BACK.
mumble mumble
THAT'S WHY I AVOIDED YOU.
I DON'T GET IT.
I UNDERSTAND! IT'S BECAUSE YOU'RE DIFFERENT, SANA.
AHA!
HE SENSED HIS NATURAL ENEMY BY INSTINCT.

About Hayama

Hayama is popular with all of you – as popular as Sana. I'm surprised. I was gonna try and make him popular gradually, but he was popular right off the bat. If he had a face like a monster, he might not have been... I kinda wanted to do that. Hee-hee. He's pretty twisted, like me, but really I based his character on a friend of mine. He's Japanese, but he looks foreign and has funny hair. Funny in a cute way, I mean. (Don't get mad.) When the wind blows, his hair moves like some kind of an animal. I wish I could show that to you guys!

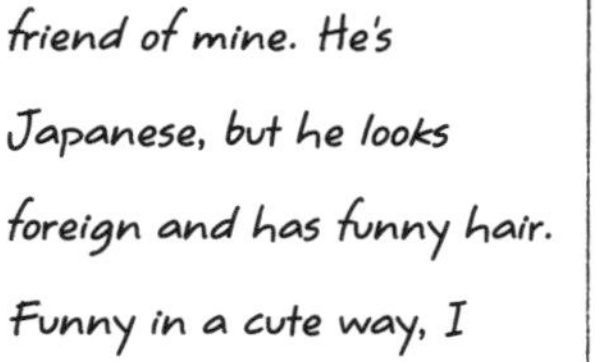
blow
blow
blow
HEE HEE
What's so funny?
Nothing.

Anyway, speaking of Hayama... to be continued.

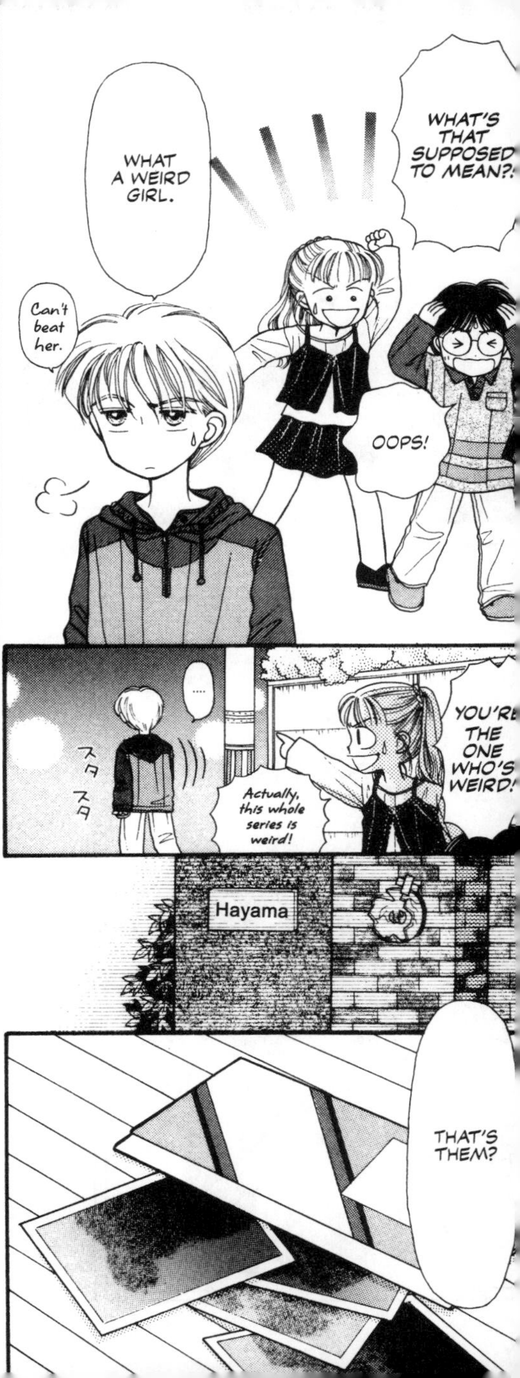
WHAT A WEIRD GIRL.
WHAT'S THAT SUPPOSED TO MEAN?!
Can't beat her.
OOPS!
....
スタ スタ
YOU'RE THE ONE WHO'S WEIRD!
Actually, this whole series is weird!
Hayama
THAT'S THEM?

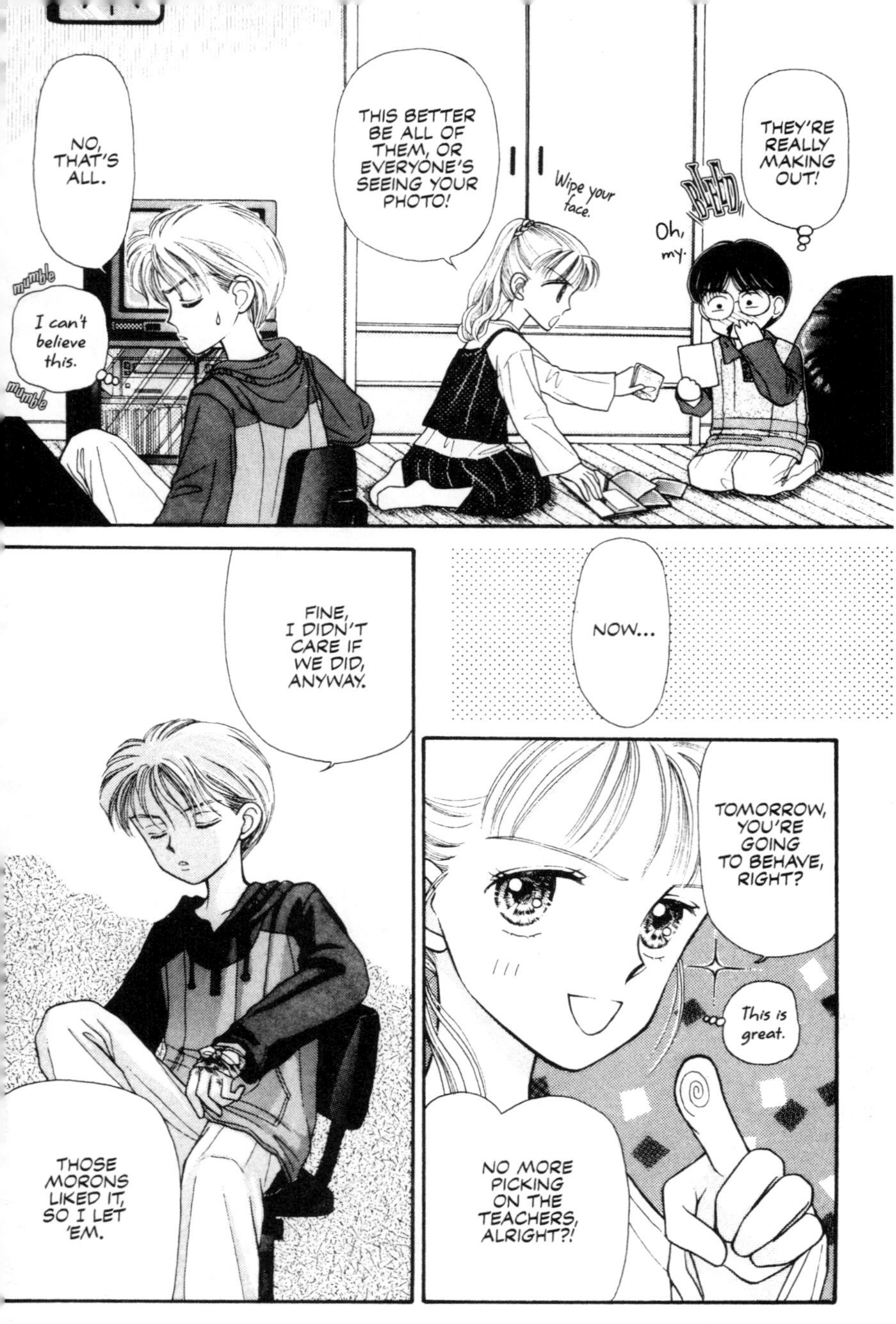
THEY'RE REALLY MAKING OUT!
BLEED
Oh, my.
Wipe your face.
THIS BETTER BE ALL OF THEM, OR EVERYONE'S SEEING YOUR PHOTO!
NO, THAT'S ALL.
mumble
I can't believe this.
mumble
NOW...
TOMORROW, YOU'RE GOING TO BEHAVE, RIGHT?
This is great.
NO MORE PICKING ON THE TEACHERS, ALRIGHT?!
FINE, I DIDN'T CARE IF WE DID, ANYWAY.
THOSE MORONS LIKED IT, SO I LET 'EM.

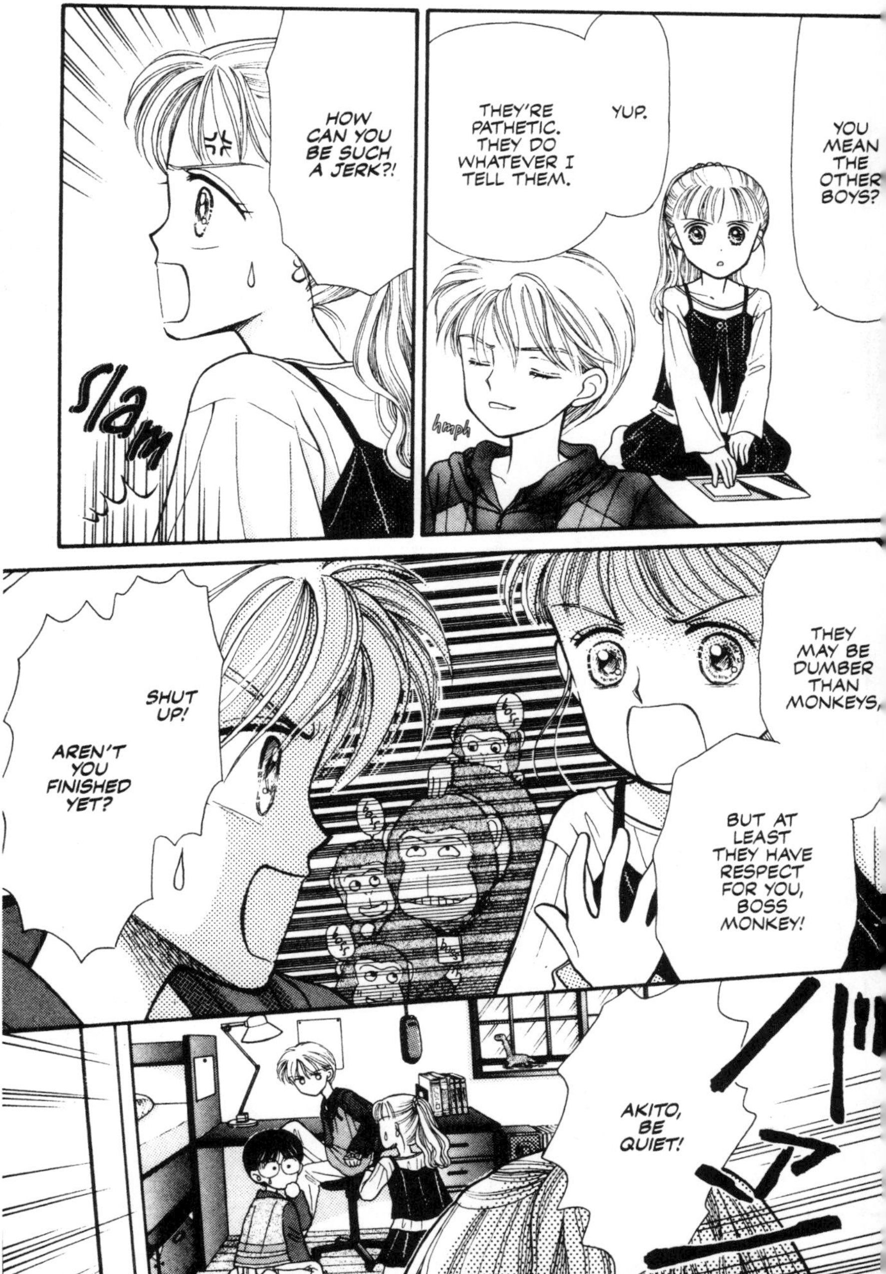
YOU MEAN THE OTHER BOYS?
YUP.
THEY'RE PATHETIC. THEY DO WHATEVER I TELL THEM.
hmph
HOW CAN YOU BE SUCH A JERK?!
slam
THEY MAY BE DUMBER THAN MONKEYS,
BUT AT LEAST THEY HAVE RESPECT FOR YOU, BOSS MONKEY!
SHUT UP!
AREN'T YOU FINISHED YET?
AKITO, BE QUIET!

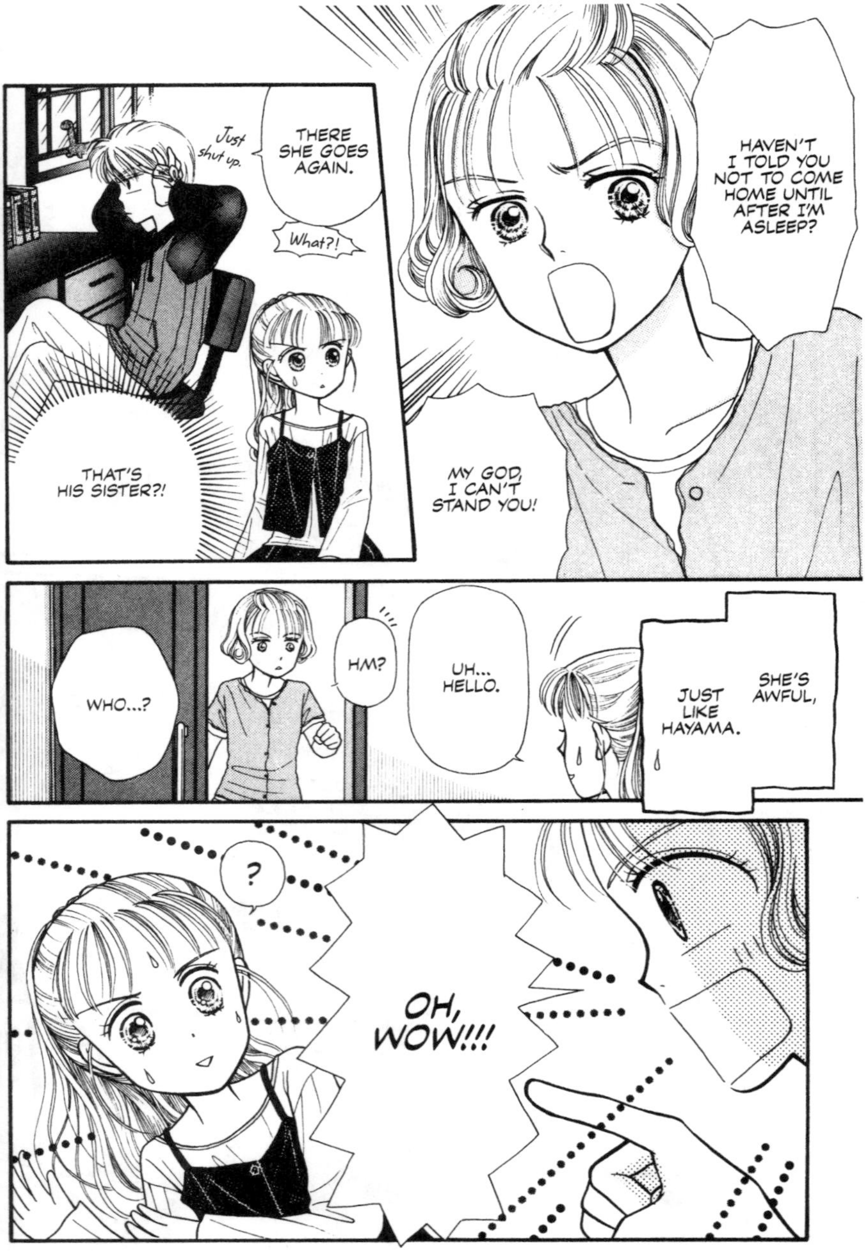

HAVEN'T I TOLD YOU NOT TO COME HOME UNTIL AFTER I'M ASLEEP?
MY GOD, I CAN'T STAND YOU!
THERE SHE GOES AGAIN.
Just shut up.
What?!
THAT'S HIS SISTER?!
SHE'S AWFUL, JUST LIKE HAYAMA.
UH... HELLO.
HM?
WHO...?
OH, WOW!!!
?

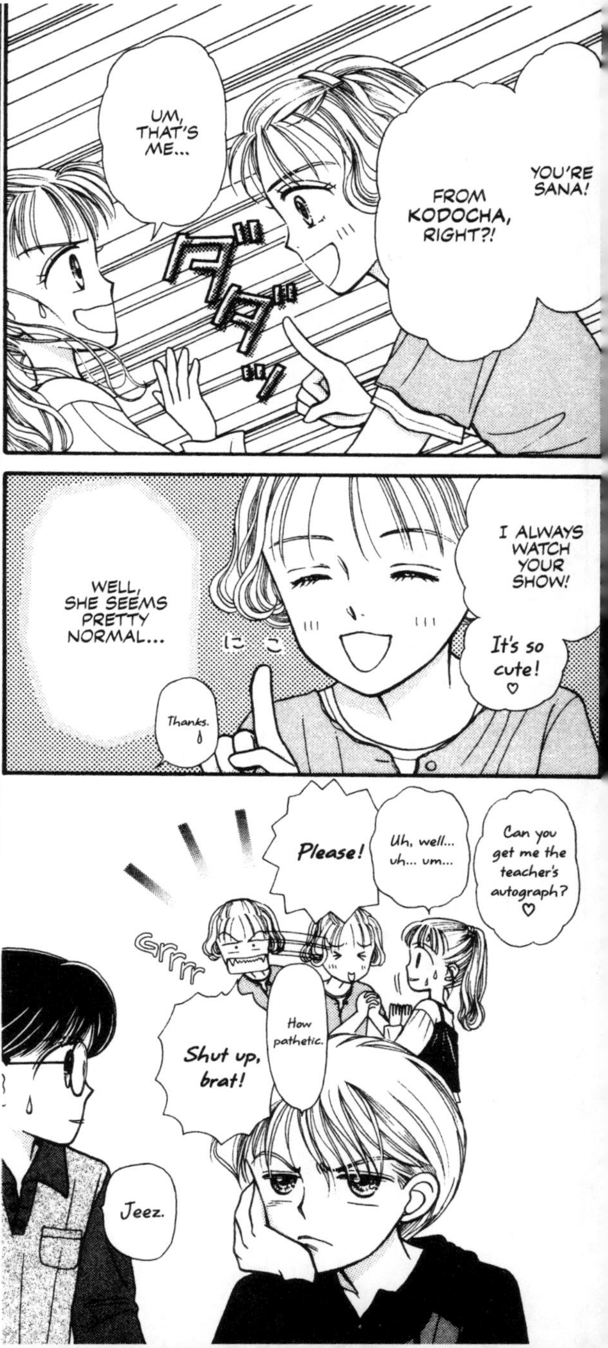
YOU'RE SANA!
FROM KODOCHA, RIGHT?!
UM, THAT'S ME...
I ALWAYS WATCH YOUR SHOW!
It's so cute! ♡
WELL, SHE SEEMS PRETTY NORMAL...
Thanks.
Can you get me the teacher's autograph? ♡
Uh, well... uh... um...
Please!
Grrrr
How pathetic.
Shut up, brat!
Jeez.

Part II

So, like I was saying, Hayama's kind-of twisted like me -- but I'm like Sana, too, of course. We're both like, "Don't be like that! Let's enjoy life!" (Ha!) I think maybe we all have opposite sides to our natures. (Maybe I have a dual personality.) So, both Hayama's and Sana's opinions are my opinion. But I favor Sana... I mean, I wanna take the good parts from both of them. I want both characters to make up for each other's weaknesses, and that will strengthen their spiritual relationship. I think it's too early for them to get physical though... (ha!) But I may do it anyway!

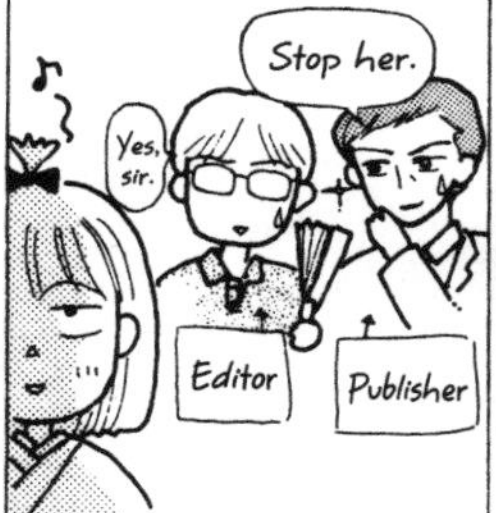
Stop her.
Yes, sir.
Editor
Publisher

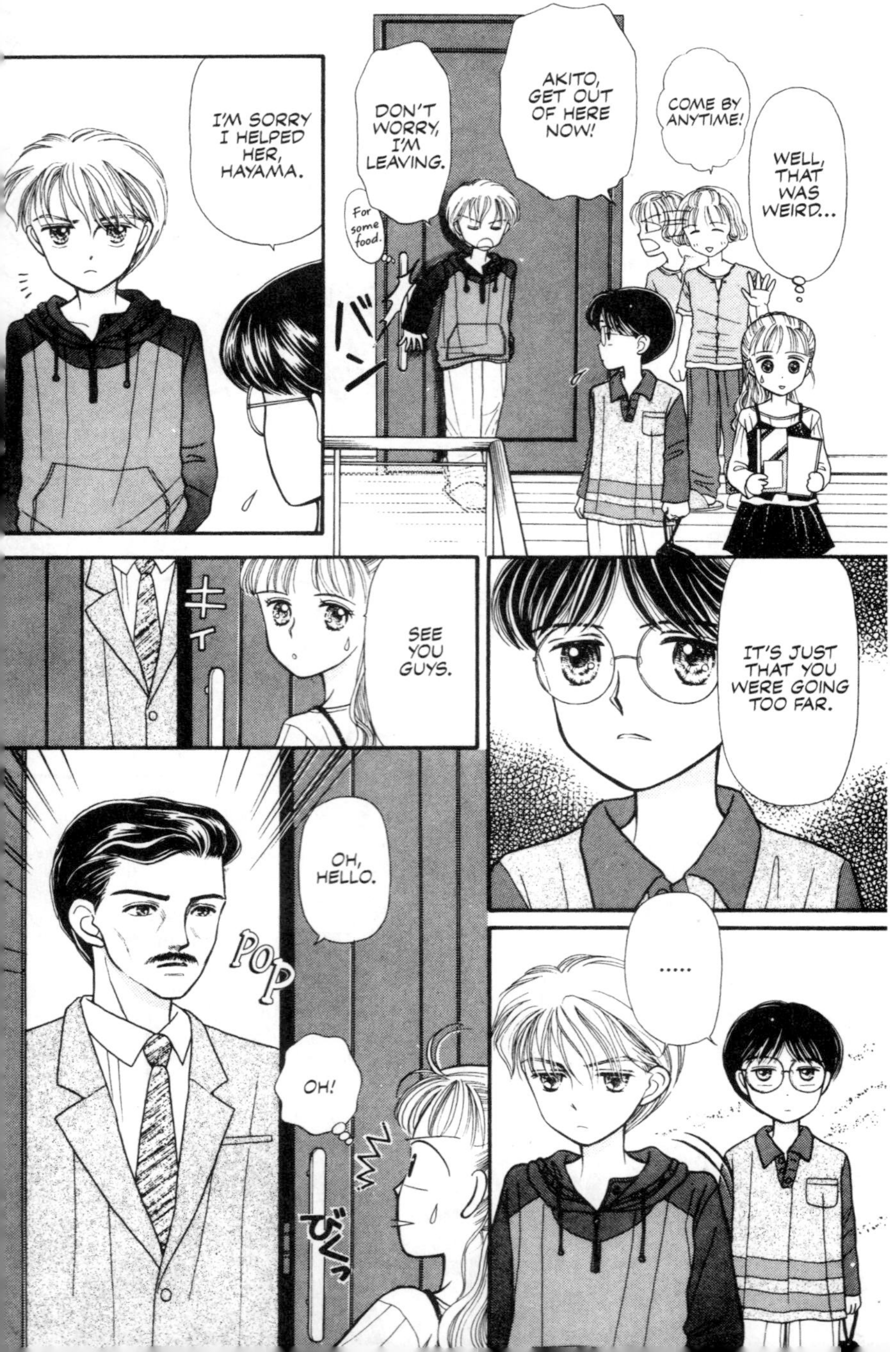
WELL, THAT WAS WEIRD...
COME BY ANYTIME!
AKITO, GET OUT OF HERE NOW!
DON'T WORRY, I'M LEAVING.
For some food.
バン
I'M SORRY I HELPED HER, HAYAMA.
IT'S JUST THAT YOU WERE GOING TOO FAR.
.....
SEE YOU GUYS.
キイ
OH, HELLO.
POP
OH!
びくっ

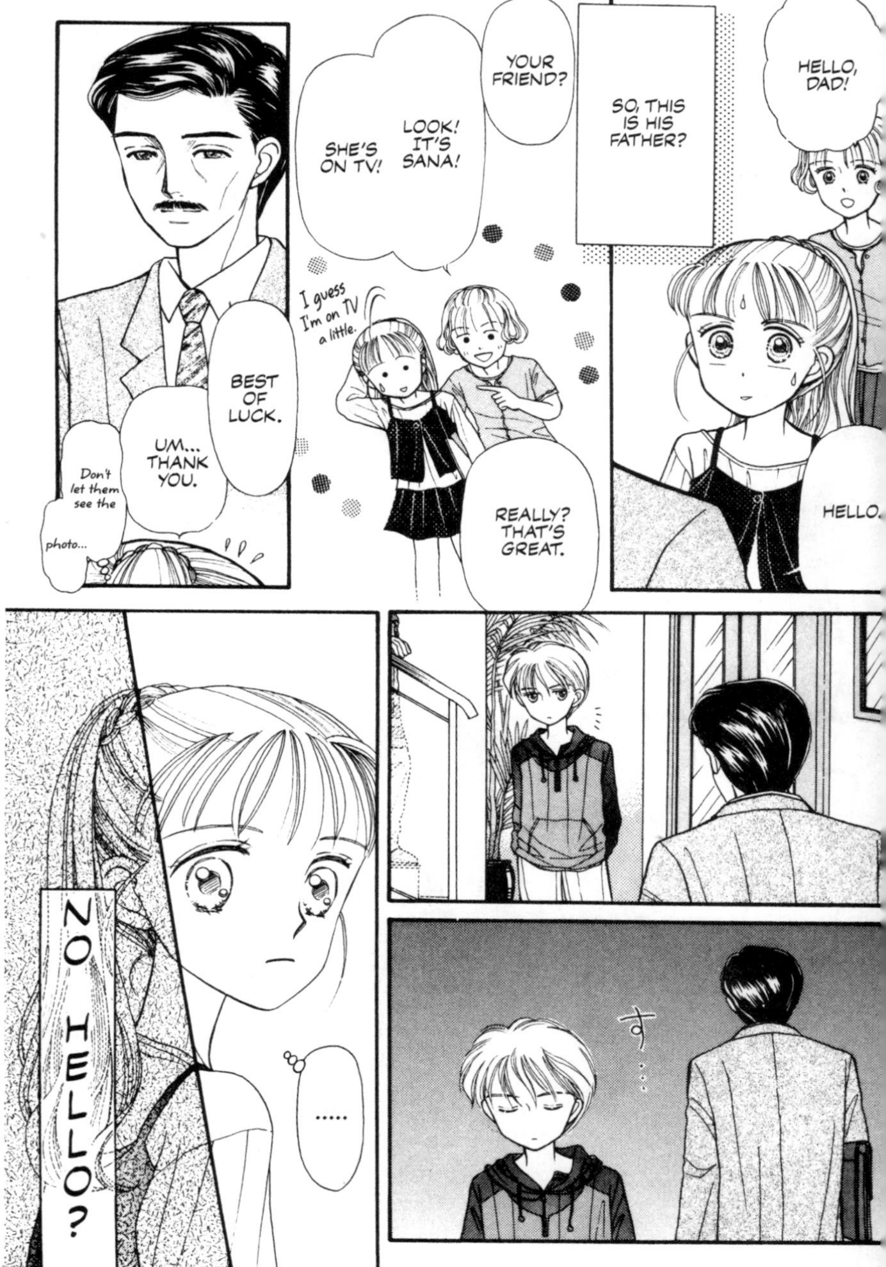
HELLO, DAD!
SO, THIS IS HIS FATHER?
HELLO.
YOUR FRIEND?
LOOK! IT'S SANA!
SHE'S ON TV!
I guess I'm on TV a little.
REALLY? THAT'S GREAT.
BEST OF LUCK.
UM... THANK YOU.
Don't let them see the photo...
す...
NO HELLO?
......

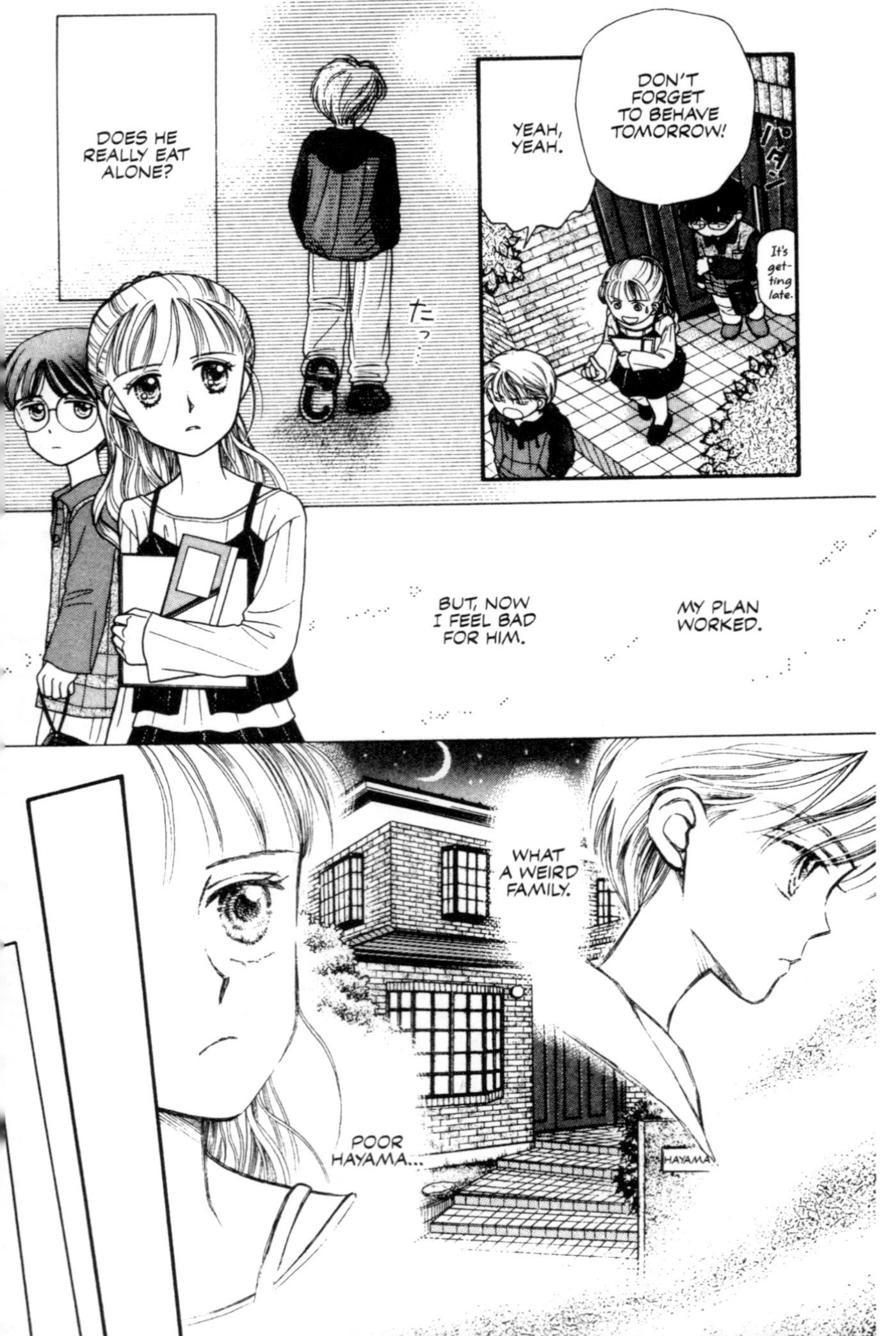
DON'T FORGET TO BEHAVE TOMORROW!
YEAH, YEAH.
It's getting late.
DOES HE REALLY EAT ALONE?
たっ
MY PLAN WORKED.
BUT, NOW I FEEL BAD FOR HIM.
WHAT A WEIRD FAMILY.
HAYAMA
POOR HAYAMA...

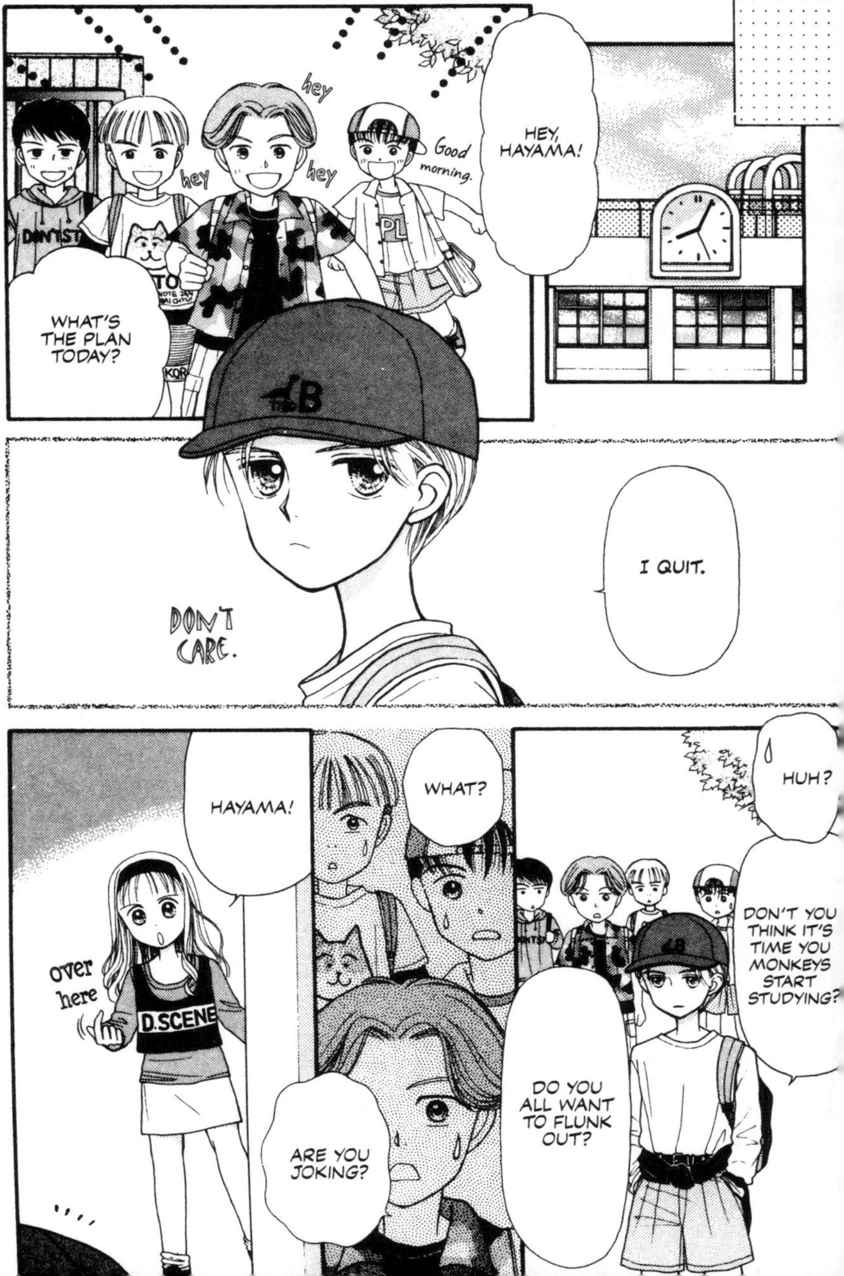
HEY, HAYAMA!
Good morning.
hey
hey
hey
WHAT'S THE PLAN TODAY?
I QUIT.
DON'T CARE.
HUH?
DON'T YOU THINK IT'S TIME YOU MONKEYS START STUDYING?
DO YOU ALL WANT TO FLUNK OUT?
WHAT?
ARE YOU JOKING?
HAYAMA!
over here
...

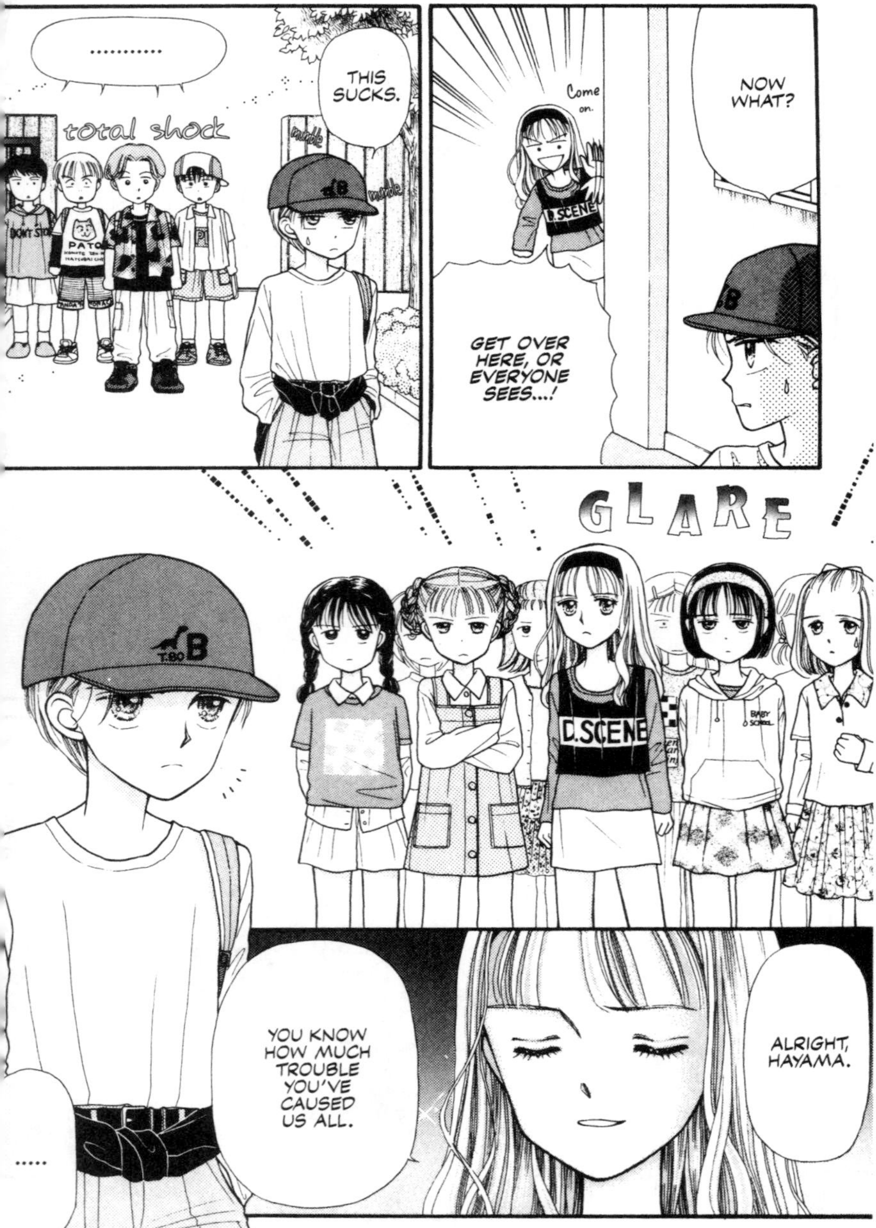
NOW WHAT?
Come on.
GET OVER HERE, OR EVERYONE SEES...!
THIS SUCKS.
....
total shock
mumble
mumble
GLARE
ALRIGHT, HAYAMA.
YOU KNOW HOW MUCH TROUBLE YOU'VE CAUSED US ALL.
.....

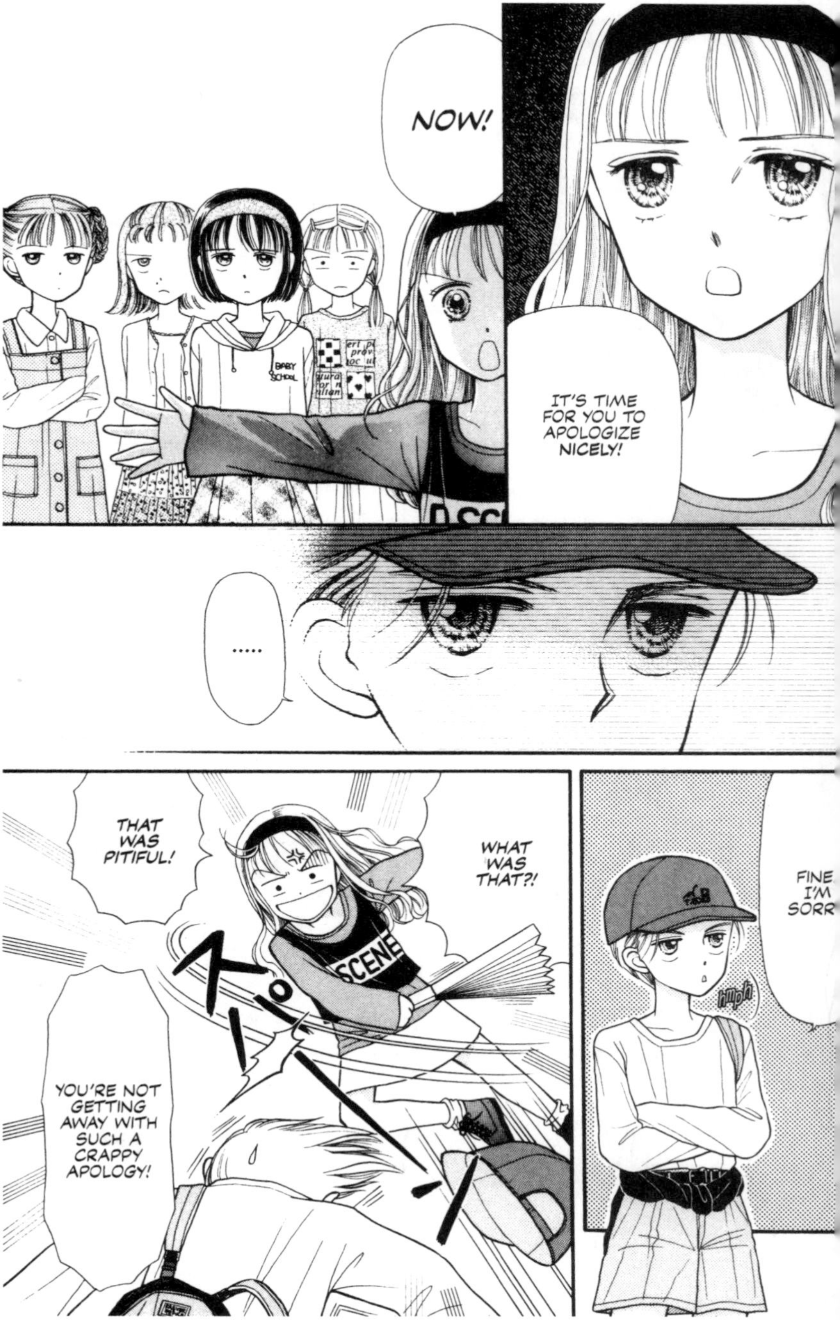
IT'S TIME FOR YOU TO APOLOGIZE NICELY!
NOW!
......
FINE. I'M SORR
hmph
WHAT WAS THAT?!
THAT WAS PITIFUL!
YOU'RE NOT GETTING AWAY WITH SUCH A CRAPPY APOLOGY!

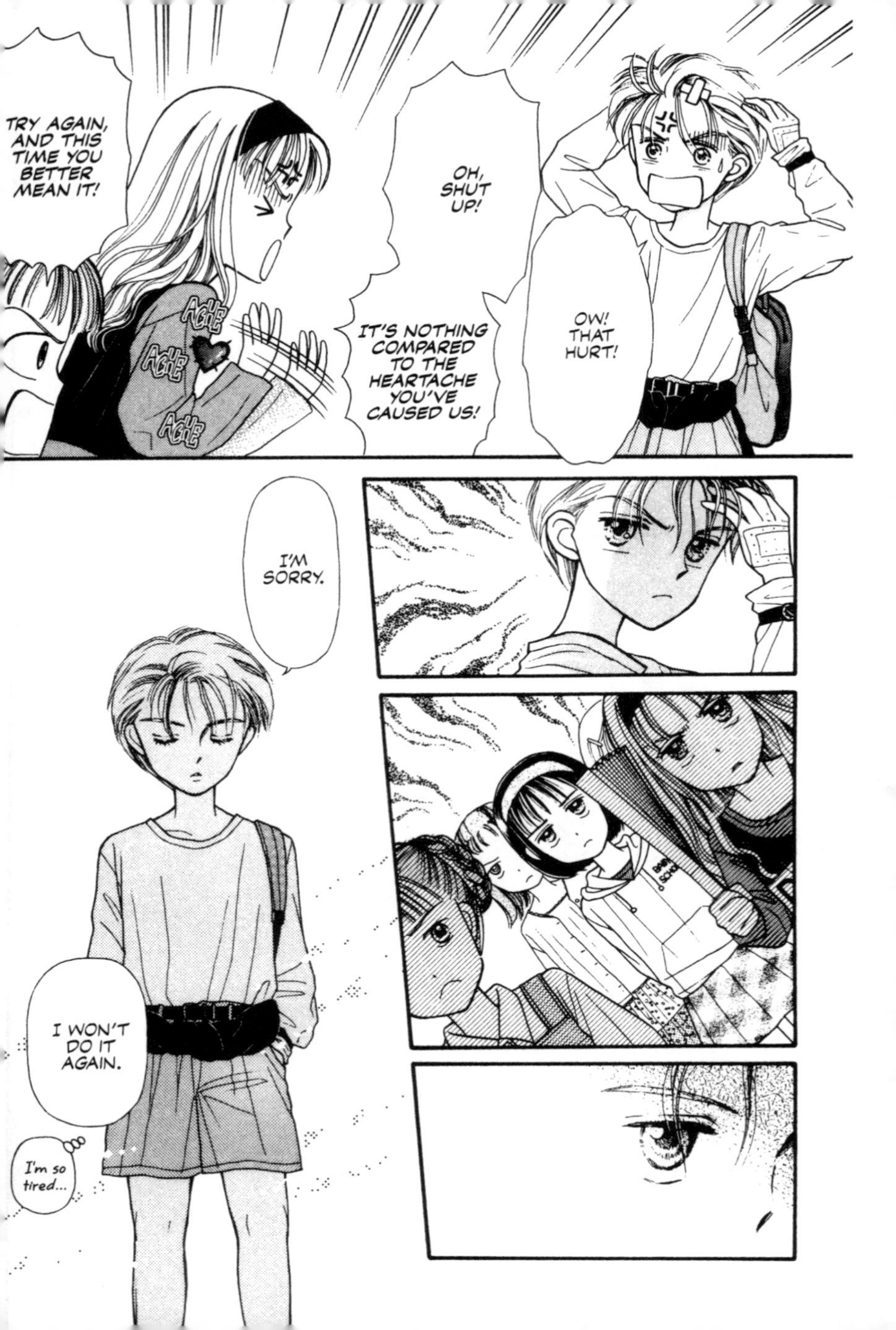
OW! THAT HURT!
OH, SHUT UP!
IT'S NOTHING COMPARED TO THE HEARTACHE YOU'VE CAUSED US!
TRY AGAIN, AND THIS TIME YOU BETTER MEAN IT!
I'M SORRY.
I WON'T DO IT AGAIN.
I'm so tired...

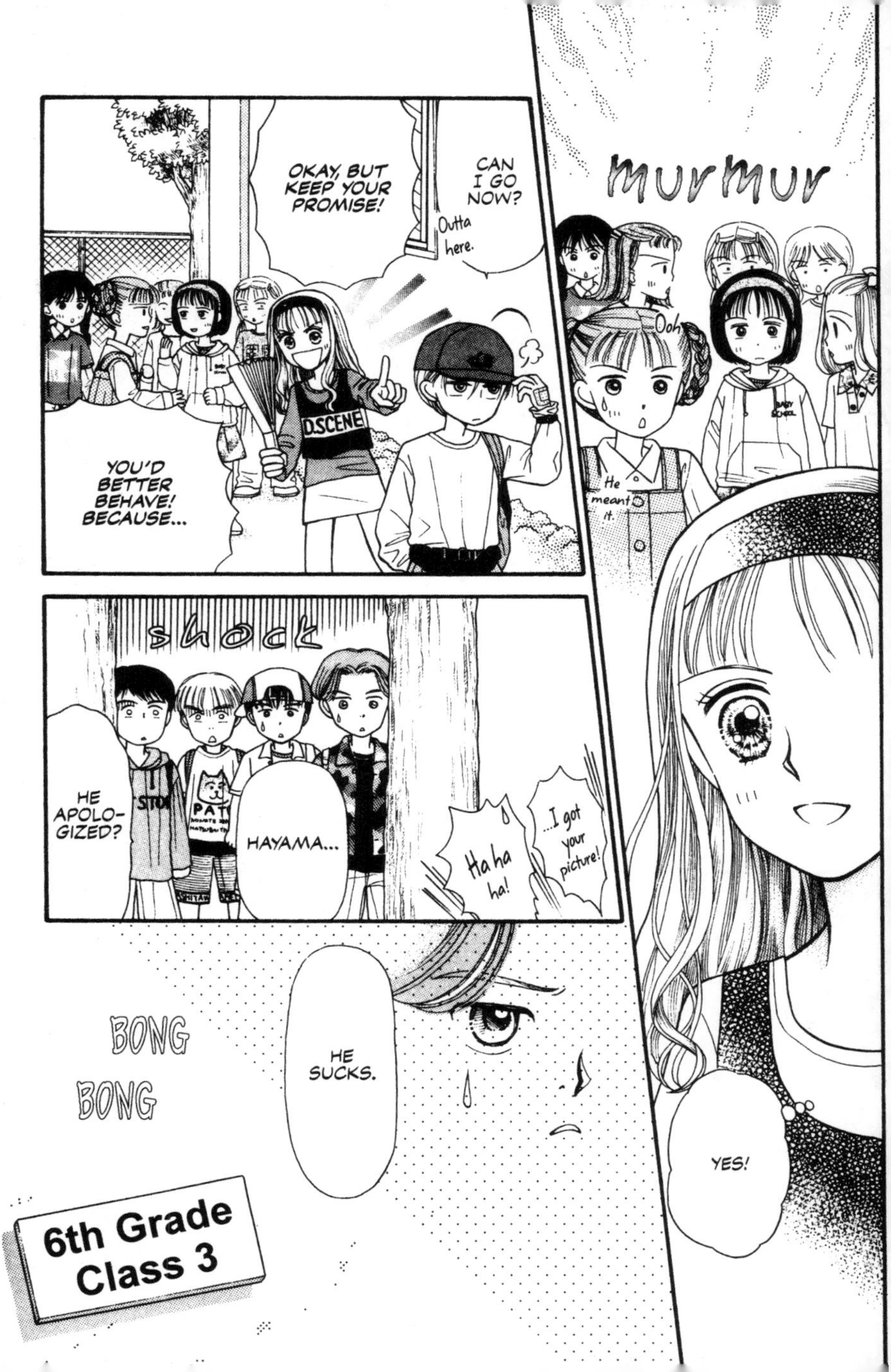
murmur
Ooh
He meant it.
YES!
CAN I GO NOW?
Outta here.
OKAY, BUT KEEP YOUR PROMISE!
YOU'D BETTER BEHAVE! BECAUSE...
shock
...I got your picture!
Ha ha ha!
HAYAMA...
HE APOLOGIZED?
HE SUCKS.
BONG
BONG
6th Grade Class 3

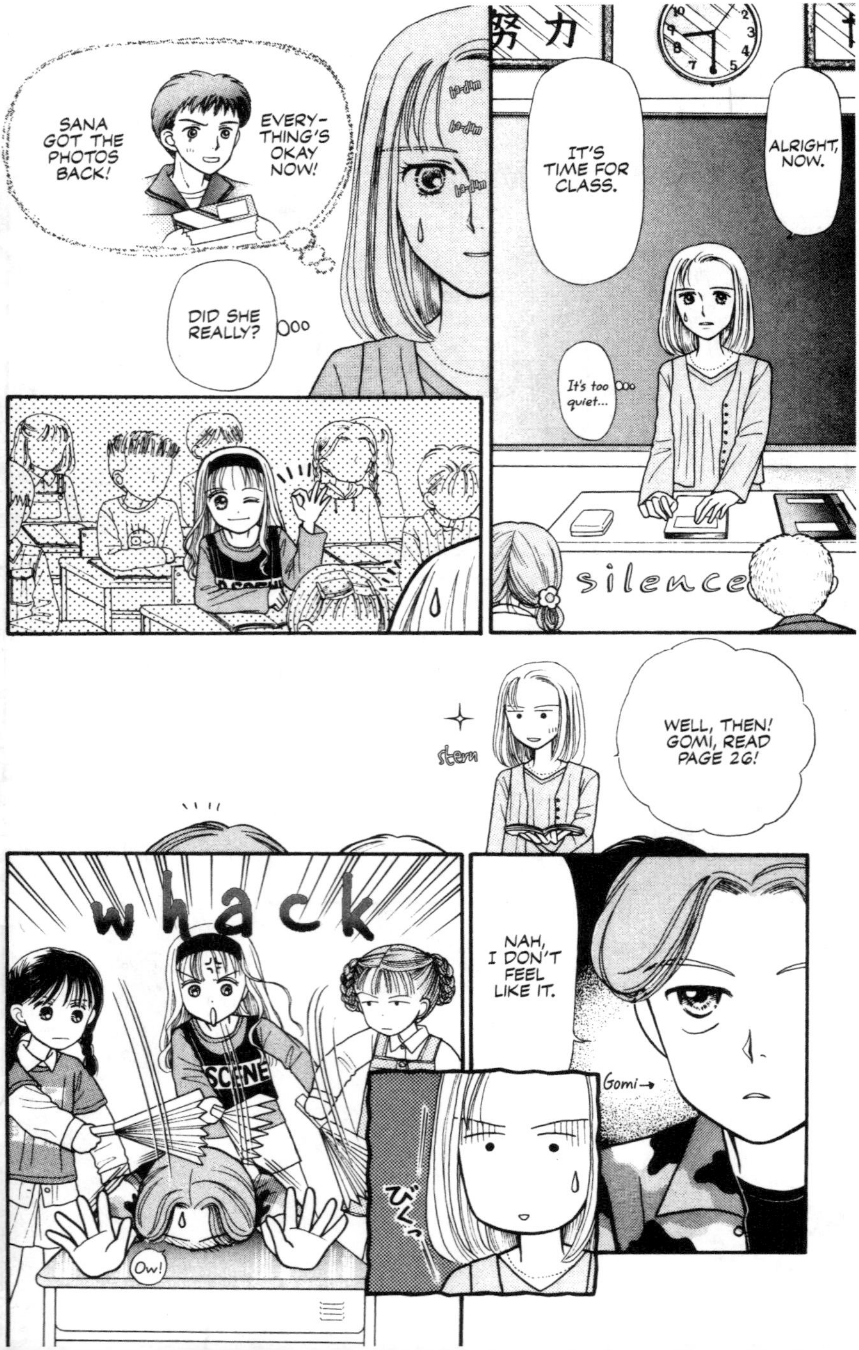
ALRIGHT, NOW.
IT'S TIME FOR CLASS.
It's too quiet...
silence
ba-dum
ba-dum
ba-dum
SANA GOT THE PHOTOS BACK! EVERY-THING'S OKAY NOW!
DID SHE REALLY?
WELL, THEN! GOMI, READ PAGE 26!
stern
NAH, I DON'T FEEL LIKE IT.
Gomi→
びくっ
whack
Ow!

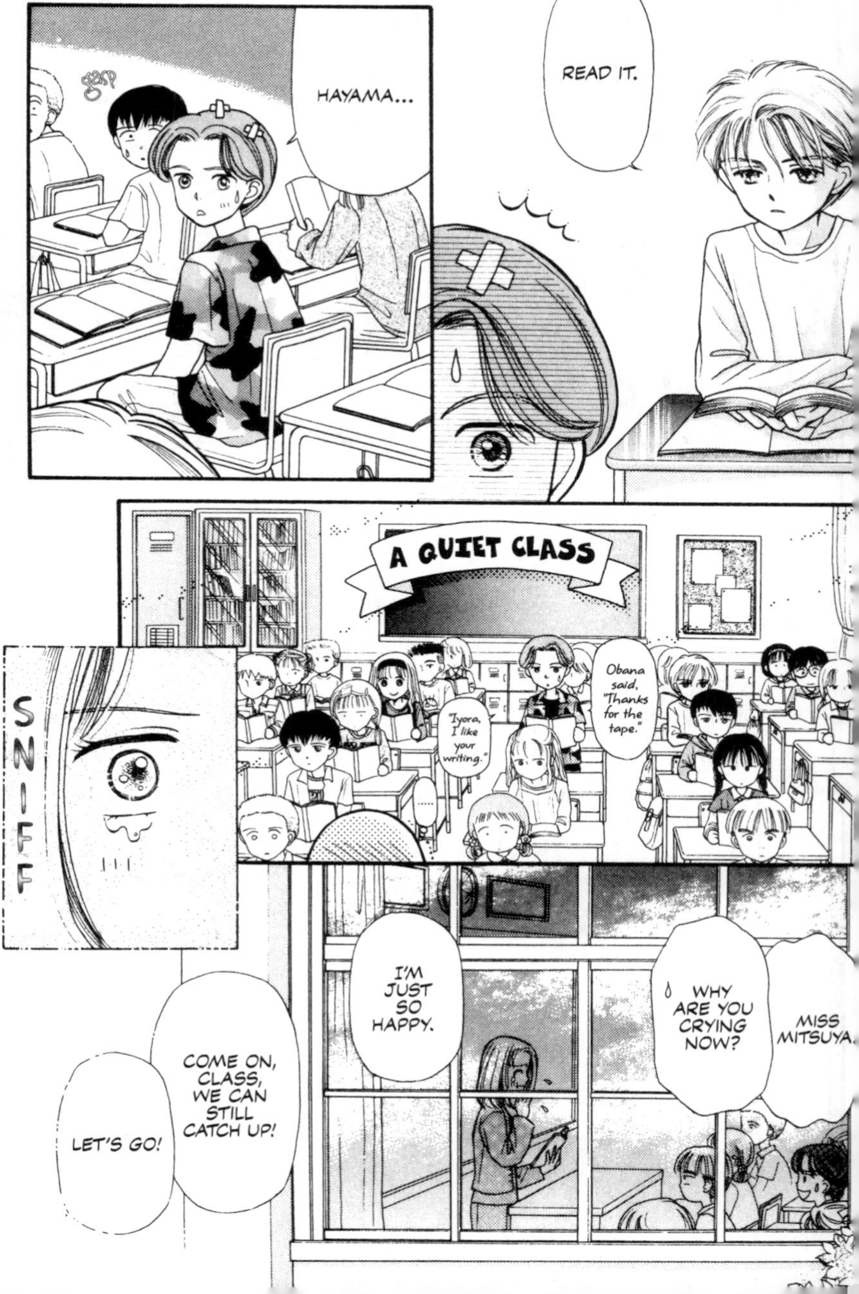
READ IT.
gasp
HAYAMA...
A QUIET CLASS
Obana said, "Thanks for the tape."
"Iyora, I like your writing."
......
SNIFF
MISS MITSUYA.
WHY ARE YOU CRYING NOW?
I'M JUST SO HAPPY.
COME ON, CLASS, WE CAN STILL CATCH UP!
LET'S GO!

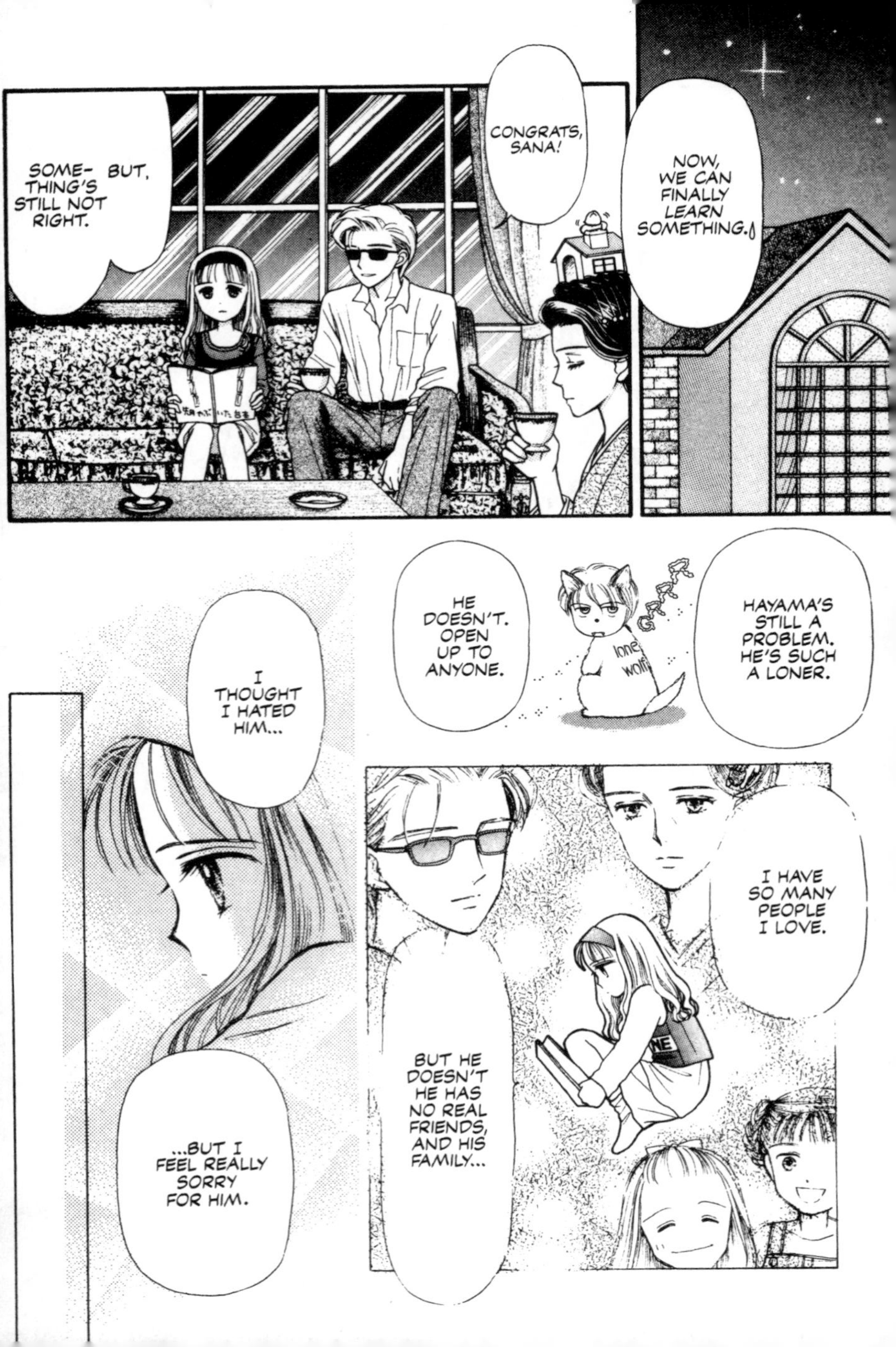
NOW, WE CAN FINALLY LEARN SOMETHING.♪
CONGRATS, SANA!
BUT, SOME- THING'S STILL NOT RIGHT.
HAYAMA'S STILL A PROBLEM. HE'S SUCH A LONER.
HE DOESN'T. OPEN UP TO ANYONE.
lone wolf
I HAVE SO MANY PEOPLE I LOVE.
BUT HE DOESN'T HE HAS NO REAL FRIENDS, AND HIS FAMILY...
I THOUGHT I HATED HIM...
...BUT I FEEL REALLY SORRY FOR HIM.

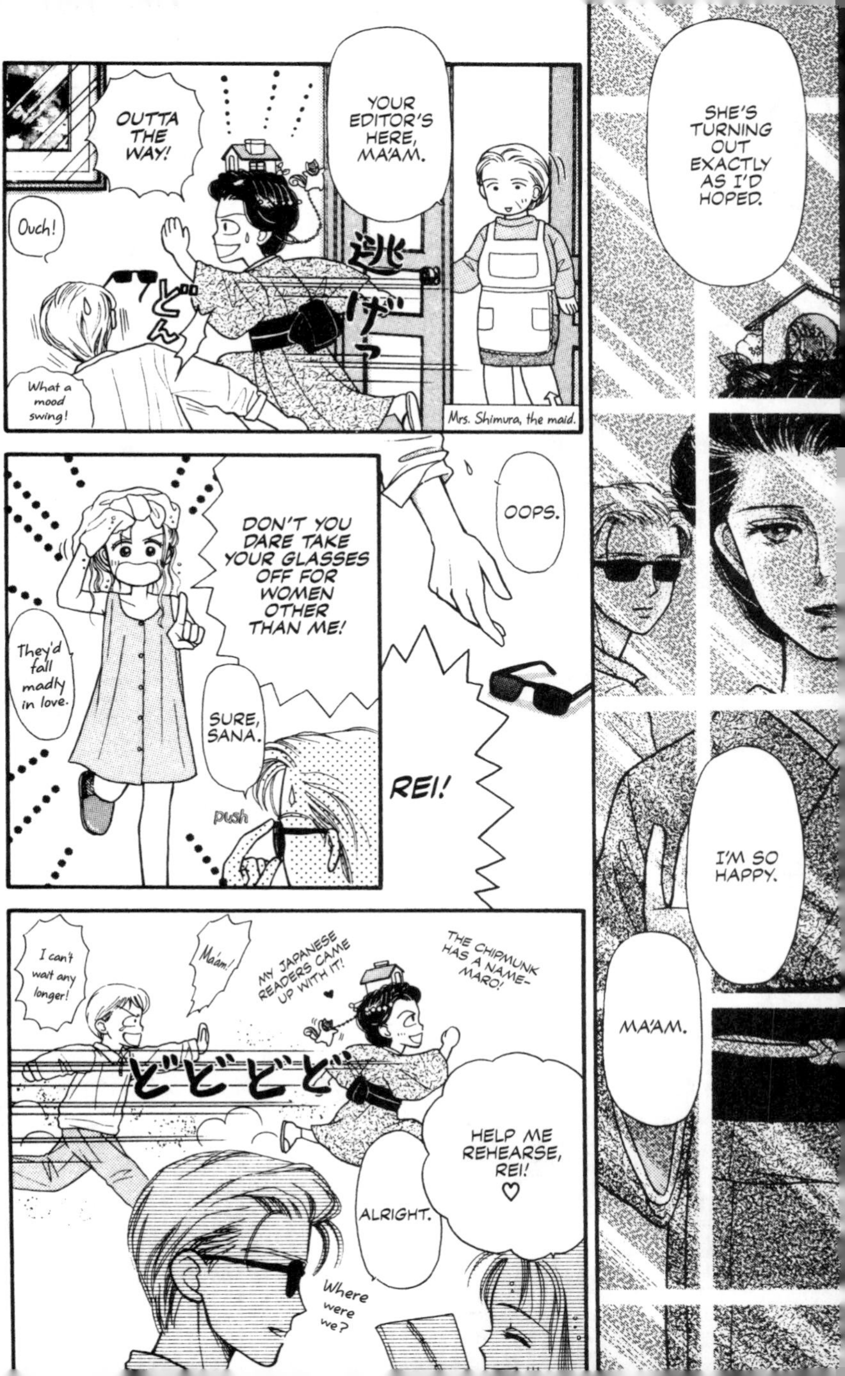
SHE'S TURNING OUT EXACTLY AS I'D HOPED.
I'M SO HAPPY.
MA'AM.
YOUR EDITOR'S HERE, MA'AM.
Mrs. Shimura, the maid.
逃げっ
OUTTA THE WAY!
どん
Ouch!
What a mood swing!
OOPS.
REI!
DON'T YOU DARE TAKE YOUR GLASSES OFF FOR WOMEN OTHER THAN ME!
SURE, SANA.
push
They'd fall madly in love.
THE CHIPMUNK HAS A NAME— MARO!
MY JAPANESE READERS CAME UP WITH IT!
Ma'am!
I can't wait any longer!
どどどどど
HELP ME REHEARSE, REI! ♡
ALRIGHT.
Where were we?

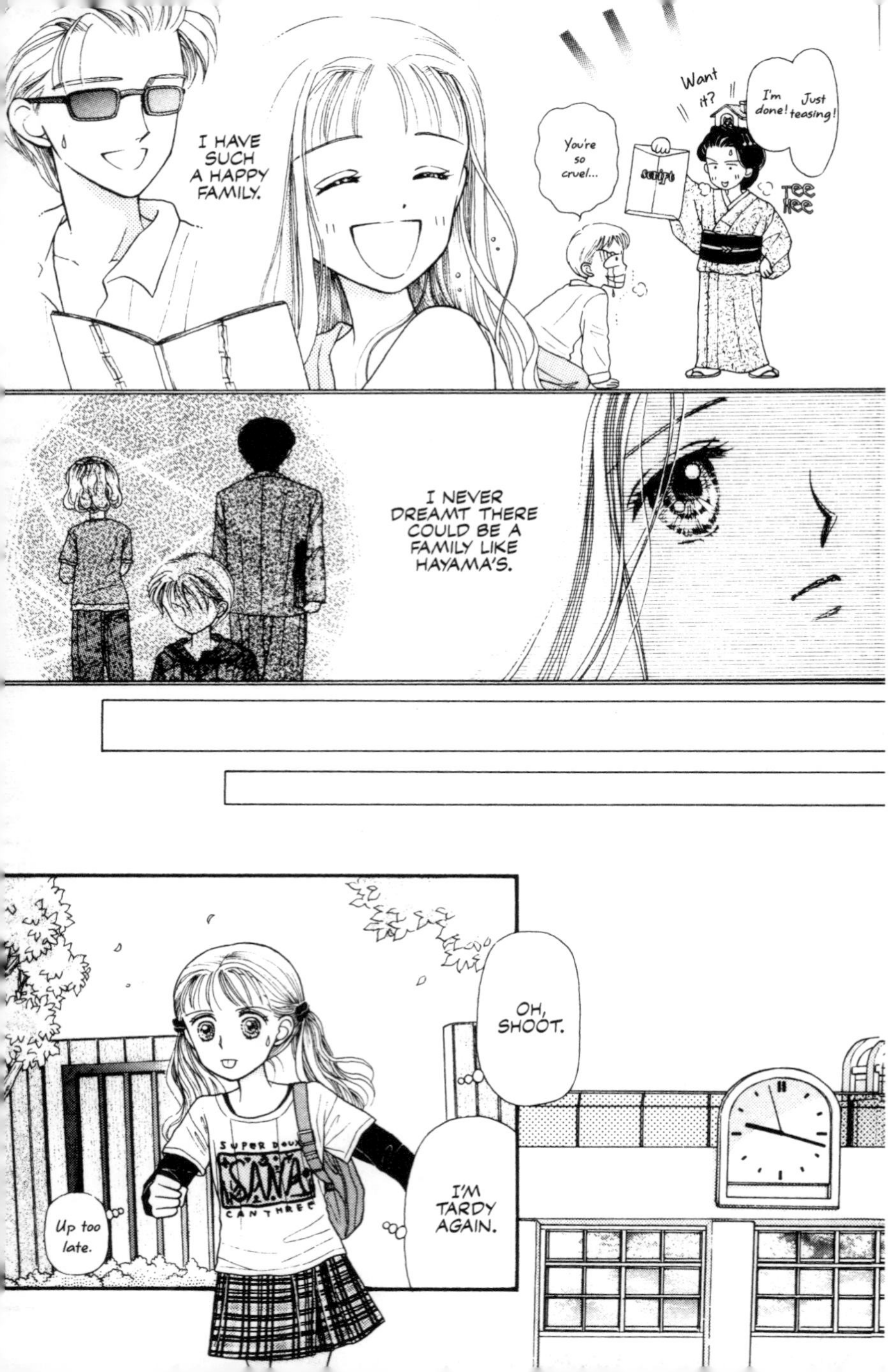
Want it?
I'm done! Just teasing!
TEE HEE
script
You're so cruel...
I HAVE SUCH A HAPPY FAMILY.
I NEVER DREAMT THERE COULD BE A FAMILY LIKE HAYAMA'S.
OH, SHOOT.
I'M TARDY AGAIN.
SANA
Up too late.

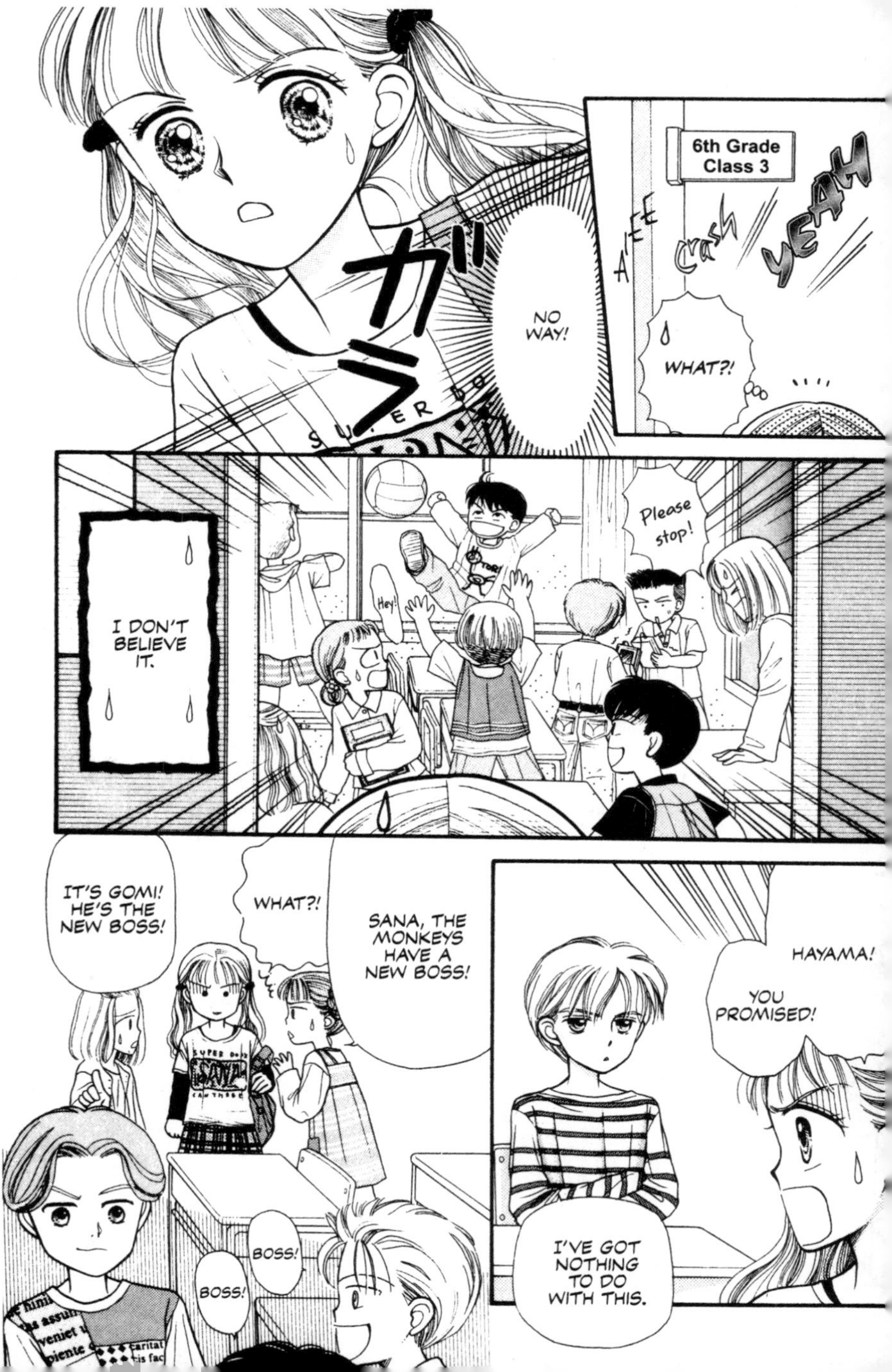
6th Grade Class 3
AIEE
crash
YEAH
WHAT?!
ガラ
NO WAY!
Please stop!
Hey!
I DON'T BELIEVE IT.
HAYAMA!
YOU PROMISED!
I'VE GOT NOTHING TO DO WITH THIS.
SANA, THE MONKEYS HAVE A NEW BOSS!
WHAT?!
IT'S GOMI! HE'S THE NEW BOSS!
BOSS!
BOSS!

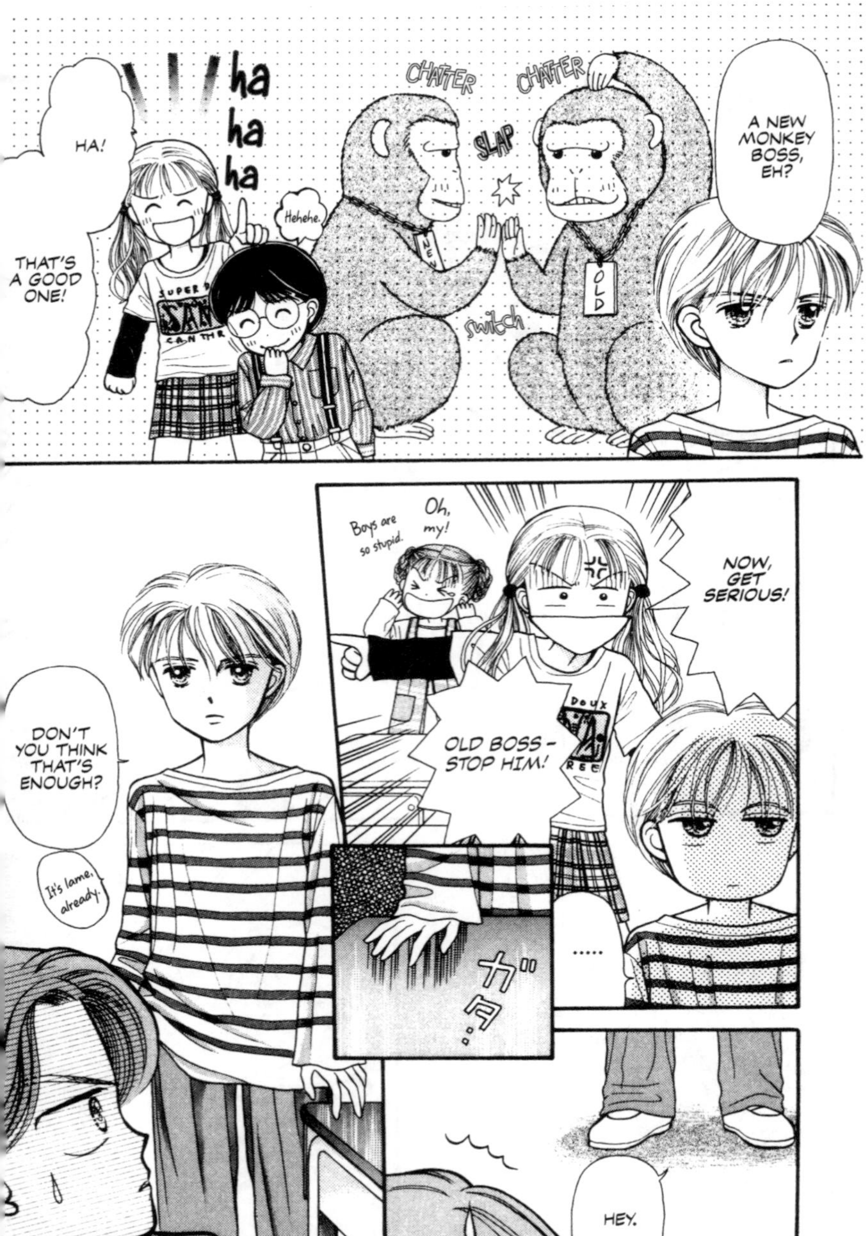
A NEW MONKEY BOSS, EH?
CHATTER
CHATTER
SLAP
switch
NEW
OLD
Hehehe.
ha ha ha
HA!
THAT'S A GOOD ONE!
NOW, GET SERIOUS!
Oh, my!
Boys are so stupid.
OLD BOSS - STOP HIM!
.....
ガタ
HEY.
DON'T YOU THINK THAT'S ENOUGH?
It's lame, already.

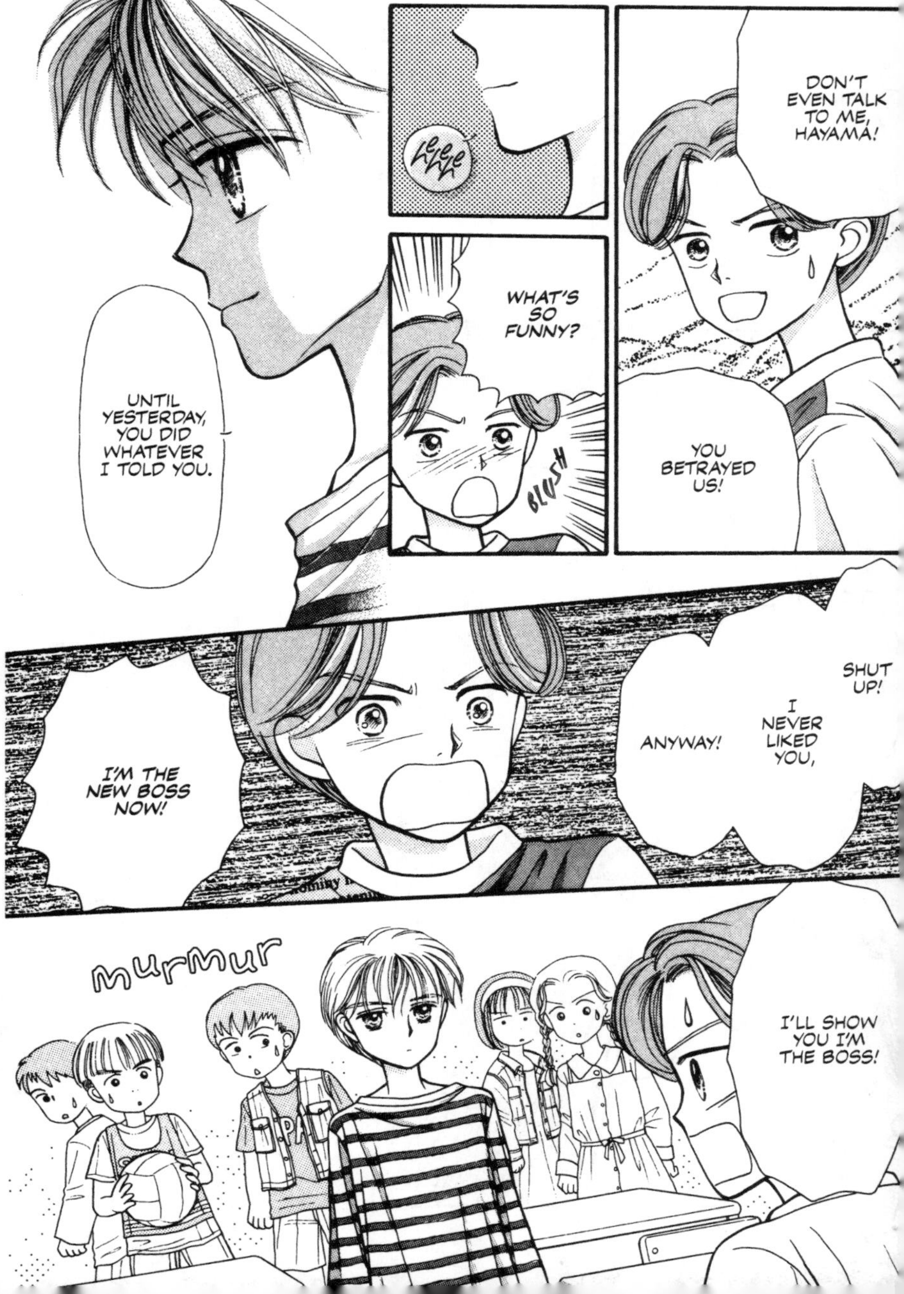
DON'T EVEN TALK TO ME, HAYAMA!
YOU BETRAYED US!
WHAT'S SO FUNNY?
BLUSH
UNTIL YESTERDAY, YOU DID WHATEVER I TOLD YOU.
SHUT UP!
I NEVER LIKED YOU,
ANYWAY!
I'M THE NEW BOSS NOW!
I'LL SHOW YOU I'M THE BOSS!
MURMUR

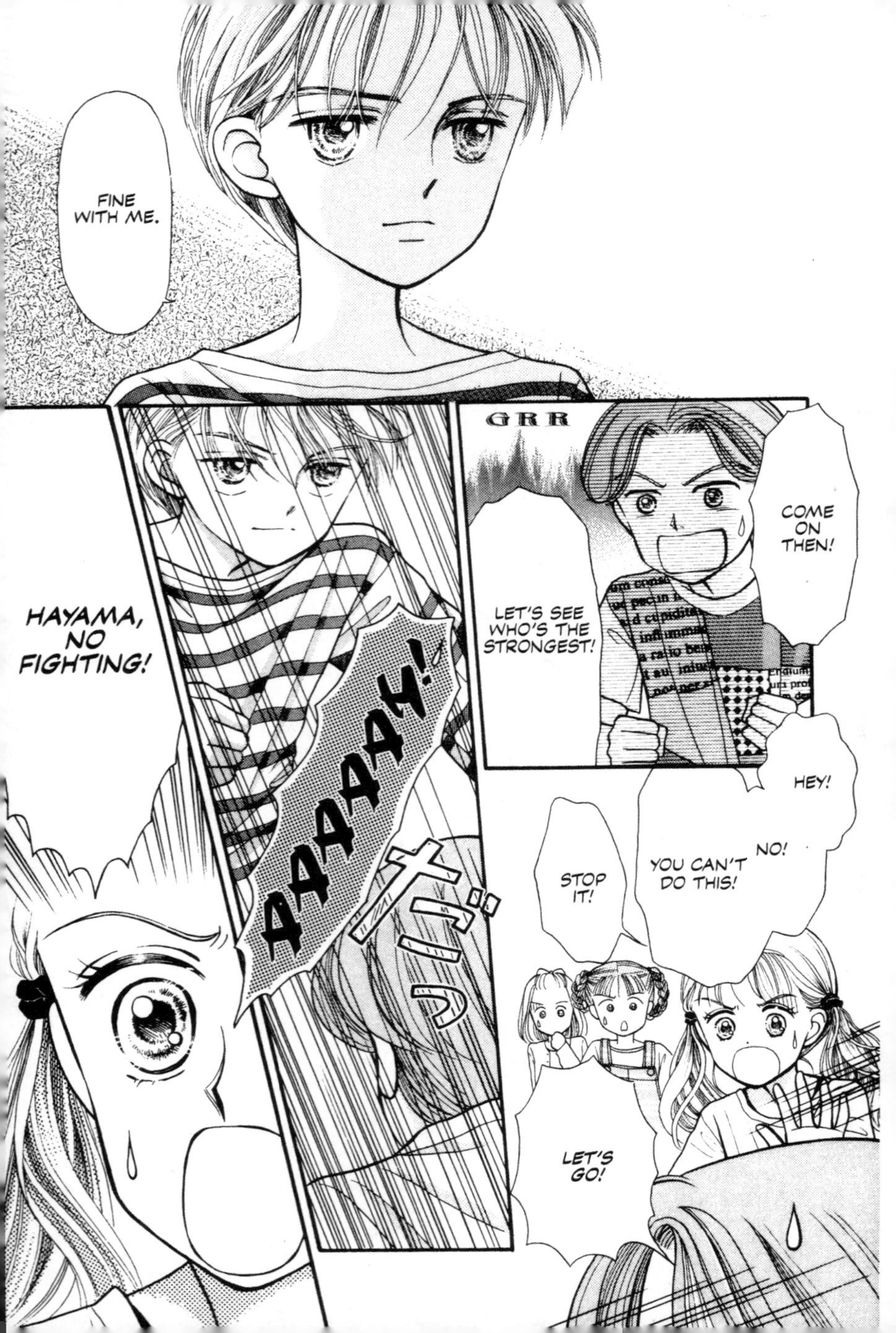
FINE WITH ME.
GRR
COME ON THEN!
LET'S SEE WHO'S THE STRONGEST!
AAAAAH!
HEY!
NO!
YOU CAN'T DO THIS!
STOP IT!
LET'S GO!
HAYAMA, NO FIGHTING!

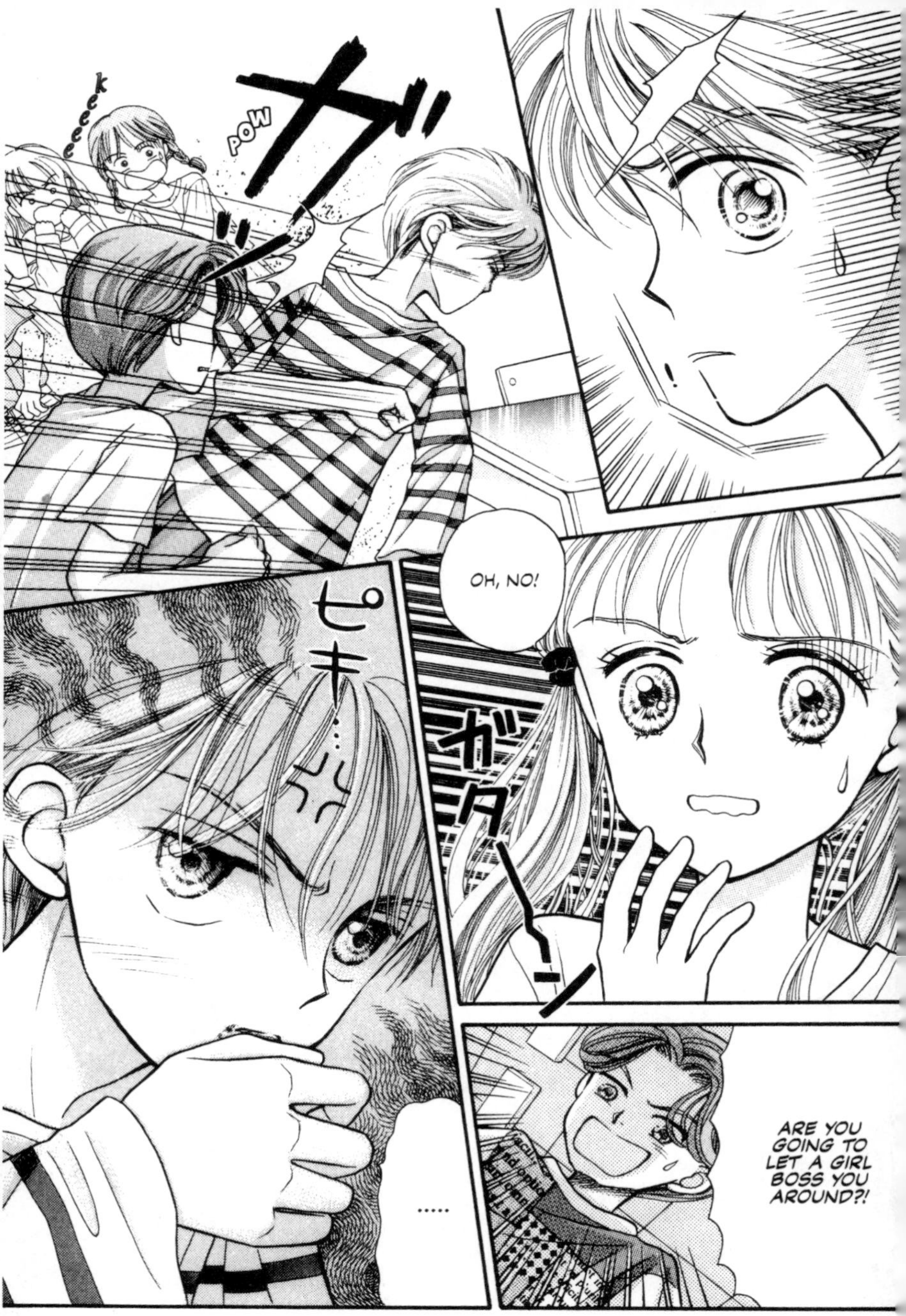

!
keeeee
POW
ガ
OH, NO!
ガタ
ARE YOU GOING TO LET A GIRL BOSS YOU AROUND?!
ピキ
.....

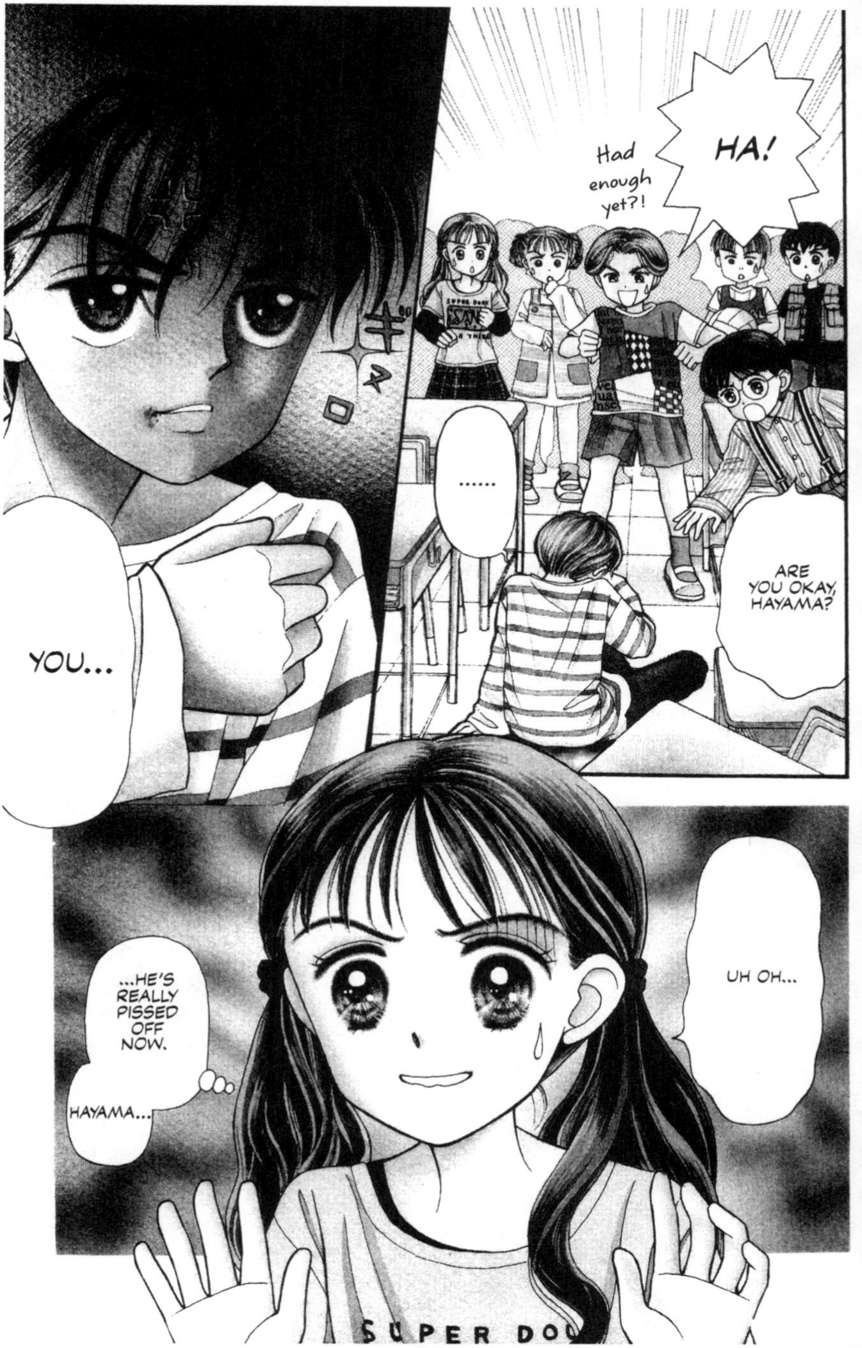
HA!
Had enough yet?!
ARE YOU OKAY, HAYAMA?
......
YOU...
UH OH...
...HE'S REALLY PISSED OFF NOW.
HAYAMA...
SUPER DOU

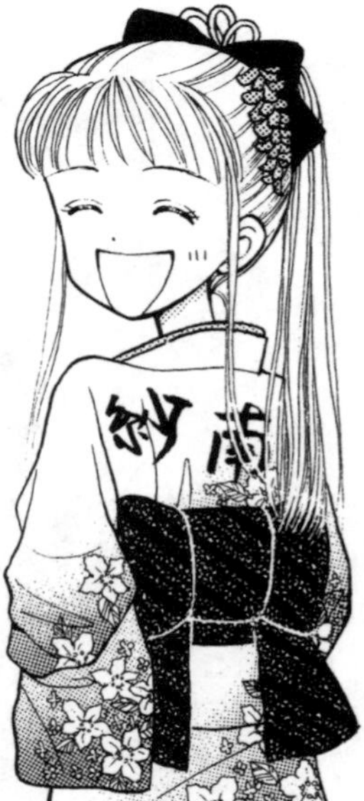
紗南

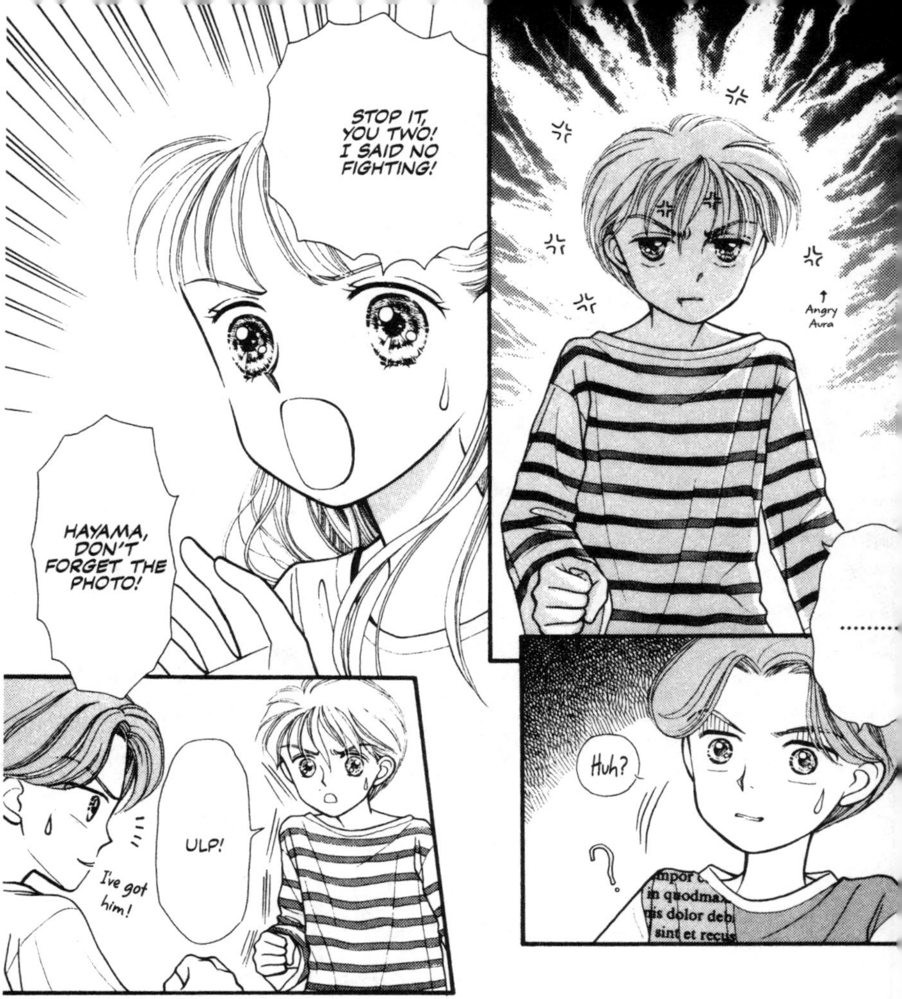
Angry Aura
STOP IT, YOU TWO! I SAID NO FIGHTING!
HAYAMA, DON'T FORGET THE PHOTO!
Huh?
ULP!
I've got him!

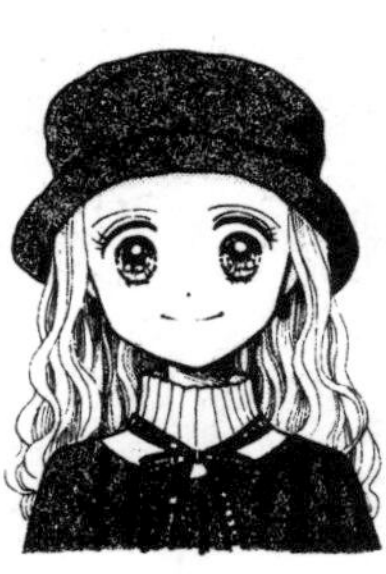

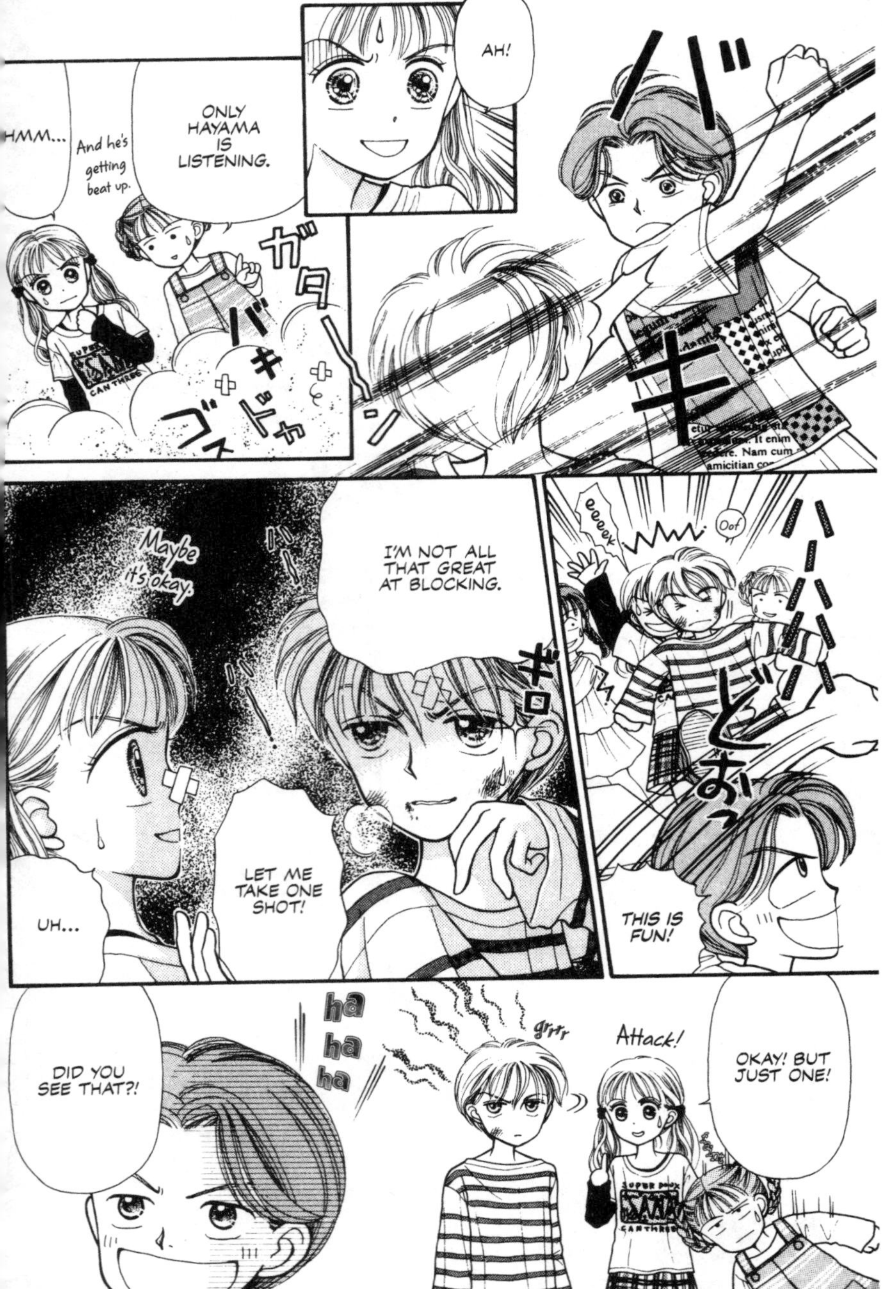
AH!
ONLY HAYAMA IS LISTENING.
And he's getting beat up.
HMM...
eeeek
Oof
THIS IS FUN!
I'M NOT ALL THAT GREAT AT BLOCKING.
Maybe it's okay.
LET ME TAKE ONE SHOT!
UH...
OKAY! BUT JUST ONE!
Attack!
grrr
ha ha ha ha
DID YOU SEE THAT?!

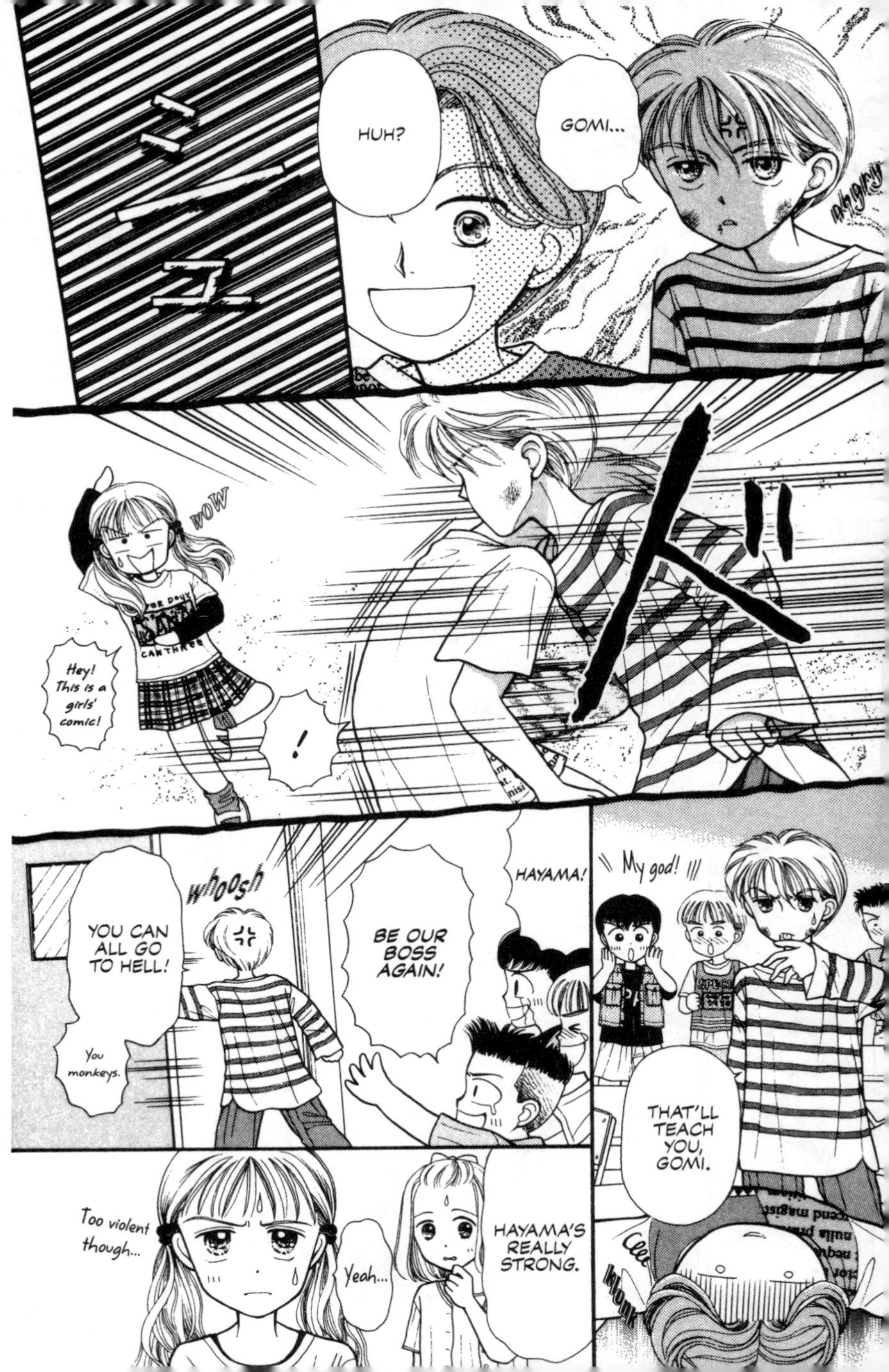
GOMI...
HUH?
WOW
!
Hey! This is a girls' comic!
My god!
THAT'LL TEACH YOU, GOMI.
HAYAMA!
BE OUR BOSS AGAIN!
whoosh
YOU CAN ALL GO TO HELL!
You monkeys.
HAYAMA'S REALLY STRONG.
Yeah...
Too violent though...

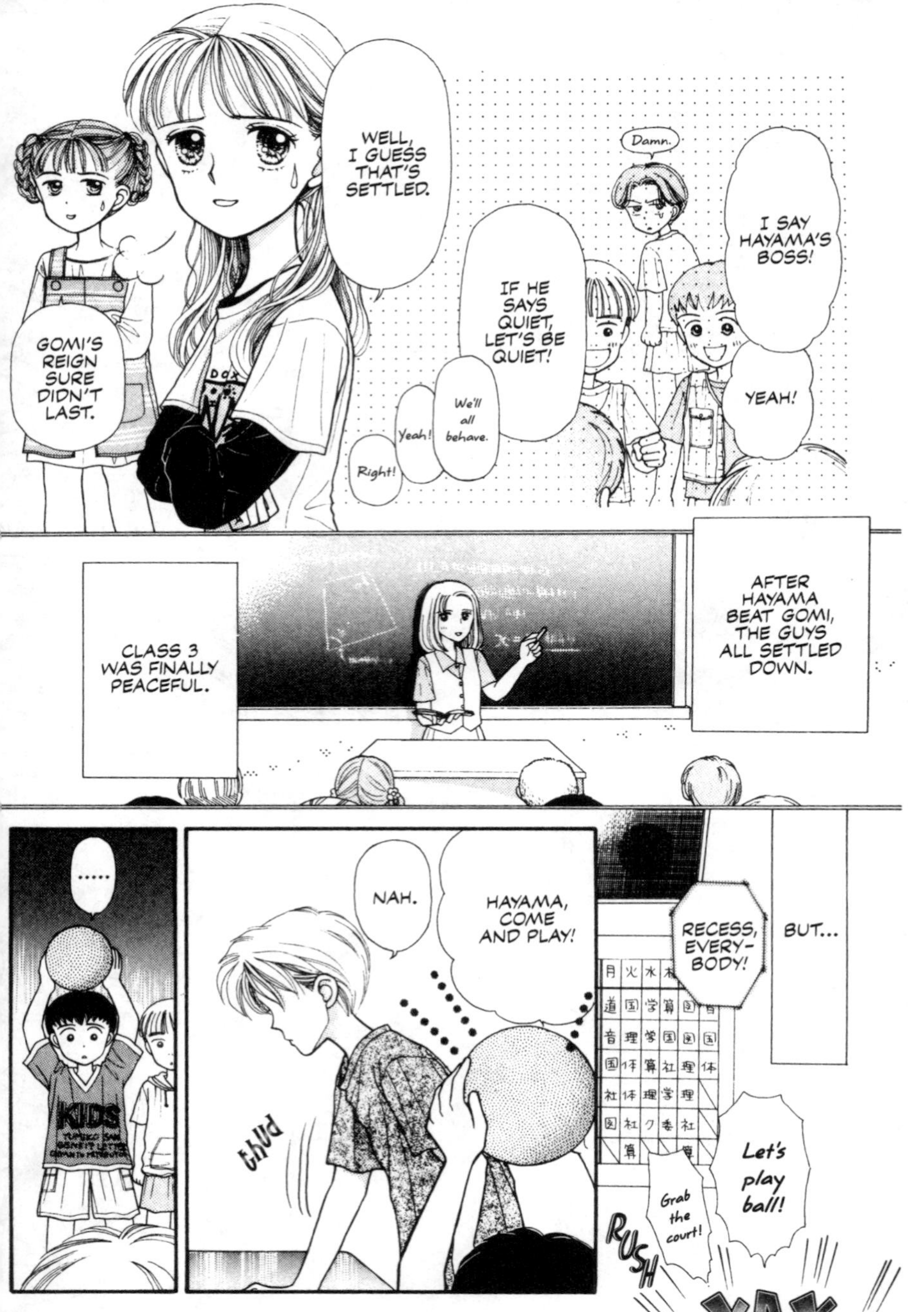
Damn.
I SAY HAYAMA'S BOSS!
YEAH!
IF HE SAYS QUIET, LET'S BE QUIET!
We'll all behave.
Yeah!
Right!
WELL, I GUESS THAT'S SETTLED.
GOMI'S REIGN SURE DIDN'T LAST.
AFTER HAYAMA BEAT GOMI, THE GUYS ALL SETTLED DOWN.
CLASS 3 WAS FINALLY PEACEFUL.
BUT...
RECESS, EVERY-BODY!
Let's play ball!
Grab the court!
RUSH
YAY
HAYAMA, COME AND PLAY!
NAH.
thud
......

About Monchichi

Do you remember Monchichi? Maybe you guys are too young. If I say, "Monchichi at 8 o'clock", you won't know what I'm talking about. That's too bad. Monchichi is a monkey doll which was very trendy when I was in elementary school. It was really cute, popular, and you could find them everywhere. I was so into Monchichi! Anyway, my Monchichi has a blue beard now. The color came off its nose, so I tried to fix it with a pen, but then I smeared it with my arm by accident! (I often make the same mistake at work.) And the paint dried before I could clean it off. Poor Bluebeard...

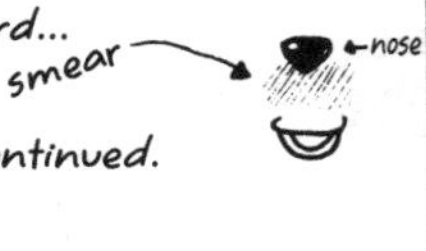
smear
nose

To be continued.

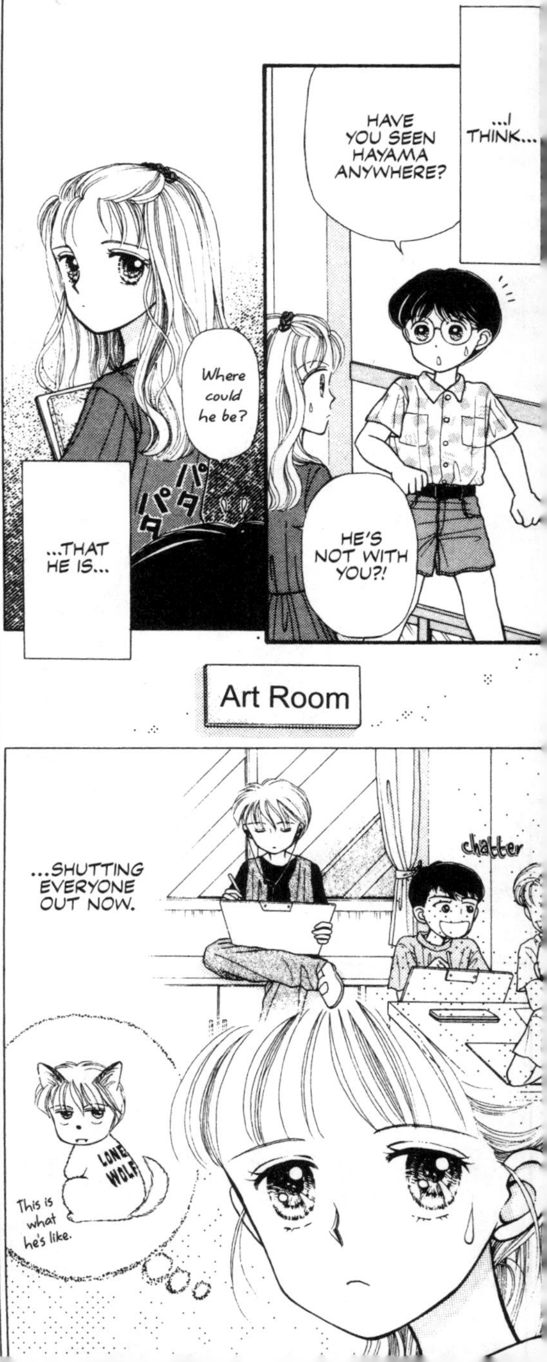
...I THINK...
HAVE YOU SEEN HAYAMA ANYWHERE?
HE'S NOT WITH YOU?!
Where could he be?
...THAT HE IS...
Art Room
chatter
...SHUTTING EVERYONE OUT NOW.
LONE WOLF
This is what he's like.

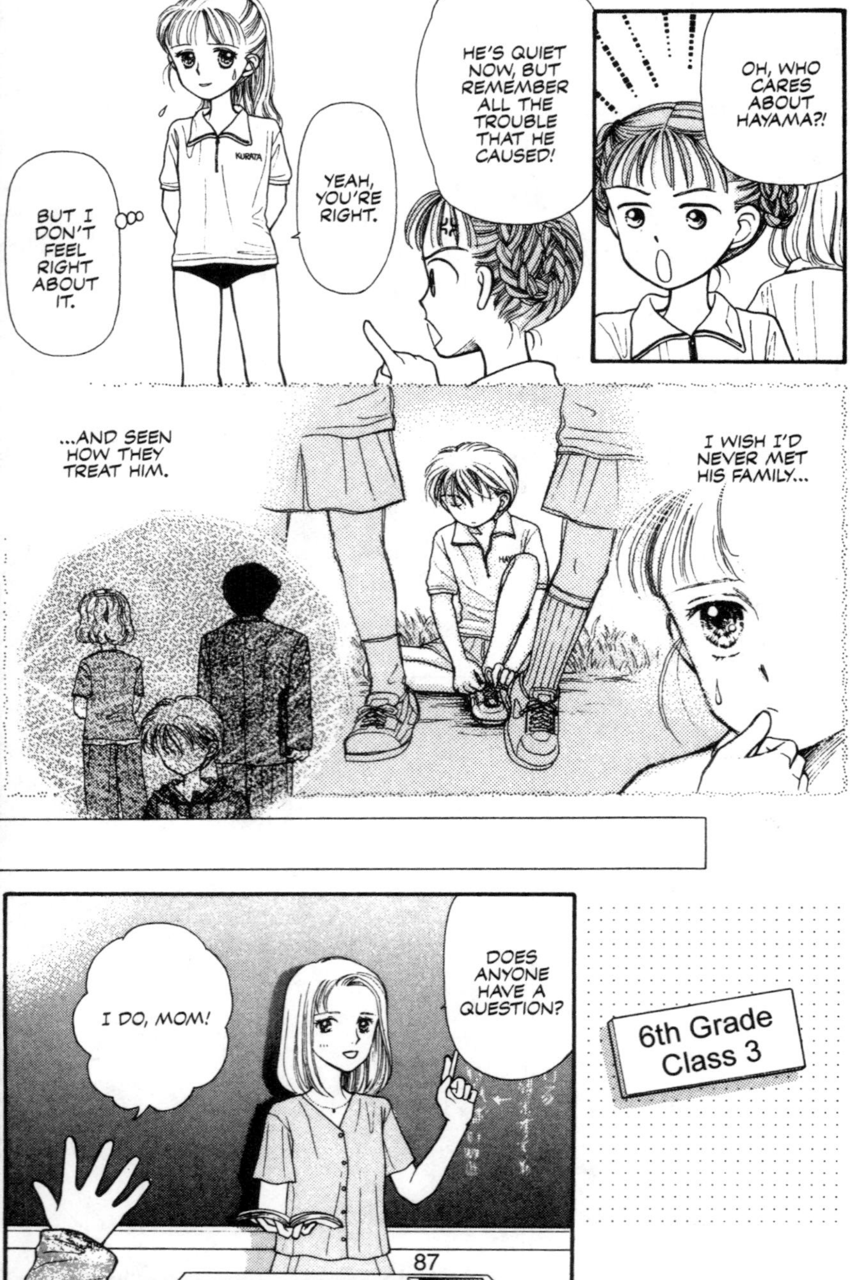
OH, WHO CARES ABOUT HAYAMA?!
HE'S QUIET NOW, BUT REMEMBER ALL THE TROUBLE THAT HE CAUSED!
YEAH, YOU'RE RIGHT.
BUT I DON'T FEEL RIGHT ABOUT IT.
I WISH I'D NEVER MET HIS FAMILY...
...AND SEEN HOW THEY TREAT HIM.
6th Grade Class 3
DOES ANYONE HAVE A QUESTION?
I DO, MOM!

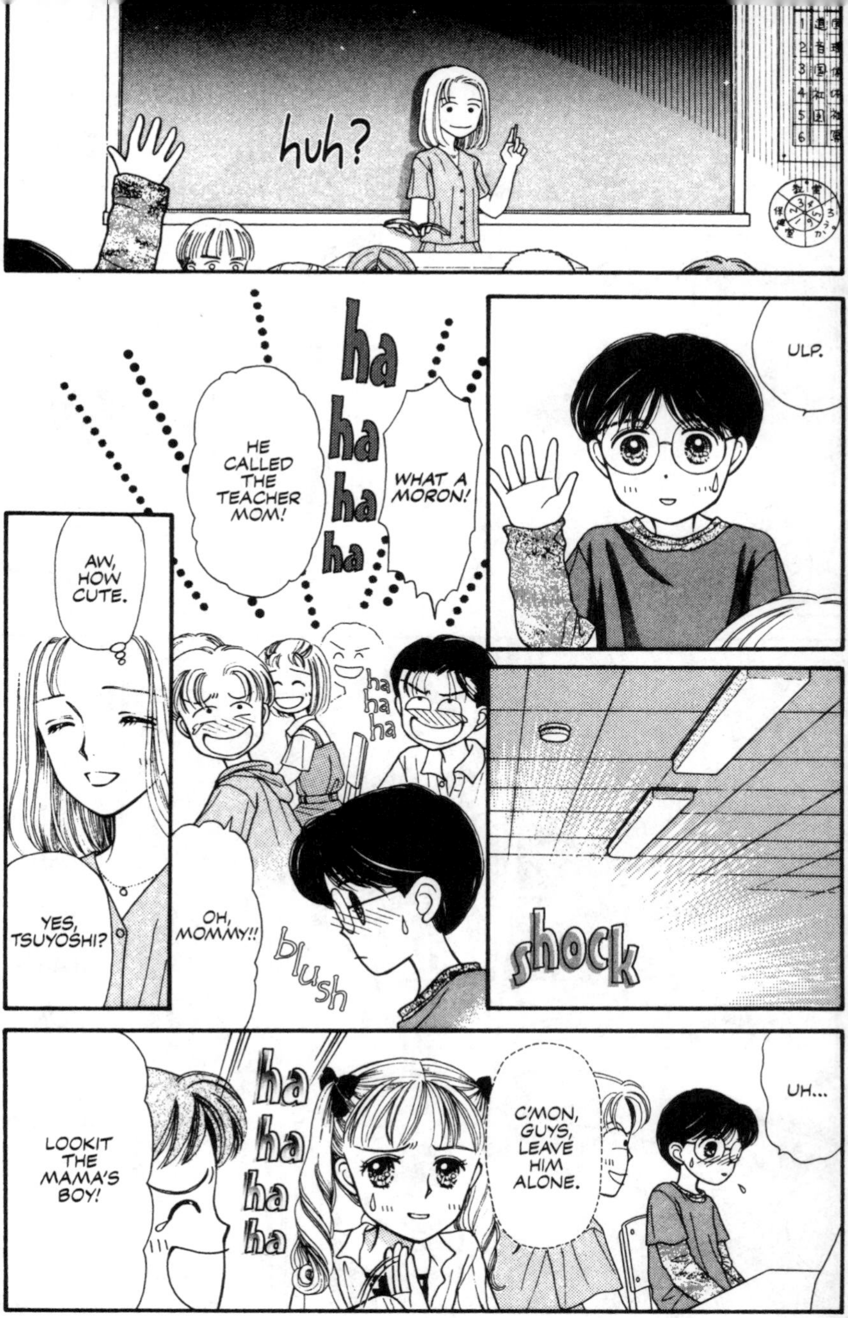
huh?
ULP.
shock
WHAT A MORON!
ha ha ha ha ha
HE CALLED THE TEACHER MOM!
ha ha ha
OH, MOMMY!!
blush
AW, HOW CUTE.
YES, TSUYOSHI?
UH...
C'MON, GUYS, LEAVE HIM ALONE.
ha ha ha ha
LOOKIT THE MAMA'S BOY!

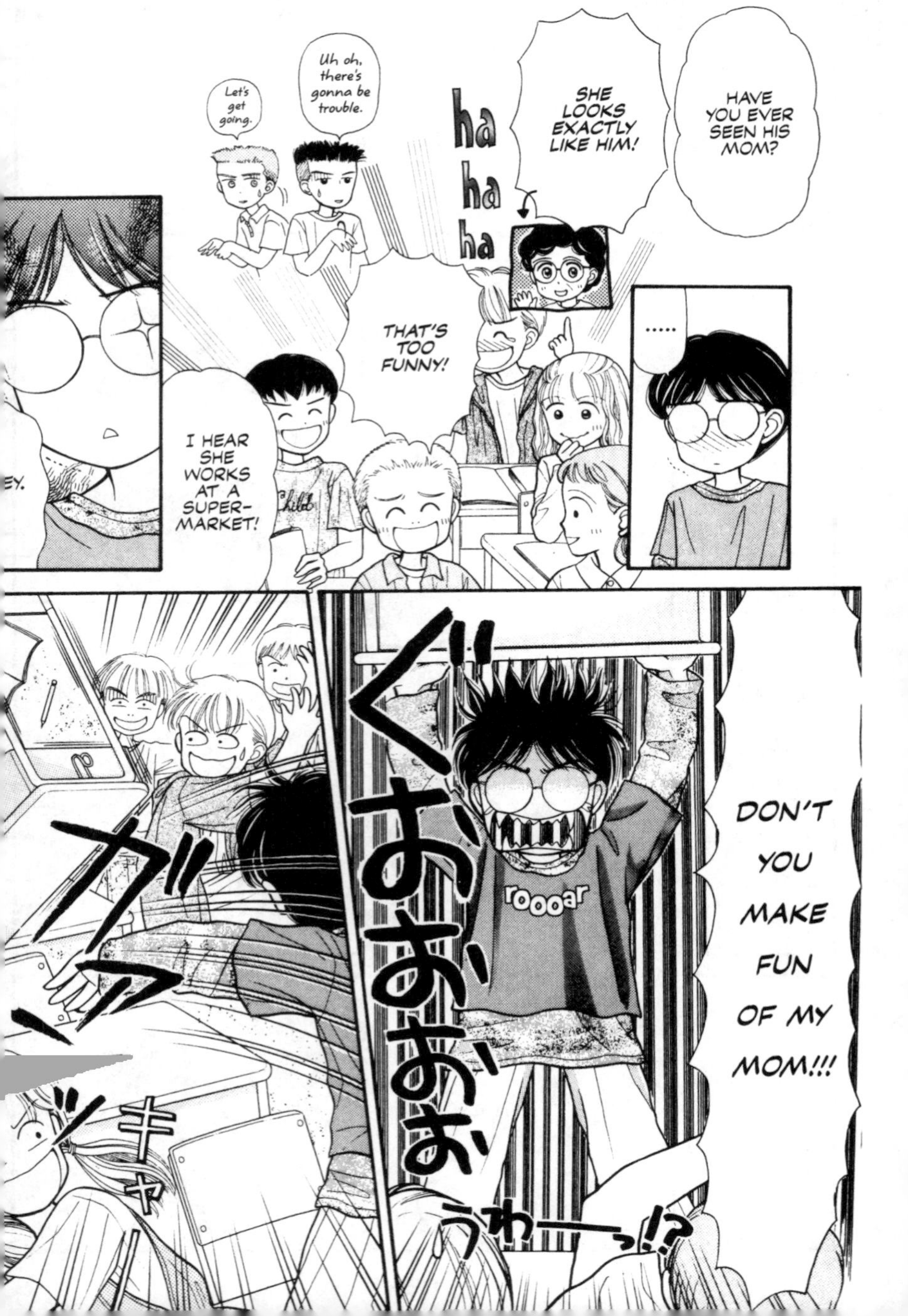
HAVE YOU EVER SEEN HIS MOM?
SHE LOOKS EXACTLY LIKE HIM!
ha ha ha
Uh oh, there's gonna be trouble.
Let's get going.
......
THAT'S TOO FUNNY!
I HEAR SHE WORKS AT A SUPER-MARKET!
DON'T YOU MAKE FUN OF MY MOM!!!
ぐぉぉぉぉ
roooar
うわーっ!?
ガァ

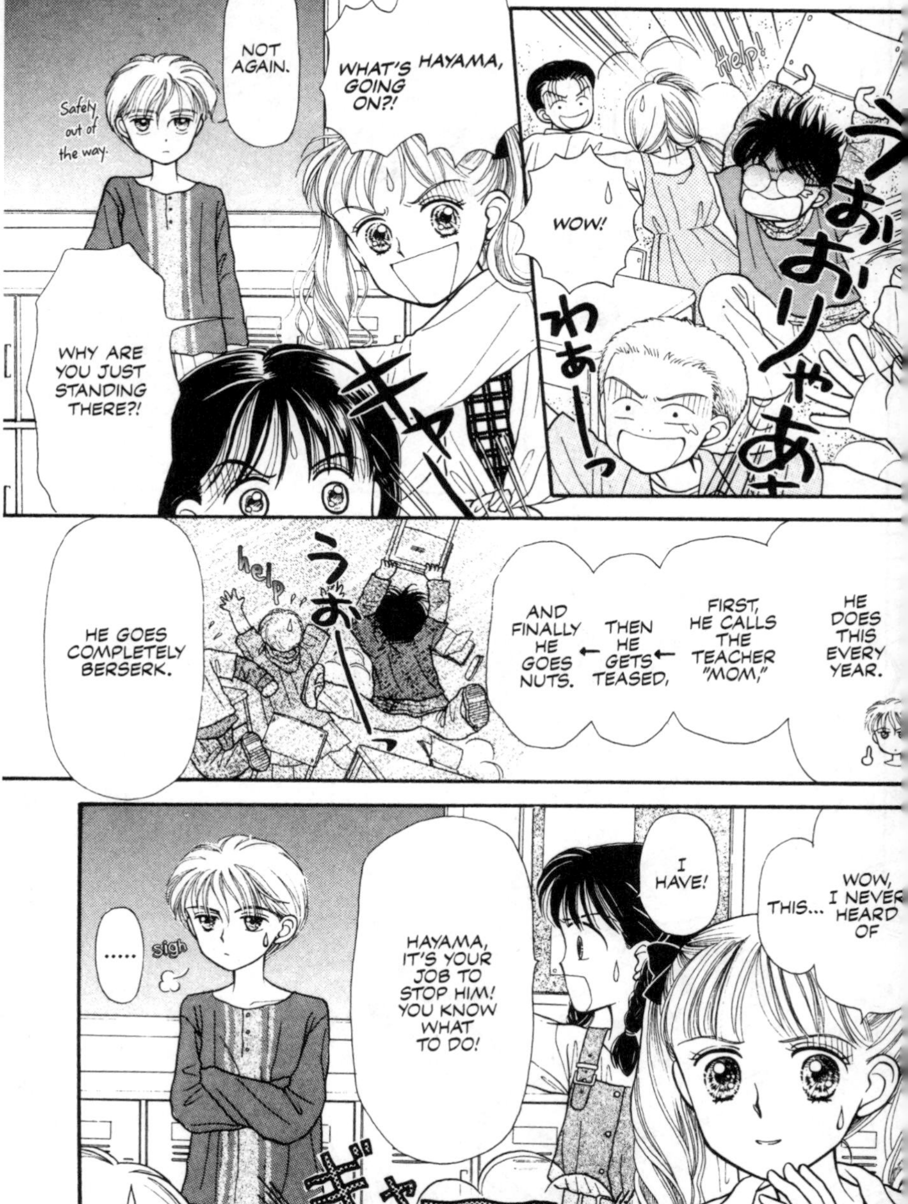
Help!
WOW!
うおおりゃあ
わぁーっ
HAYAMA, WHAT'S GOING ON?!
NOT AGAIN.
Safely out of the way.
WHY ARE YOU JUST STANDING THERE?!
キャー
HE DOES THIS EVERY YEAR.
FIRST, HE CALLS THE TEACHER "MOM," ← THEN HE GETS TEASED, ← AND FINALLY HE GOES NUTS.
help
うおーっ
HE GOES COMPLETELY BERSERK.
WOW, I NEVER HEARD OF THIS...
I HAVE!
HAYAMA, IT'S YOUR JOB TO STOP HIM! YOU KNOW WHAT TO DO!
......
sigh
ギャーー

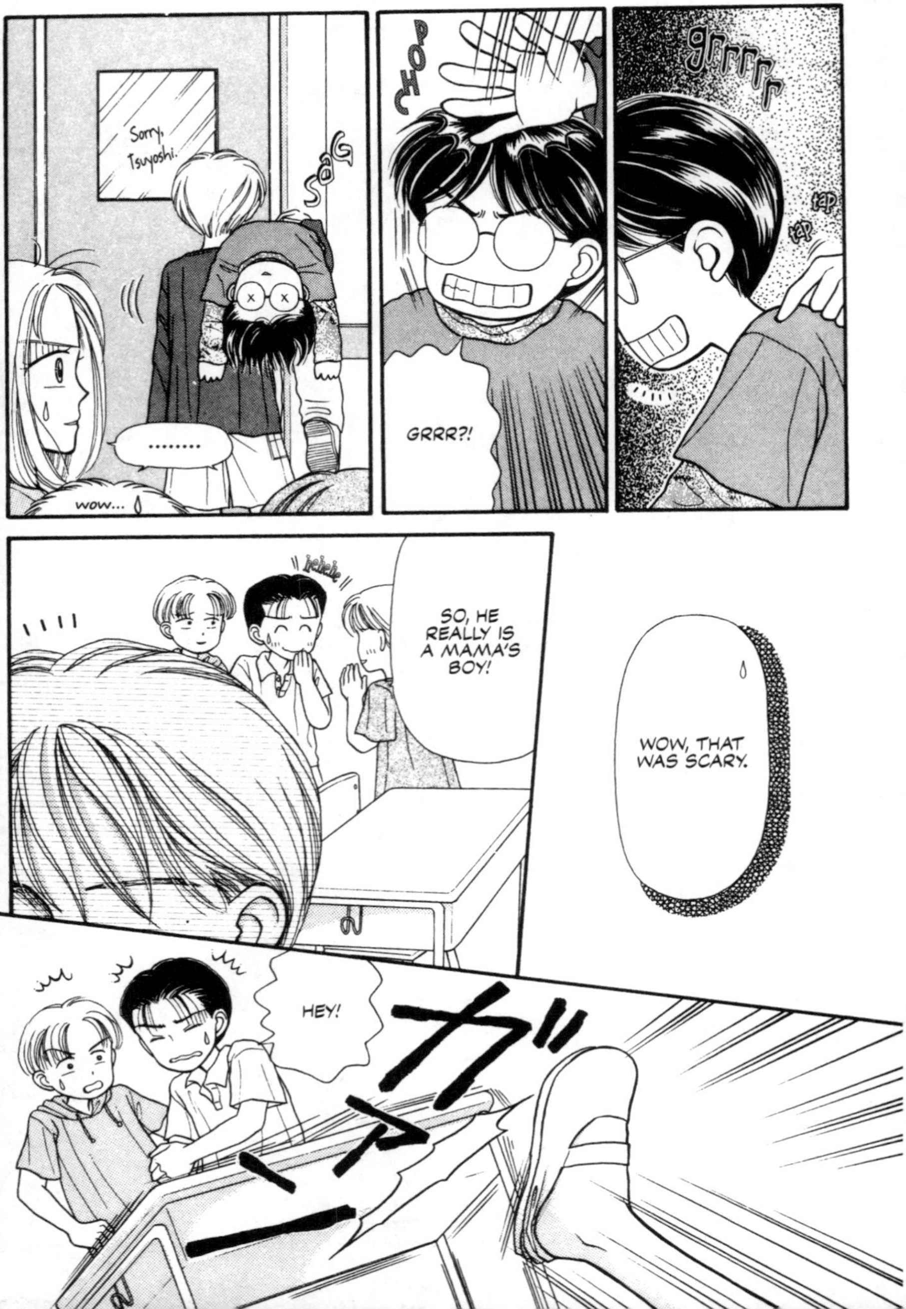
grrrrr
tap
tap
CHOP
GRRR?!
Sorry, Tsuyoshi.
SAG
....
wow...
WOW, THAT WAS SCARY.
SO, HE REALLY IS A MAMA'S BOY!
hehehe
HEY!

About Monchichi Part II

So, Monchi (short for Monchichi) costs exactly ten bucks. (There was no sales tax in Japan back then.) Ten bucks was a lot of money for an elementary school kid. It took my parents a while to get me one. So, I started looking at everything in terms of how many Monchichis it was worth. And I still do this! I'll get my check for drawing a comic, and when I look at the total, I start thinking, "This will buy me this many Monchichis"! Weird things stay with you, you know? Oh, my Monchichi... How many times did I say Monchichi this time? Oh, please... don't count them.

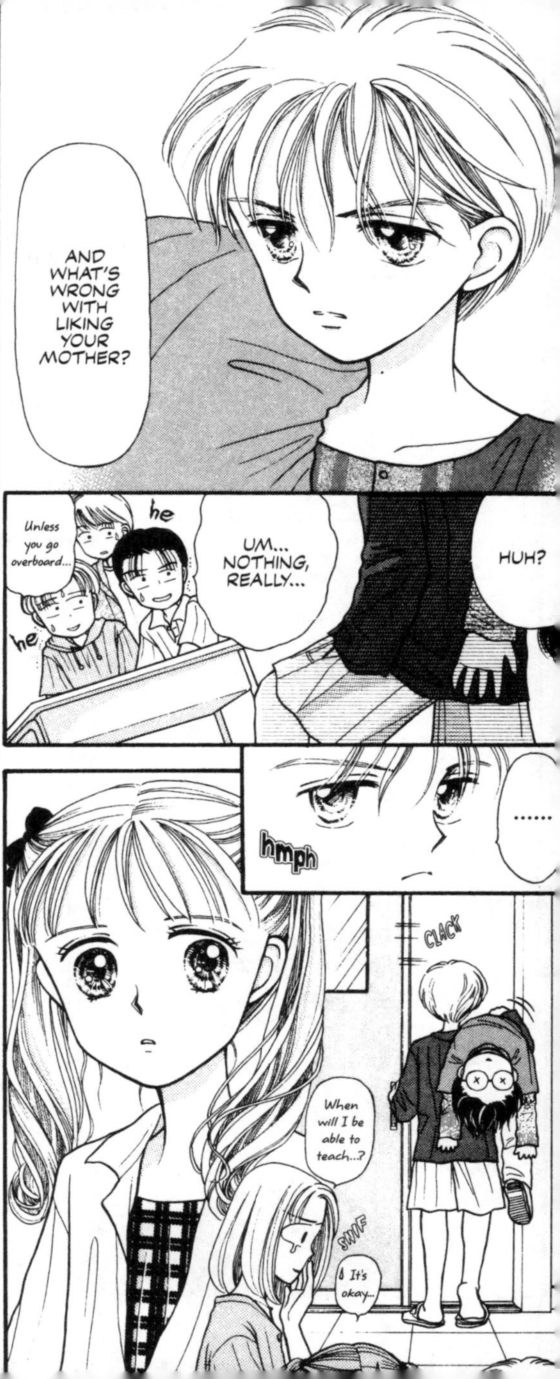
AND WHAT'S WRONG WITH LIKING YOUR MOTHER?
HUH?
UM... NOTHING, REALLY...
he
Unless you go overboard...
he
......
hmph
CLACK
When will I be able to teach...?
SNIF
It's okay...

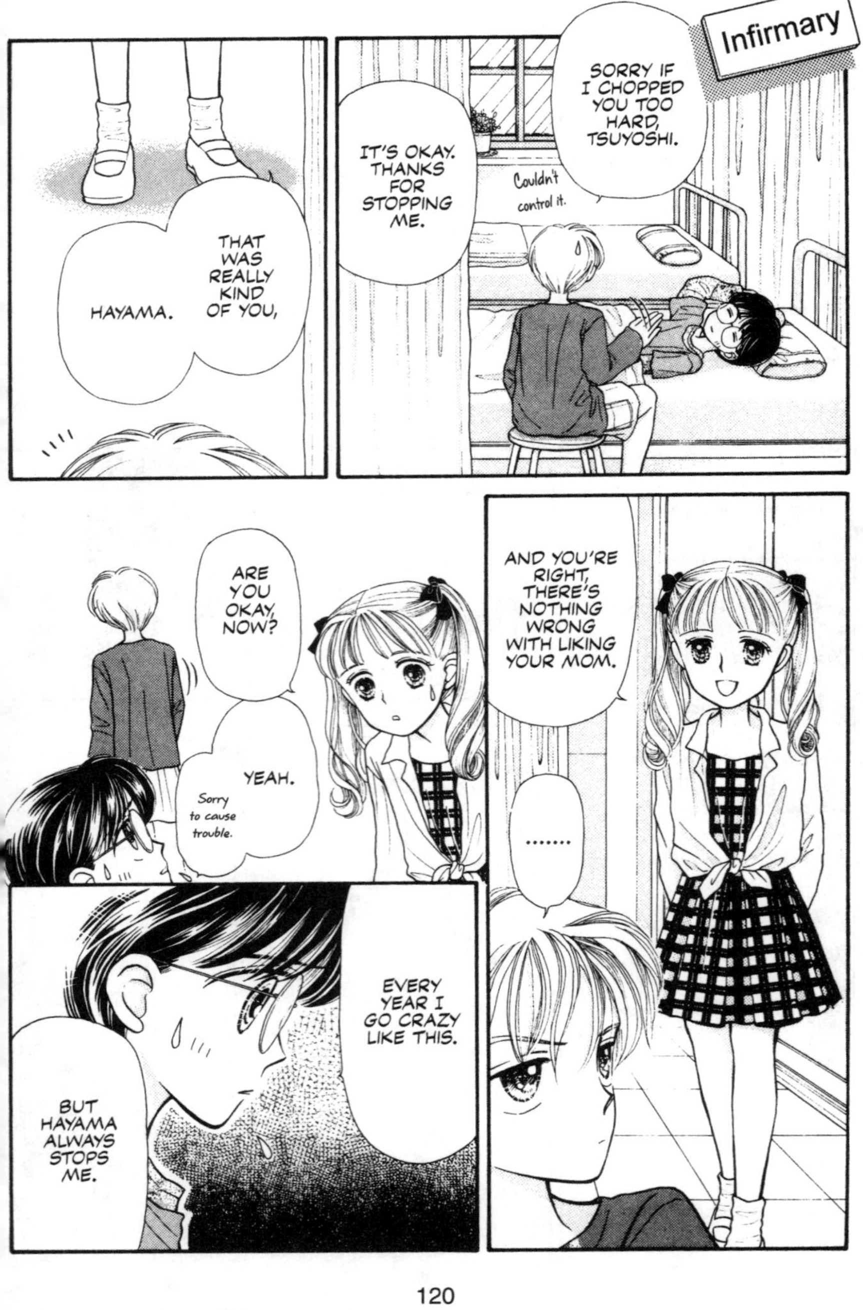
Infirmary
SORRY IF I CHOPPED YOU TOO HARD, TSUYOSHI.
IT'S OKAY. THANKS FOR STOPPING ME.
Couldn't control it.
THAT WAS REALLY KIND OF YOU,
HAYAMA.
AND YOU'RE RIGHT, THERE'S NOTHING WRONG WITH LIKING YOUR MOM.
....
ARE YOU OKAY, NOW?
YEAH.
Sorry to cause trouble.
EVERY YEAR I GO CRAZY LIKE THIS.
BUT HAYAMA ALWAYS STOPS ME.

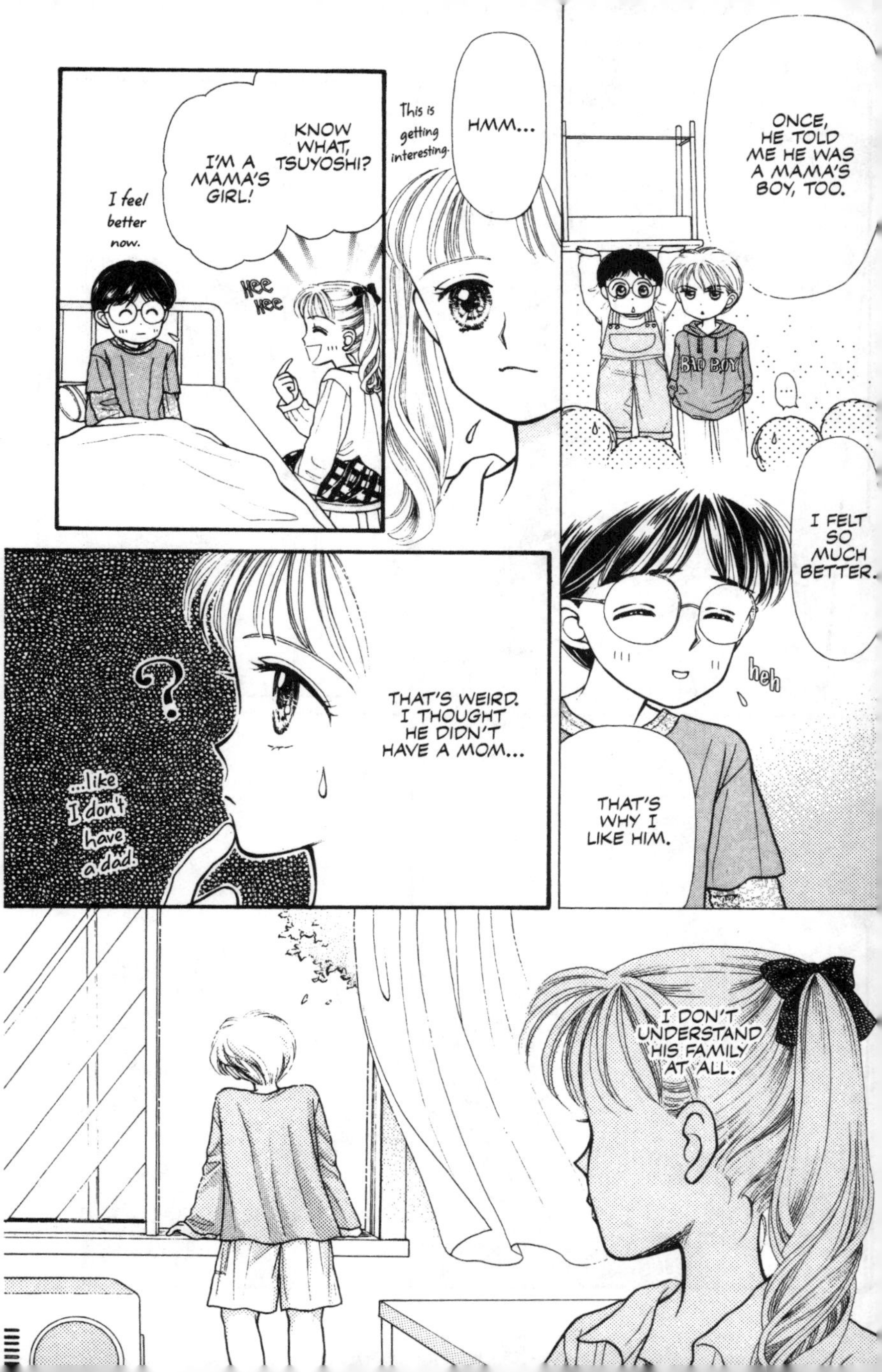
ONCE, HE TOLD ME HE WAS A MAMA'S BOY, TOO.
...
I FELT SO MUCH BETTER.
heh
THAT'S WHY I LIKE HIM.
HMM...
This is getting interesting.
KNOW WHAT, TSUYOSHI?
I'M A MAMA'S GIRL!
HEE HEE
I feel better now.
THAT'S WEIRD. I THOUGHT HE DIDN'T HAVE A MOM...
?
...like I don't have a dad.
I DON'T UNDERSTAND HIS FAMILY AT ALL.

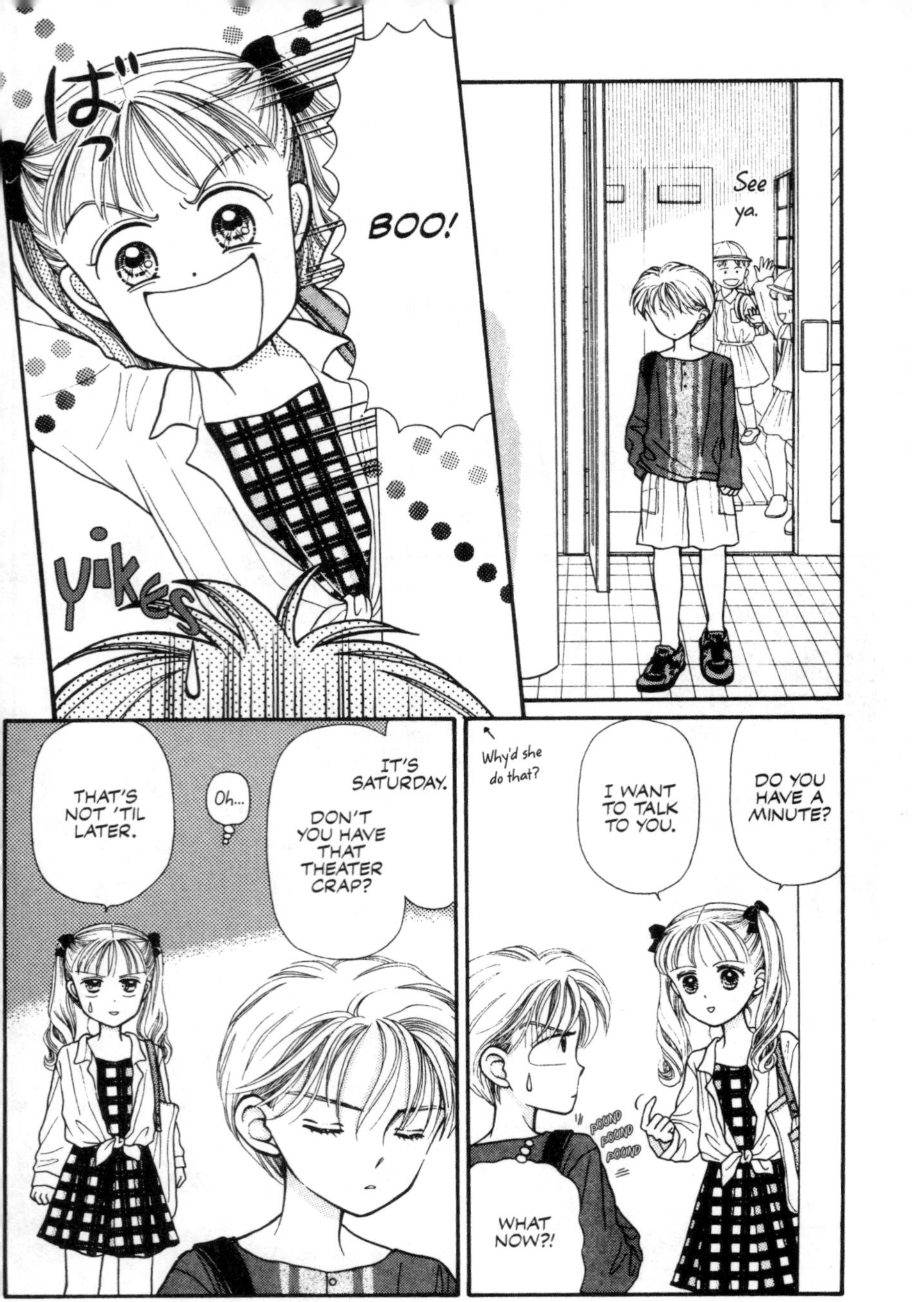
See ya.
BOO!
ばっ
yikes
DO YOU HAVE A MINUTE?
I WANT TO TALK TO YOU.
Why'd she do that?
POUND POUND POUND
WHAT NOW?!
IT'S SATURDAY.
DON'T YOU HAVE THAT THEATER CRAP?
Oh...
THAT'S NOT 'TIL LATER.

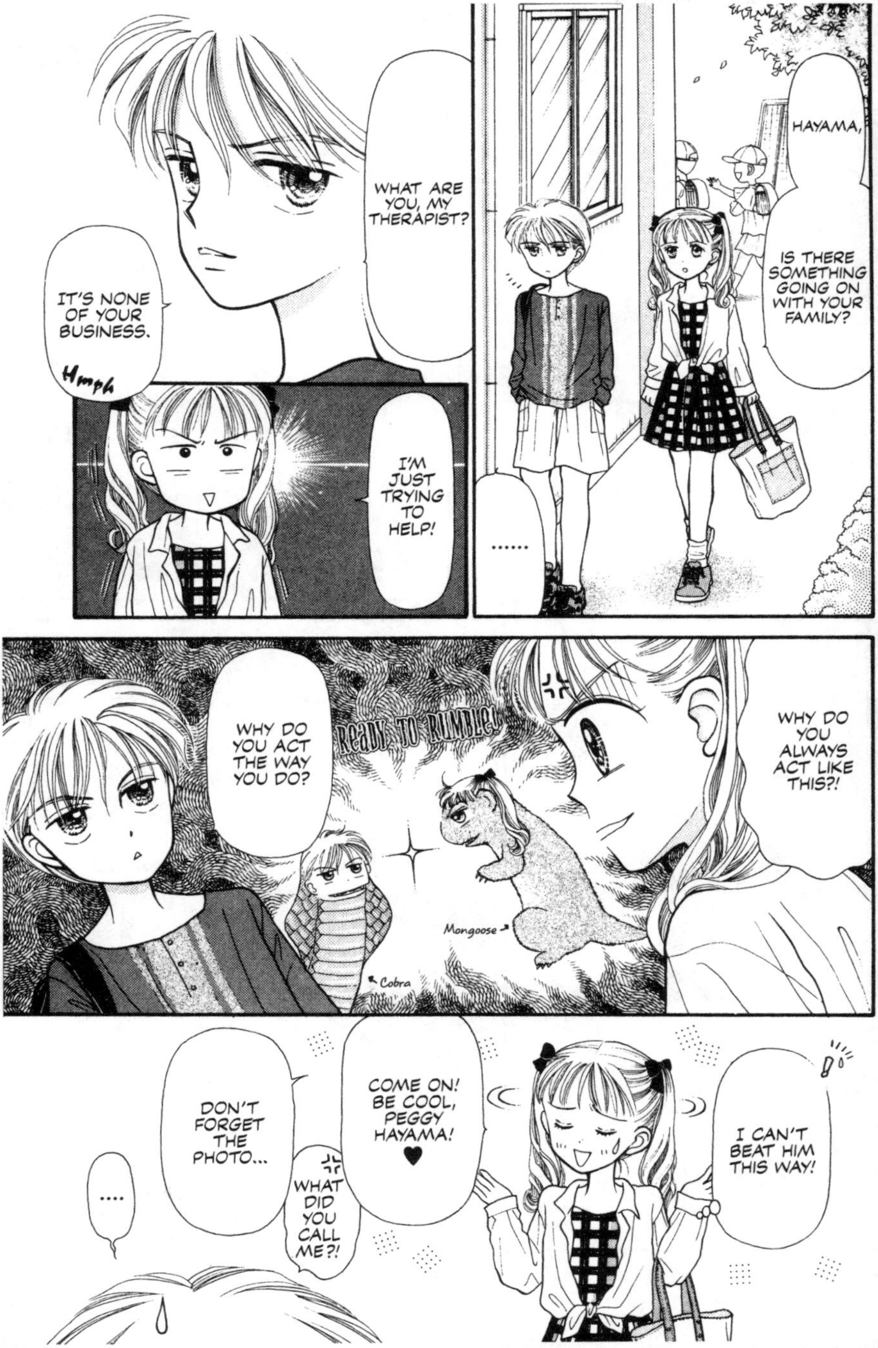
HAYAMA,
IS THERE SOMETHING GOING ON WITH YOUR FAMILY?
......
WHAT ARE YOU, MY THERAPIST?
IT'S NONE OF YOUR BUSINESS.
Hmph
I'M JUST TRYING TO HELP!
WHY DO YOU ALWAYS ACT LIKE THIS?!
WHY DO YOU ACT THE WAY YOU DO?
READY TO RUMBLE!
Mongoose
Cobra
I CAN'T BEAT HIM THIS WAY!
COME ON! BE COOL, PEGGY HAYAMA! ♥
WHAT DID YOU CALL ME?!
DON'T FORGET THE PHOTO...
....

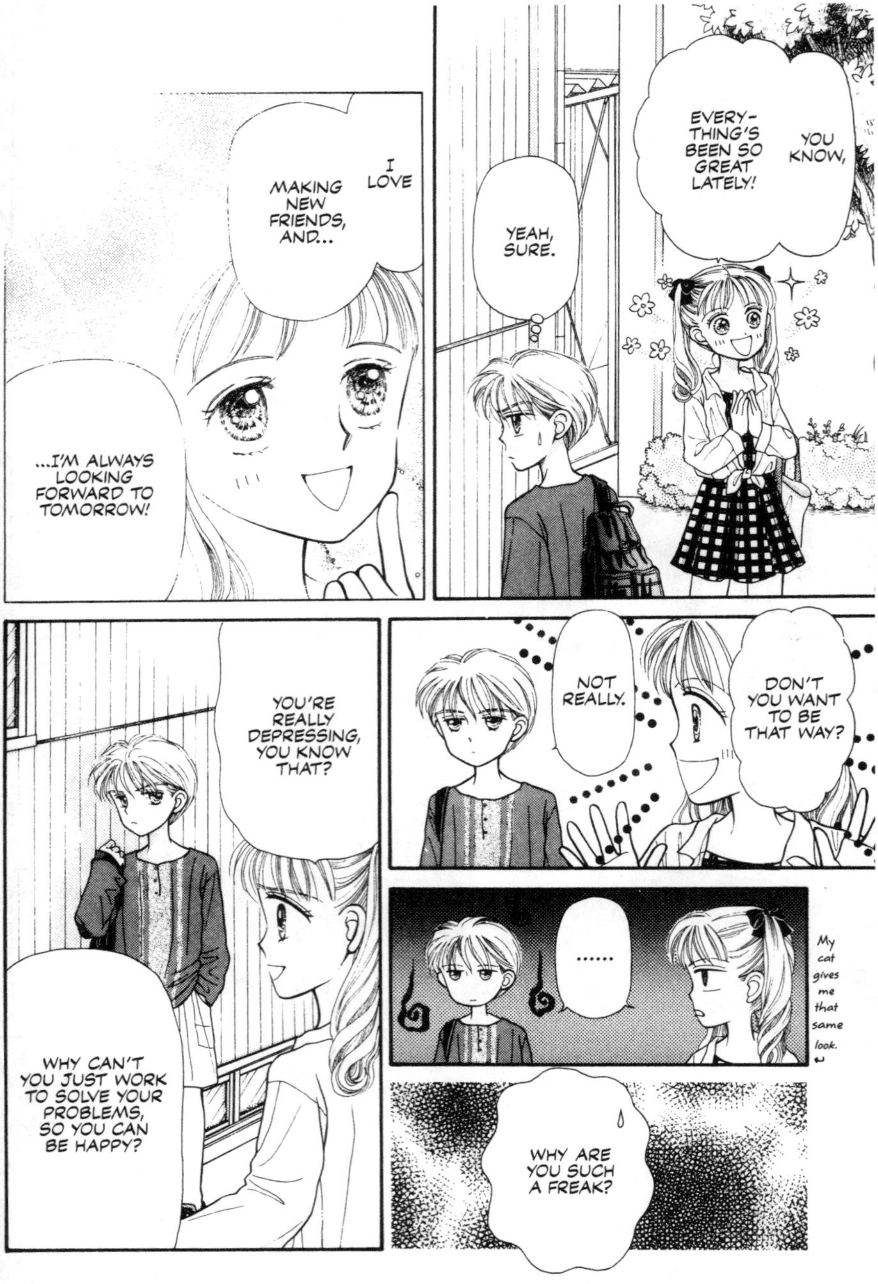
YOU KNOW,
EVERY-THING'S BEEN SO GREAT LATELY!
YEAH, SURE.
I LOVE
MAKING NEW FRIENDS, AND...
...I'M ALWAYS LOOKING FORWARD TO TOMORROW!
DON'T YOU WANT TO BE THAT WAY?
NOT REALLY.
......
My cat gives me that same look.
WHY ARE YOU SUCH A FREAK?
YOU'RE REALLY DEPRESSING, YOU KNOW THAT?
WHY CAN'T YOU JUST WORK TO SOLVE YOUR PROBLEMS, SO YOU CAN BE HAPPY?

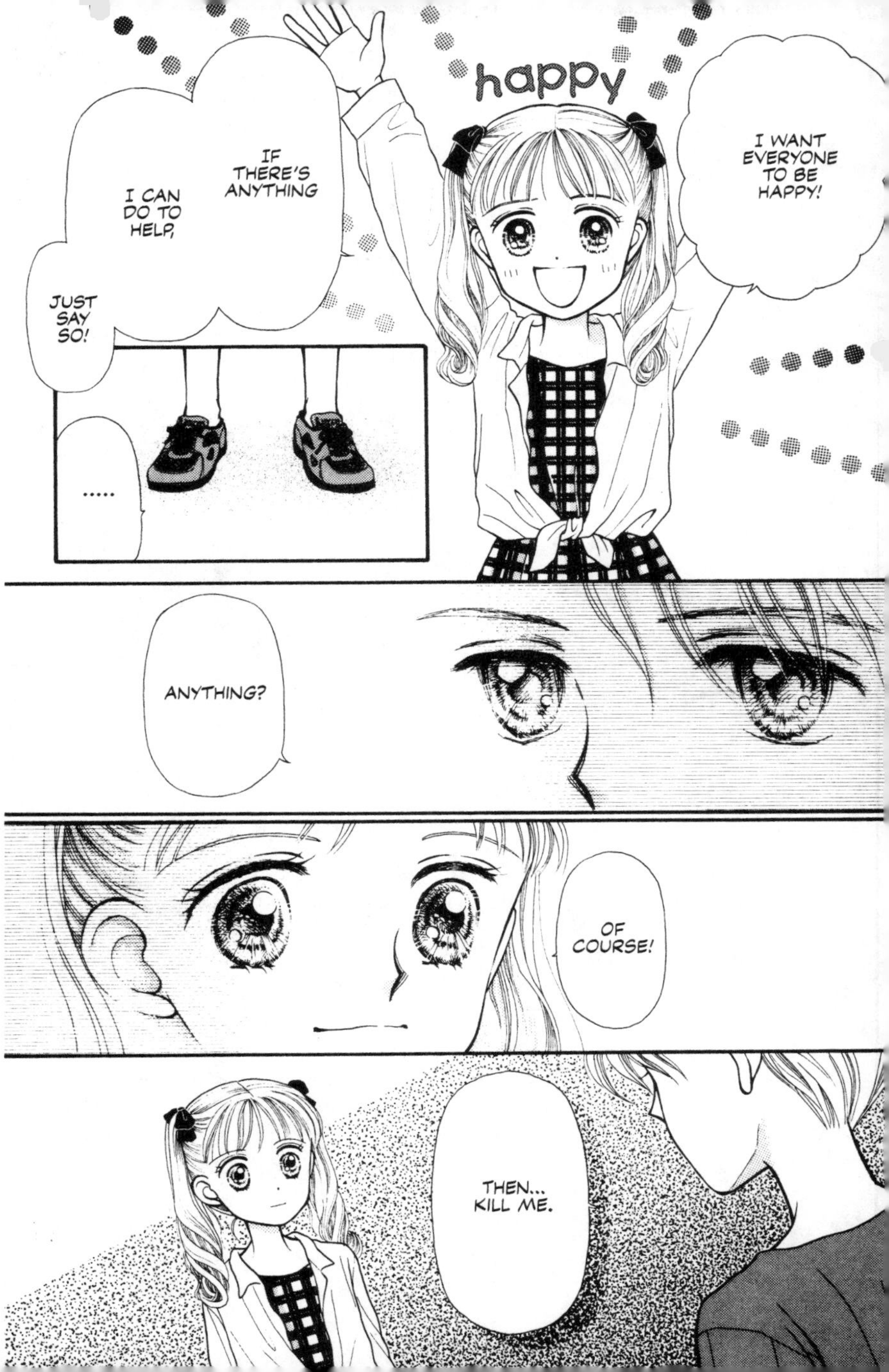
happy
I WANT EVERYONE TO BE HAPPY!
IF THERE'S ANYTHING I CAN DO TO HELP, JUST SAY SO!
.....
ANYTHING?
OF COURSE!
THEN... KILL ME.

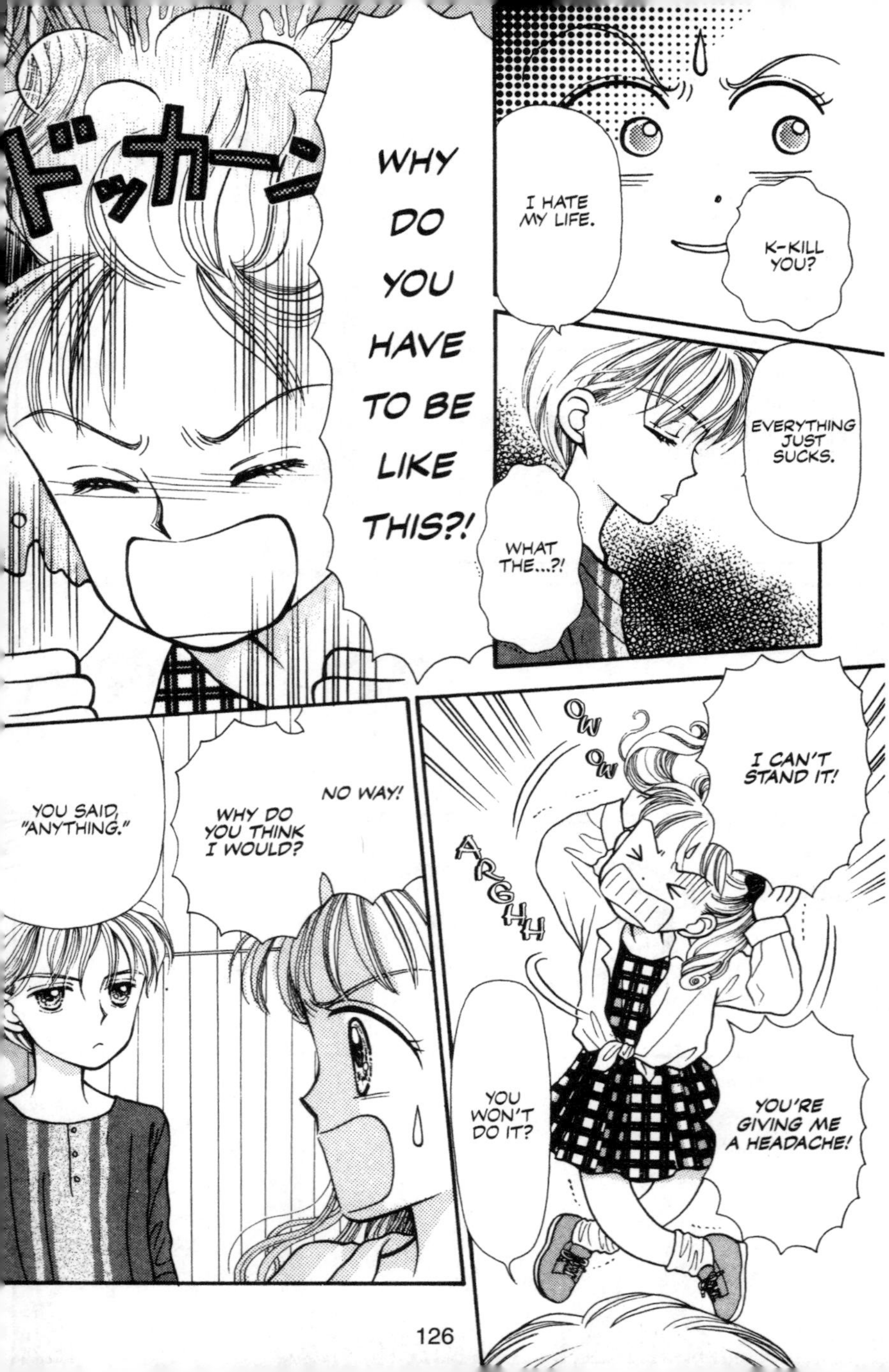
K-KILL YOU?
I HATE MY LIFE.
EVERYTHING JUST SUCKS.
WHAT THE...?!
ドッカーン
WHY DO YOU HAVE TO BE LIKE THIS?!
I CAN'T STAND IT!
OW OW
ARGHH
YOU'RE GIVING ME A HEADACHE!
YOU WON'T DO IT?
NO WAY!
WHY DO YOU THINK I WOULD?
YOU SAID, "ANYTHING."

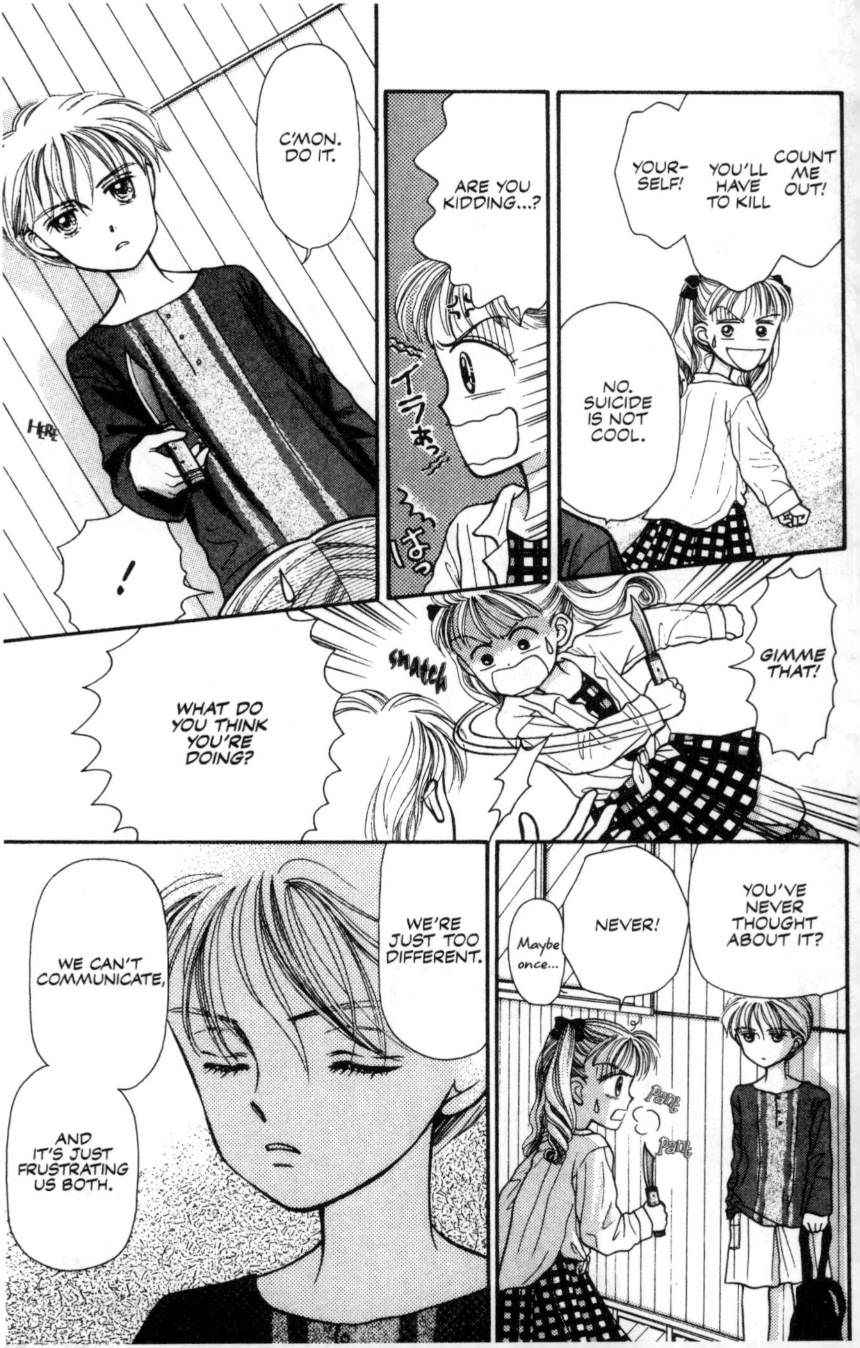
COUNT ME OUT! YOU'LL HAVE TO KILL YOURSELF!
NO. SUICIDE IS NOT COOL.
ARE YOU KIDDING...?
イラあっ
C'MON. DO IT.
HERE
!
GIMME THAT!
SNATCH
WHAT DO YOU THINK YOU'RE DOING?
YOU'VE NEVER THOUGHT ABOUT IT?
NEVER!
Maybe once...
PANT
PANT
WE'RE JUST TOO DIFFERENT.
WE CAN'T COMMUNICATE,
AND IT'S JUST FRUSTRATING US BOTH.

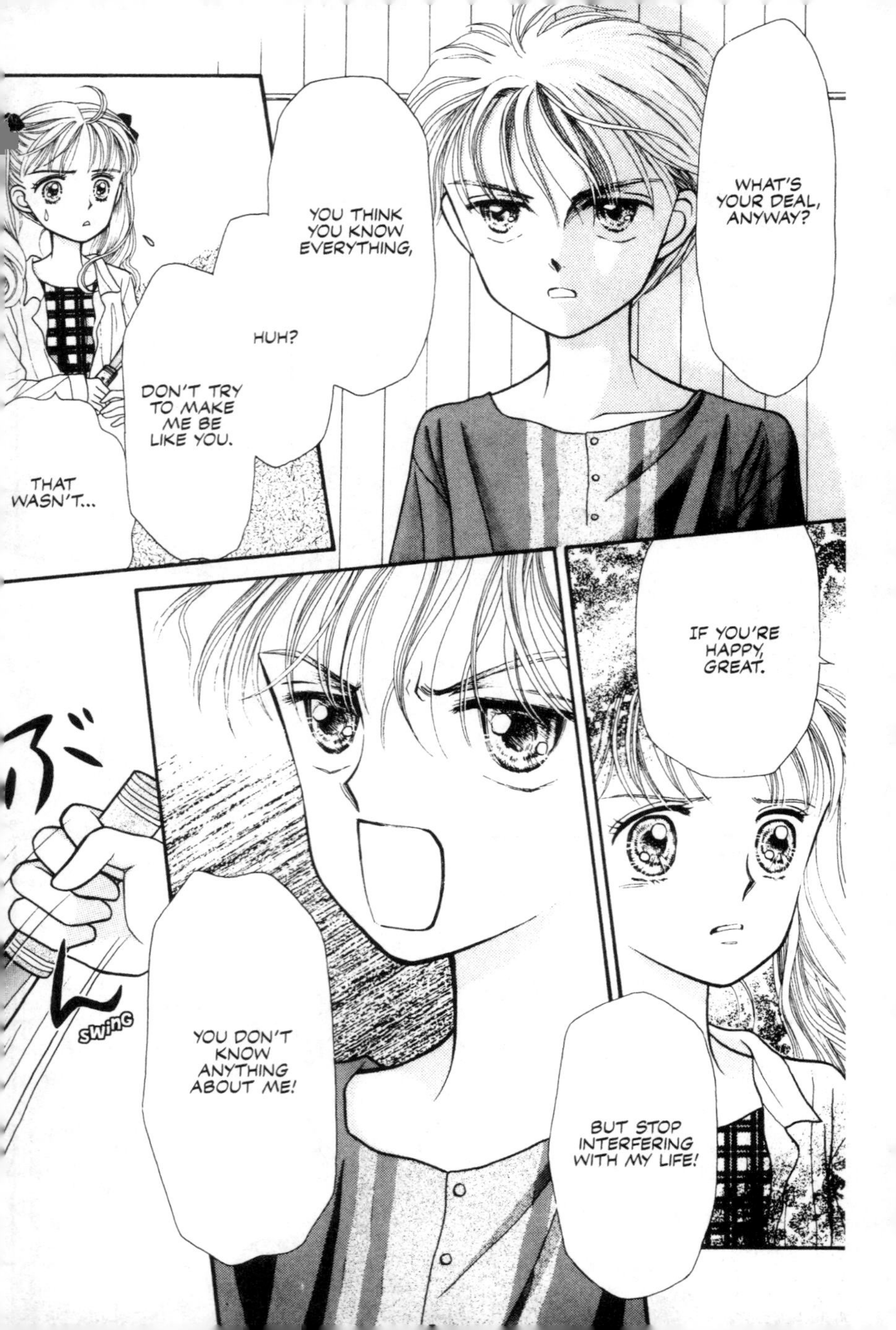
WHAT'S YOUR DEAL, ANYWAY?
YOU THINK YOU KNOW EVERYTHING,
HUH?
DON'T TRY TO MAKE ME BE LIKE YOU.
THAT WASN'T...
IF YOU'RE HAPPY, GREAT.
BUT STOP INTERFERING WITH MY LIFE!
YOU DON'T KNOW ANYTHING ABOUT ME!
ぶん
SWING

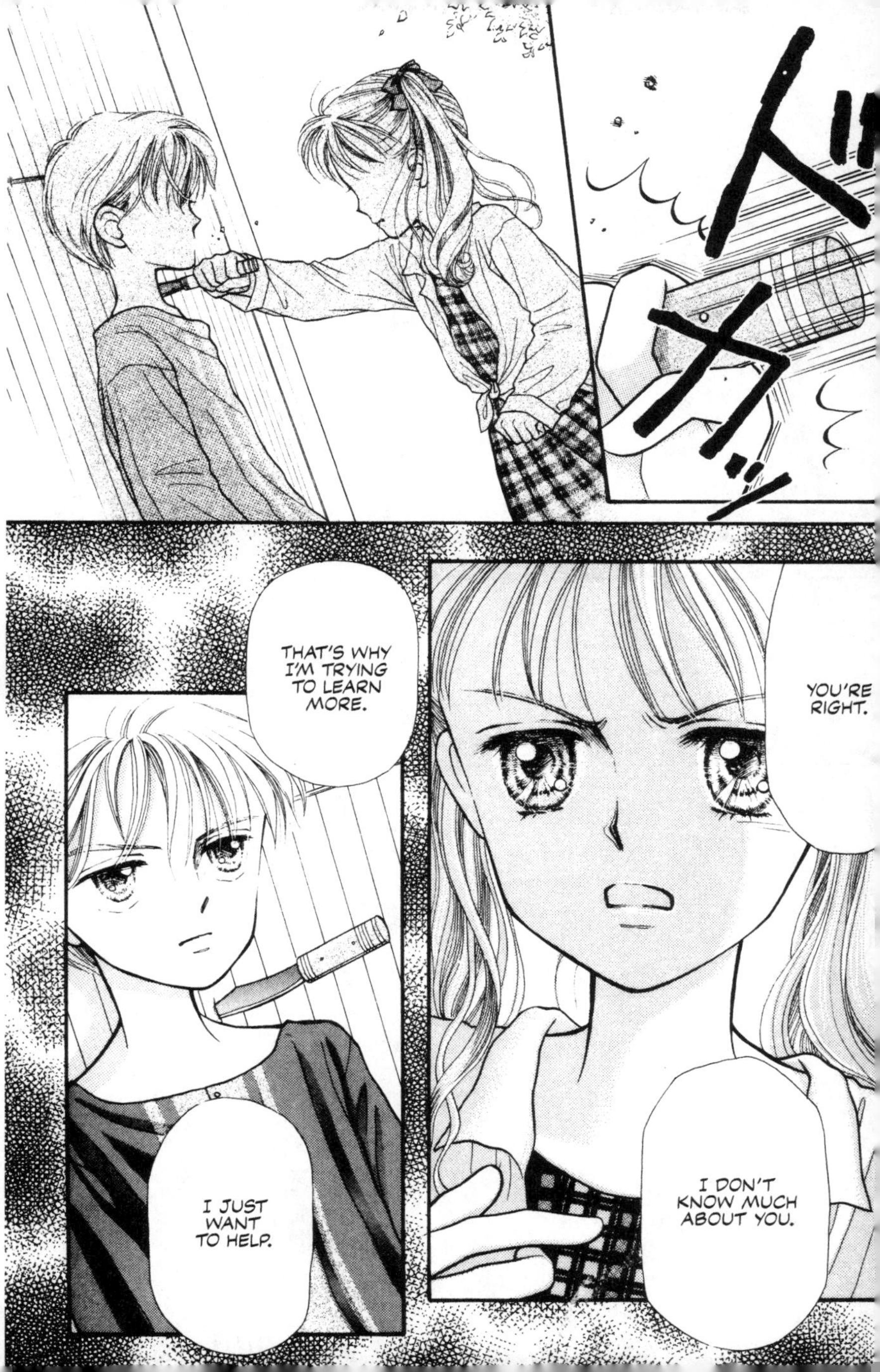
ドカッ
YOU'RE RIGHT.
I DON'T KNOW MUCH ABOUT YOU.
THAT'S WHY I'M TRYING TO LEARN MORE.
I JUST WANT TO HELP.

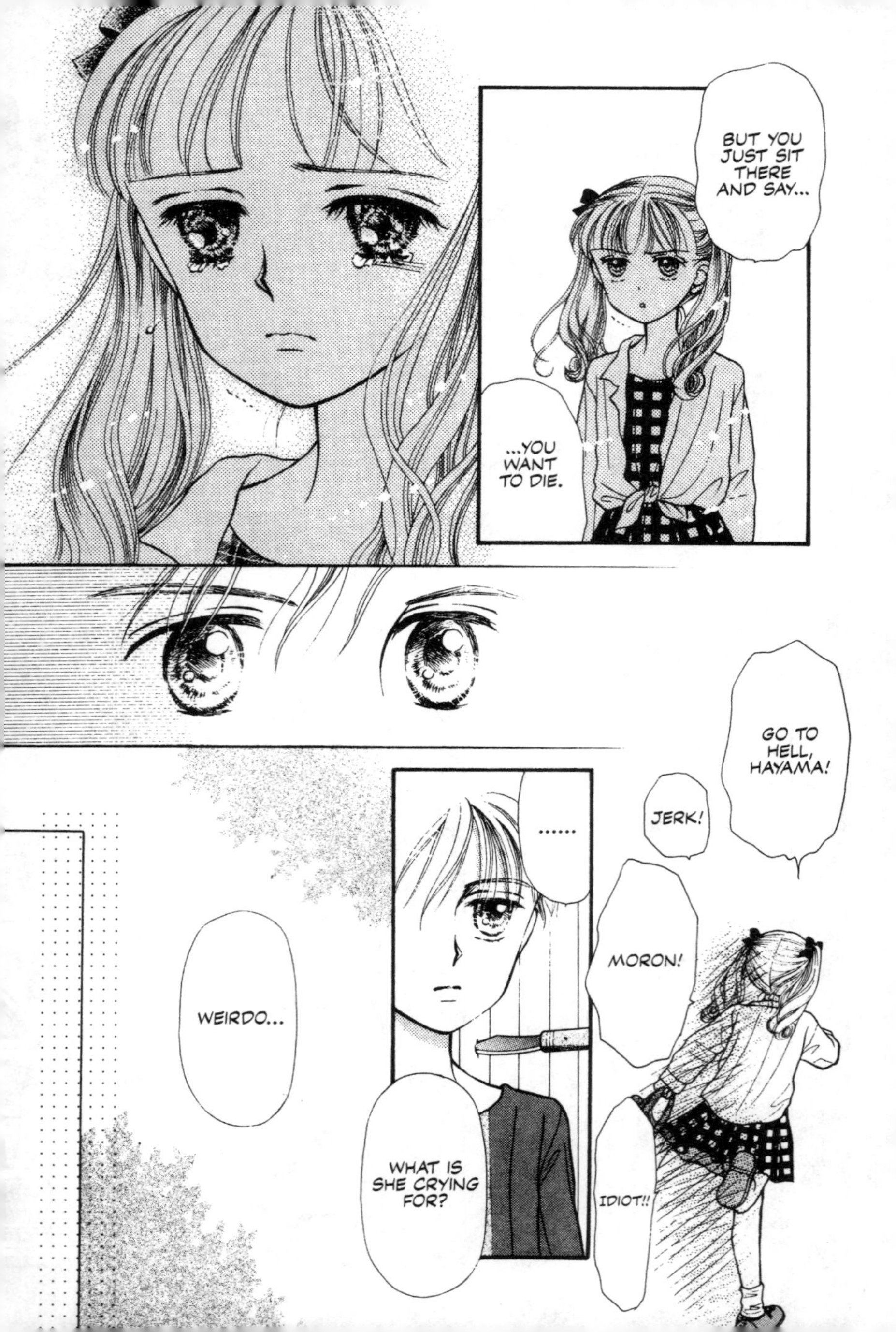
BUT YOU JUST SIT THERE AND SAY...
...YOU WANT TO DIE.
GO TO HELL, HAYAMA!
JERK!
MORON!
IDIOT!!
......
WHAT IS SHE CRYING FOR?
WEIRDO...

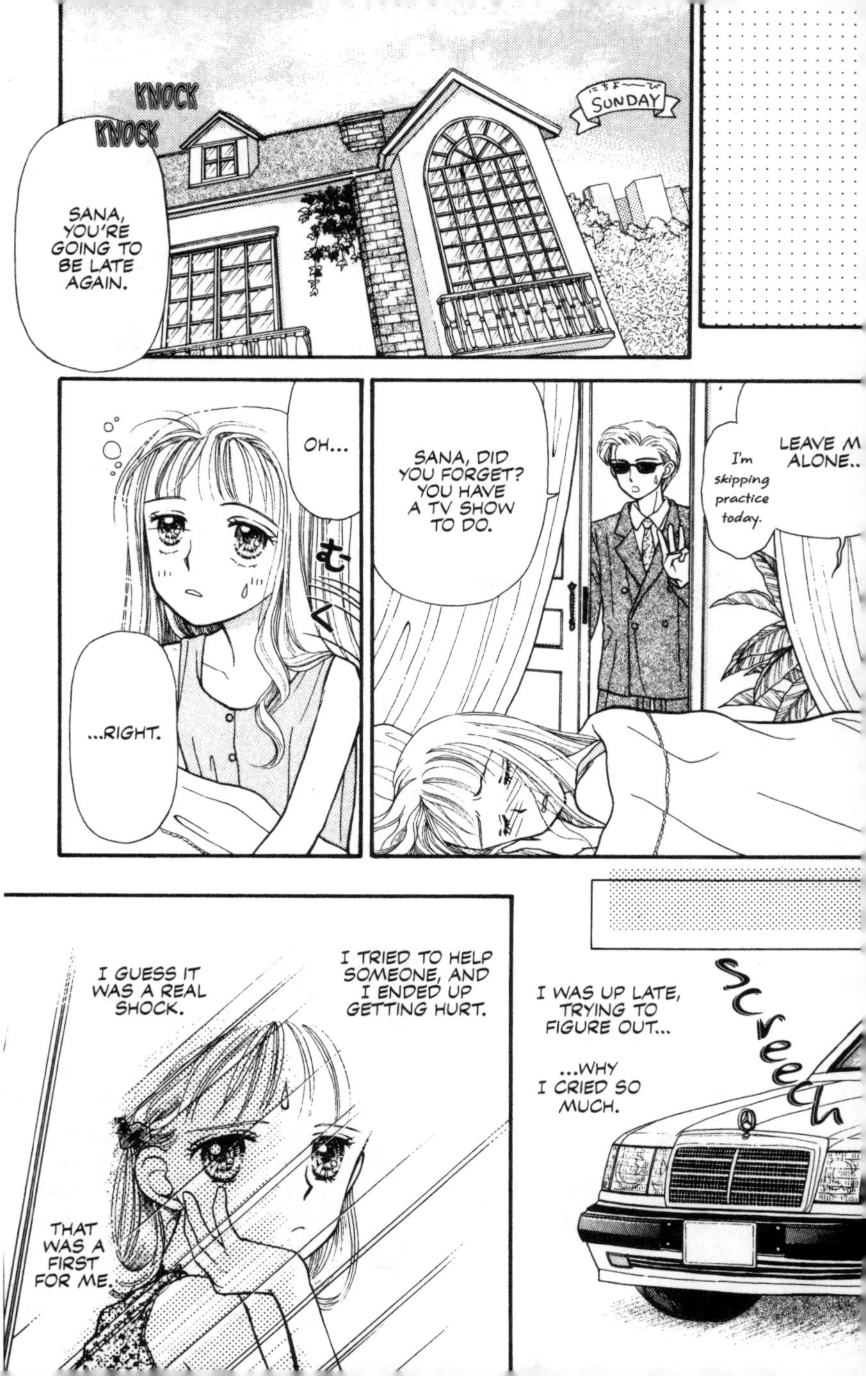
SUNDAY
KNOCK
KNOCK
SANA, YOU'RE GOING TO BE LATE AGAIN.
LEAVE M ALONE..
I'm skipping practice today.
SANA, DID YOU FORGET? YOU HAVE A TV SHOW TO DO.
OH...
むく
...RIGHT.
screech
I WAS UP LATE, TRYING TO FIGURE OUT...
...WHY I CRIED SO MUCH.
I TRIED TO HELP SOMEONE, AND I ENDED UP GETTING HURT.
I GUESS IT WAS A REAL SHOCK.
THAT WAS A FIRST FOR ME.

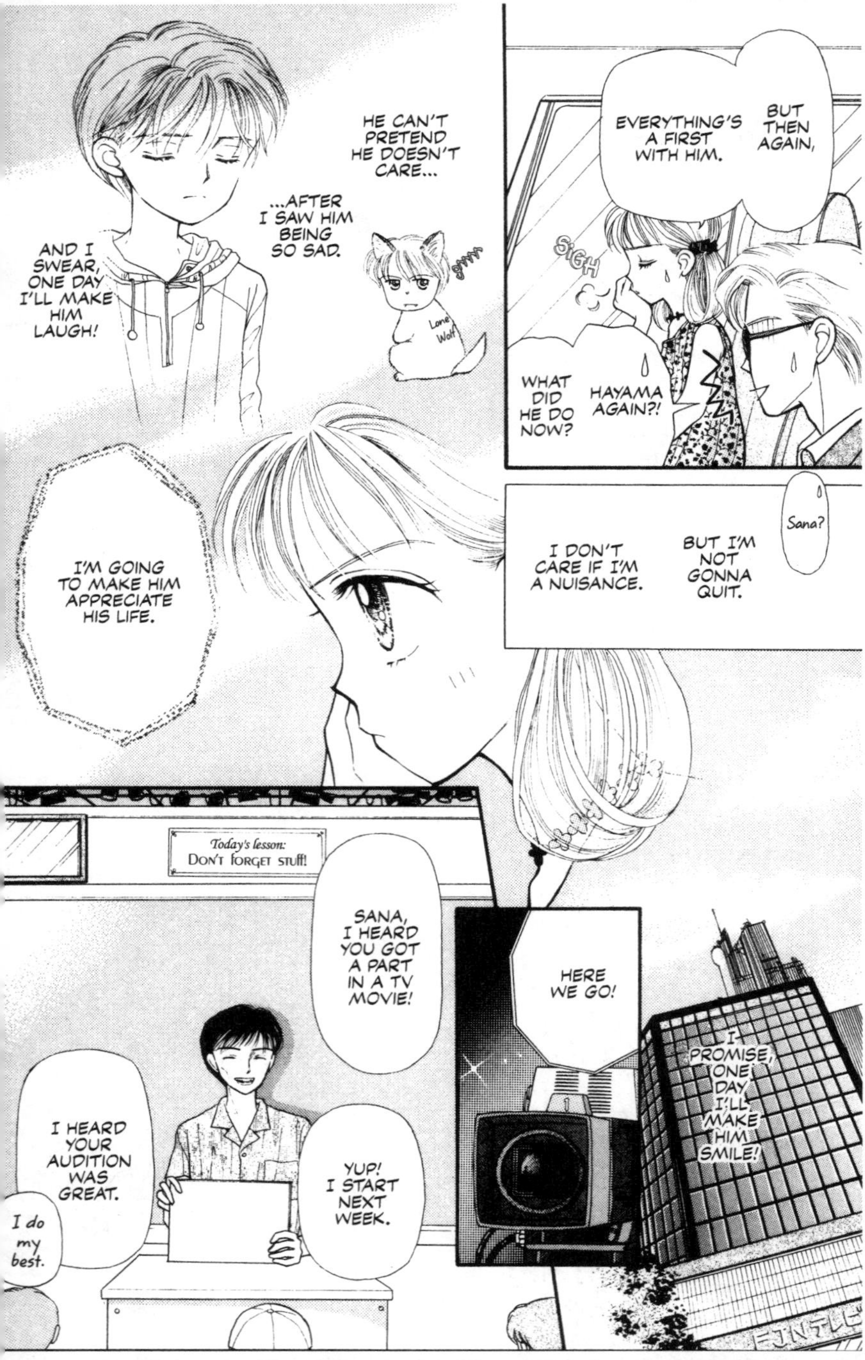
BUT THEN AGAIN,
EVERYTHING'S A FIRST WITH HIM.
SIGH
HAYAMA AGAIN?!
WHAT DID HE DO NOW?
Sana?
BUT I'M NOT GONNA QUIT.
I DON'T CARE IF I'M A NUISANCE.
HE CAN'T PRETEND HE DOESN'T CARE...
...AFTER I SAW HIM BEING SO SAD.
AND I SWEAR, ONE DAY I'LL MAKE HIM LAUGH!
grrr
Lone Wolf
I'M GOING TO MAKE HIM APPRECIATE HIS LIFE.
I PROMISE, ONE DAY I'LL MAKE HIM SMILE!
HERE WE GO!
Today's lesson:
Don't forget stuff!
SANA, I HEARD YOU GOT A PART IN A TV MOVIE!
YUP! I START NEXT WEEK.
I HEARD YOUR AUDITION WAS GREAT.
I do my best.

About Rei

Have you ever heard of "Abunai Deka*"? It was in reruns for ages, so you may have seen it if you were in Japan. It was really popular when I was in high school (in reruns, that is). My friend was a hard-core fan and had taped all the episodes, so we all went to his house and watched it one day. The next day, we brought sunglasses to school and played the characters. That was fun.

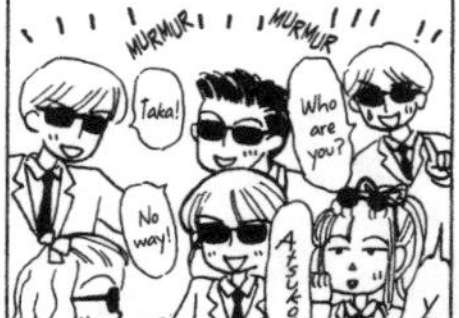
MURMUR
MURMUR
Taka!
Who are you?
No way!

I still giggle when I think about it, so I based Rei on one of the characters on the show. Many readers want to see Sana and Rei hook up. You'll learn a lot more about him in Book 2!

*Abunai Deka- an old Japanese detective show with 2 main characters, Taka & Yuji.

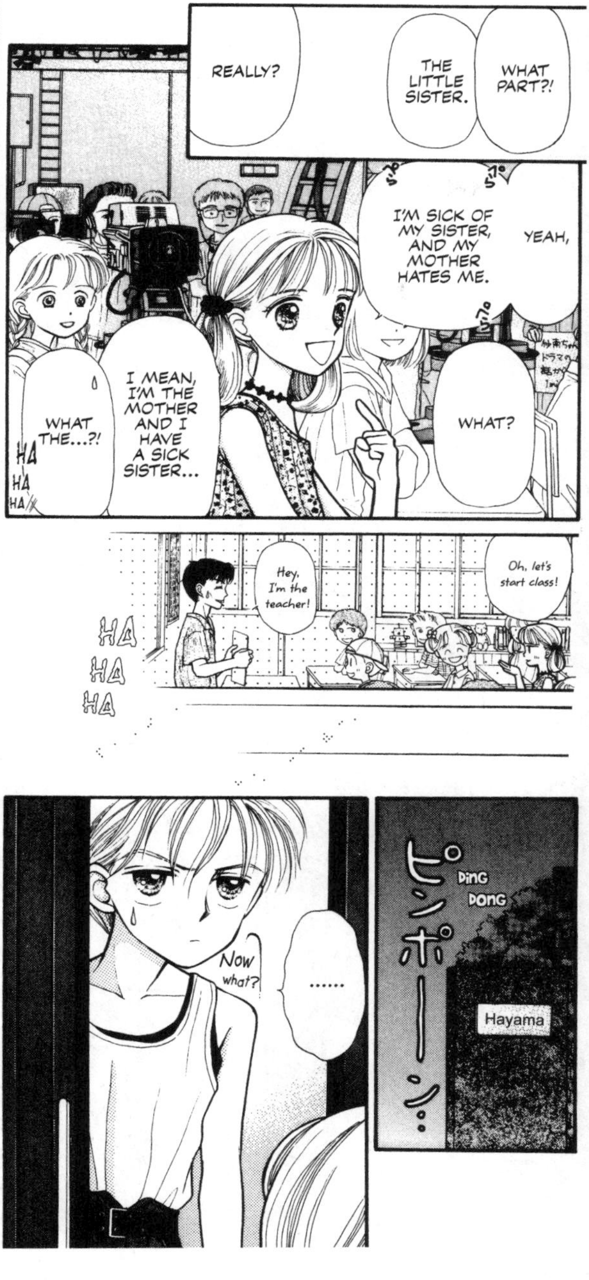
WHAT PART?!
THE LITTLE SISTER.
REALLY?
YEAH,
I'M SICK OF MY SISTER, AND MY MOTHER HATES ME.
WHAT?
I MEAN, I'M THE MOTHER AND I HAVE A SICK SISTER...
WHAT THE...?!
HA HA HA
Oh, let's start class!
Hey, I'm the teacher!
HA HA HA
ピンポーン
DING DONG
Hayama
......
Now what?

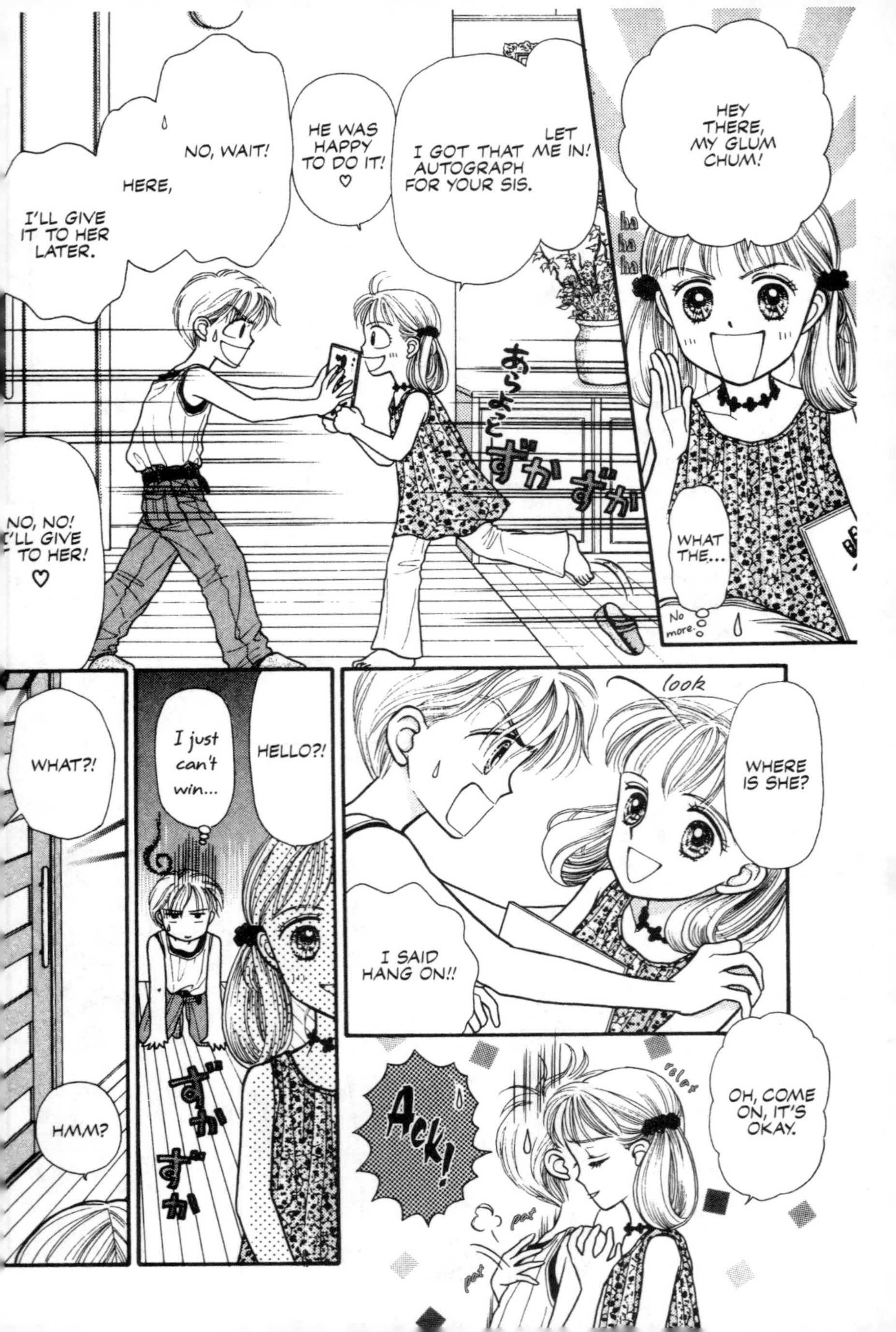
HEY THERE, MY GLUM CHUM!
ha ha ha
WHAT THE...
No more.
LET ME IN!
I GOT THAT AUTOGRAPH FOR YOUR SIS.
HE WAS HAPPY TO DO IT! ♡
あらよっと
ずかずか
NO, WAIT!
HERE,
I'LL GIVE IT TO HER LATER.
NO, NO! I'LL GIVE TO HER! ♡
look
WHERE IS SHE?
I SAID HANG ON!!
relax
OH, COME ON, IT'S OKAY.
Ack!
pat pat
HELLO?!
I just can't win...
ずかずか
WHAT?!
HMM?

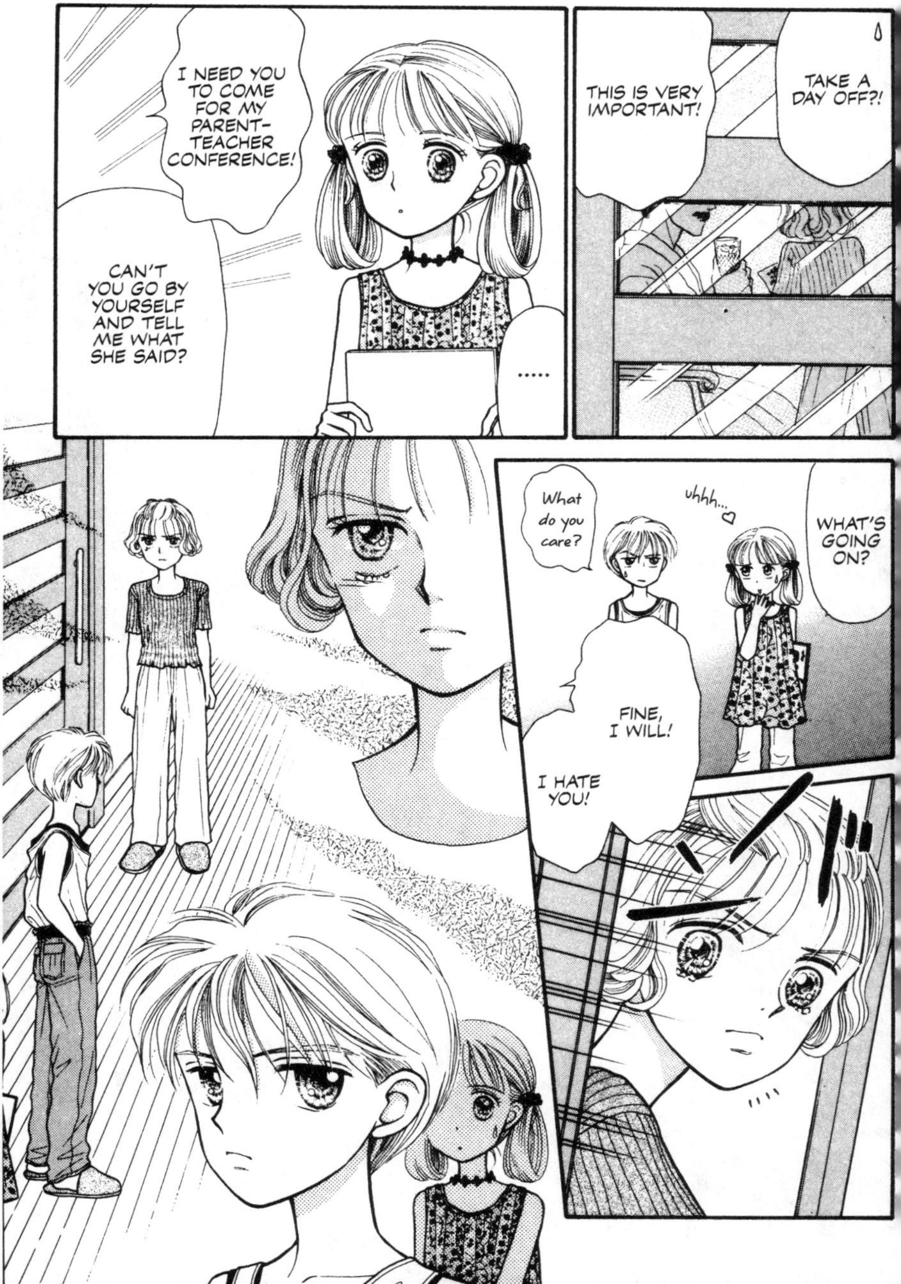
TAKE A DAY OFF?!
THIS IS VERY IMPORTANT!
I NEED YOU TO COME FOR MY PARENT-TEACHER CONFERENCE!
CAN'T YOU GO BY YOURSELF AND TELL ME WHAT SHE SAID?
.....
WHAT'S GOING ON?
uhhh...♡
What do you care?
FINE, I WILL!
I HATE YOU!

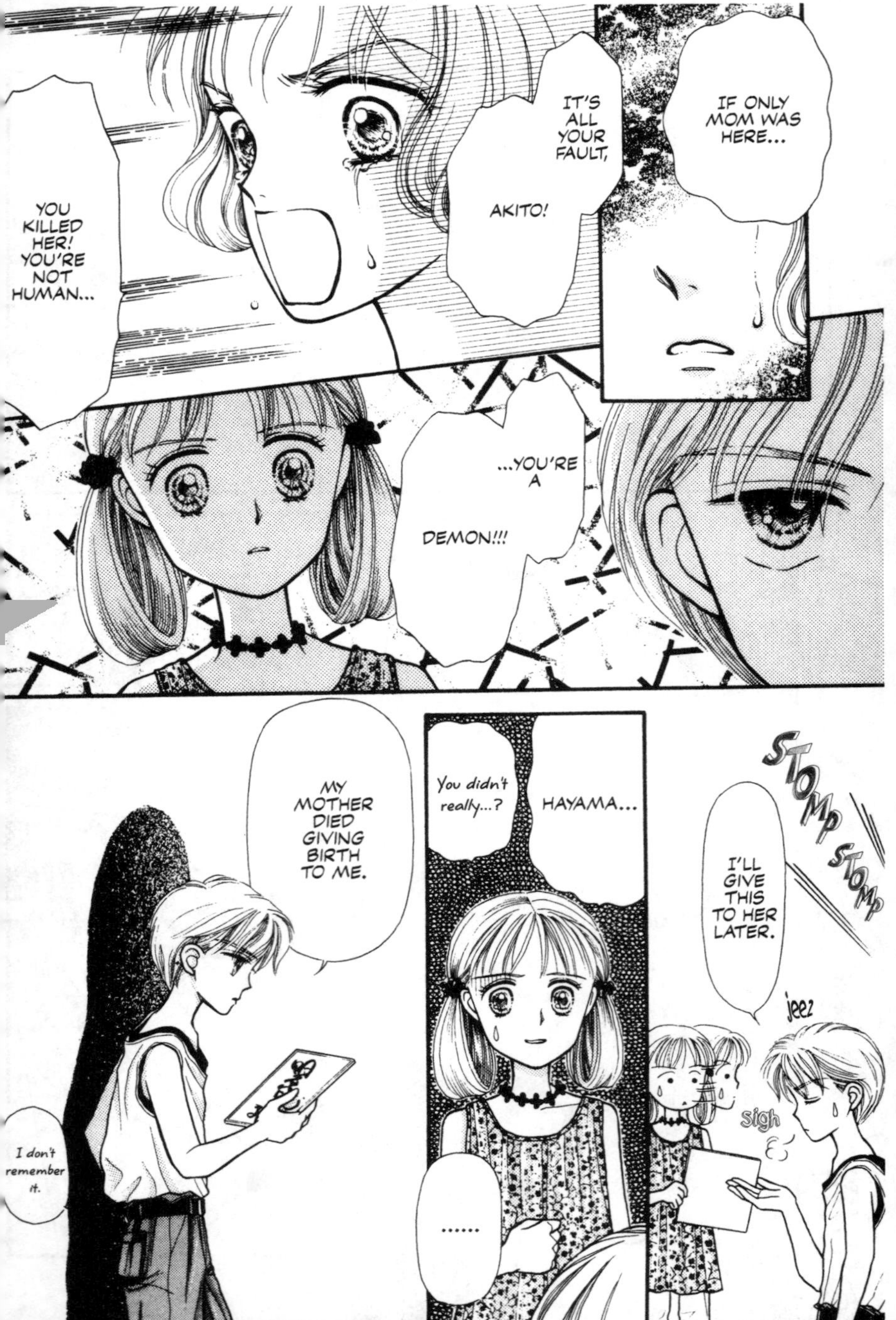
IF ONLY MOM WAS HERE...
IT'S ALL YOUR FAULT,
AKITO!
YOU KILLED HER! YOU'RE NOT HUMAN...
...YOU'RE A
DEMON!!!
STOMP STOMP
I'LL GIVE THIS TO HER LATER.
jeez
sigh
HAYAMA...
You didn't really...?
......
MY MOTHER DIED GIVING BIRTH TO ME.
I don't remember it.

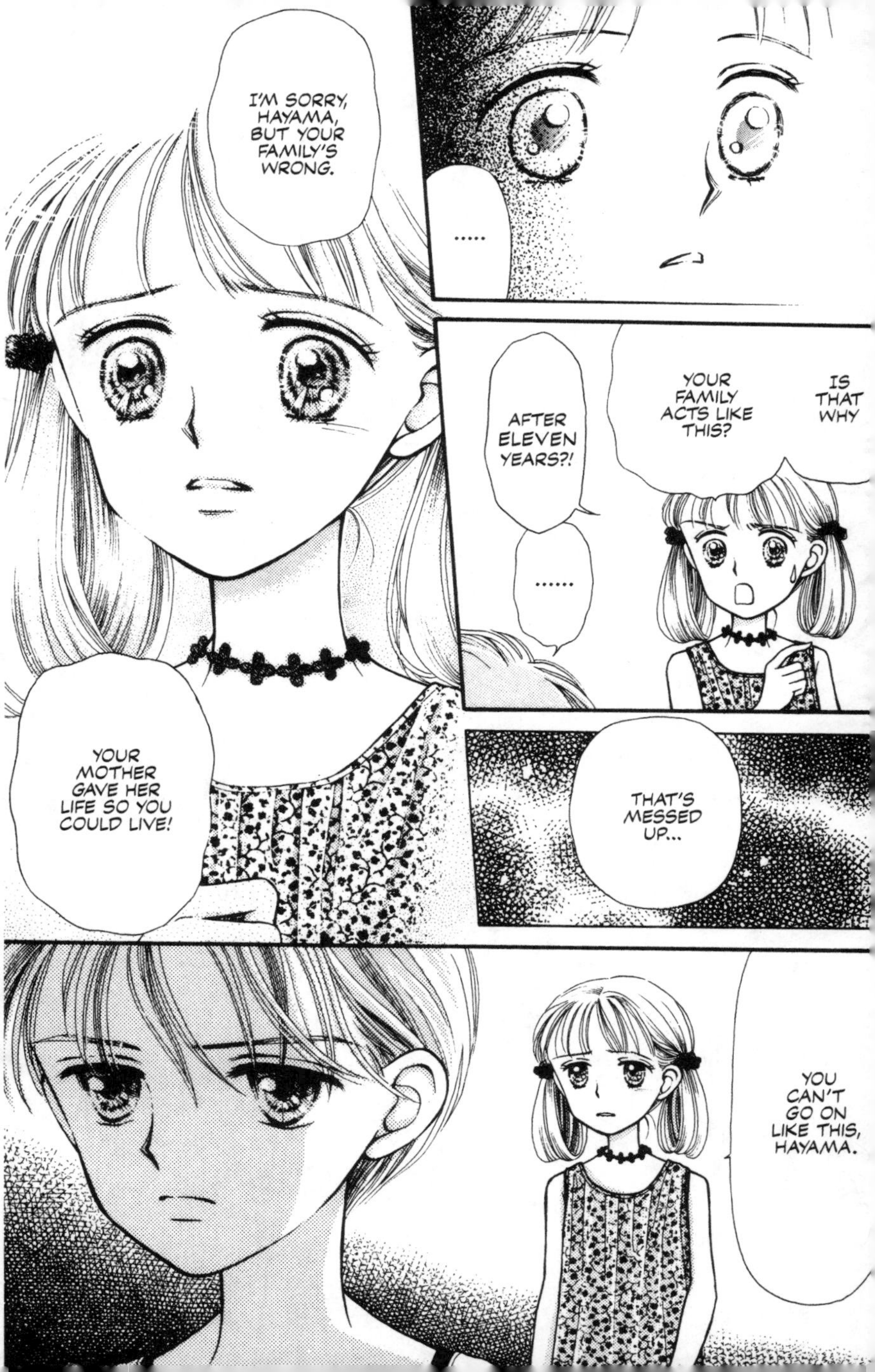
......
IS THAT WHY YOUR FAMILY ACTS LIKE THIS?
AFTER ELEVEN YEARS?!
......
THAT'S MESSED UP...
I'M SORRY, HAYAMA, BUT YOUR FAMILY'S WRONG.
YOUR MOTHER GAVE HER LIFE SO YOU COULD LIVE!
YOU CAN'T GO ON LIKE THIS, HAYAMA.

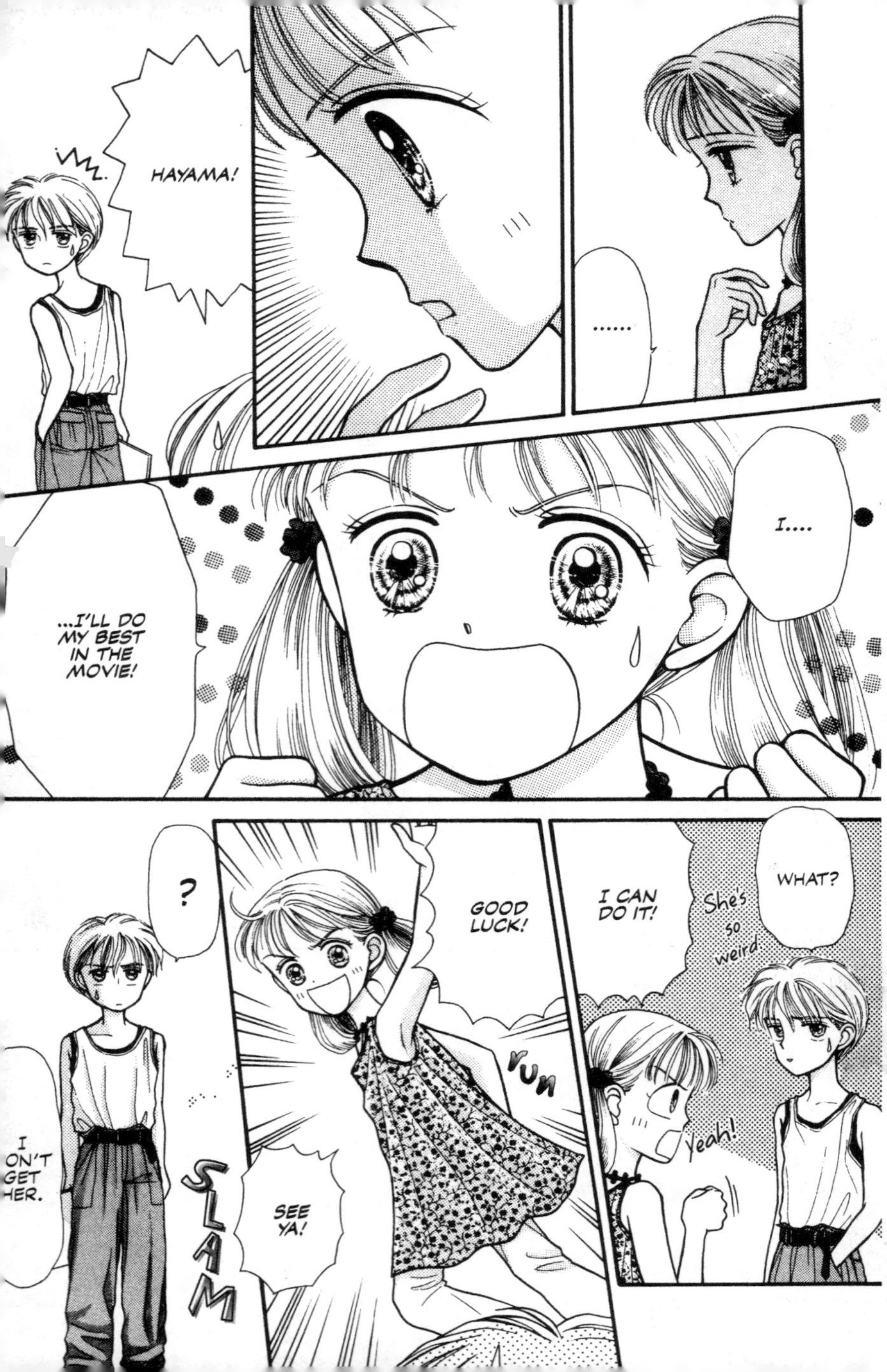
......
HAYAMA!
I....
...I'LL DO MY BEST IN THE MOVIE!
WHAT?
I CAN DO IT!
She's so weird
Yeah!
GOOD LUCK!
YUN
SEE YA!
SLAM
?
I ON'T GET HER.

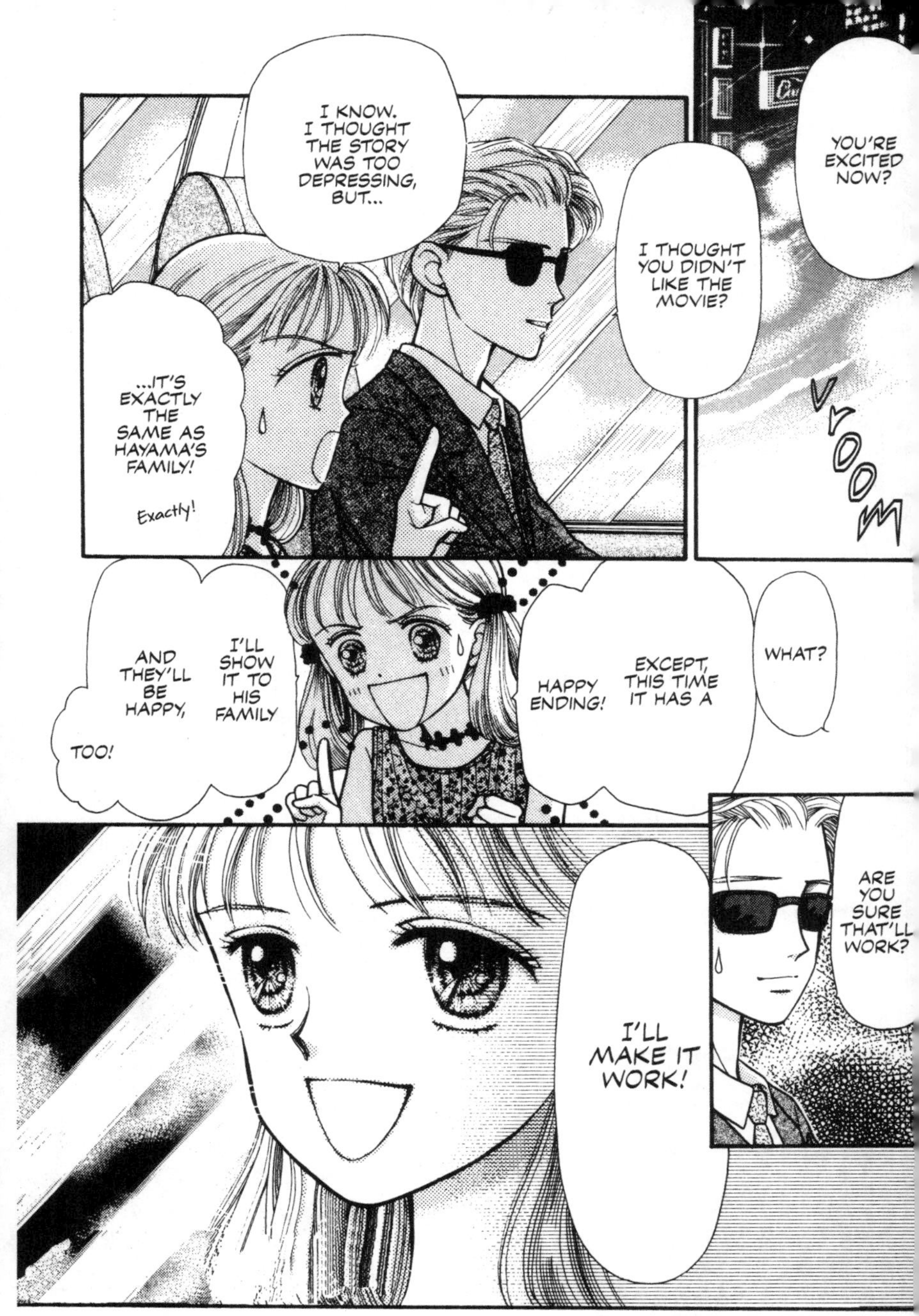
YOU'RE EXCITED NOW?
I THOUGHT YOU DIDN'T LIKE THE MOVIE?
VROOM
I KNOW. I THOUGHT THE STORY WAS TOO DEPRESSING, BUT...
...IT'S EXACTLY THE SAME AS HAYAMA'S FAMILY!
Exactly!
WHAT?
EXCEPT, THIS TIME IT HAS A
HAPPY ENDING!
I'LL SHOW IT TO HIS FAMILY
AND THEY'LL BE HAPPY,
TOO!
ARE YOU SURE THAT'LL WORK?
I'LL MAKE IT WORK!

COME ON DOWN, GUEST!

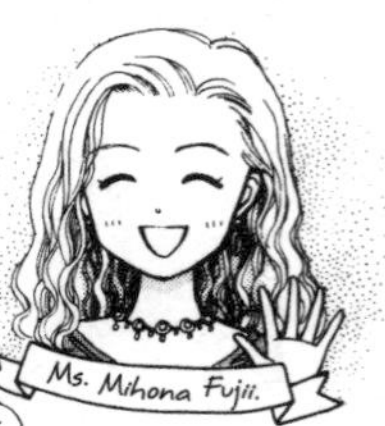

Ms. Mihona Fujii.

Hello! Let me introduce Ms. Mihona Fujii. She's like a sister to me. (She's even the same age as my real sister!) She's so nice and always forgives me when I do dumb things. She's been going to school and working at the same time.

Although, somehow she can never get my cat's name right. She calls "Nao-no-suke", "Gengoro" or "Tame-no-suke".

She will focus on comic books this year, and I know she'll do great!

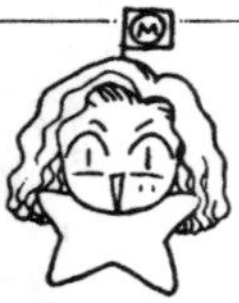

Hello, I'm Mihona Fujii!

CONGRATULATIONS TO MIHO ON PUBLISHING BOOK 1 OF KODOCHA!

Ms. Obana and I have been close for a very long time. We really are just like sisters! (Take care of me, sis!) We've even put our characters (Sana & Erika) in each other's comics, but no one believes us! Grrr! It's true -- when Ms. Obana came over to my place, we drew our characters on each other's artwork. (We were drinking. Hee-hee. Let's do it again!) Ms. Obana's the best sister I could ask for. I have a lot to learn from her. Her work is really deep, compared to mine. I wish I could have her insight. My favorite character is Rei, because he's nice -- and so cool! Be happy with your strong spirit, Sana! I'll be here for you!

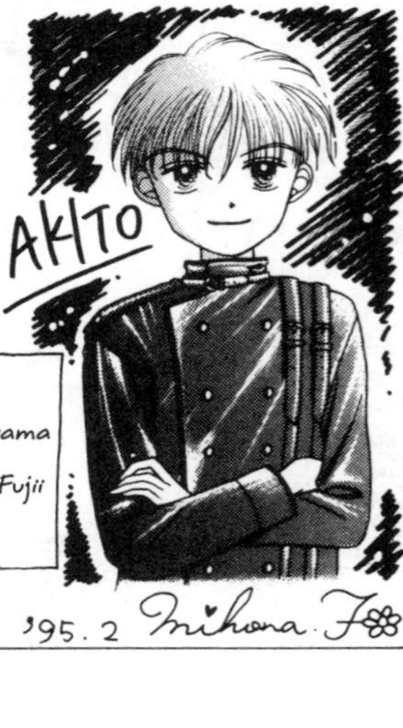

AKITO
Hayama by Fujii

Alright, guys, bye!

P.S. Let's go drinking again, Ms. Obana!

HEE-HEE-HEE♫ '95. 2 Mihona F

P.S. to Fujii: Yeah, let's go! Let's ditch work!

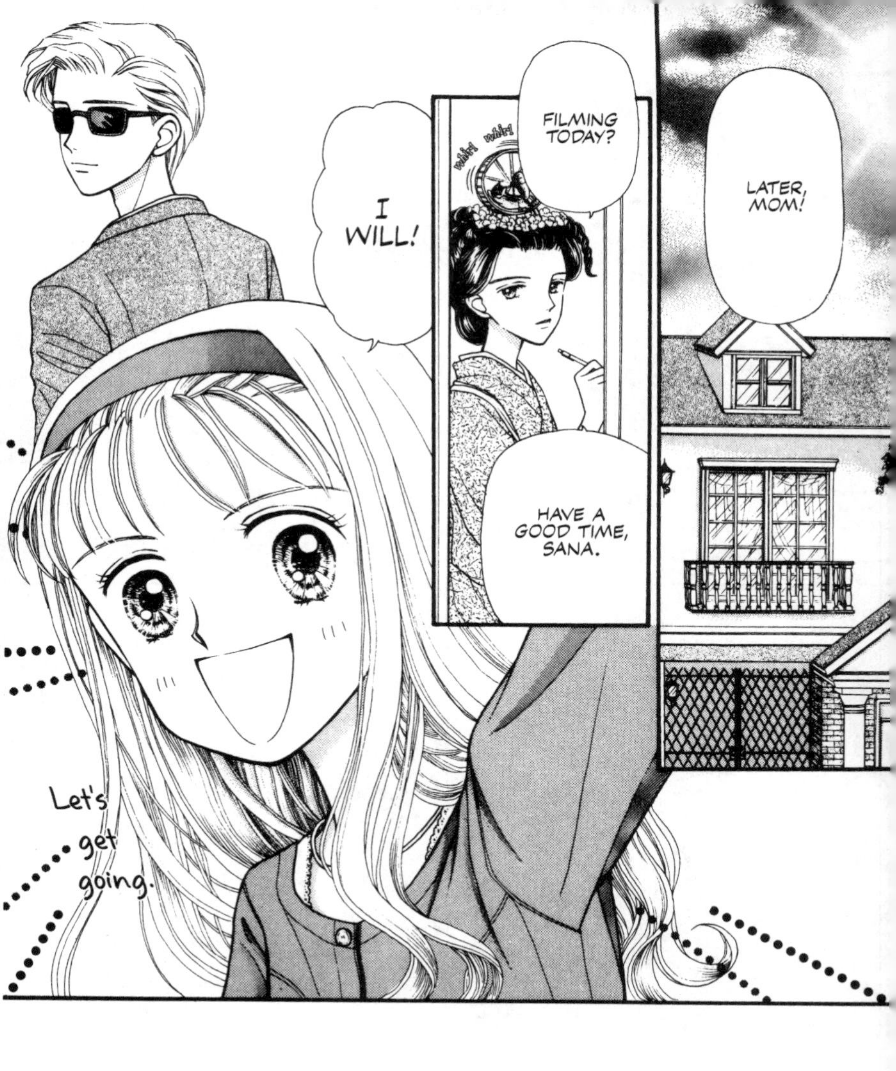
LATER, MOM!
FILMING TODAY?
HAVE A GOOD TIME, SANA.
I WILL!
Let's get going.

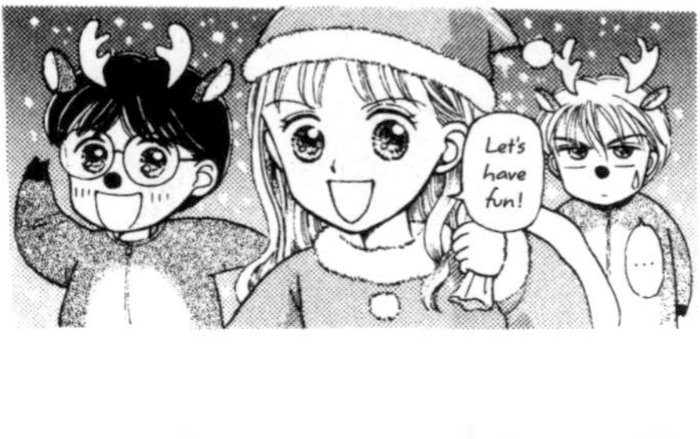
Let's have fun!
...

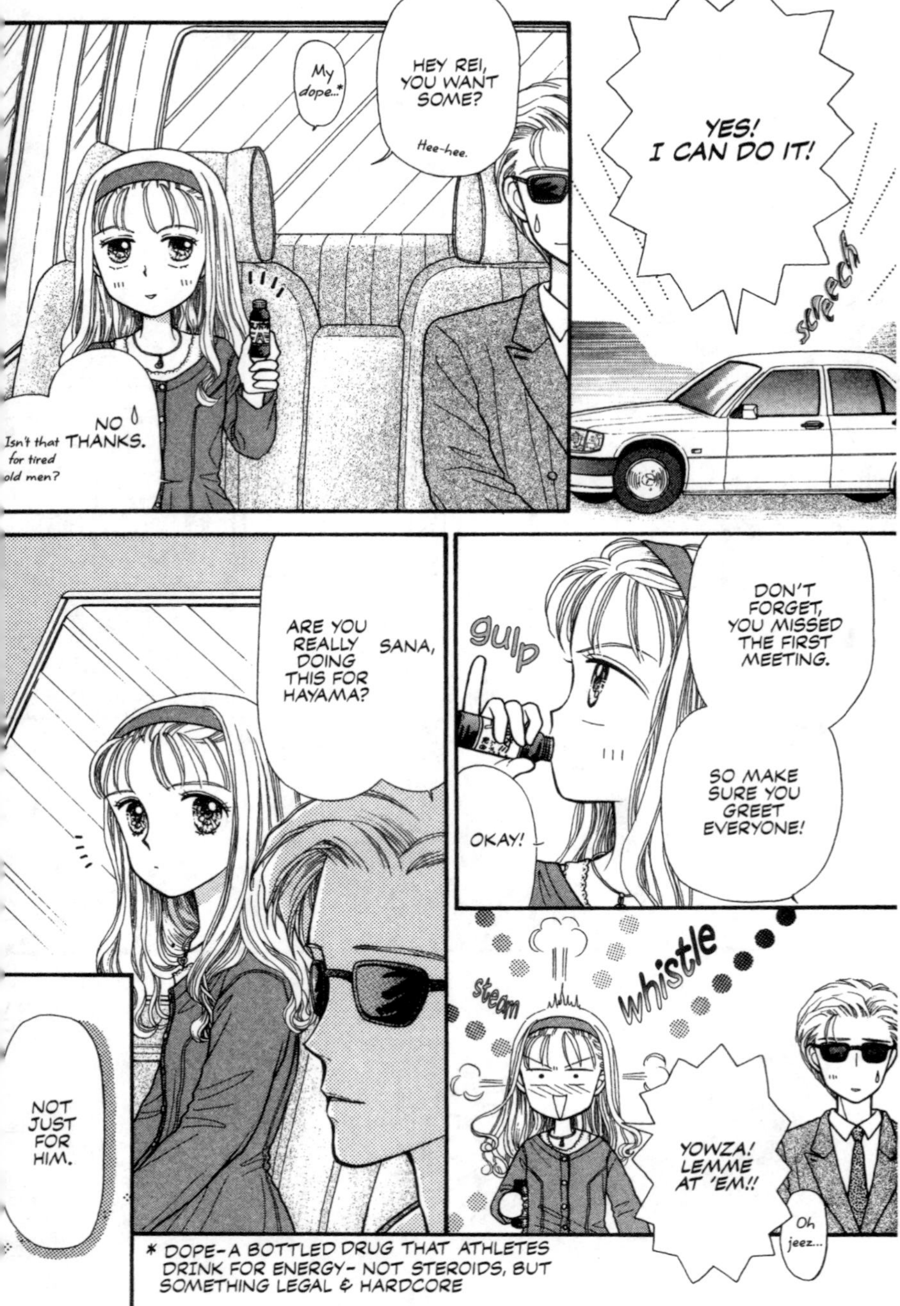
YES! I CAN DO IT!
screech
HEY REI, YOU WANT SOME?
Hee-hee.
My dope...*
NO THANKS.
Isn't that for tired old men?
DON'T FORGET, YOU MISSED THE FIRST MEETING.
gulp
SO MAKE SURE YOU GREET EVERYONE!
OKAY!
whistle
steam
YOWZA! LEMME AT 'EM!!
Oh jeez...
SANA, ARE YOU REALLY DOING THIS FOR HAYAMA?
NOT JUST FOR HIM.

* DOPE–A BOTTLED DRUG THAT ATHLETES DRINK FOR ENERGY– NOT STEROIDS, BUT SOMETHING LEGAL & HARDCORE

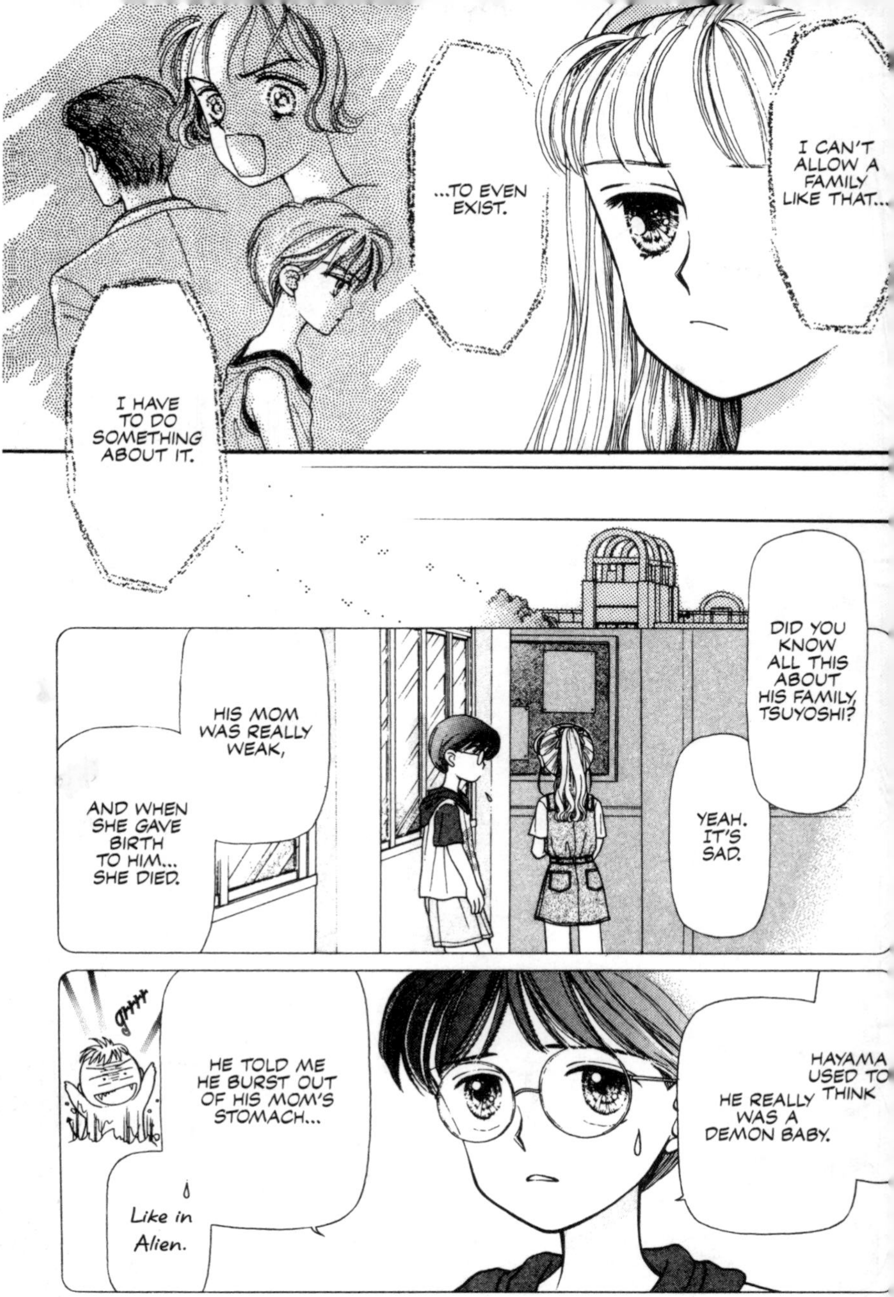
I CAN'T ALLOW A FAMILY LIKE THAT...
...TO EVEN EXIST.
I HAVE TO DO SOMETHING ABOUT IT.
DID YOU KNOW ALL THIS ABOUT HIS FAMILY, TSUYOSHI?
YEAH. IT'S SAD.
HIS MOM WAS REALLY WEAK,
AND WHEN SHE GAVE BIRTH TO HIM... SHE DIED.
HAYAMA USED TO THINK HE REALLY WAS A DEMON BABY.
HE TOLD ME HE BURST OUT OF HIS MOM'S STOMACH...
Like in Alien.

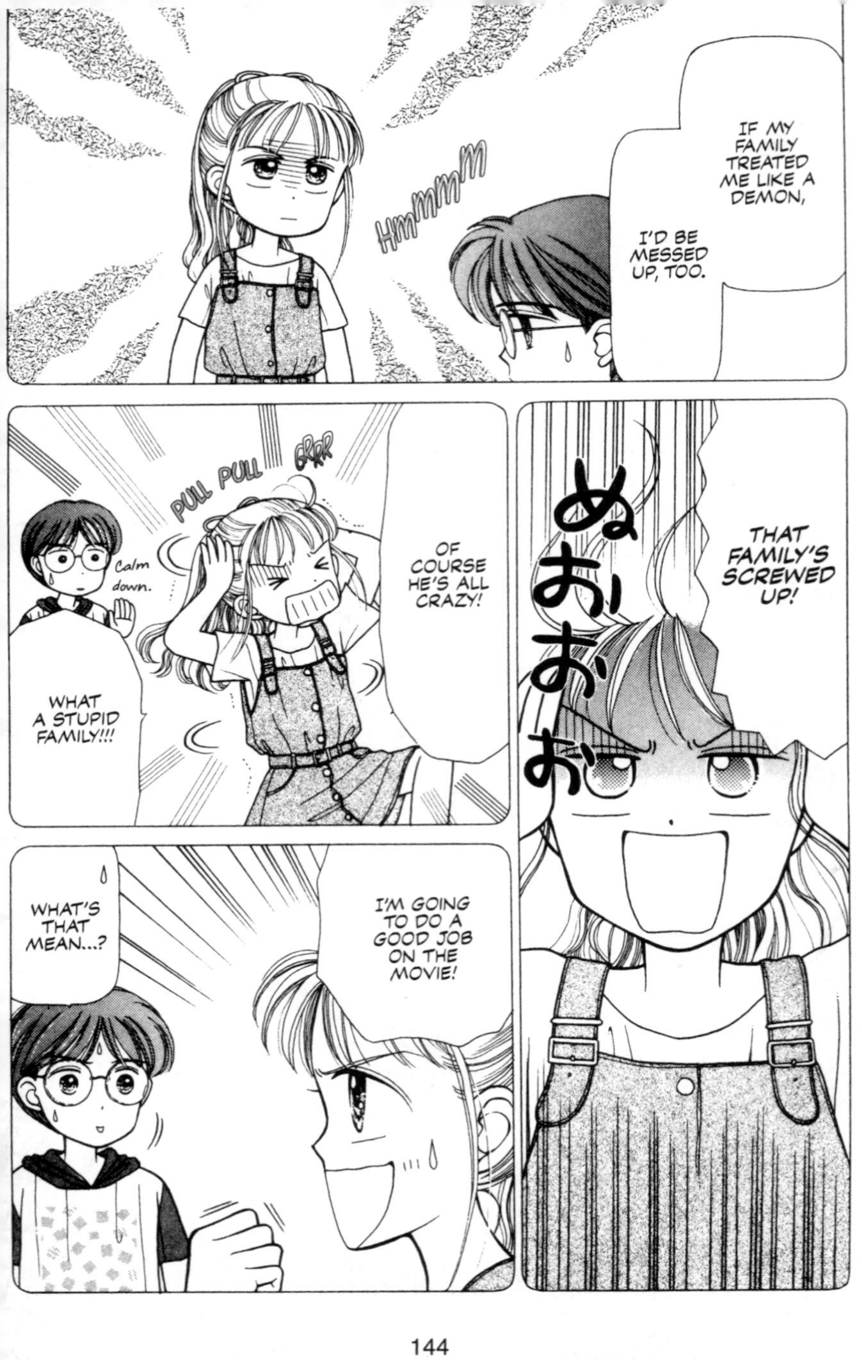
IF MY FAMILY TREATED ME LIKE A DEMON,
I'D BE MESSED UP, TOO.
HMMMMM
ぬおおおお
THAT FAMILY'S SCREWED UP!
OF COURSE HE'S ALL CRAZY!
GRRR
PULL PULL
Calm down.
WHAT A STUPID FAMILY!!!
I'M GOING TO DO A GOOD JOB ON THE MOVIE!
WHAT'S THAT MEAN...?

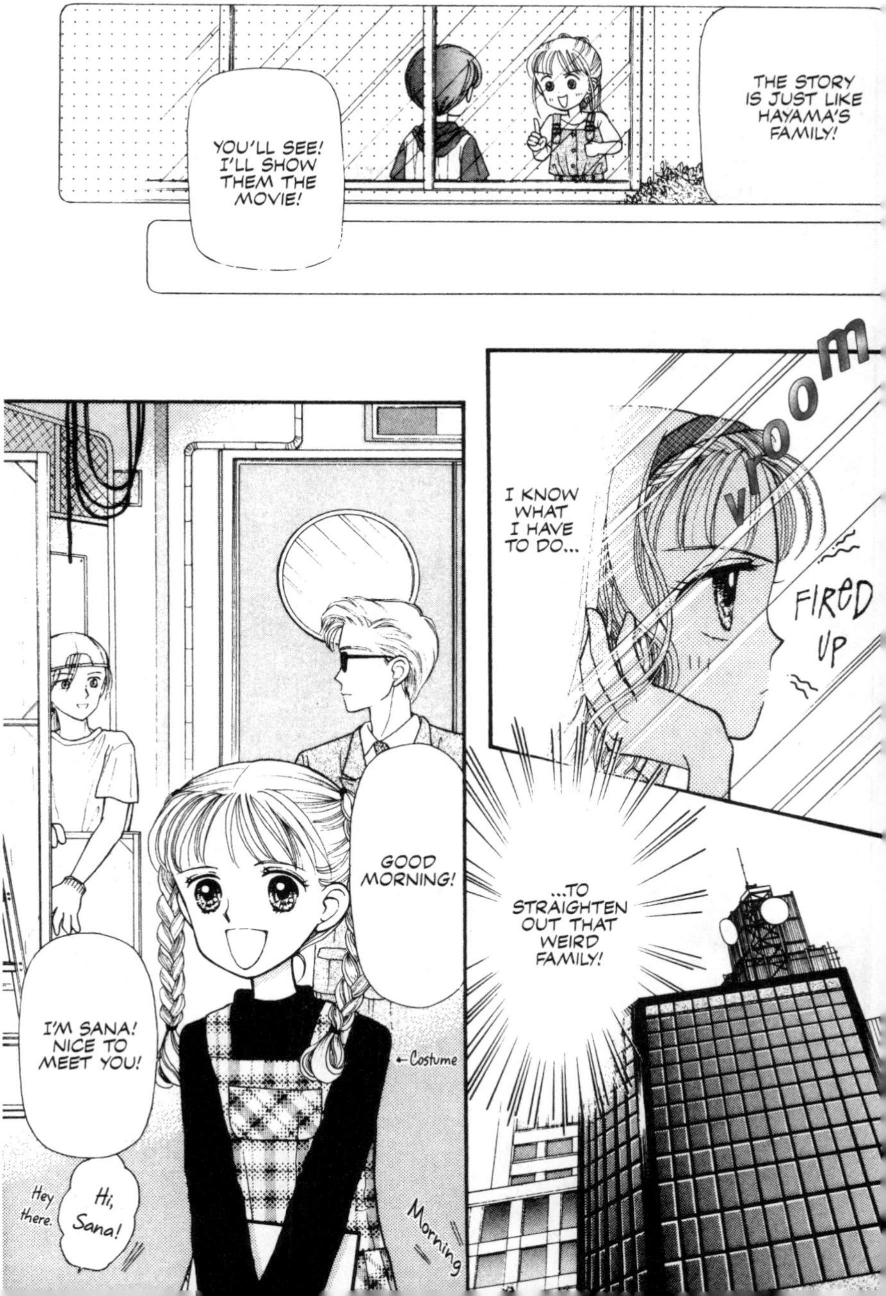
THE STORY IS JUST LIKE HAYAMA'S FAMILY!
YOU'LL SEE! I'LL SHOW THEM THE MOVIE!
I KNOW WHAT I HAVE TO DO...
vroom
FIRED UP
...TO STRAIGHTEN OUT THAT WEIRD FAMILY!
GOOD MORNING!
← Costume
I'M SANA! NICE TO MEET YOU!
Morning
Hi, Sana!
Hey there.

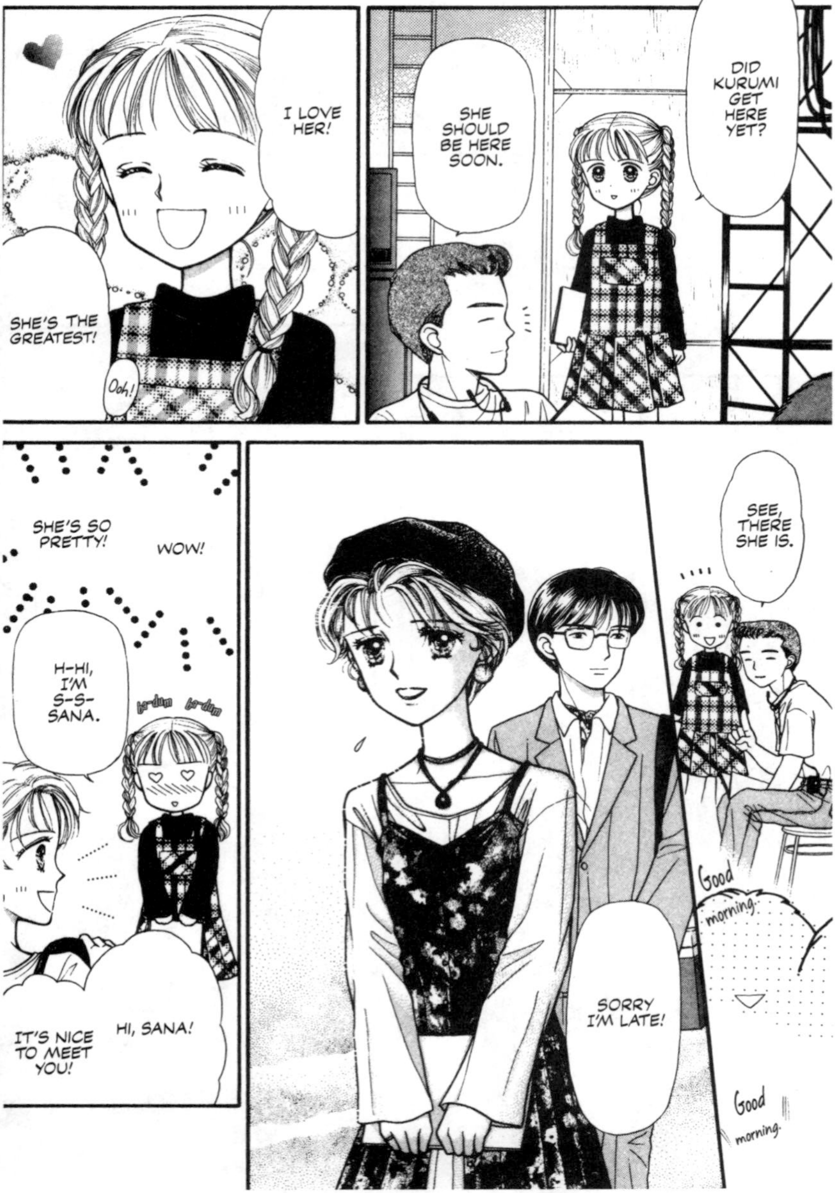
DID KURUMI GET HERE YET?
SHE SHOULD BE HERE SOON.
I LOVE HER!
SHE'S THE GREATEST!
Ooh!
SEE, THERE SHE IS.
Good morning.
SORRY I'M LATE!
Good morning.
WOW!
SHE'S SO PRETTY!
ba-dum ba-dum
H-HI, I'M S-S-SANA.
HI, SANA!
IT'S NICE TO MEET YOU!

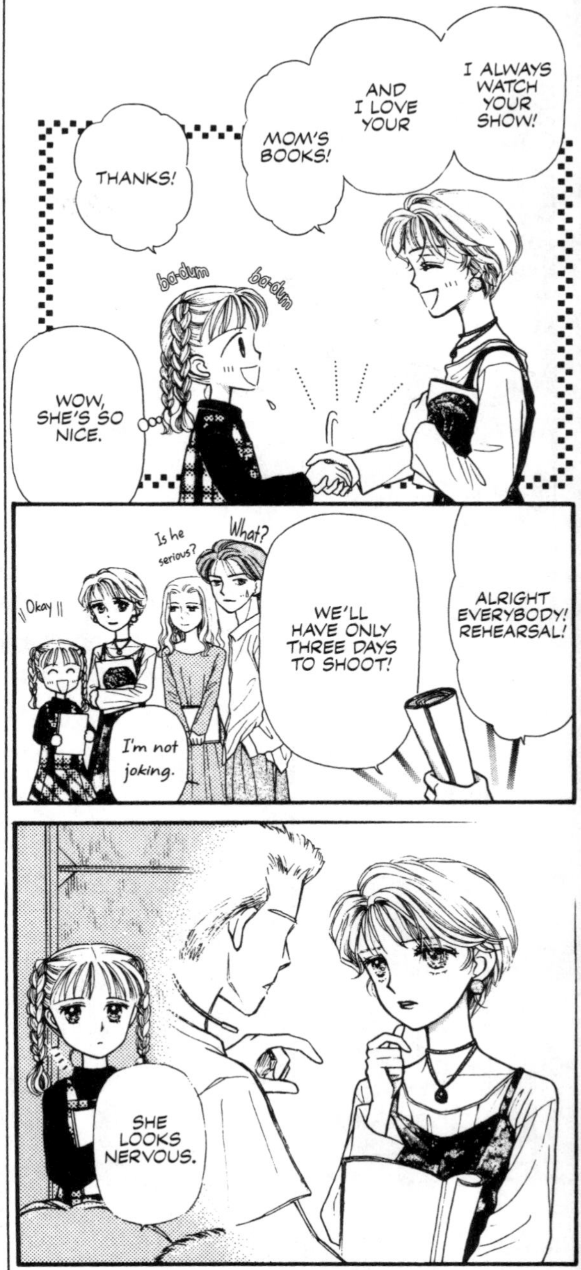
I ALWAYS WATCH YOUR SHOW!
AND I LOVE YOUR
MOM'S BOOKS!
THANKS!
ba-dum
ba-dum
WOW, SHE'S SO NICE.
ALRIGHT EVERYBODY! REHEARSAL!
WE'LL HAVE ONLY THREE DAYS TO SHOOT!
What?
Is he serious?
Okay
I'm not joking.
SHE LOOKS NERVOUS.

All About "I"

"I" was a classmate of mine from junior high. Later, he became a professional fighter. In school, he was the smallest boy in class and everyone used to tease him. But now he's a pro boxer! After he went to Thailand for training, he came back for a match, so I went to check it out. (I had a chance to see one of his matches before he left, but I couldn't because of a snow storm.) He was so impressive, I couldn't believe it was him!
I videotaped him with this really cool video camera I bought. H.K. (an actor who was all over the tabloids then) was there also, so I got a good close up of him. (ha!) "I" won in the 3rd round with a TKO. He was so much cooler than H.K!
To be continued.

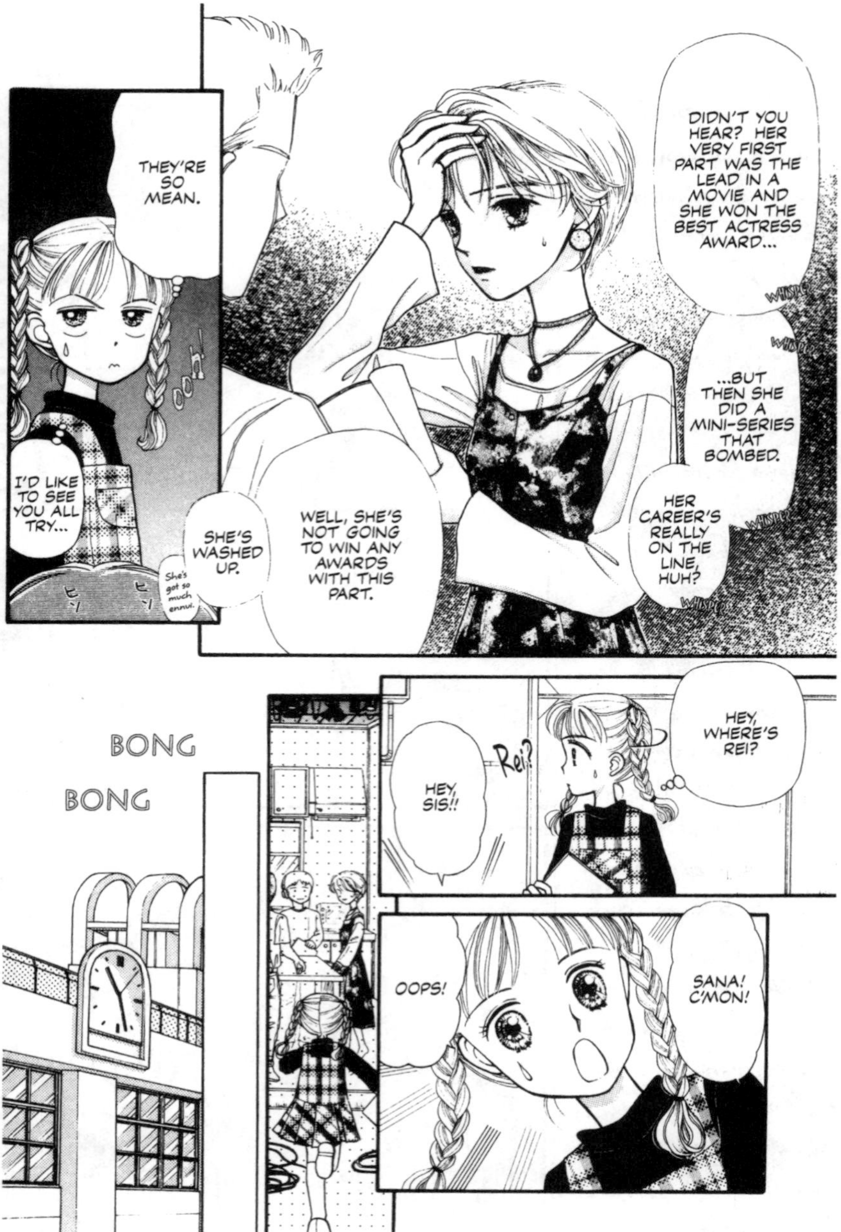
DIDN'T YOU HEAR? HER VERY FIRST PART WAS THE LEAD IN A MOVIE AND SHE WON THE BEST ACTRESS AWARD...
...BUT THEN SHE DID A MINI-SERIES THAT BOMBED.
HER CAREER'S REALLY ON THE LINE, HUH?
WELL, SHE'S NOT GOING TO WIN ANY AWARDS WITH THIS PART.
SHE'S WASHED UP.
THEY'RE SO MEAN.
Ooh!
I'D LIKE TO SEE YOU ALL TRY...
She's got so much ennui.
HEY, WHERE'S REI?
Rei?
HEY, SIS!!
SANA! C'MON!
OOPS!
BONG
BONG

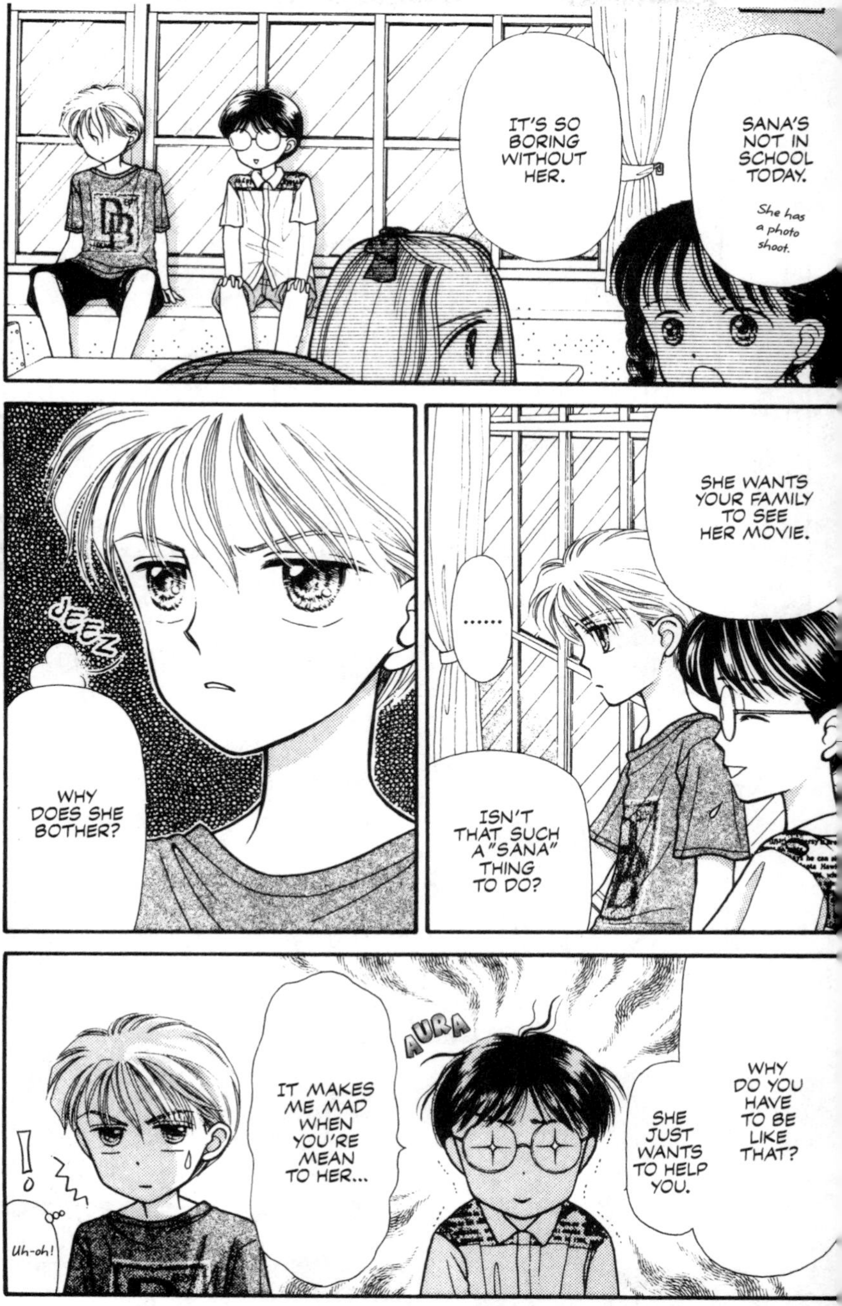
SANA'S NOT IN SCHOOL TODAY.
She has a photo shoot.
IT'S SO BORING WITHOUT HER.
SHE WANTS YOUR FAMILY TO SEE HER MOVIE.
......
ISN'T THAT SUCH A "SANA" THING TO DO?
JEEZ
WHY DOES SHE BOTHER?
WHY DO YOU HAVE TO BE LIKE THAT?
SHE JUST WANTS TO HELP YOU.
AURA
IT MAKES ME MAD WHEN YOU'RE MEAN TO HER...
!
Uh-oh!

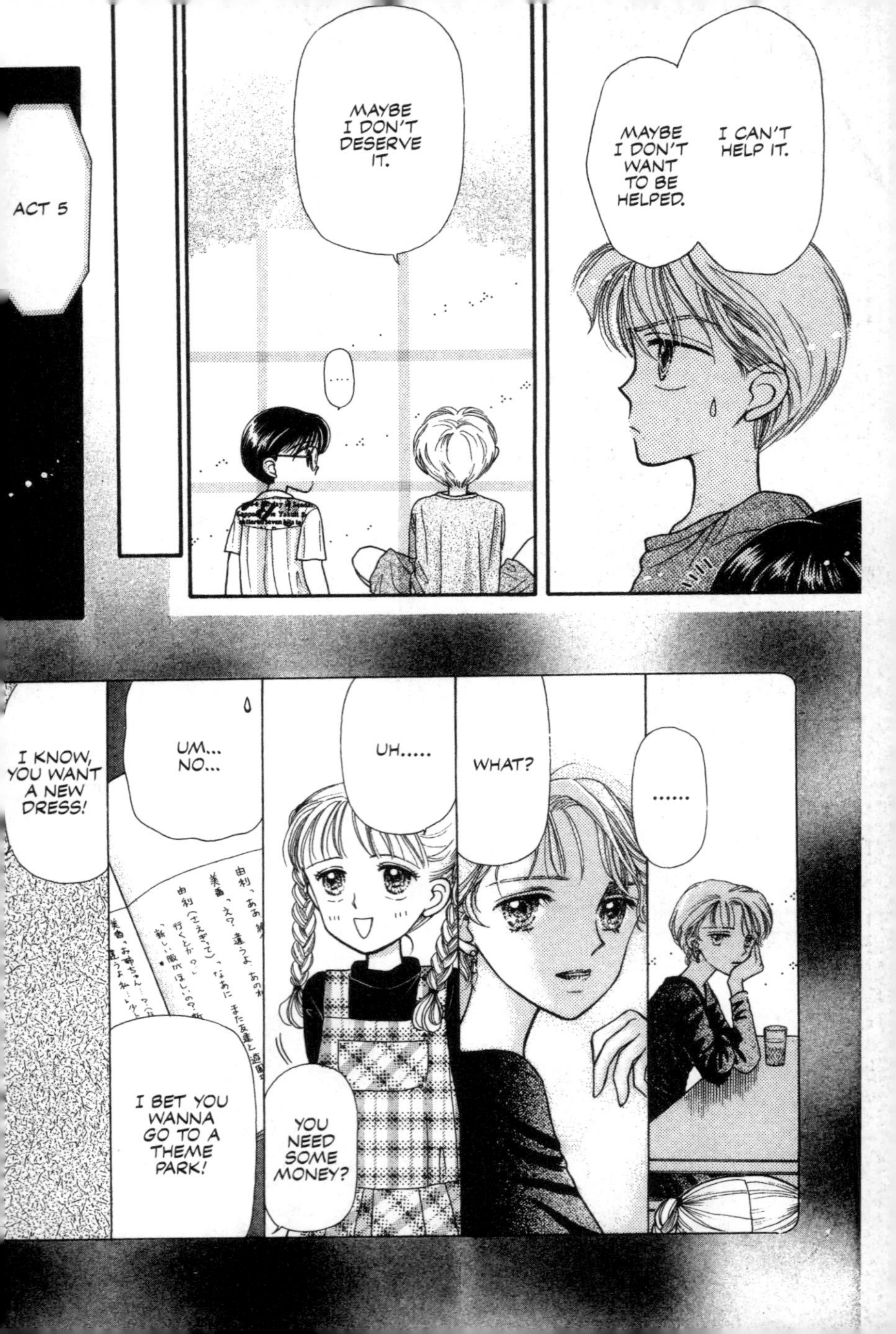
I CAN'T HELP IT.
MAYBE I DON'T WANT TO BE HELPED.
MAYBE I DON'T DESERVE IT.
.....
ACT 5
......
WHAT?
UH.....
YOU NEED SOME MONEY?
UM... NO...
I BET YOU WANNA GO TO A THEME PARK!
I KNOW, YOU WANT A NEW DRESS!

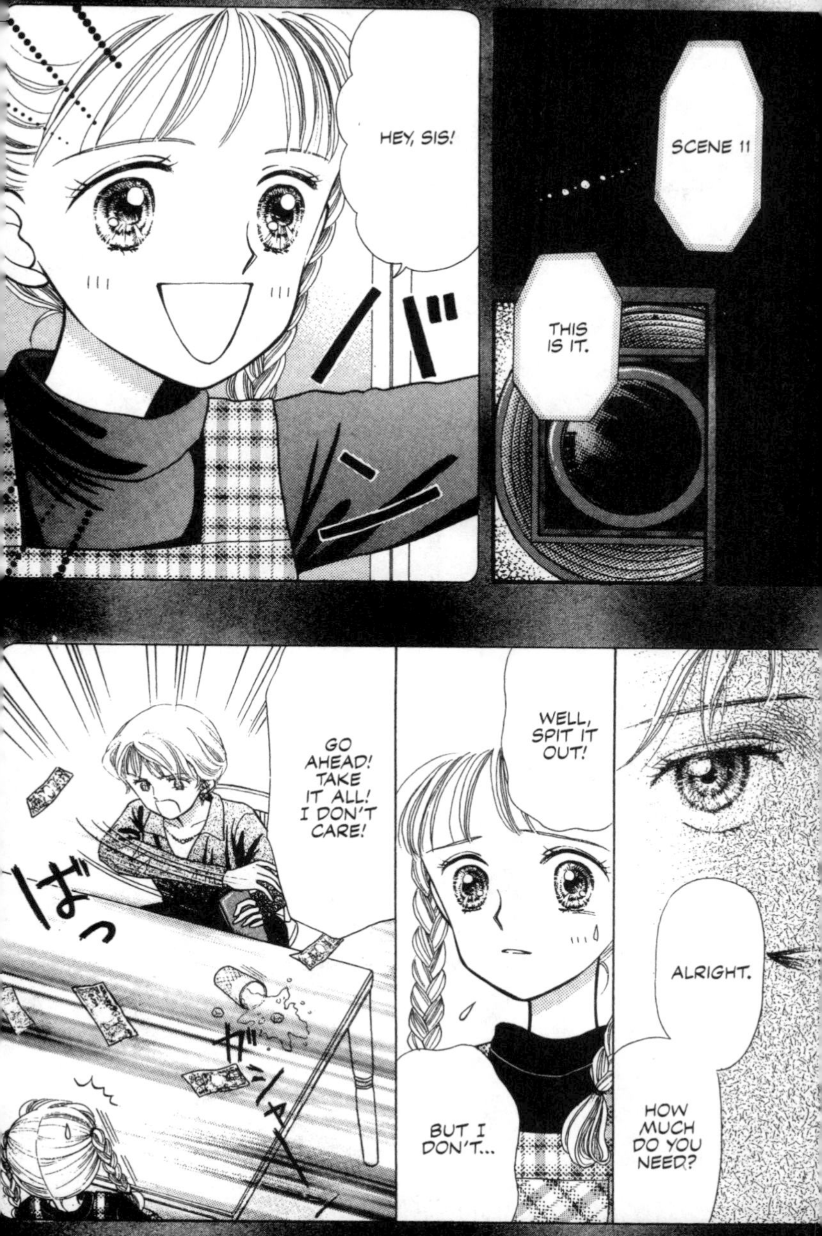
SCENE 11
THIS IS IT.
HEY, SIS!
ALRIGHT.
HOW MUCH DO YOU NEED?
WELL, SPIT IT OUT!
BUT I DON'T...
GO AHEAD! TAKE IT ALL! I DON'T CARE!

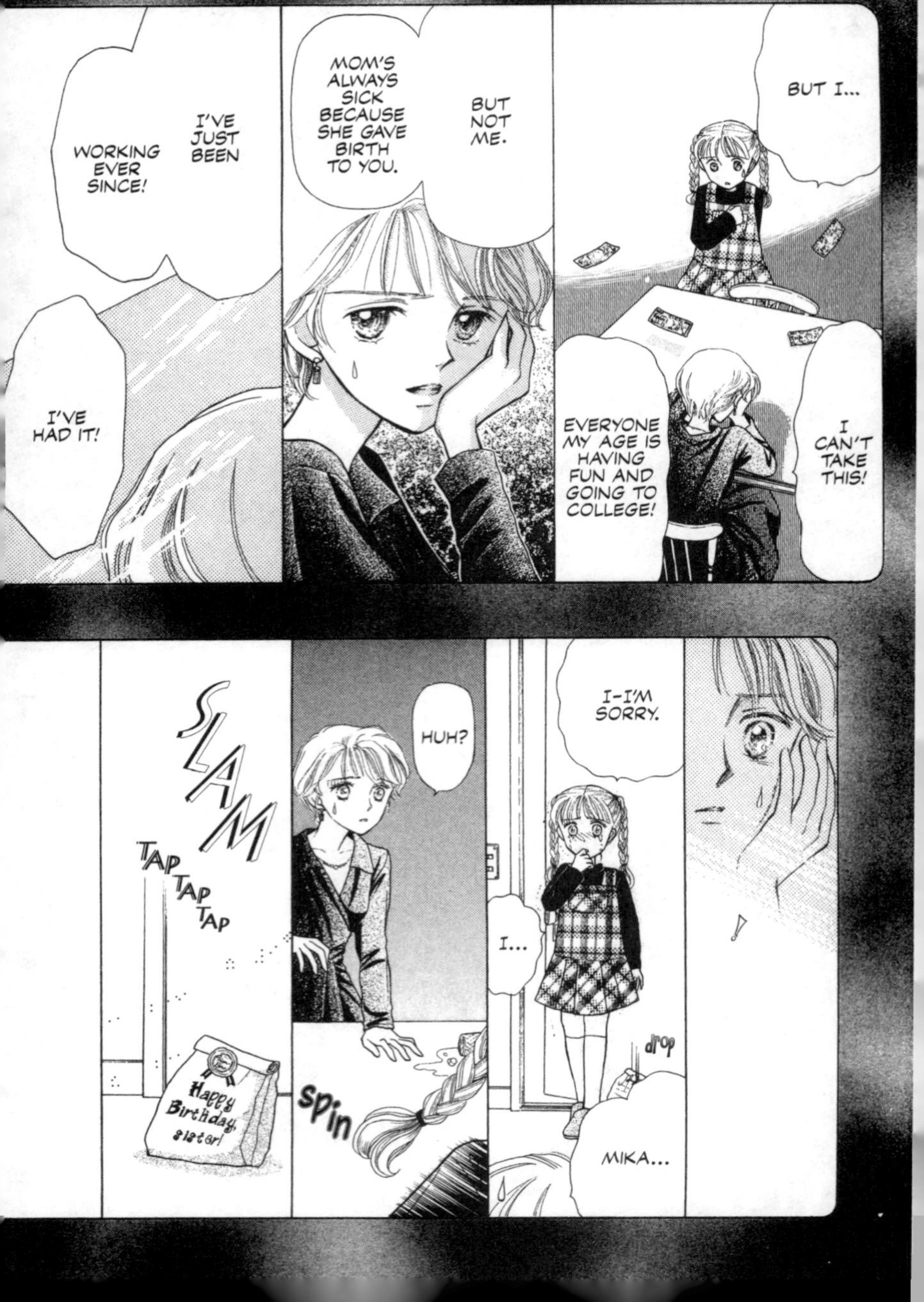
BUT I...
I CAN'T TAKE THIS!
EVERYONE MY AGE IS HAVING FUN AND GOING TO COLLEGE!
BUT NOT ME.
MOM'S ALWAYS SICK BECAUSE SHE GAVE BIRTH TO YOU.
I'VE JUST BEEN WORKING EVER SINCE!
I'VE HAD IT!
!
I-I'M SORRY.
I...
drop
MIKA...
HUH?
spin
SLAM
TAP TAP TAP
Happy Birthday, sister!

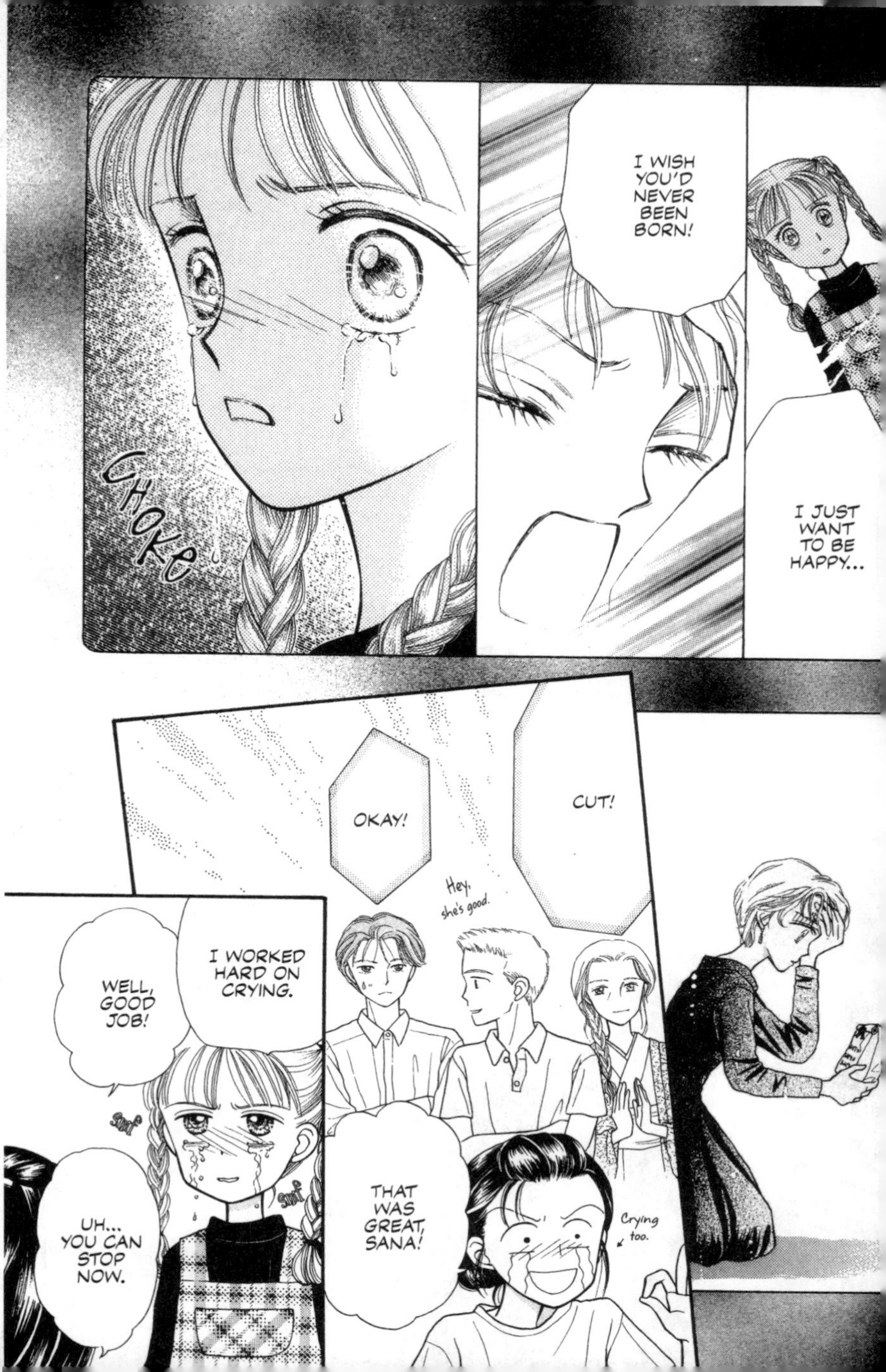
I JUST WANT TO BE HAPPY...
I WISH YOU'D NEVER BEEN BORN!
CHOKE
CUT!
OKAY!
Hey, she's good.
THAT WAS GREAT, SANA!
Crying too.
I WORKED HARD ON CRYING.
WELL, GOOD JOB!
UH... YOU CAN STOP NOW.

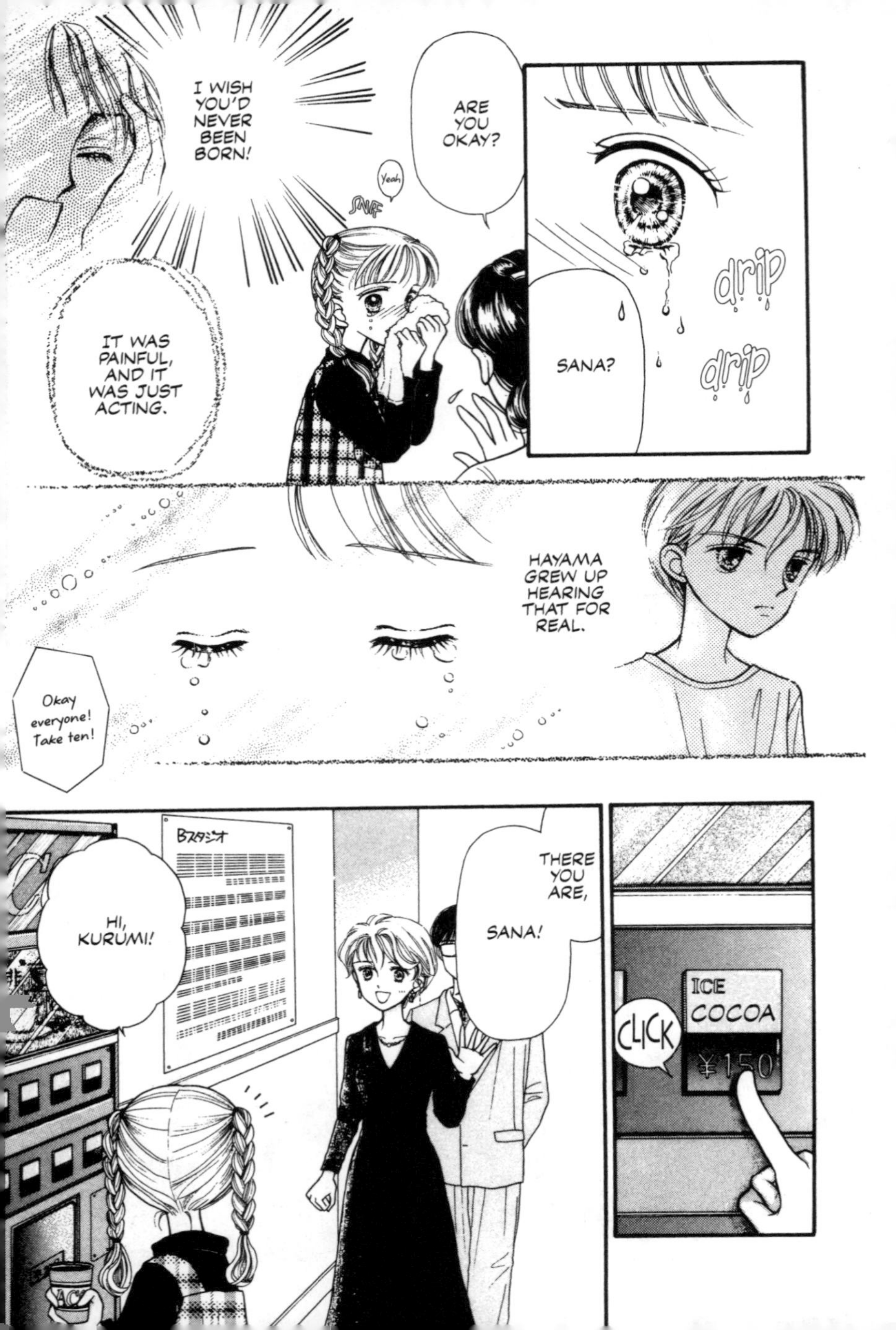
SANA?
drip
drip
ARE YOU OKAY?
Yeah
SNIFF
I WISH YOU'D NEVER BEEN BORN!
IT WAS PAINFUL, AND IT WAS JUST ACTING.
HAYAMA GREW UP HEARING THAT FOR REAL.
Okay everyone! Take ten!
CLICK
ICE COCOA
¥150
THERE YOU ARE,
SANA!
Bスタジオ
HI, KURUMI!

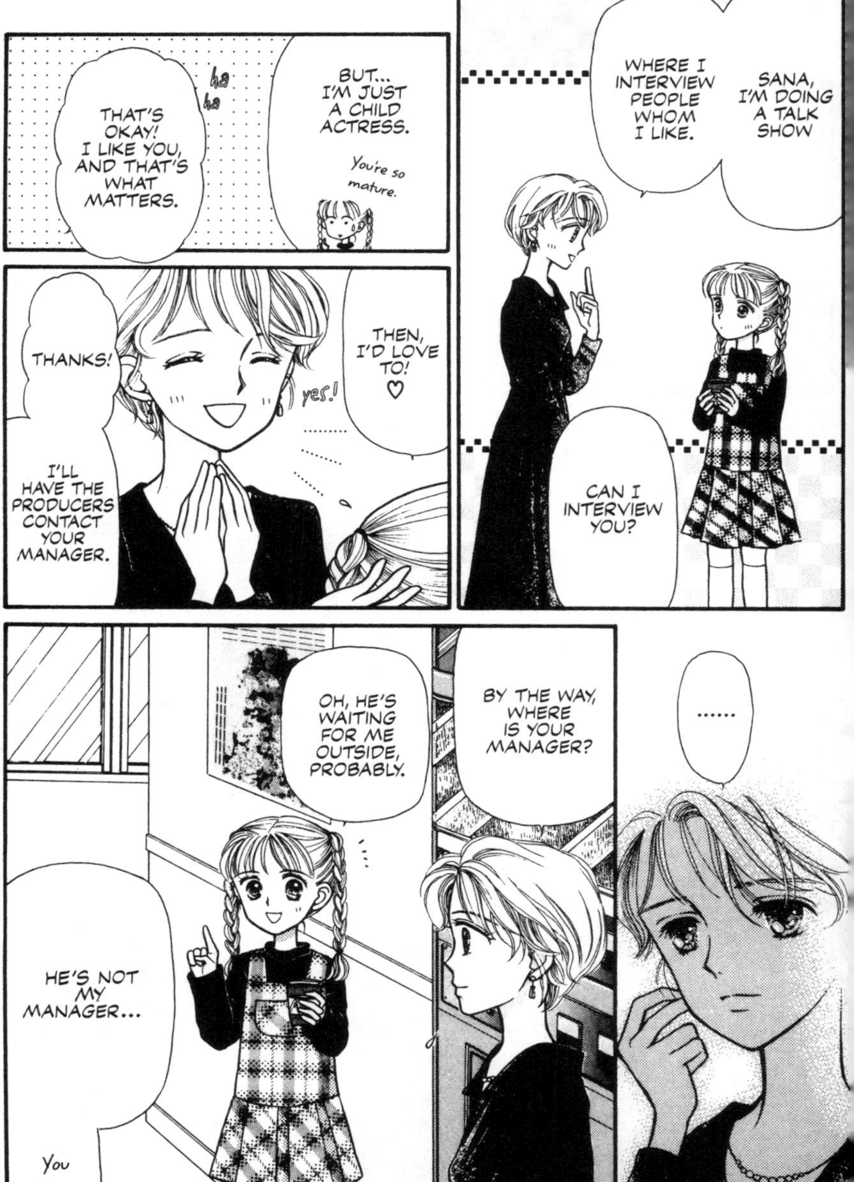
SANA, I'M DOING A TALK SHOW
WHERE I INTERVIEW PEOPLE WHOM I LIKE.
CAN I INTERVIEW YOU?
BUT... I'M JUST A CHILD ACTRESS.
You're so mature.
ha ha
THAT'S OKAY! I LIKE YOU, AND THAT'S WHAT MATTERS.
THEN, I'D LOVE TO! ♡
yes!
THANKS!
I'LL HAVE THE PRODUCERS CONTACT YOUR MANAGER.
......
BY THE WAY, WHERE IS YOUR MANAGER?
OH, HE'S WAITING FOR ME OUTSIDE, PROBABLY.
HE'S NOT MY MANAGER...
You know.

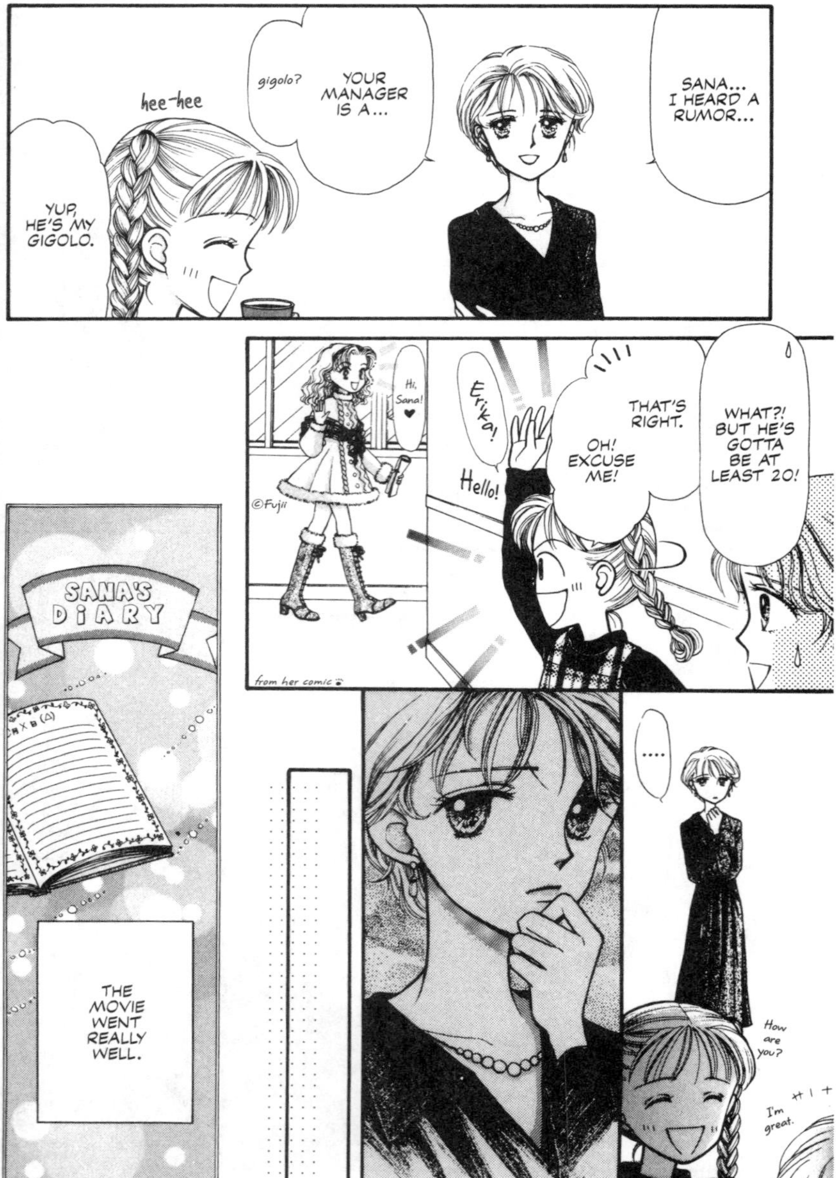
SANA... I HEARD A RUMOR...
YOUR MANAGER IS A...
gigolo?
hee-hee
YUP, HE'S MY GIGOLO.
WHAT?! BUT HE'S GOTTA BE AT LEAST 20!
THAT'S RIGHT.
OH! EXCUSE ME!
Erika!
Hello!
Hi, Sana!
©Fujii
from her comic
....
How are you?
I'm great.
SANA'S DIARY
THE MOVIE WENT REALLY WELL.

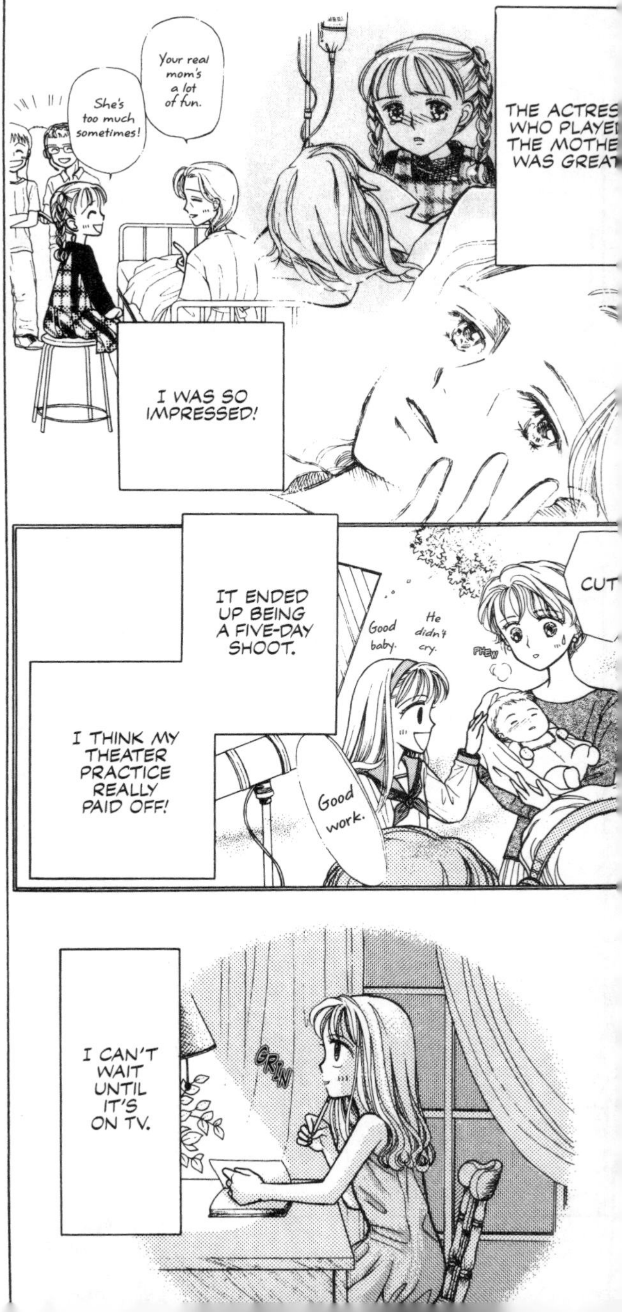
THE ACTRES WHO PLAYE THE MOTHE WAS GREAT
Your real mom's a lot of fun.
She's too much sometimes!
I WAS SO IMPRESSED!
CUT
PHEW
He didn't cry.
Good baby.
IT ENDED UP BEING A FIVE-DAY SHOOT.
Good work.
I THINK MY THEATER PRACTICE REALLY PAID OFF!
GRIN
I CAN'T WAIT UNTIL IT'S ON TV.

"I", Part II

It was the first time I had ever seen boxing matches. I felt sorry for the losers and couldn't really applaud for the winners. But for "I"'s match, I cheered for him really loudly . I did feel sorry for his opponent, but I tried to comfort him by saying, "you did well" and "good luck." (Ha!) I like athletes. None of my friends were athletes, so the way the boxers were so serious and stoic was refreshing. All my friends were into bikes, bands, or working part-time for cash. I wish I could draw a comic about athletes someday! Maybe I'll give it a try...

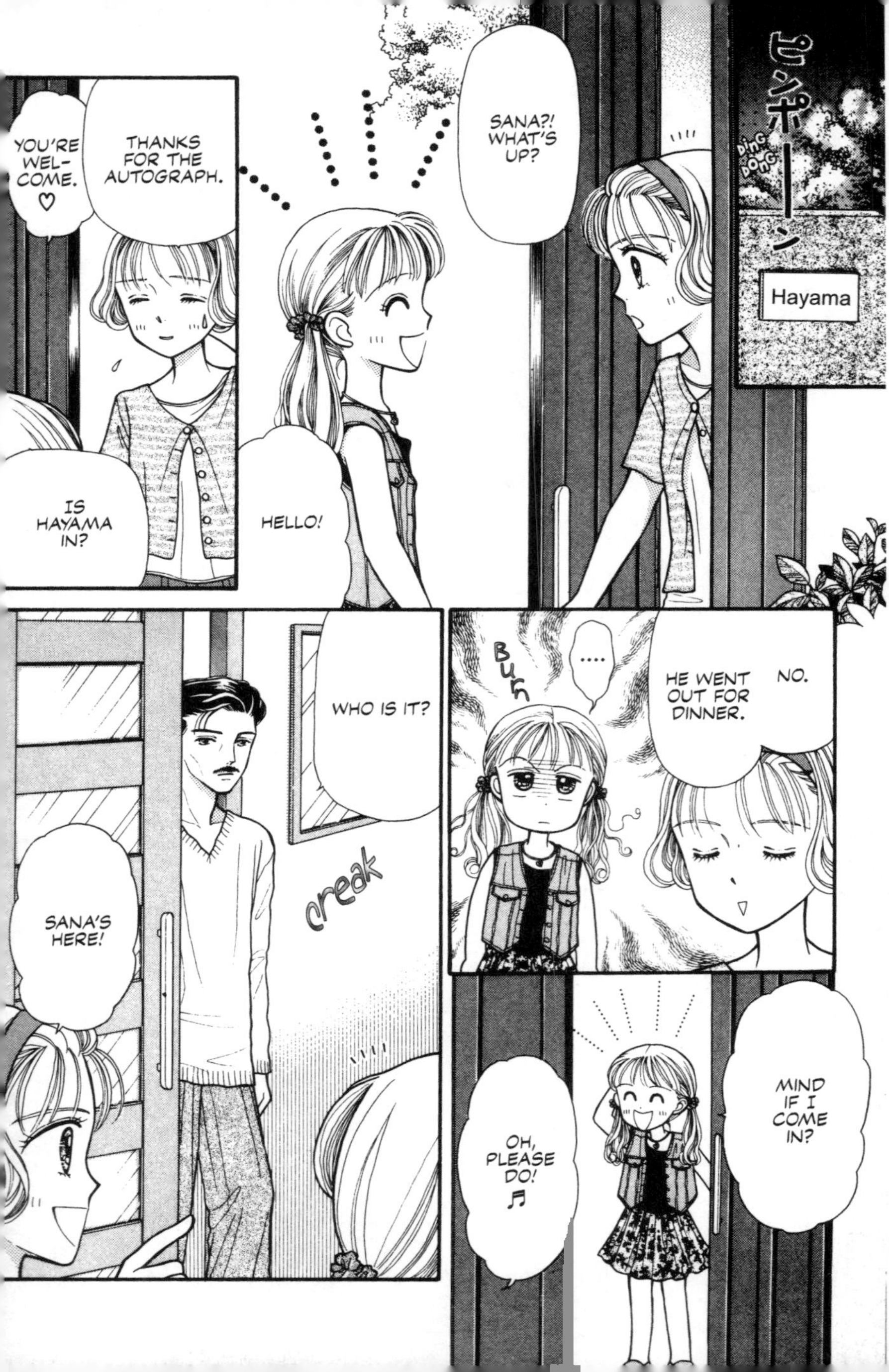
ピンポーン
DING DONG
Hayama
SANA?! WHAT'S UP?
HELLO!
IS HAYAMA IN?
THANKS FOR THE AUTOGRAPH.
YOU'RE WEL-COME. ♡
NO.
HE WENT OUT FOR DINNER.
....
BURN
MIND IF I COME IN?
OH, PLEASE DO! ♫
WHO IS IT?
creak
SANA'S HERE!

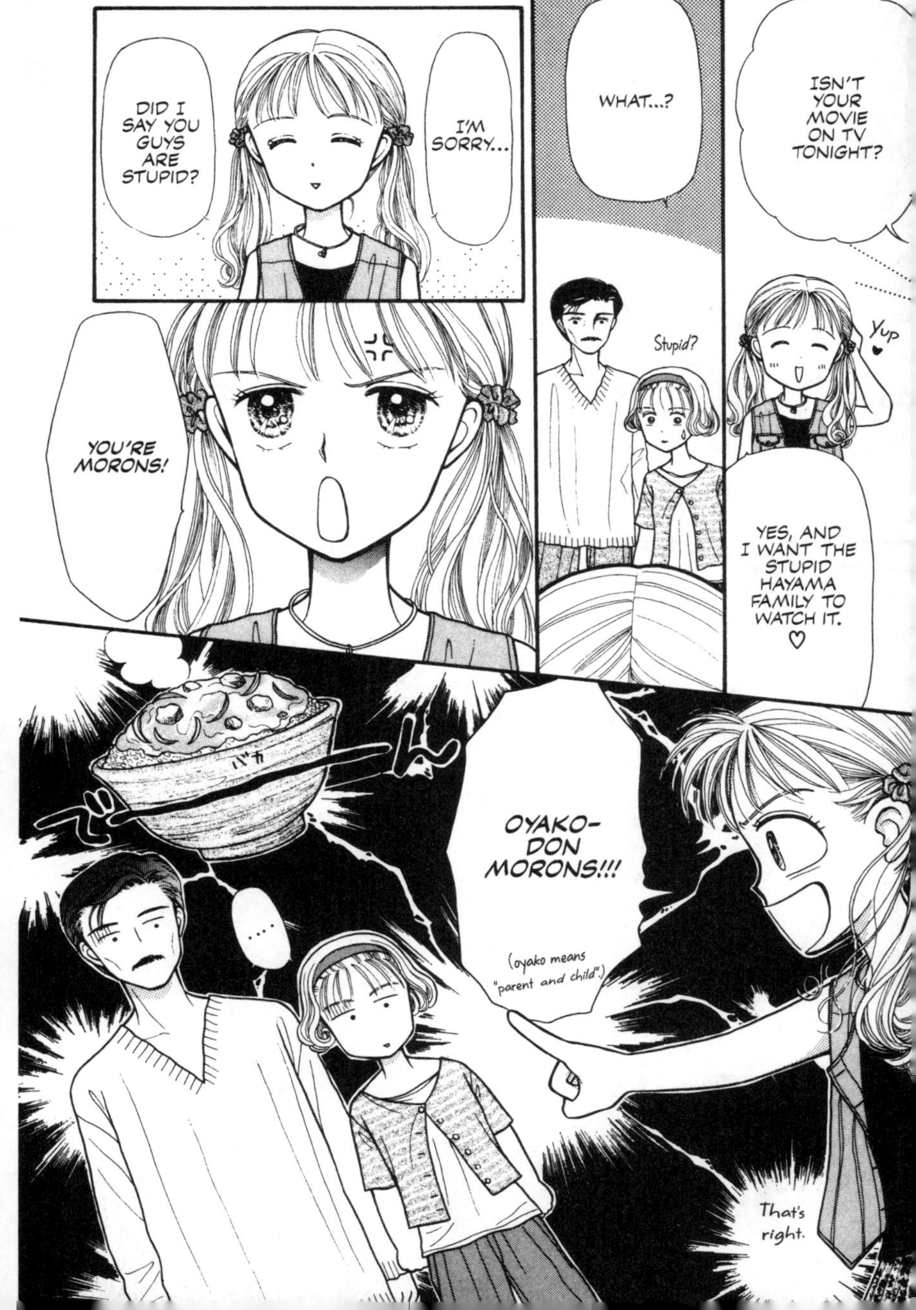

ISN'T YOUR MOVIE ON TV TONIGHT?
Yup ♥
YES, AND I WANT THE STUPID HAYAMA FAMILY TO WATCH IT. ♡
WHAT...?
Stupid?
I'M SORRY...
DID I SAY YOU GUYS ARE STUPID?
YOU'RE MORONS!
OYAKO-DON MORONS!!!
(oyako means "parent and child".)
バカ
...
That's right.

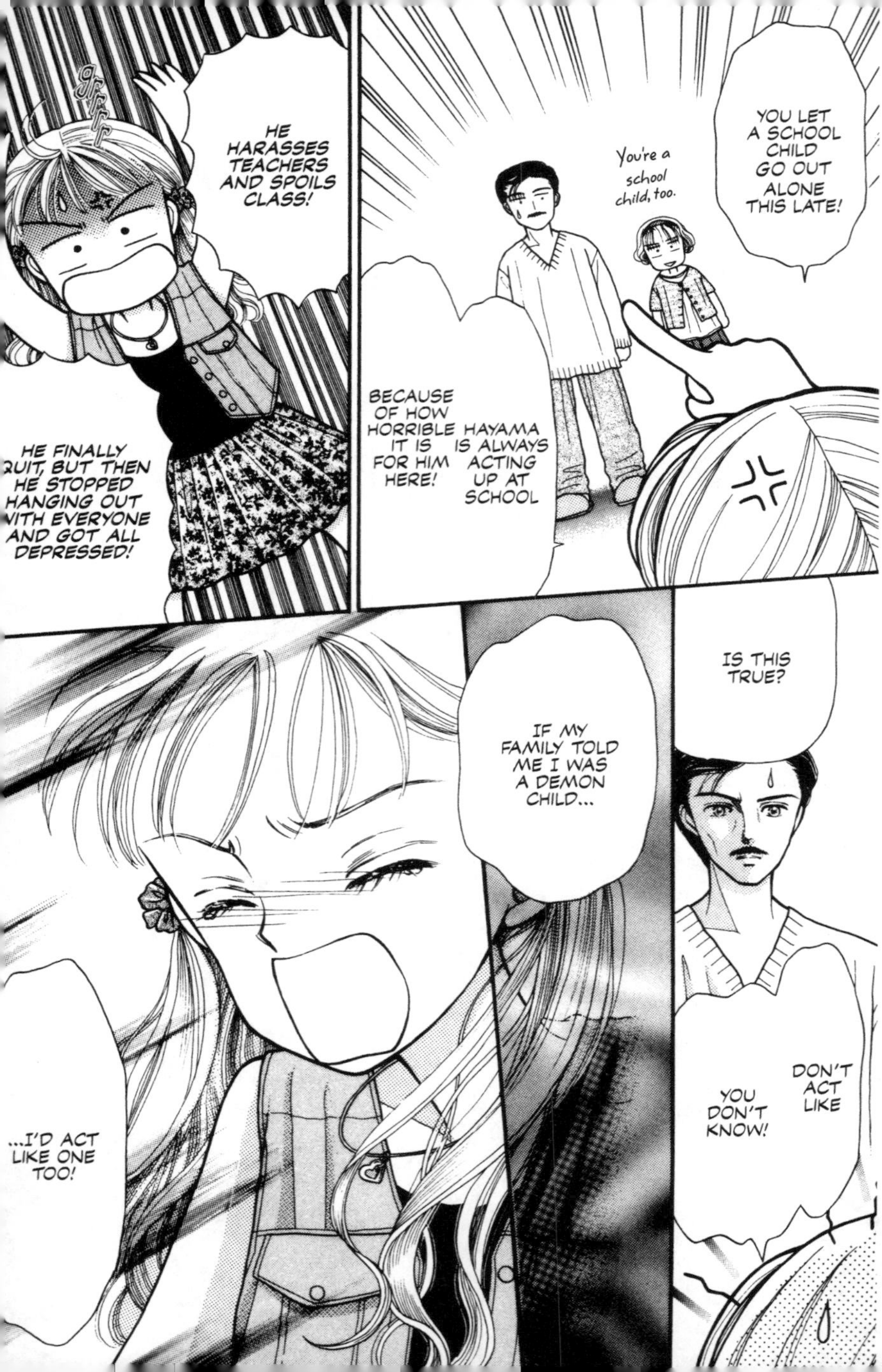
YOU LET A SCHOOL CHILD GO OUT ALONE THIS LATE!
You're a school child, too.
HAYAMA IS ALWAYS ACTING UP AT SCHOOL
BECAUSE OF HOW HORRIBLE IT IS FOR HIM HERE!
grrr
HE HARASSES TEACHERS AND SPOILS CLASS!
HE FINALLY QUIT, BUT THEN HE STOPPED HANGING OUT WITH EVERYONE AND GOT ALL DEPRESSED!
IS THIS TRUE?
DON'T ACT LIKE YOU DON'T KNOW!
IF MY FAMILY TOLD ME I WAS A DEMON CHILD...
...I'D ACT LIKE ONE TOO!

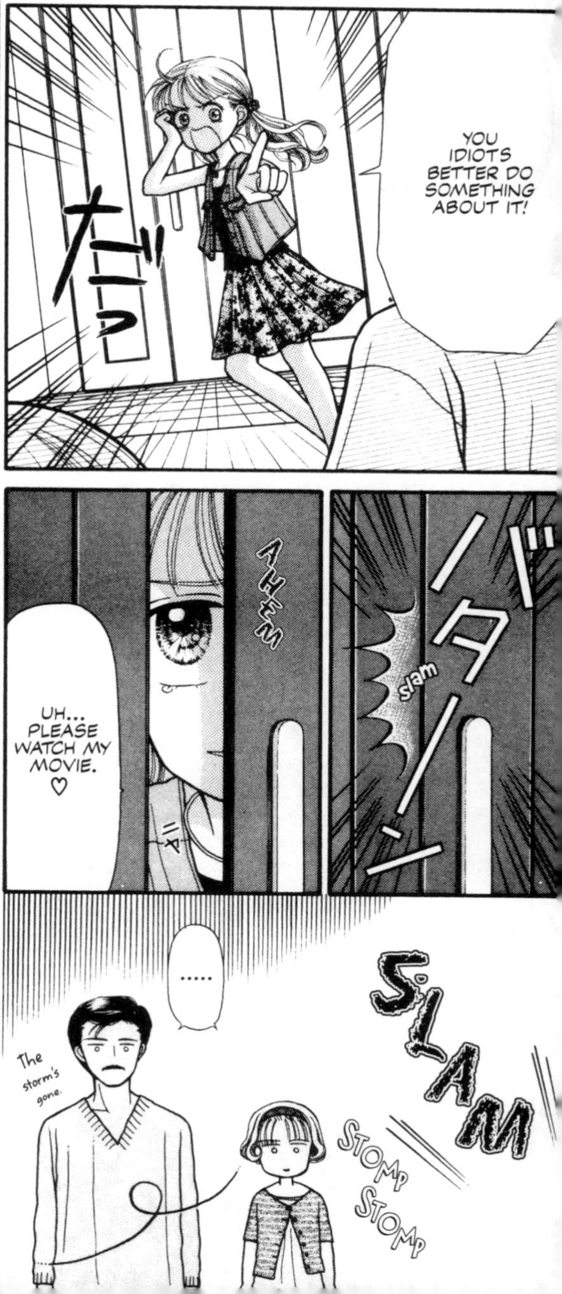
YOU IDIOTS BETTER DO SOMETHING ABOUT IT!
slam
AHEM
UH... PLEASE WATCH MY MOVIE. ♡
......
The storm's gone.
SLAM
STOMP STOMP

Information on Coming Kodocha

Because the story seems to be going so fast, many fans have been worried that the series will end soon. Hayama really settled down fast, didn't he? I'd like to make it to book 4, so I'm working on more story. And be warned -- I'm planning on a cult quiz for the last book. It's gonna be a really tough one; so tough only I would know all the answers! Hee-hee. So pay attention, guys! Tee-hee.

Also, the animated video of Kodocha will be released this summer (1995) in Japan. I'm going on a national tour for the premiere of the movie, just like a band touring for an album. I'll be making a lot of boyfriends here and there... No! Just kidding! Let me calm down. Uh... the video isn't finished yet, so check out book 2 for further info. And save up to buy it this summer, guys! Thanks!

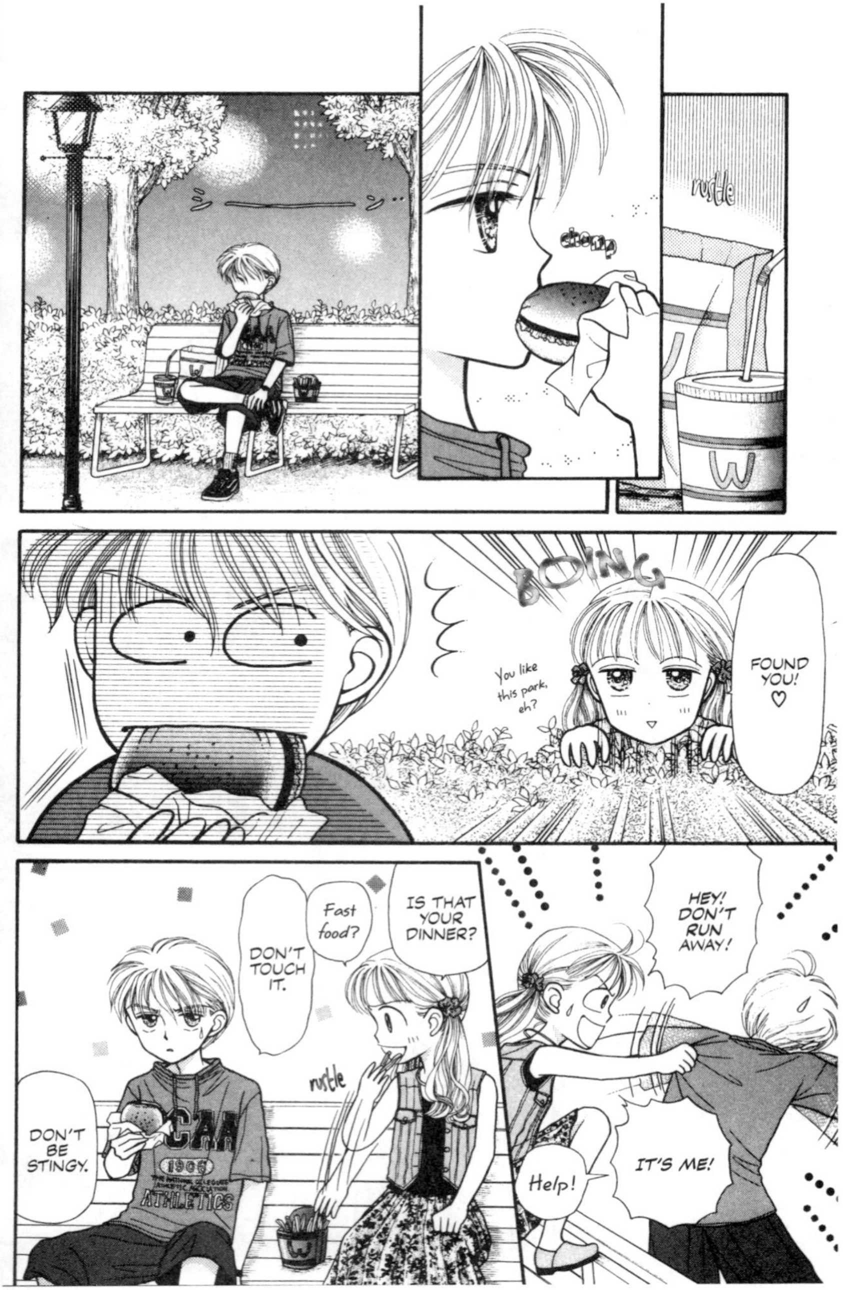

rustle
chomp
シ―――――ン‥
BOING
FOUND YOU! ♡
You like this park, eh?
HEY! DON'T RUN AWAY!
IT'S ME!
Help!
IS THAT YOUR DINNER?
Fast food?
DON'T TOUCH IT.
rustle
DON'T BE STINGY.

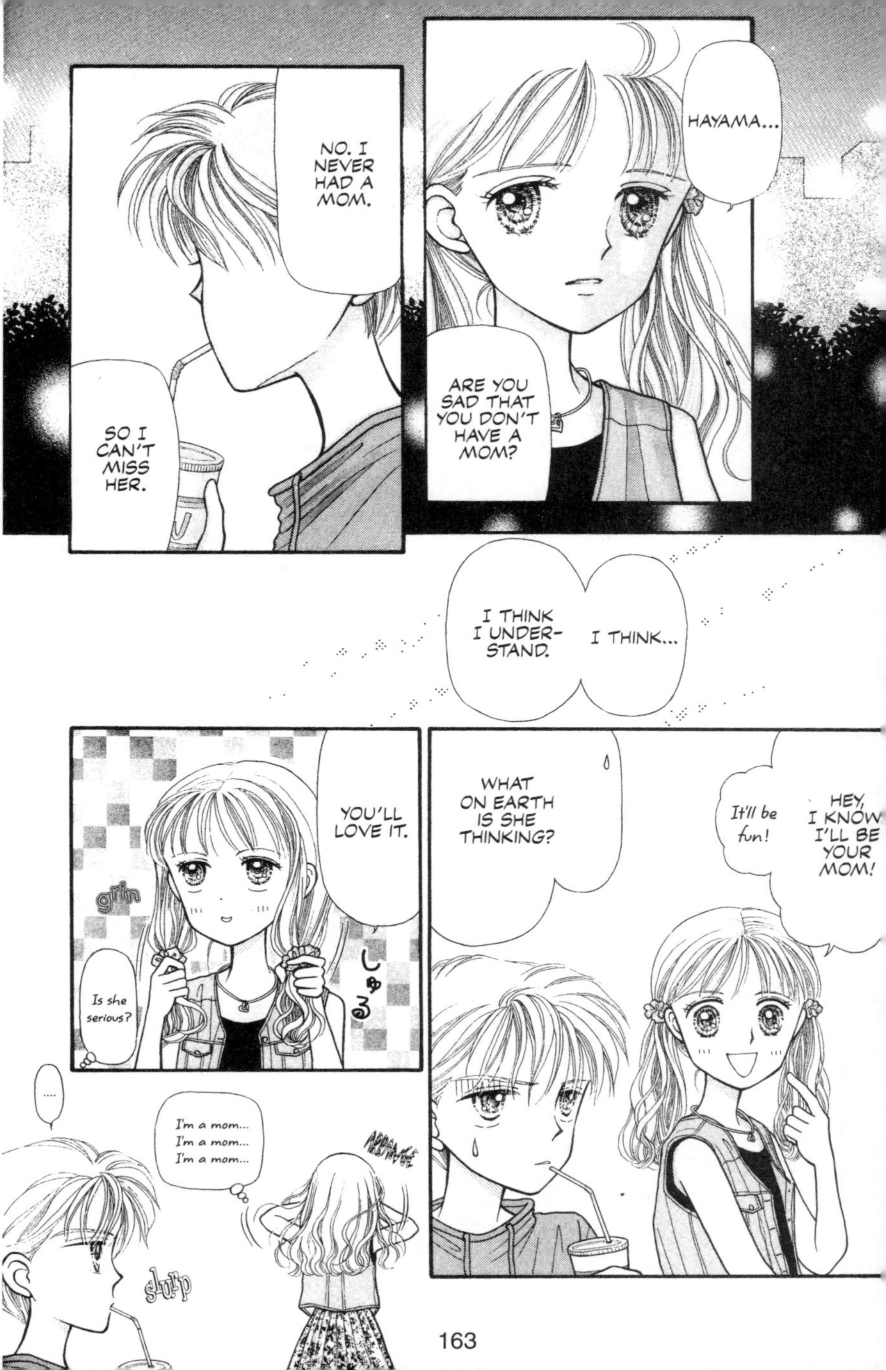
HAYAMA...
ARE YOU SAD THAT YOU DON'T HAVE A MOM?
NO. I NEVER HAD A MOM.
SO I CAN'T MISS HER.
I THINK...
I THINK I UNDERSTAND.
HEY, I KNOW I'LL BE YOUR MOM!
It'll be fun!
WHAT ON EARTH IS SHE THINKING?
YOU'LL LOVE IT.
grin
しゅる
Is she serious?
ARRANGE
I'm a mom... I'm a mom... I'm a mom...
....
slurp

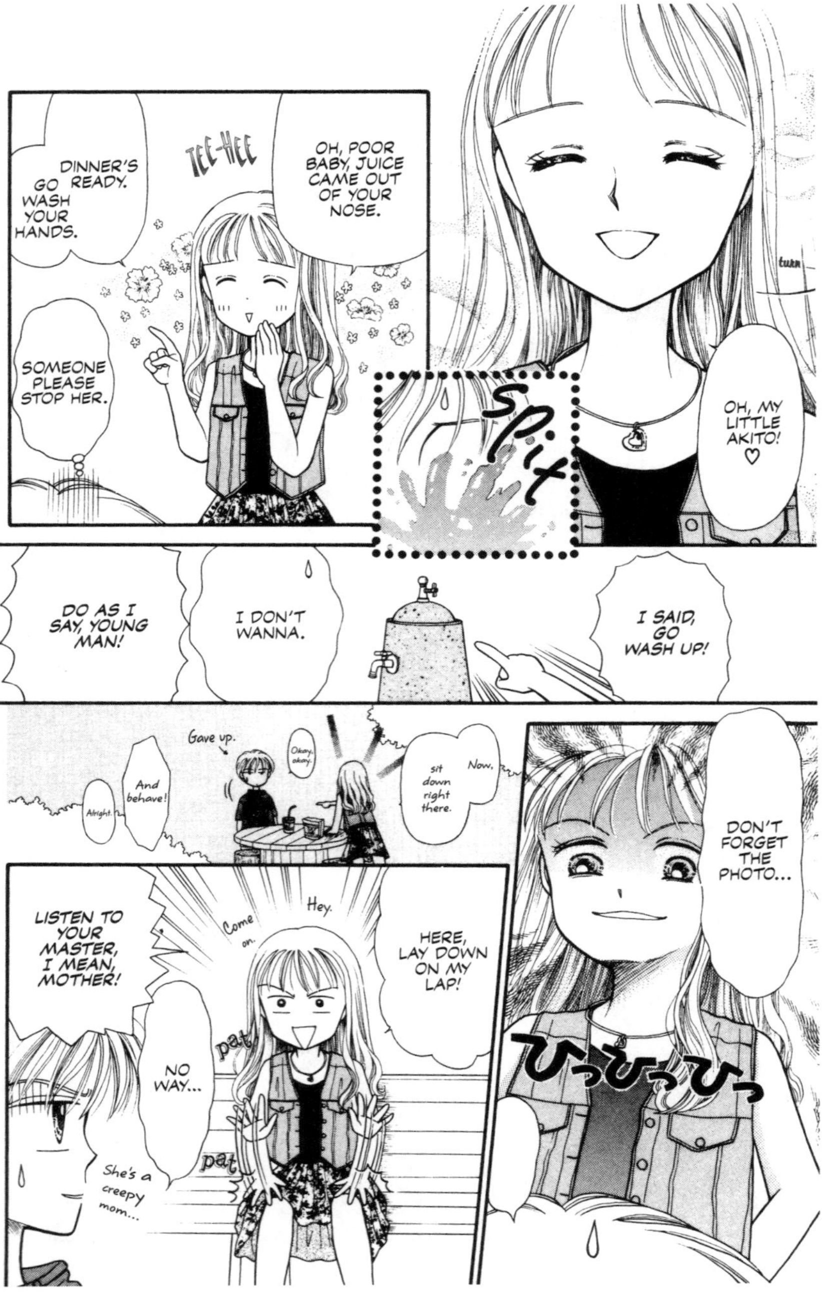
turn
OH, MY LITTLE AKITO! ♡
spit
OH, POOR BABY, JUICE CAME OUT OF YOUR NOSE.
TEE-HEE
DINNER'S READY. GO WASH YOUR HANDS.
SOMEONE PLEASE STOP HER.
I SAID, GO WASH UP!
I DON'T WANNA.
DO AS I SAY, YOUNG MAN!
DON'T FORGET THE PHOTO...
ひっひっひっ
Now, sit down right there.
Okay, okay.
Gave up.
And behave!
Alright.
HERE, LAY DOWN ON MY LAP!
Hey.
Come on.
LISTEN TO YOUR MASTER, I MEAN, MOTHER!
pat
pat
NO WAY...
She's a creepy mom...

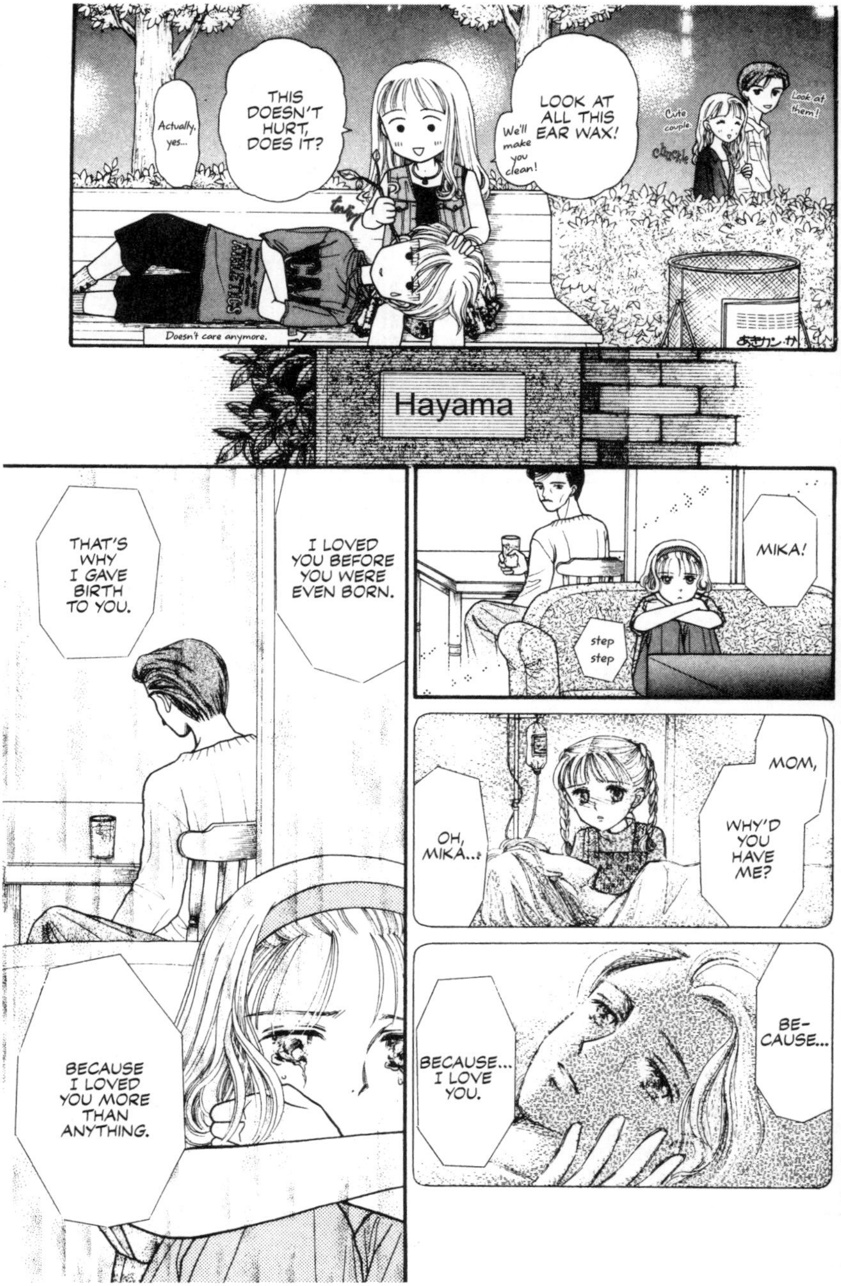
Look at them!
Cute couple.
chuckle
LOOK AT ALL THIS EAR WAX!
We'll make you clean!
THIS DOESN'T HURT, DOES IT?
Actually, yes...
Doesn't care anymore.
Hayama
MIKA!
step step
MOM,
WHY'D YOU HAVE ME?
OH, MIKA...
BE-CAUSE...
BECAUSE... I LOVE YOU.
I LOVED YOU BEFORE YOU WERE EVEN BORN.
THAT'S WHY I GAVE BIRTH TO YOU.
BECAUSE I LOVED YOU MORE THAN ANYTHING.

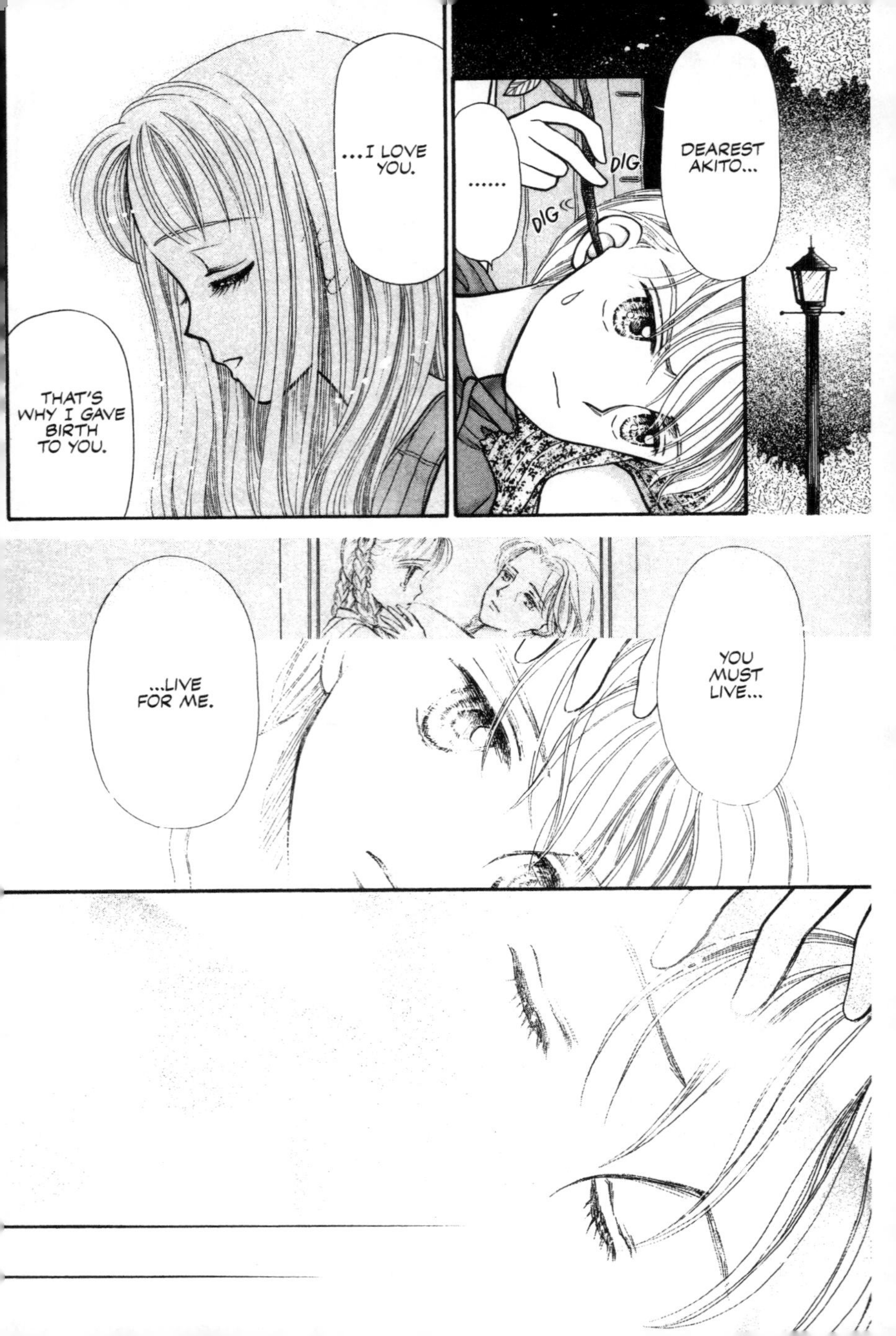
DEAREST AKITO...
DIG
DIG
......
...I LOVE YOU.
THAT'S WHY I GAVE BIRTH TO YOU.
YOU MUST LIVE...
...LIVE FOR ME.

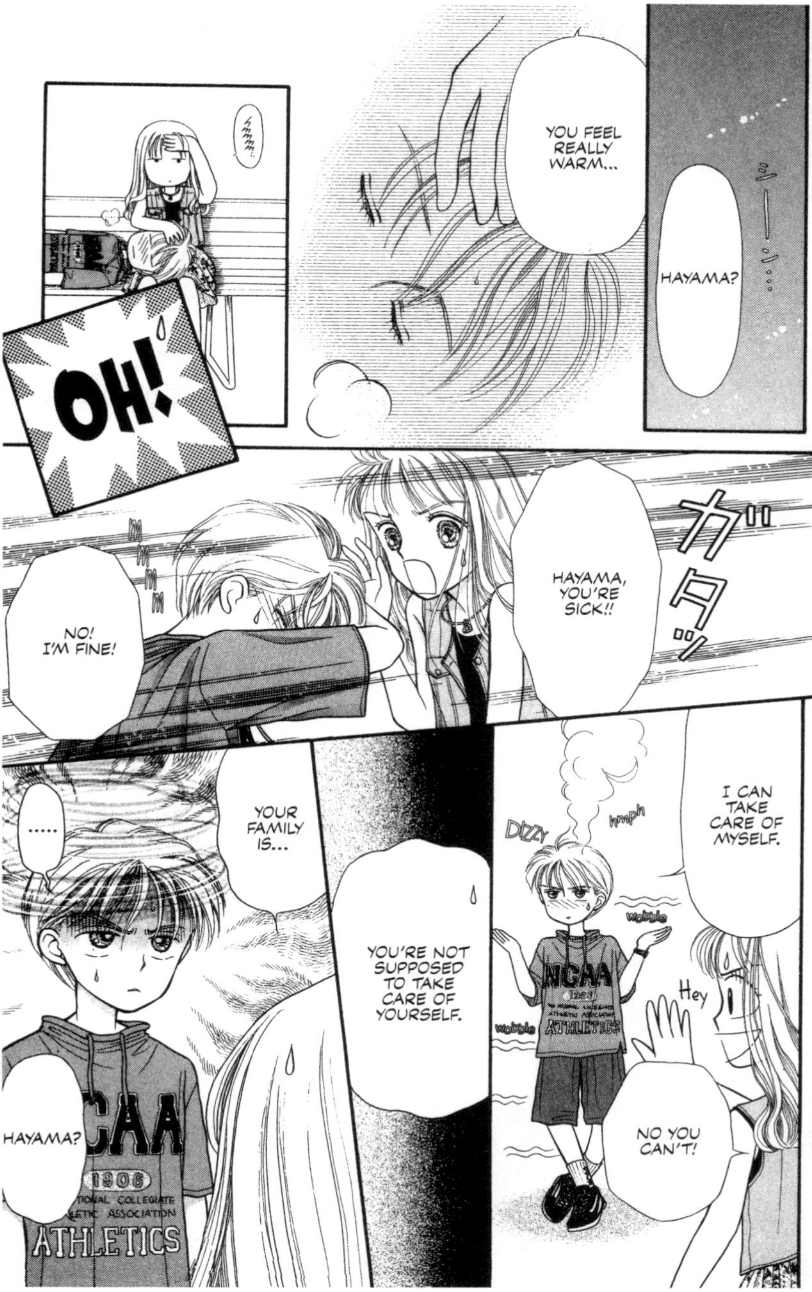
HAYAMA?
シーーン…
YOU FEEL REALLY WARM...
OH!
HAYAMA, YOU'RE SICK!!
ガタッ
NO! I'M FINE!
mmmm
I CAN TAKE CARE OF MYSELF.
DIZZY
hmph
wobble
wobble
Hey
NO YOU CAN'T!
YOUR FAMILY IS...
YOU'RE NOT SUPPOSED TO TAKE CARE OF YOURSELF.
.....
HAYAMA?

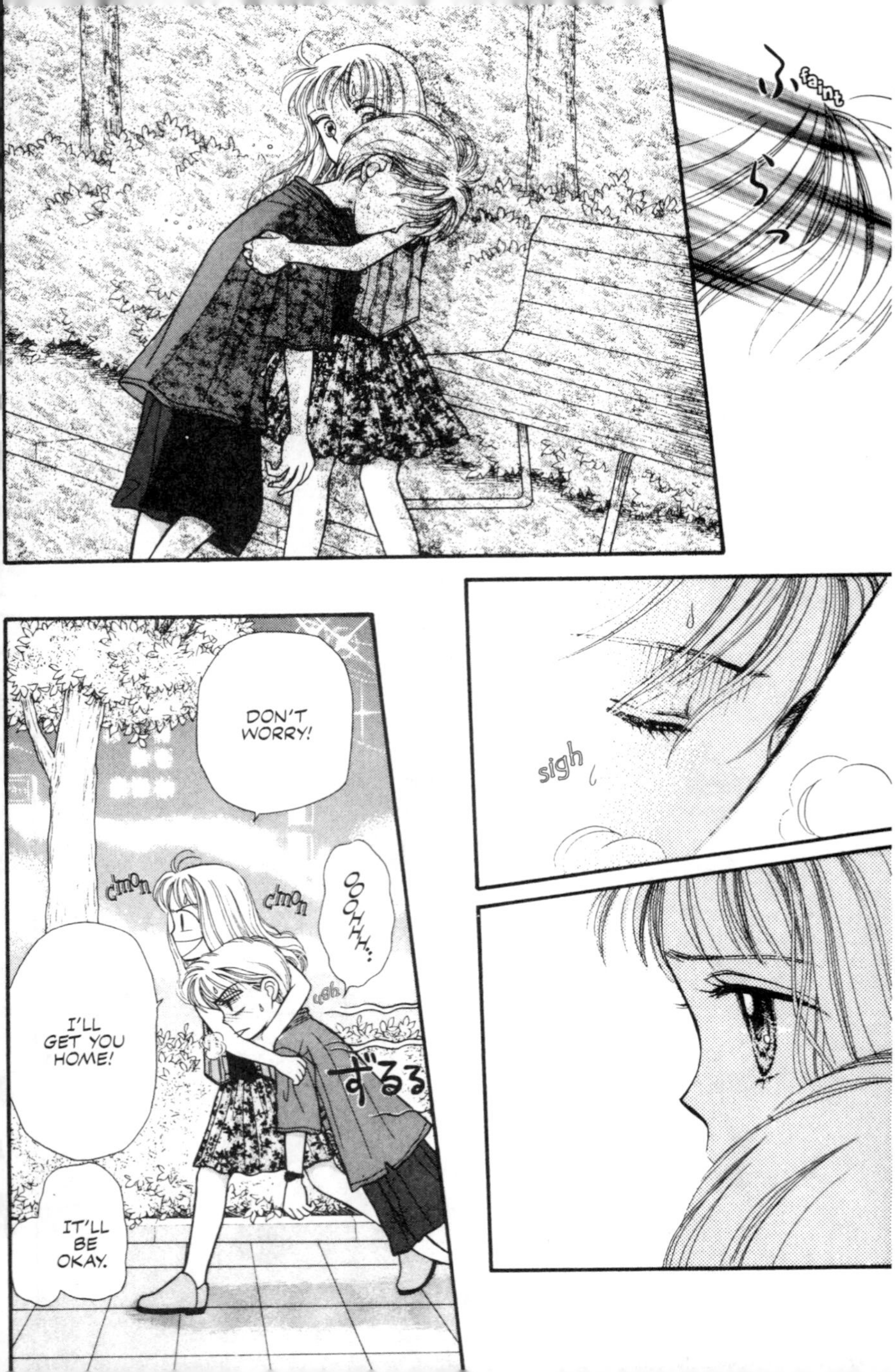
ふらっ
faint
sigh
DON'T WORRY!
OOOHHH...
c'mon
c'mon
ugh
ずるる
I'LL GET YOU HOME!
IT'LL BE OKAY.

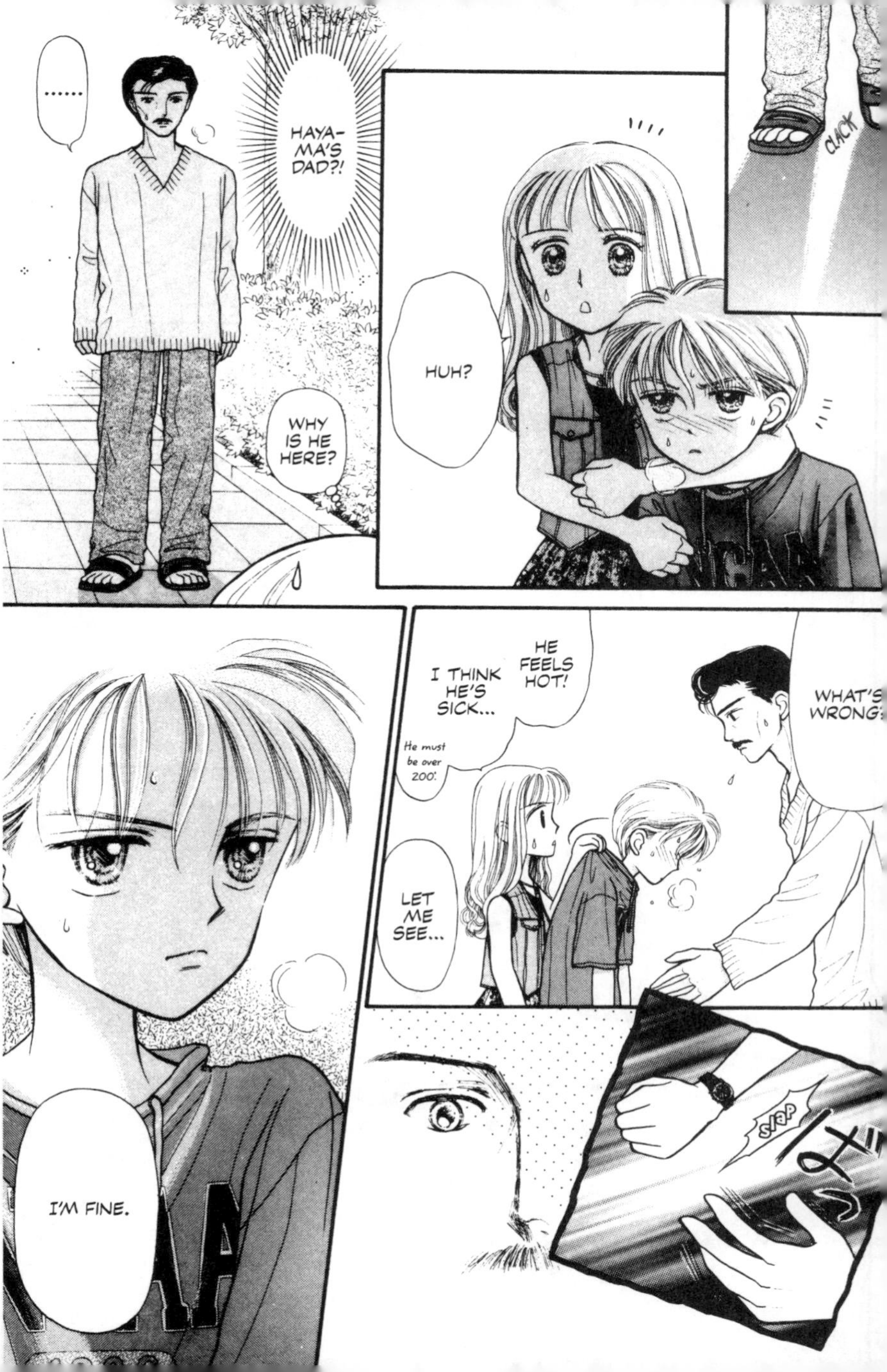
CLACK
HUH?
HAYA-MA'S DAD?!
....
WHY IS HE HERE?
WHAT'S WRONG?
HE FEELS HOT!
I THINK HE'S SICK...
He must be over 200°.
LET ME SEE...
slap
I'M FINE.

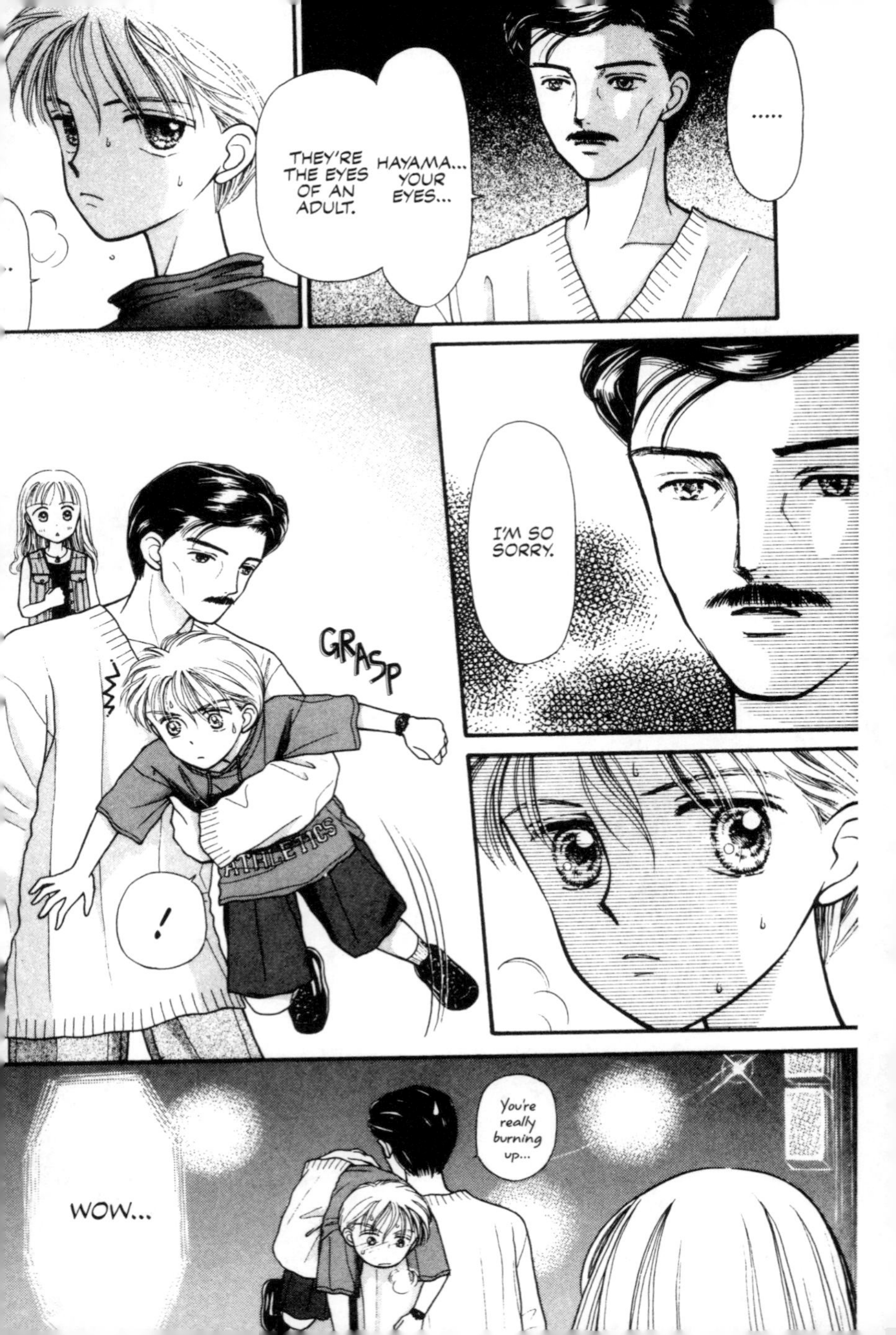
.....
HAYAMA... YOUR EYES...
THEY'RE THE EYES OF AN ADULT.
I'M SO SORRY.
GRASP
!
You're really burning up...
WOW...

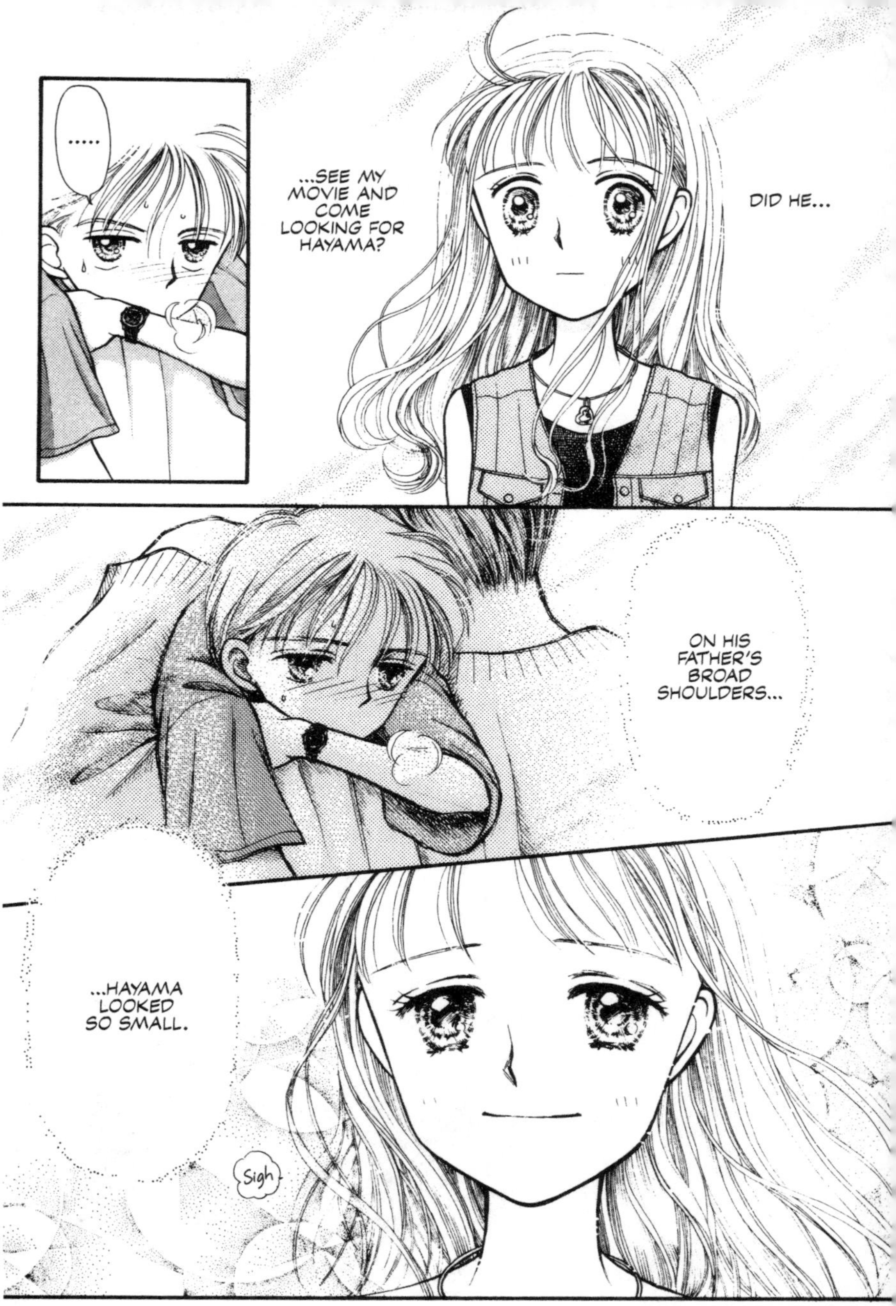
DID HE...
...SEE MY MOVIE AND COME LOOKING FOR HAYAMA?
......
ON HIS FATHER'S BROAD SHOULDERS...
...HAYAMA LOOKED SO SMALL.
Sigh

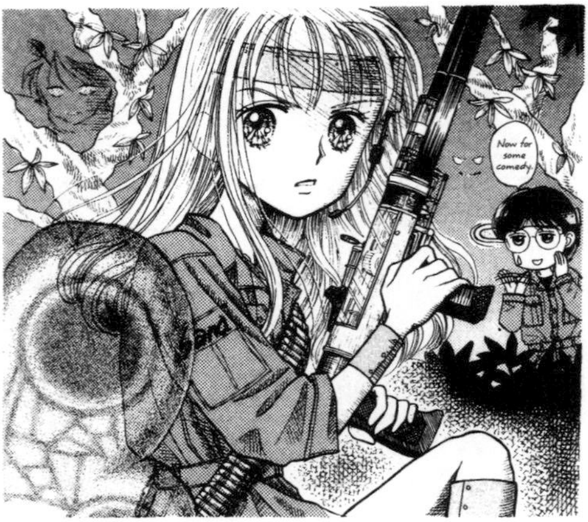
Now for some comedy.

CHILD'S TOY EXTRA: DESTROY THE HAYAMA MONSTER!

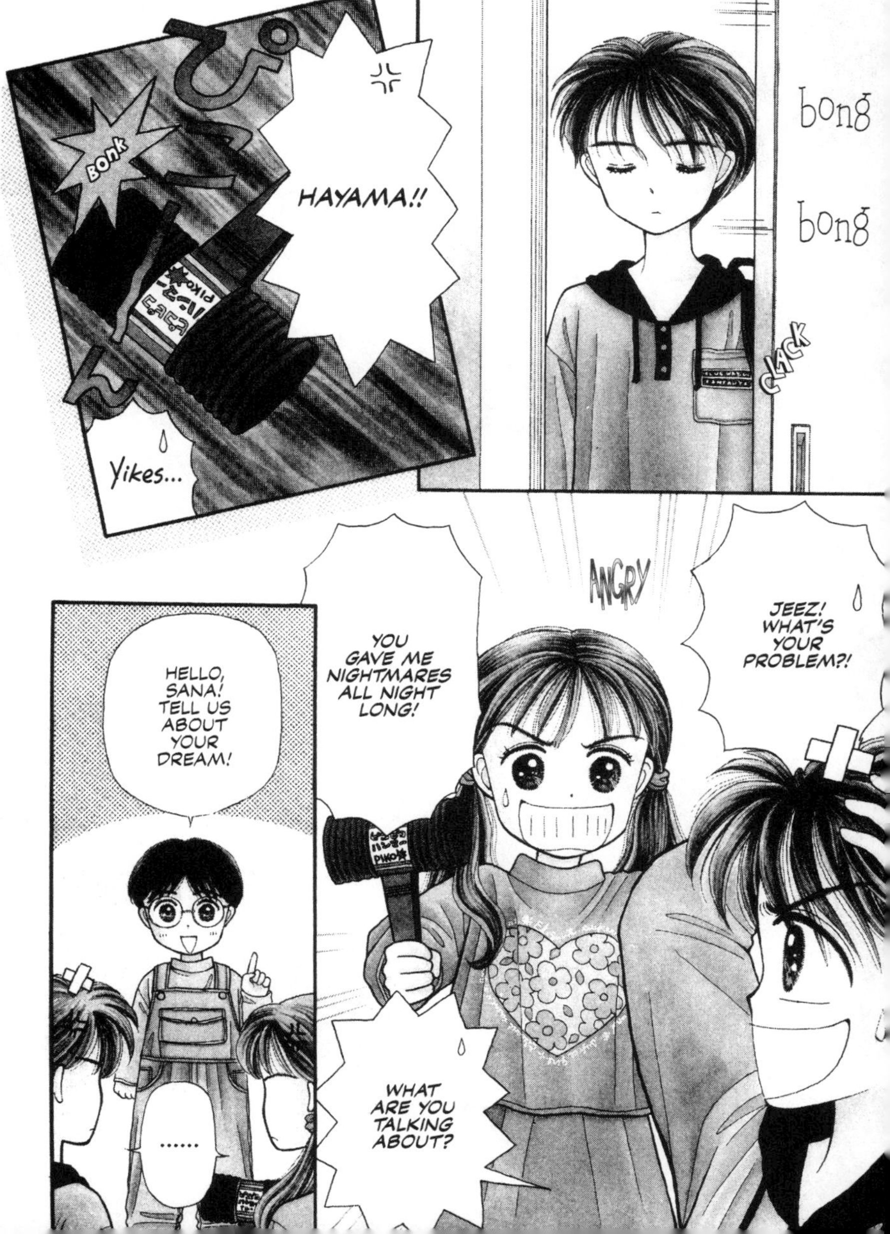

bong
bong
CLACK
HAYAMA!!
BONK
Yikes...
JEEZ! WHAT'S YOUR PROBLEM?!
ANGRY
YOU GAVE ME NIGHTMARES ALL NIGHT LONG!
WHAT ARE YOU TALKING ABOUT?
HELLO, SANA! TELL US ABOUT YOUR DREAM!
......

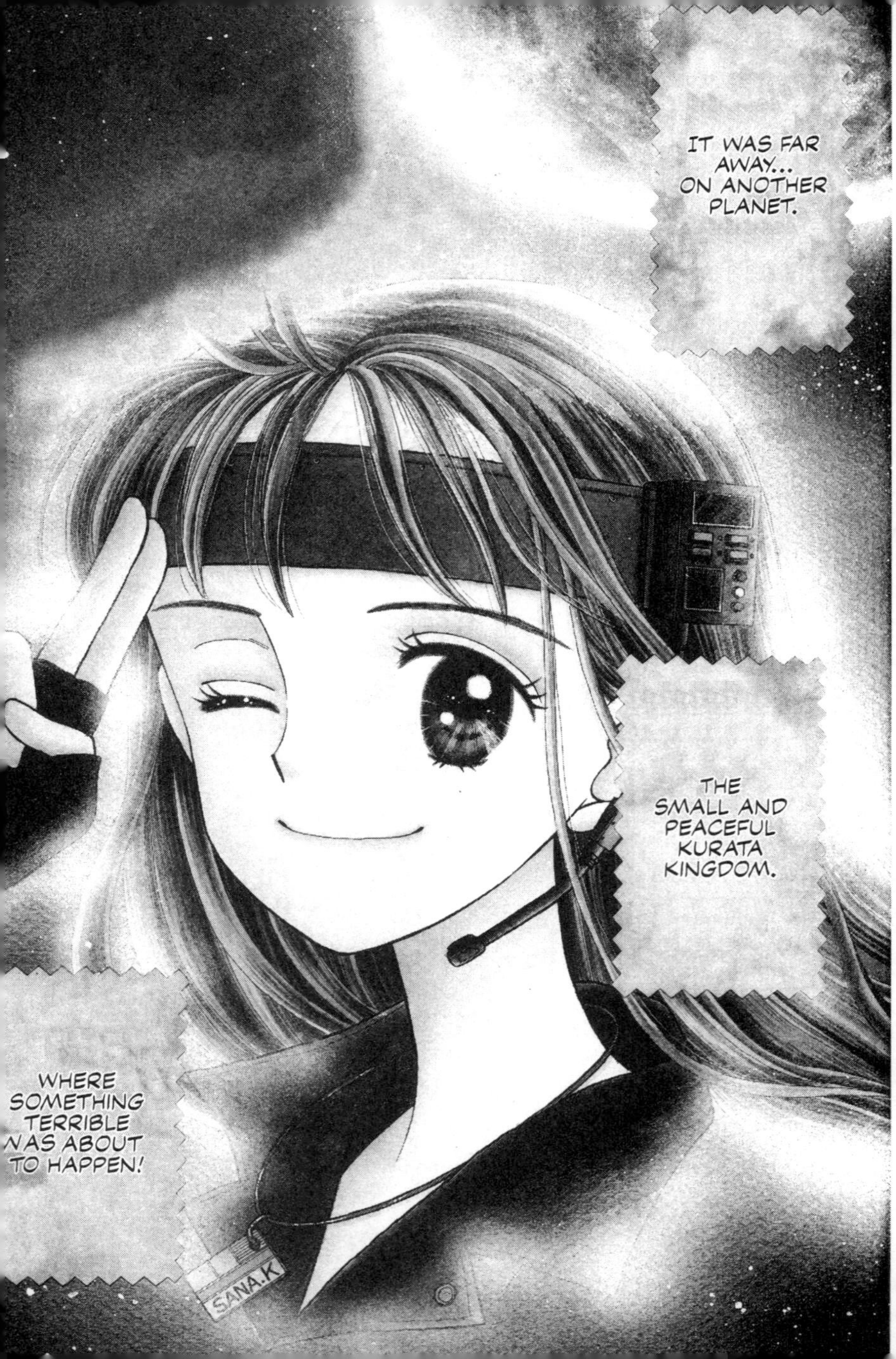
IT WAS FAR AWAY... ON ANOTHER PLANET.
THE SMALL AND PEACEFUL KURATA KINGDOM.
WHERE SOMETHING TERRIBLE WAS ABOUT TO HAPPEN!
SANA.K

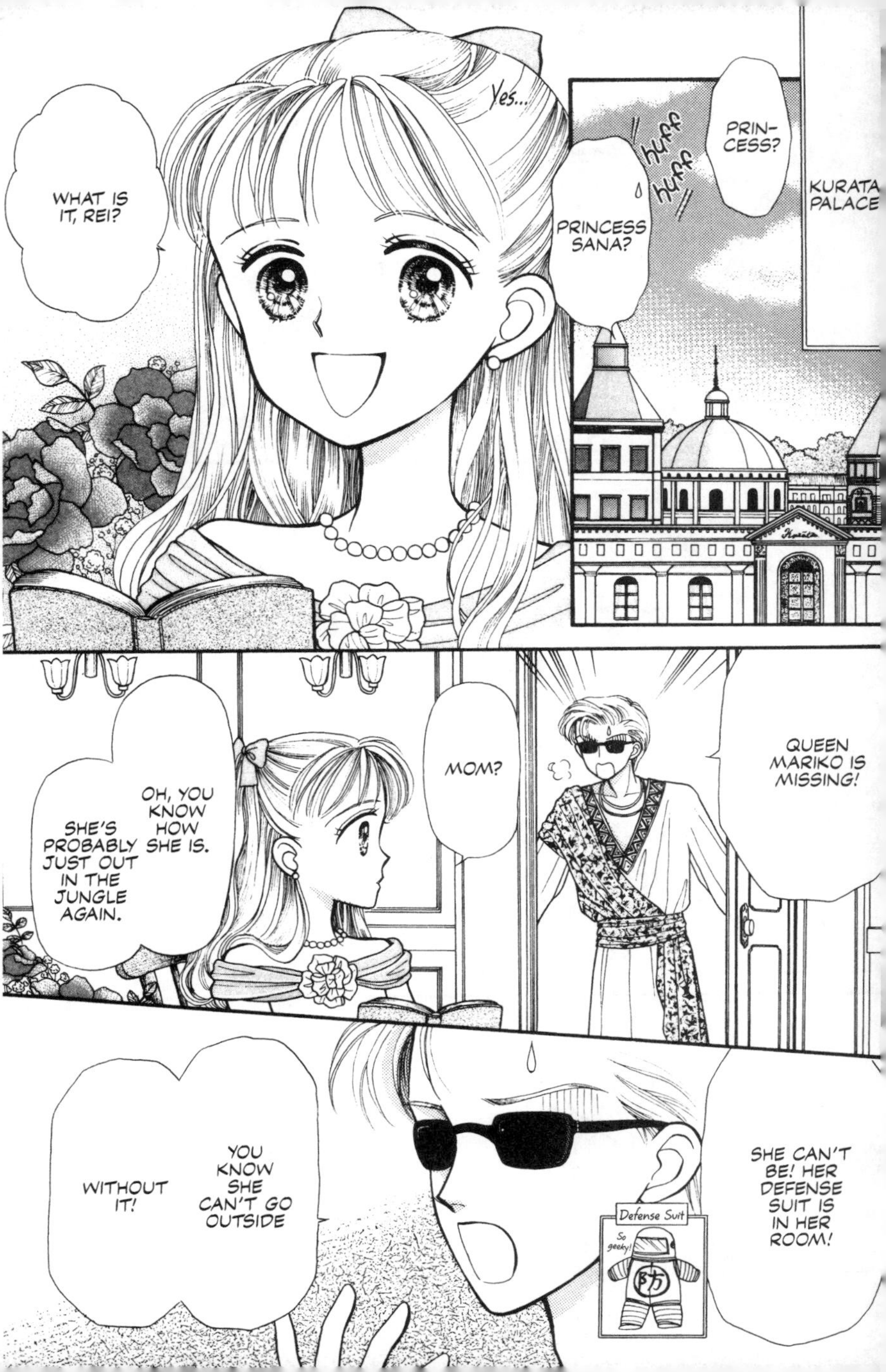
KURATA PALACE
PRIN-CESS?
huff huff
PRINCESS SANA?
Yes...
WHAT IS IT, REI?
QUEEN MARIKO IS MISSING!
MOM?
OH, YOU KNOW HOW SHE IS.
SHE'S PROBABLY JUST OUT IN THE JUNGLE AGAIN.
SHE CAN'T BE! HER DEFENSE SUIT IS IN HER ROOM!
Defense Suit
So geeky!
YOU KNOW SHE CAN'T GO OUTSIDE
WITHOUT IT!

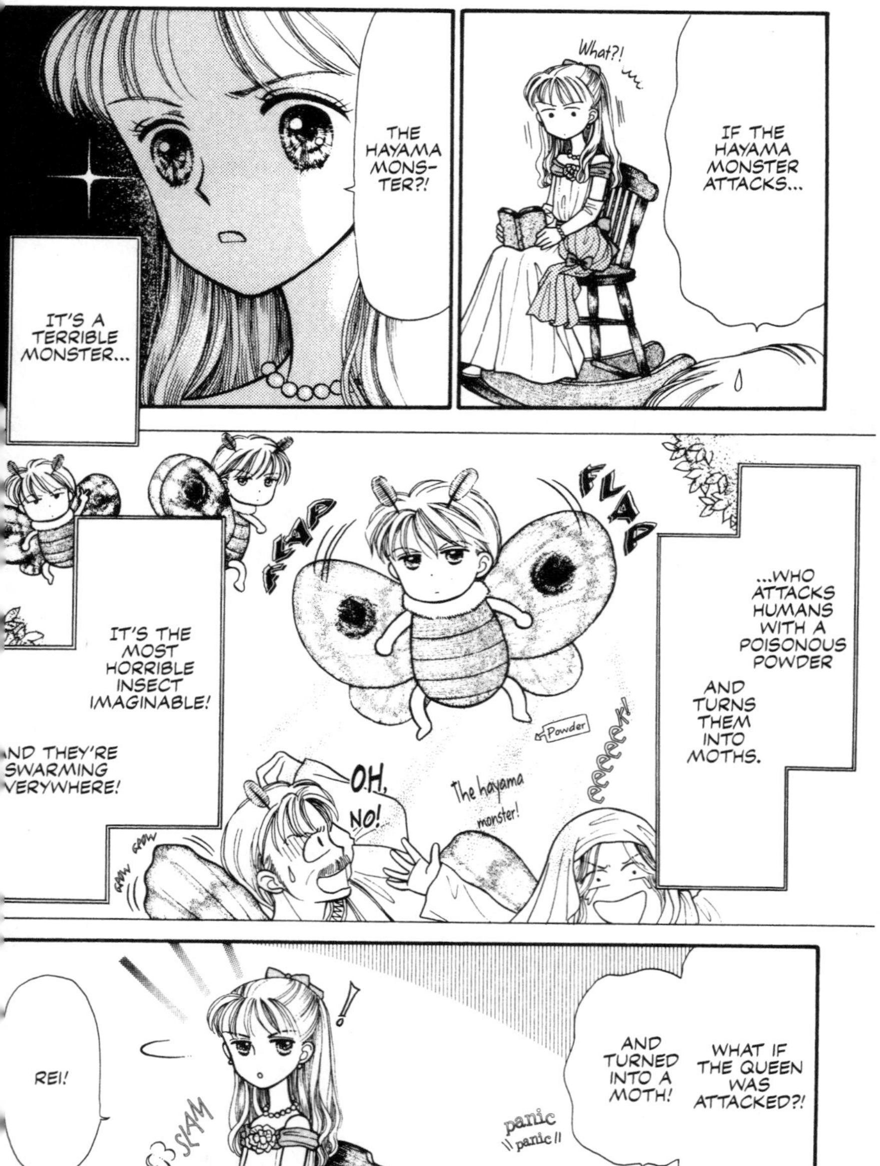
What?!
IF THE HAYAMA MONSTER ATTACKS...
THE HAYAMA MONSTER?!
IT'S A TERRIBLE MONSTER...
...WHO ATTACKS HUMANS WITH A POISONOUS POWDER
AND TURNS THEM INTO MOTHS.
FLAP
FLAP
Powder
eeeeek!
The hayama monster!
OH, NO!
GROW GROW
IT'S THE MOST HORRIBLE INSECT IMAGINABLE!
ND THEY'RE SWARMING VERYWHERE!
WHAT IF THE QUEEN WAS ATTACKED?!
AND TURNED INTO A MOTH!
panic panic
!
SLAM
REI!

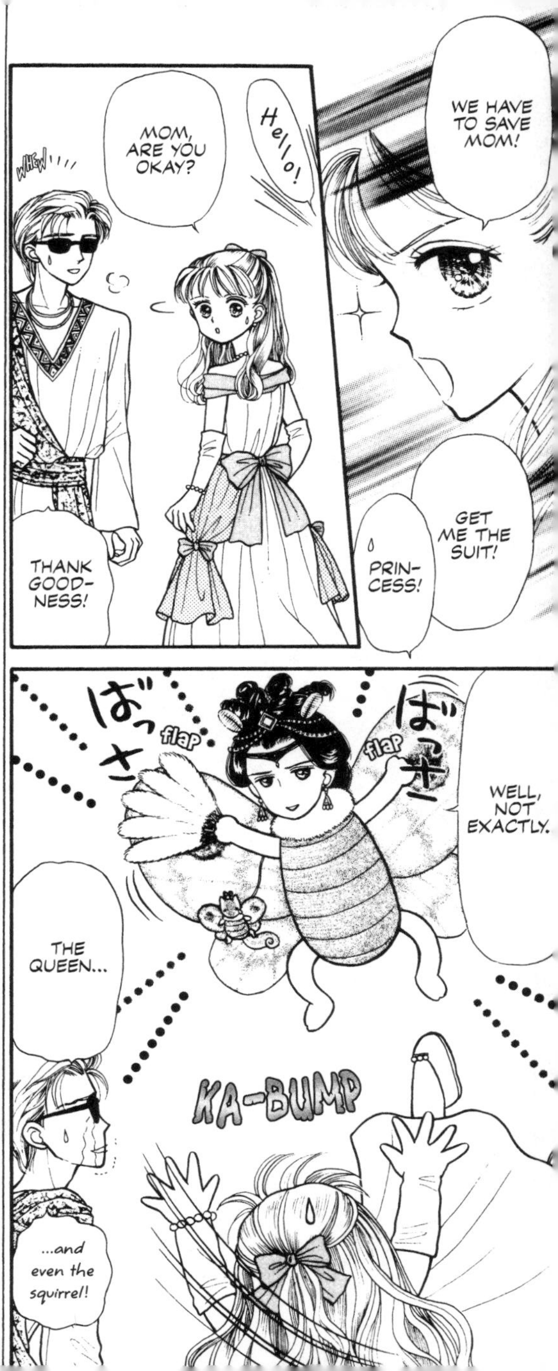
WE HAVE TO SAVE MOM!
GET ME THE SUIT!
PRIN-CESS!
Hello!
MOM, ARE YOU OKAY?
WHEW
THANK GOOD-NESS!
WELL, NOT EXACTLY.
flap
flap
THE QUEEN...
...and even the squirrel!
KA-BUMP

This Extra....is a parody of an awful nightmare I had when I was in junior high. It was about a bunch of moths attacking our school with some weird poisonous powder. I left my best friend, Y, behind and ran! It was a bad dream - but still! How could I?!

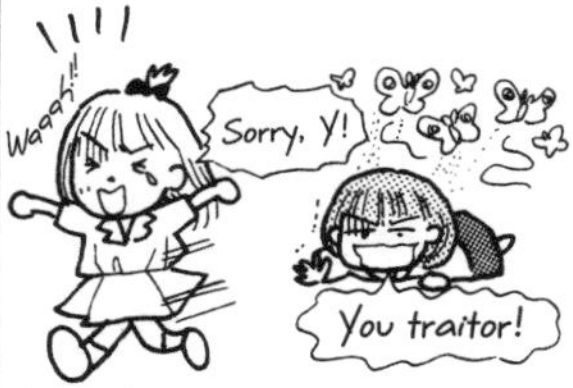
Waaah!!
Sorry, Y!
You traitor!

The Hayama Monster is the product of Sana's imagination, and I think it's a little happier than the real Hayama, don't you? For one thing, it laughs! Check it out! Anyway, this is the last of my incoherent babbling for this volume.

Thank you ♥♥♥♥♥

It was pretty incoherent, wasn't it? But I actually talk like this. You must be a nice person to have read this far!!♡ Thank you so much! And I hope you'll check out book 2.

Miho Obana.
'95. 2.

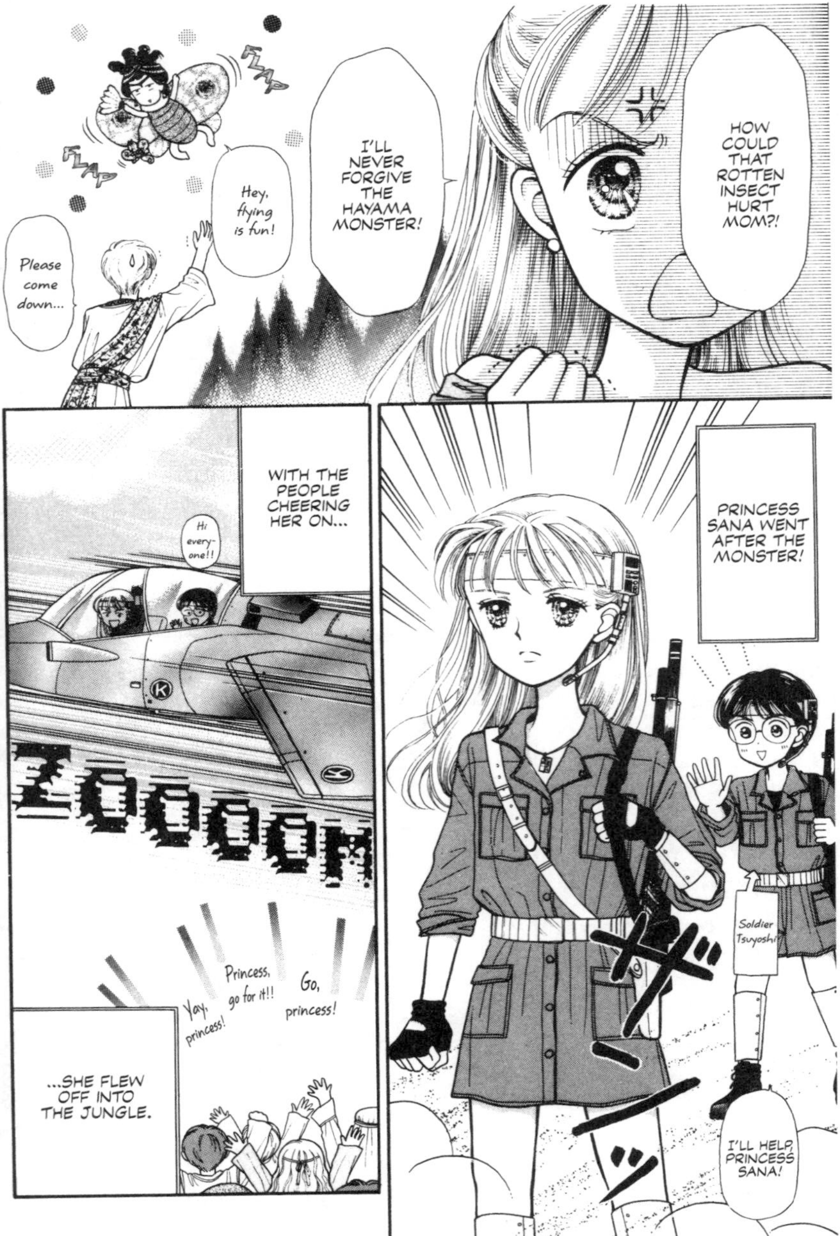
HOW COULD THAT ROTTEN INSECT HURT MOM?!
I'LL NEVER FORGIVE THE HAYAMA MONSTER!
FLAP
FLAP
Hey, flying is fun!
Please come down...
PRINCESS SANA WENT AFTER THE MONSTER!
Soldier Tsuyoshi
I'LL HELP, PRINCESS SANA!
WITH THE PEOPLE CHEERING HER ON...
Hi every-one!!
ZOOOOOM
Go, princess!
Princess, go for it!!
Yay, princess!
...SHE FLEW OFF INTO THE JUNGLE.

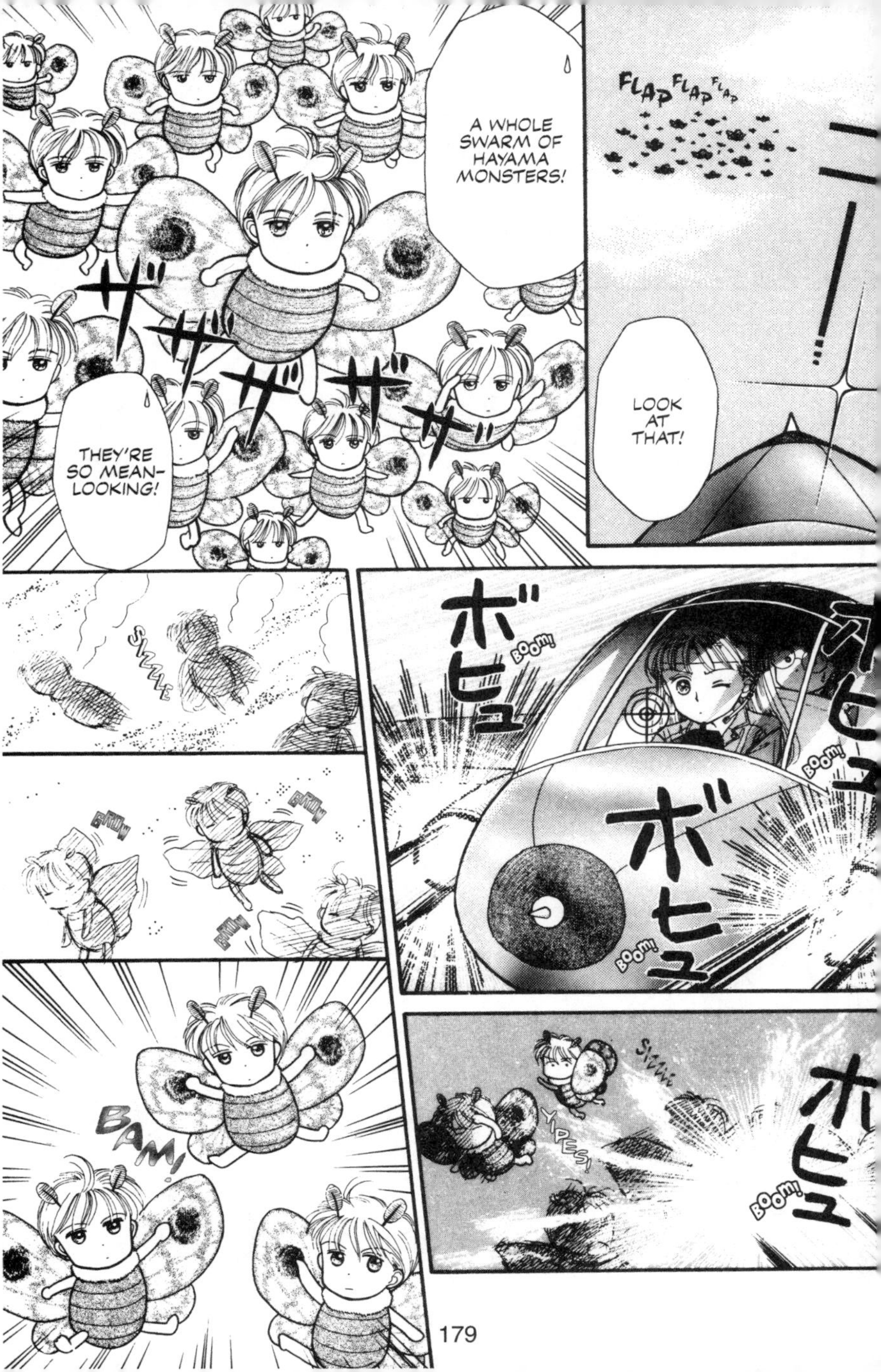
FLAP FLAP FLAP
LOOK AT THAT!
A WHOLE SWARM OF HAYAMA MONSTERS!
THEY'RE SO MEAN-LOOKING!
BOOM!
BOOM!
BOOM!
SIZZLE
SIZZLE
YIPES!
BOOM!
BAM!

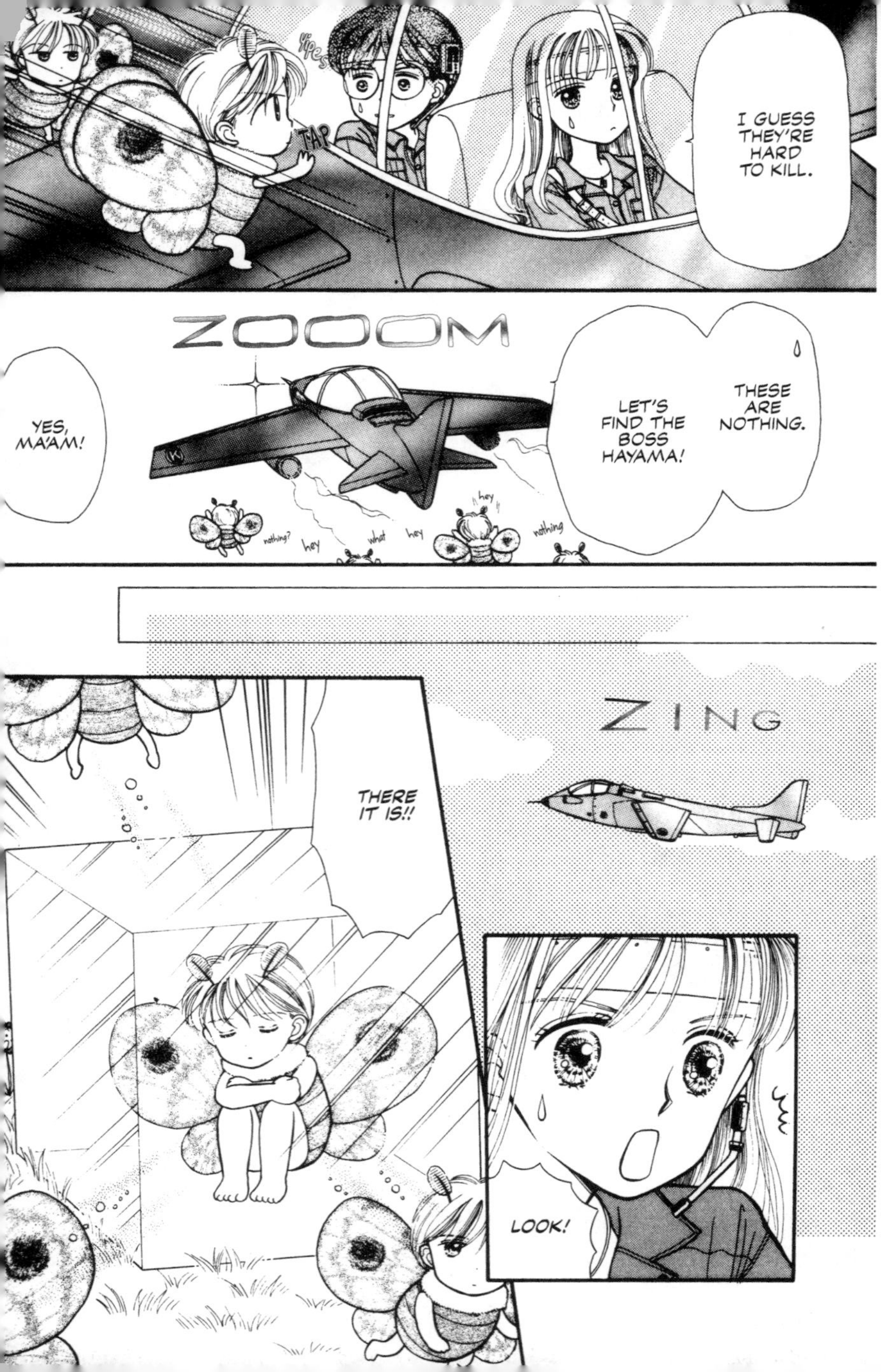

yipes
TAP
I GUESS THEY'RE HARD TO KILL.
THESE ARE NOTHING.
LET'S FIND THE BOSS HAYAMA!
ZOOOM
YES, MA'AM!
nothing
hey
hey
what
hey
nothing?
ZING
LOOK!
THERE IT IS!!

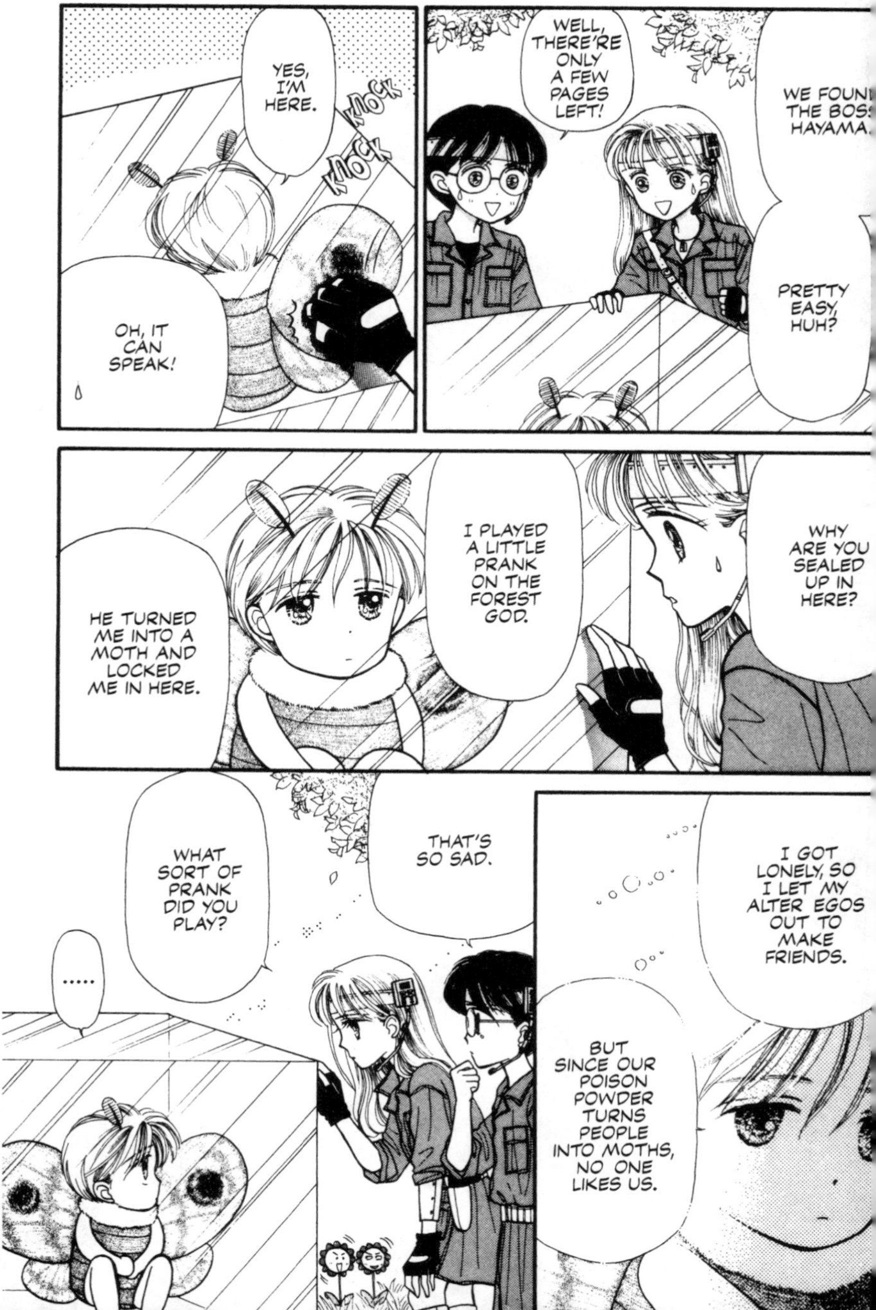
WE FOUND THE BOSS HAYAMA.
PRETTY EASY, HUH?
WELL, THERE'RE ONLY A FEW PAGES LEFT!
KNOCK
KNOCK
YES, I'M HERE.
OH, IT CAN SPEAK!
WHY ARE YOU SEALED UP IN HERE?
I PLAYED A LITTLE PRANK ON THE FOREST GOD.
HE TURNED ME INTO A MOTH AND LOCKED ME IN HERE.
I GOT LONELY, SO I LET MY ALTER EGOS OUT TO MAKE FRIENDS.
BUT SINCE OUR POISON POWDER TURNS PEOPLE INTO MOTHS, NO ONE LIKES US.
THAT'S SO SAD.
WHAT SORT OF PRANK DID YOU PLAY?
......

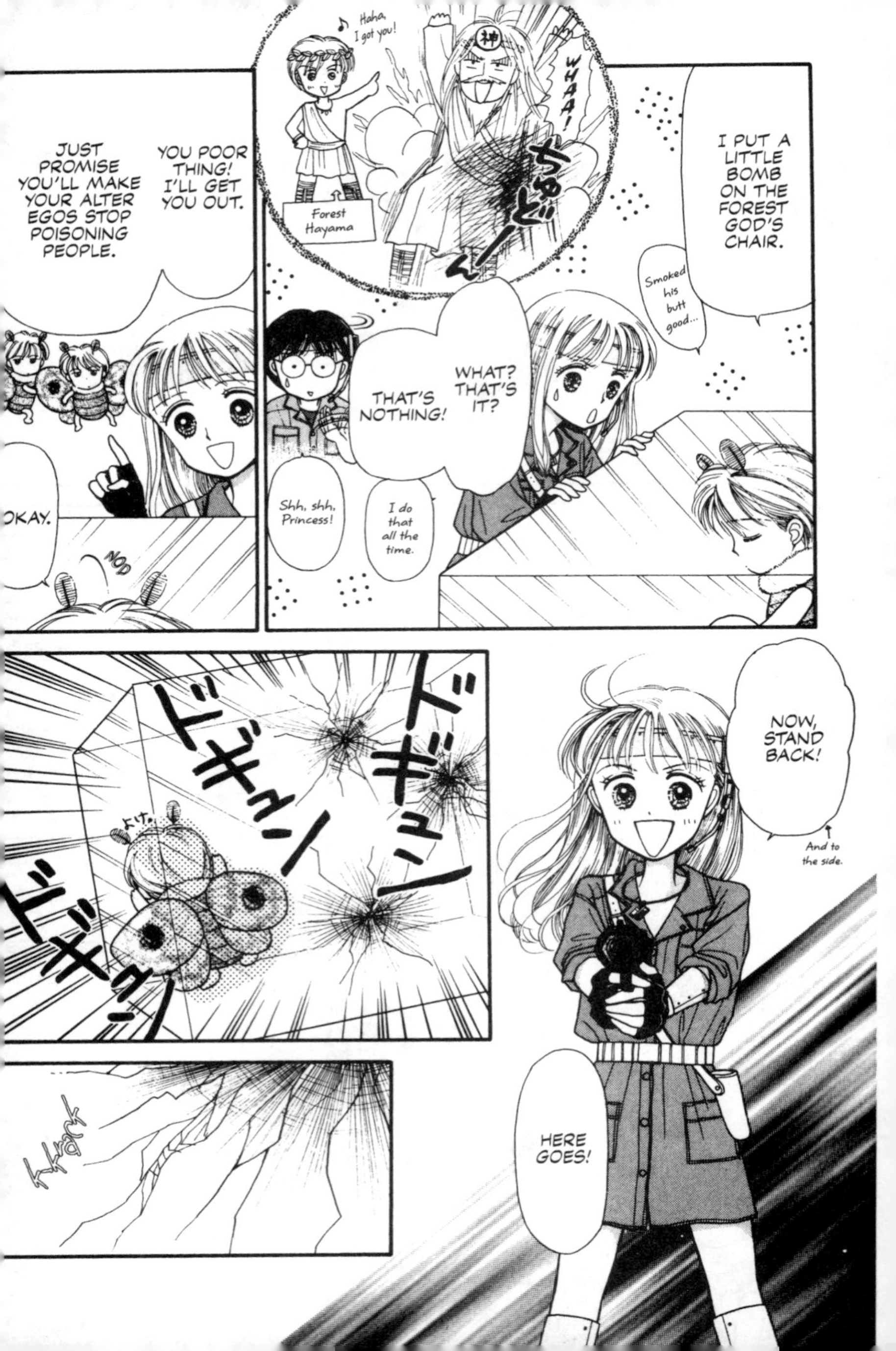
I PUT A LITTLE BOMB ON THE FOREST GOD'S CHAIR.
Smoked his butt good...
♪ Haha, I got you!
WHAAA!
ちゅどーん
Forest Hayama
WHAT? THAT'S IT?
THAT'S NOTHING!
Shh, shh, Princess!
I do that all the time.
YOU POOR THING! I'LL GET YOU OUT.
JUST PROMISE YOU'LL MAKE YOUR ALTER EGOS STOP POISONING PEOPLE.
OKAY.
NOD
NOW, STAND BACK!
And to the side.
HERE GOES!
ドギューン
ドギューン
ドギュ
よけ
kuh-krack

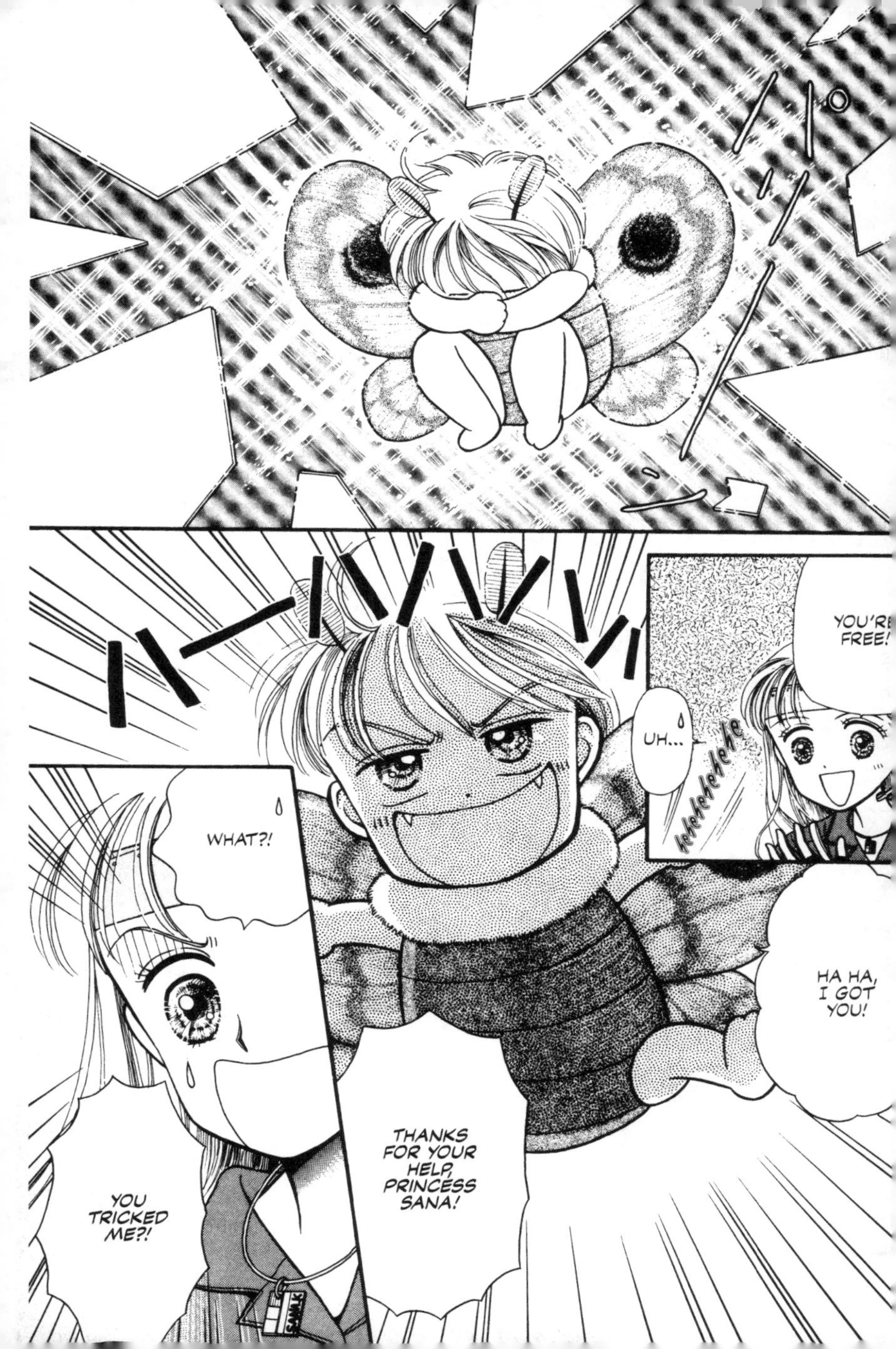

YOU'RE FREE!
UH...
hehehehehe
HA HA, I GOT YOU!
THANKS FOR YOUR HELP, PRINCESS SANA!
WHAT?!
YOU TRICKED ME?!

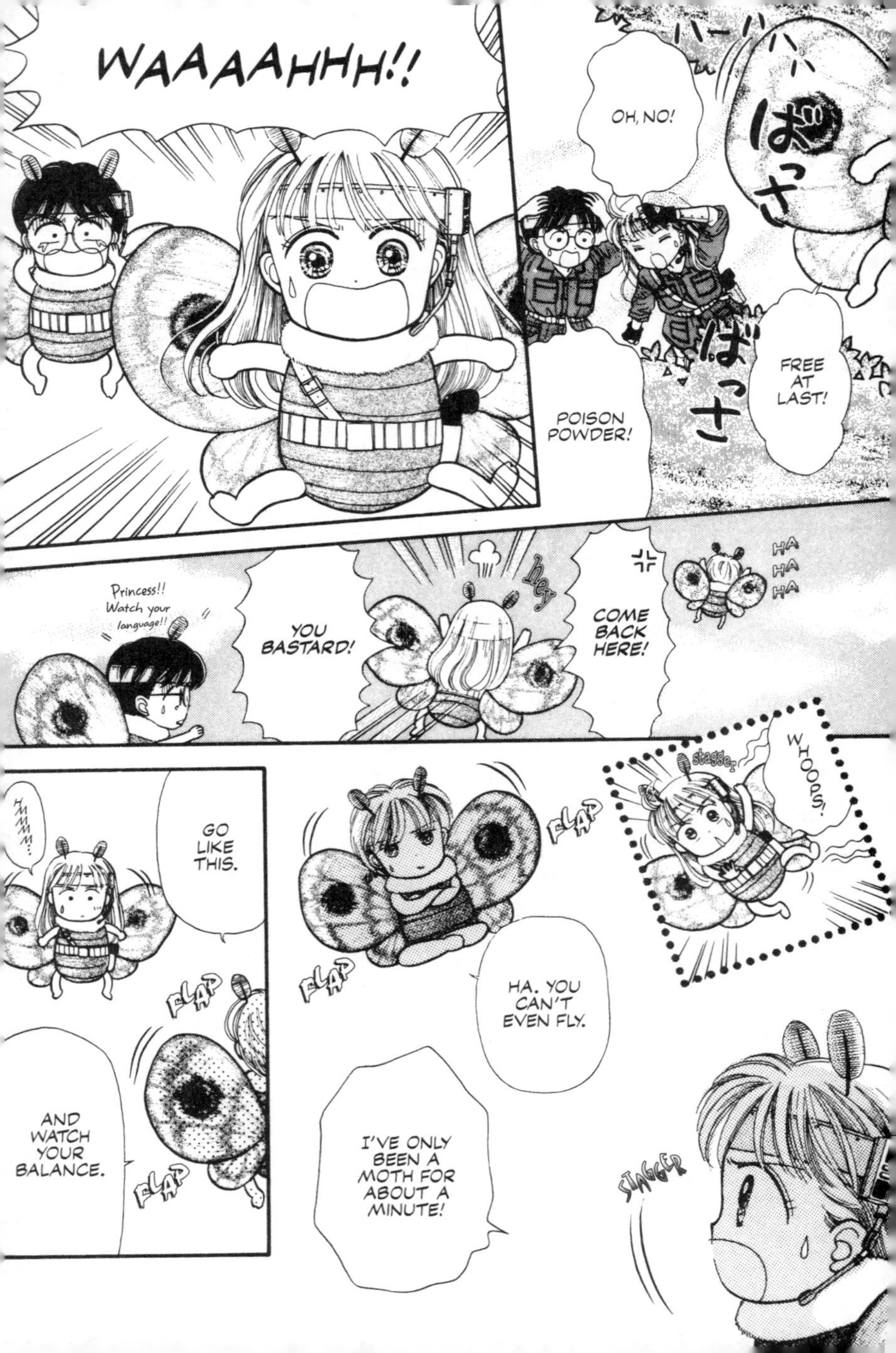

ばっさ
OH, NO!
FREE AT LAST!
ばっさ
POISON POWDER!
WAAAAHHH!!
HA HA HA
COME BACK HERE!
hey
YOU BASTARD!
Princess!! Watch your language!!
WHOOPS!
stagger
FLAP
HA. YOU CAN'T EVEN FLY.
FLAP
I'VE ONLY BEEN A MOTH FOR ABOUT A MINUTE!
STAGGER
GO LIKE THIS.
HMMM...
FLAP
AND WATCH YOUR BALANCE.
FLAP

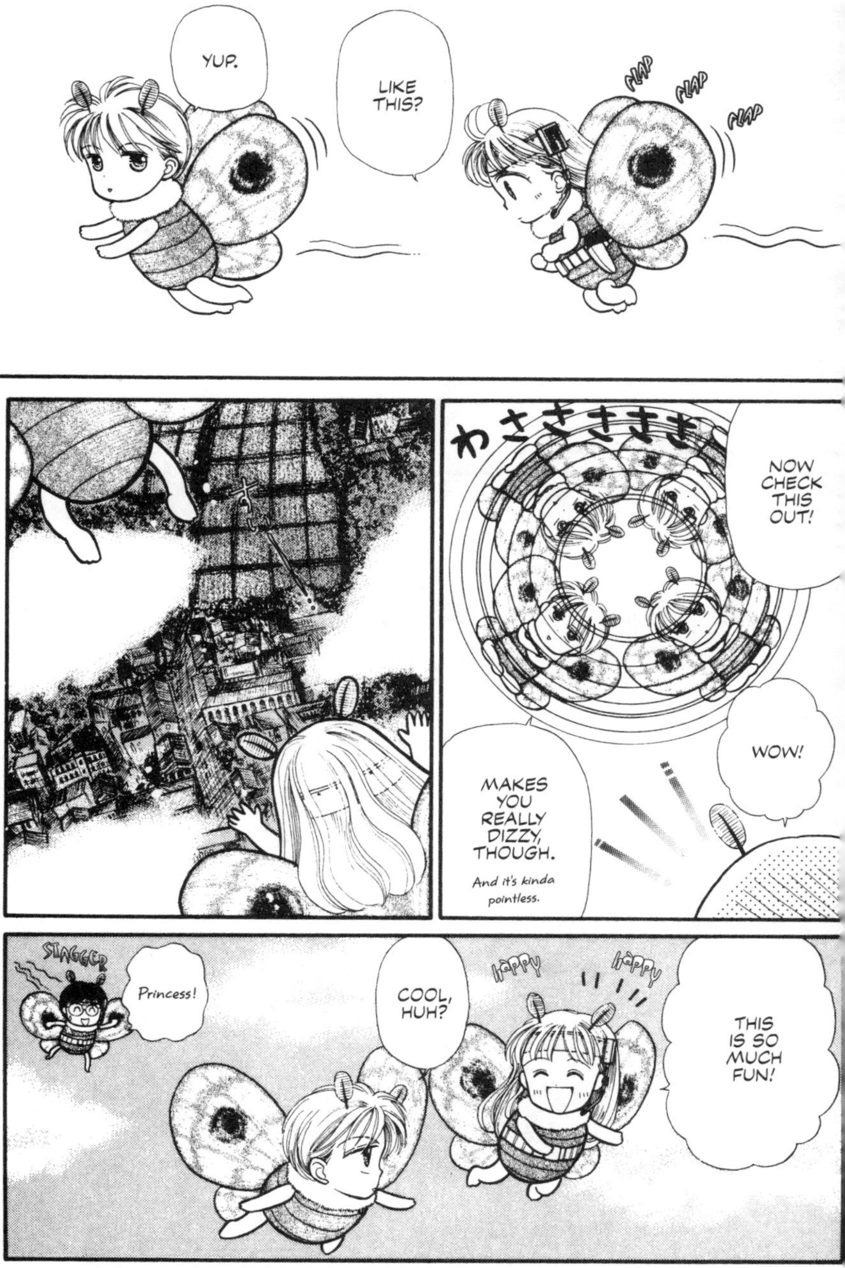
FLAP FLAP FLAP
LIKE THIS?
YUP.
わささささ
NOW CHECK THIS OUT!
WOW!
MAKES YOU REALLY DIZZY, THOUGH.
And it's kinda pointless.
THIS IS SO MUCH FUN!
happy happy
COOL, HUH?
STAGGER
Princess!

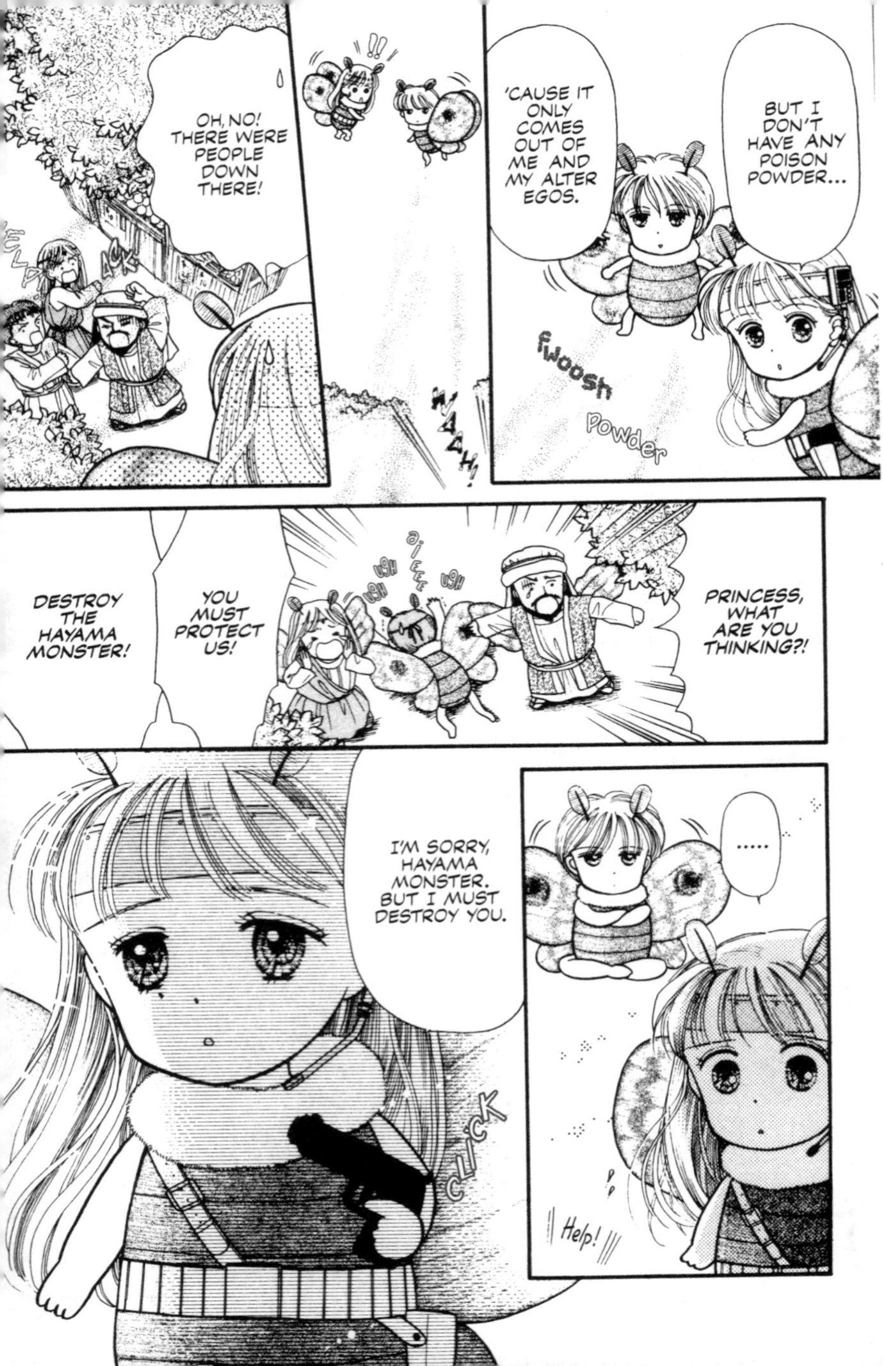
BUT I DON'T HAVE ANY POISON POWDER...
'CAUSE IT ONLY COMES OUT OF ME AND MY ALTER EGOS.
fwoosh
powder
!!
OH, NO! THERE WERE PEOPLE DOWN THERE!
ACK!
PRINCESS, WHAT ARE YOU THINKING?!
YOU MUST PROTECT US!
DESTROY THE HAYAMA MONSTER!
.....
Help!
I'M SORRY, HAYAMA MONSTER. BUT I MUST DESTROY YOU.
CLICK

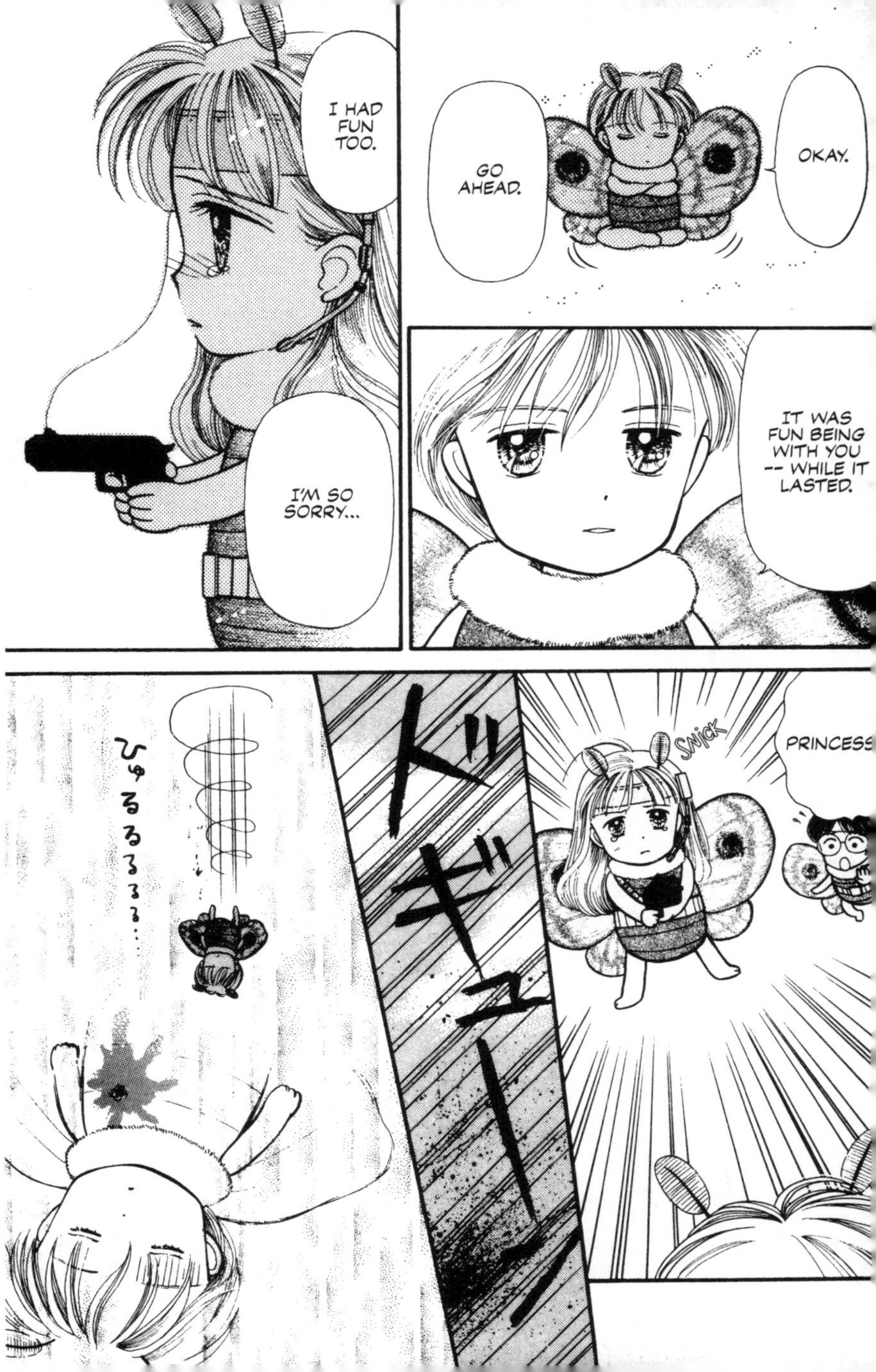
OKAY.
GO AHEAD.
IT WAS FUN BEING WITH YOU -- WHILE IT LASTED.
I HAD FUN TOO.
I'M SO SORRY...
PRINCESS
SNICK
ドギューーー
ひゅるるるる…

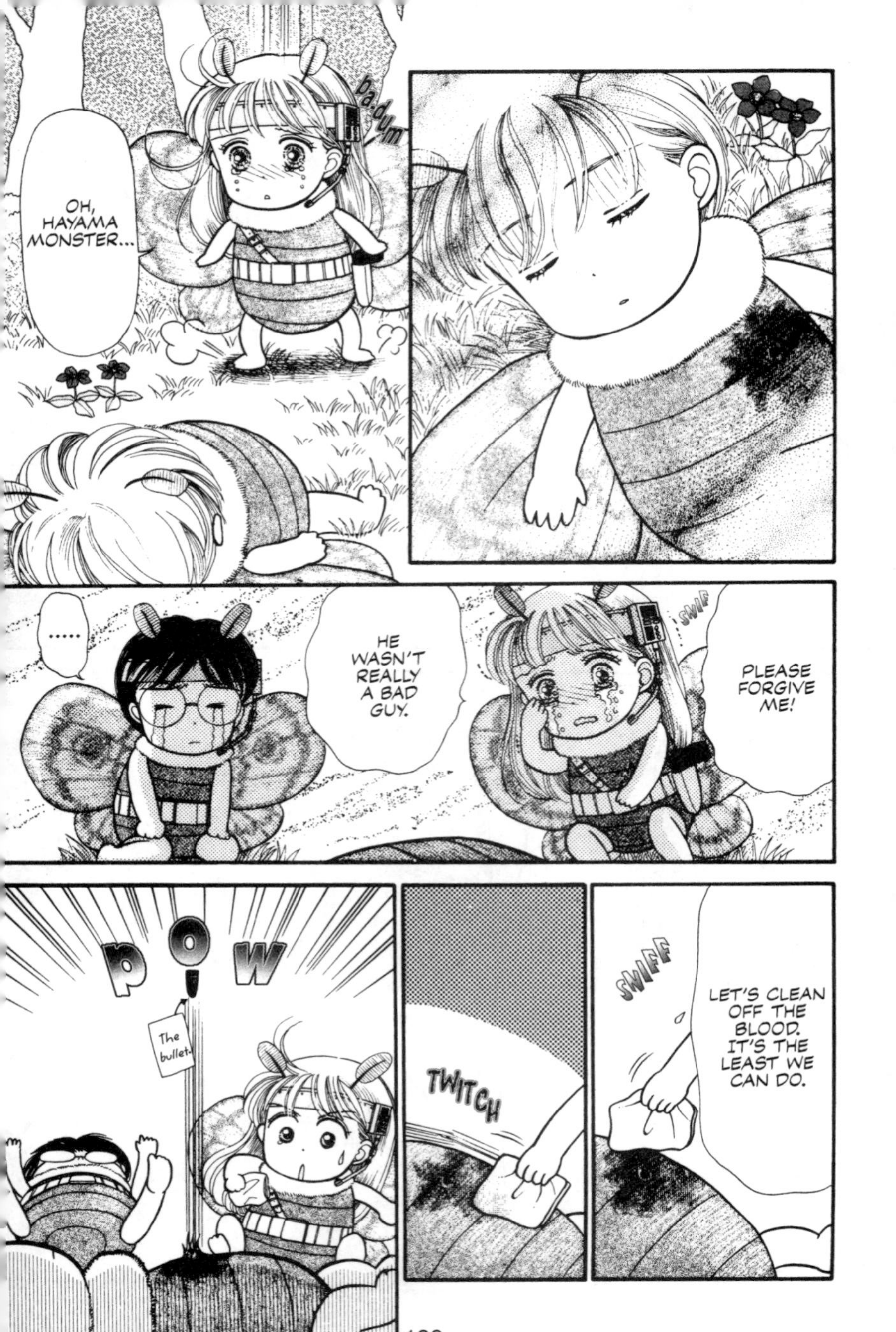
pa-dum
OH, HAYAMA MONSTER...
PLEASE FORGIVE ME!
SNIF
HE WASN'T REALLY A BAD GUY.
......
LET'S CLEAN OFF THE BLOOD. IT'S THE LEAST WE CAN DO.
SNIFF
TWITCH
POW
The bullet.

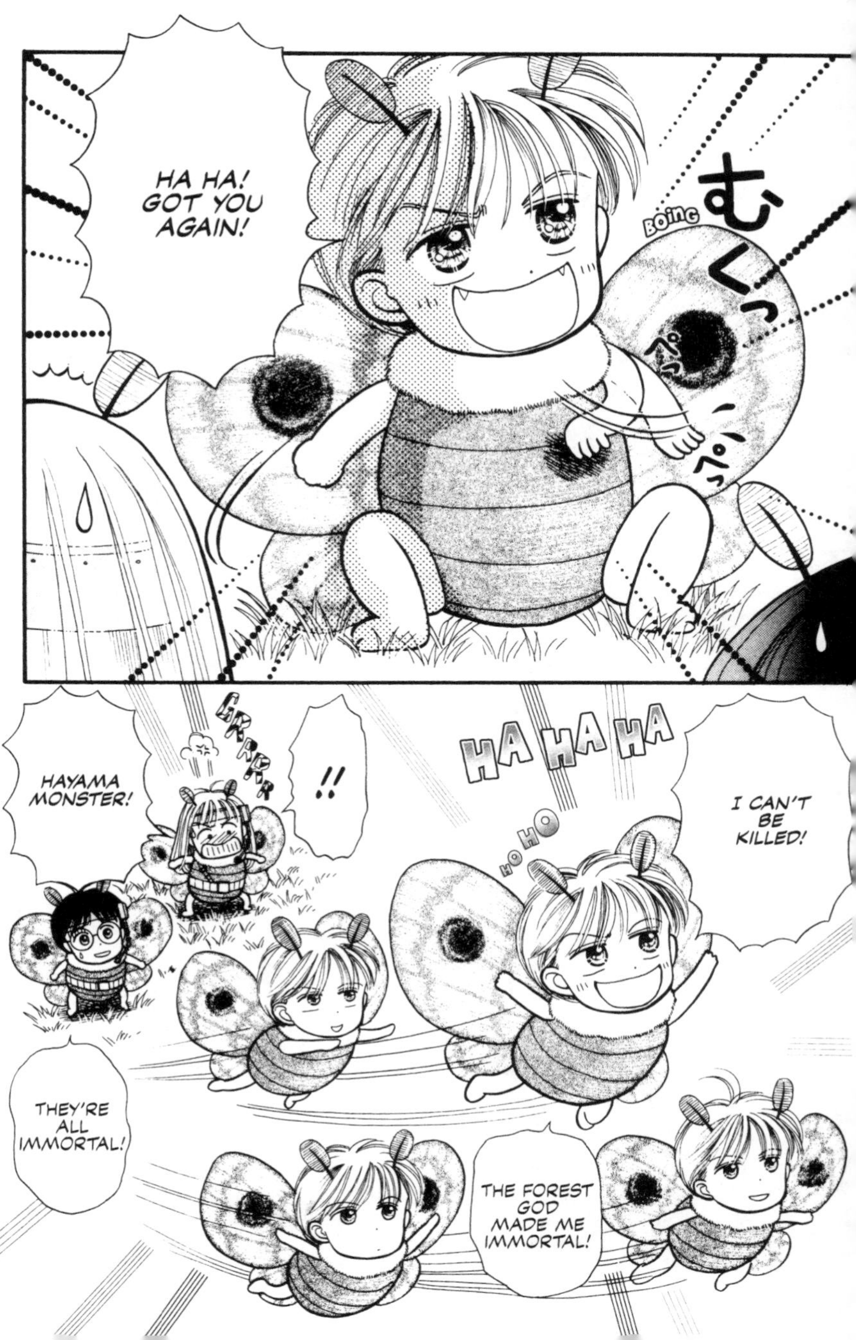

むくっ
BOING
HA HA! GOT YOU AGAIN!
I CAN'T BE KILLED!
HA HA HA HA
HO HO
!!
GRRRR
HAYAMA MONSTER!
THE FOREST GOD MADE ME IMMORTAL!
THEY'RE ALL IMMORTAL!

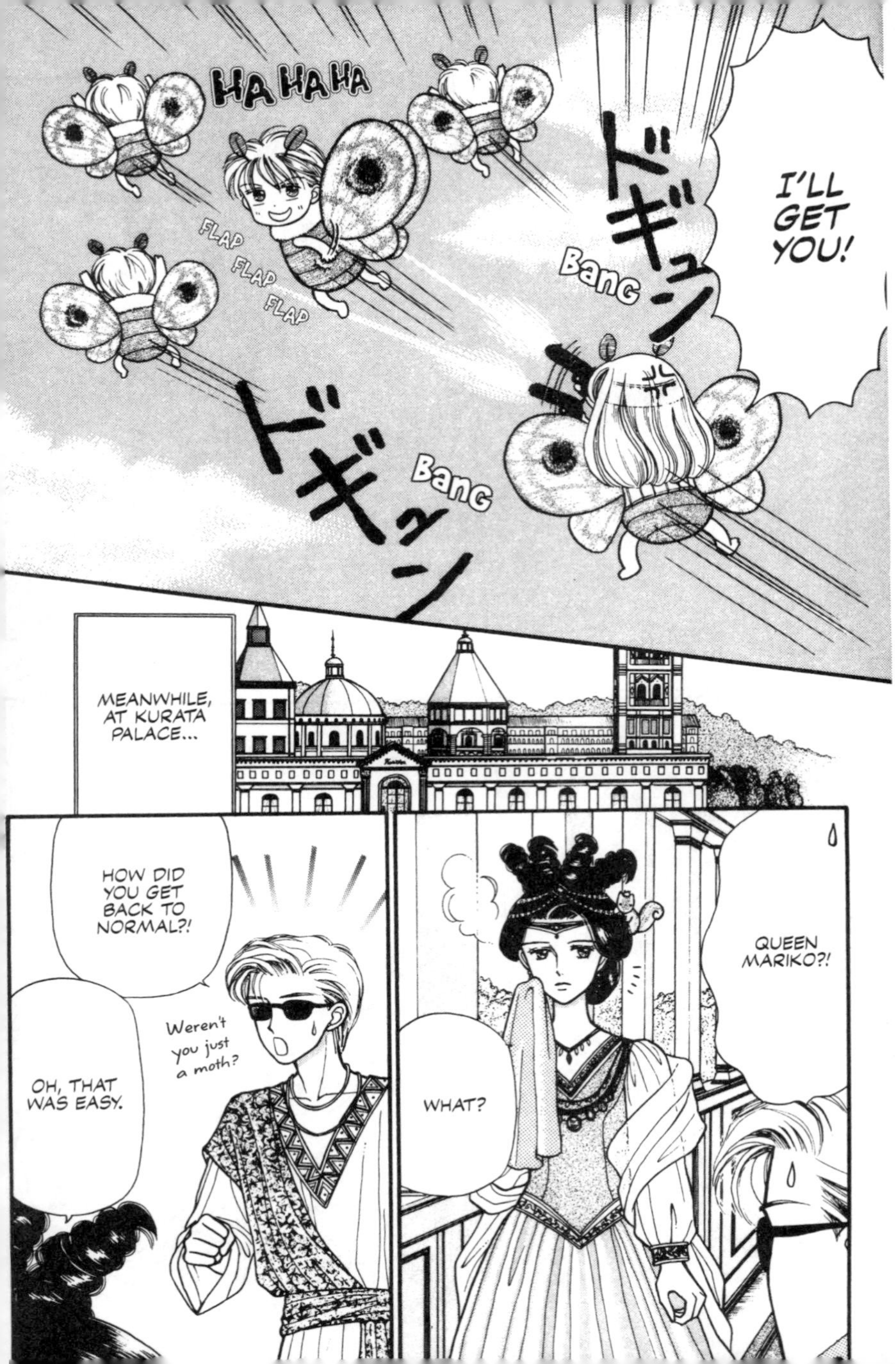
I'LL GET YOU!
ドギューン
Bang
HA HA HA
FLAP FLAP FLAP
ドギュン
Bang
MEANWHILE, AT KURATA PALACE...
QUEEN MARIKO?!
WHAT?
HOW DID YOU GET BACK TO NORMAL?!
Weren't you just a moth?
OH, THAT WAS EASY.

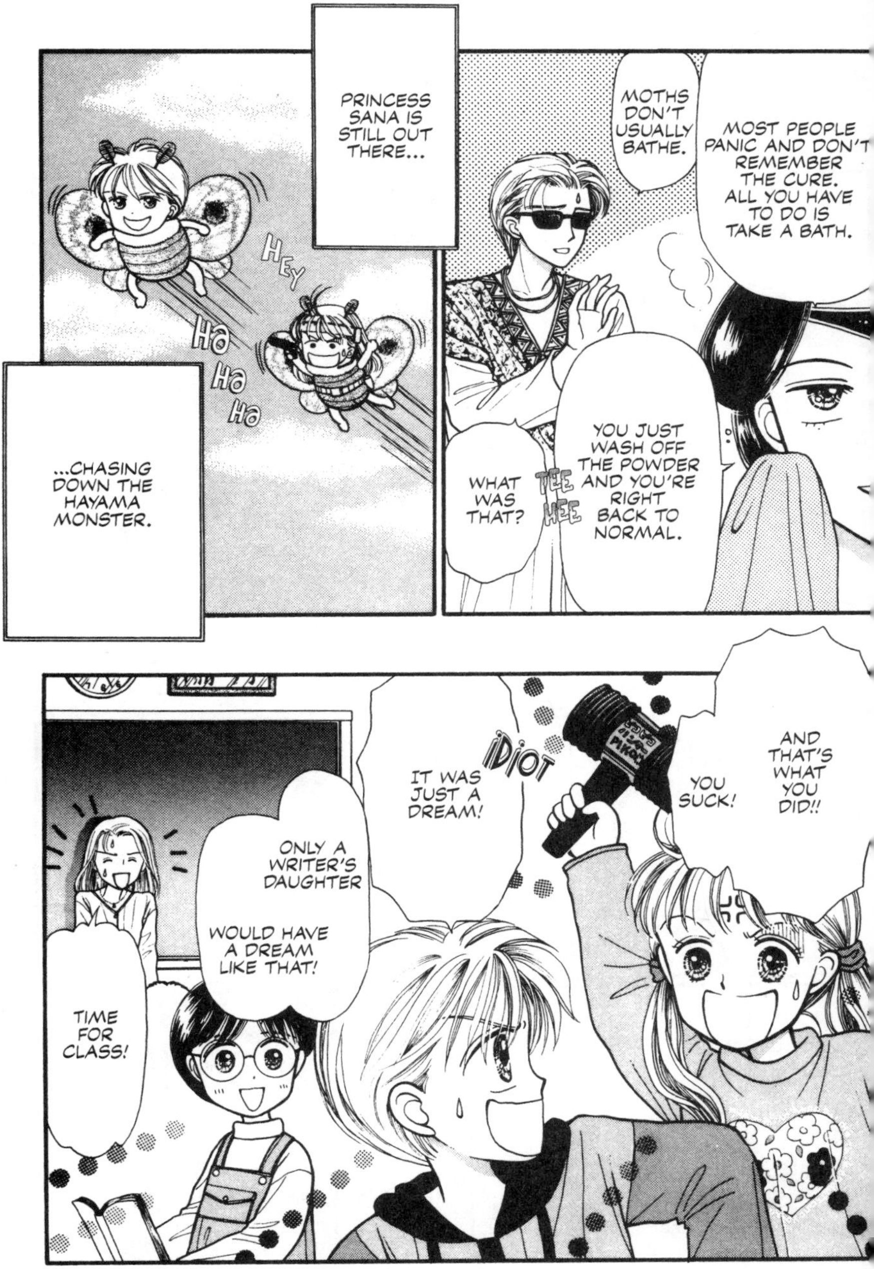
MOST PEOPLE PANIC AND DON'T REMEMBER THE CURE. ALL YOU HAVE TO DO IS TAKE A BATH.
MOTHS DON'T USUALLY BATHE.
YOU JUST WASH OFF THE POWDER AND YOU'RE RIGHT BACK TO NORMAL.
TEE HEE
WHAT WAS THAT?
PRINCESS SANA IS STILL OUT THERE...
HEY
HA HA HA HA
...CHASING DOWN THE HAYAMA MONSTER.
AND THAT'S WHAT YOU DID!!
YOU SUCK!
IDIOT
IT WAS JUST A DREAM!
ONLY A WRITER'S DAUGHTER
WOULD HAVE A DREAM LIKE THAT!
TIME FOR CLASS!

MARIKO AND MARO

THE WAY WE MET

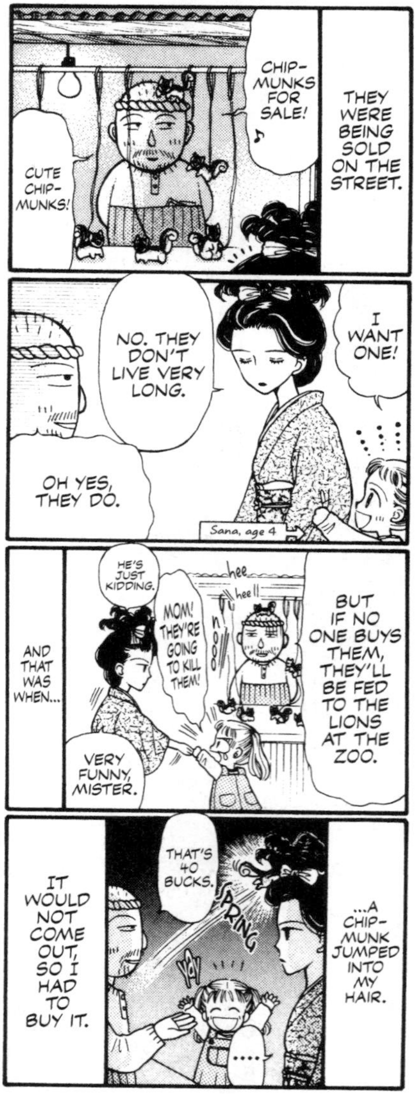

THEY WERE BEING SOLD ON THE STREET.
CHIPMUNKS FOR SALE! ♪
CUTE CHIPMUNKS!
I WANT ONE!
NO. THEY DON'T LIVE VERY LONG.
OH YES, THEY DO.
Sana, age 4
BUT IF NO ONE BUYS THEM, THEY'LL BE FED TO THE LIONS AT THE ZOO.
hee hee!!
MOM! THEY'RE GOING TO KILL THEM!
HE'S JUST KIDDING.
nooo
AND THAT WAS WHEN...
VERY FUNNY, MISTER.
...A CHIPMUNK JUMPED INTO MY HAIR.
SPRING
THAT'S 40 BUCKS.
yay
IT WOULD NOT COME OUT, SO I HAD TO BUY IT.
.....

FATE

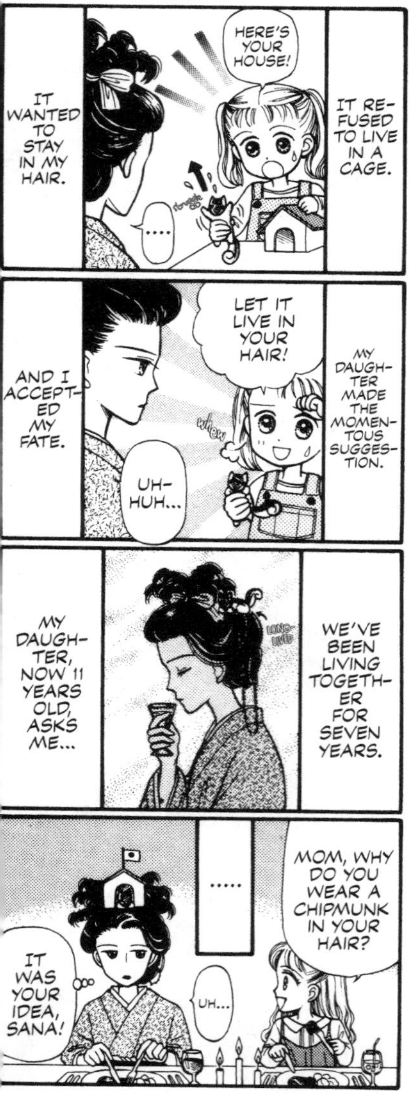

IT REFUSED TO LIVE IN A CAGE.
HERE'S YOUR HOUSE!
IT WANTED TO STAY IN MY HAIR.
.....
MY DAUGHTER MADE THE MOMENTOUS SUGGESTION.
LET IT LIVE IN YOUR HAIR!
whew
AND I ACCEPTED MY FATE.
UH-HUH...
WE'VE BEEN LIVING TOGETHER FOR SEVEN YEARS.
LONG-LIVED
MY DAUGHTER, NOW 11 YEARS OLD, ASKS ME...
MOM, WHY DO YOU WEAR A CHIPMUNK IN YOUR HAIR?
......
UH...
IT WAS YOUR IDEA, SANA!

MARIKO AND MARO

IT'S ALL IN YOUR HEAD

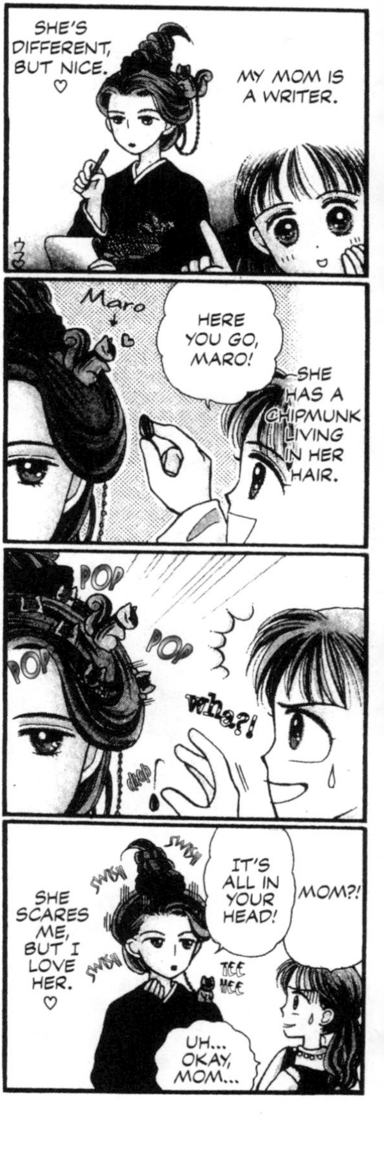
MY MOM IS A WRITER.
SHE'S DIFFERENT, BUT NICE. ♡
SHE HAS A CHIPMUNK LIVING IN HER HAIR.
HERE YOU GO, MARO!
Maro
POP
POP
wha?!
POP
drop
MOM?!
IT'S ALL IN YOUR HEAD!
SWISH
SWISH
SHE SCARES ME, BUT I LOVE HER. ♡
SWISH
TEE HEE
UH... OKAY, MOM...

IT HAPPENS A LOT

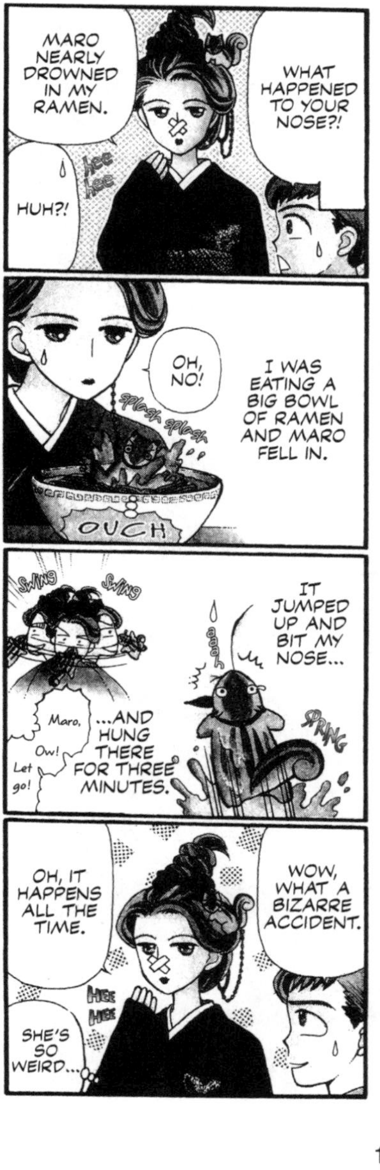
WHAT HAPPENED TO YOUR NOSE?!
MARO NEARLY DROWNED IN MY RAMEN.
hee hee
HUH?!
I WAS EATING A BIG BOWL OF RAMEN AND MARO FELL IN.
OH, NO!
splash splash
OUCH
IT JUMPED UP AND BIT MY NOSE...
SWING
SWING
SPRING
...AND HUNG THERE FOR THREE MINUTES.
Maro, Ow! Let go!
WOW, WHAT A BIZARRE ACCIDENT.
OH, IT HAPPENS ALL THE TIME.
HEE HEE
SHE'S SO WEIRD...

Coming Next!

Sana harbors a massive crush on her manager, the man she adoringly calls "gigolo" Rei. If Rei shatters Sana's adolescent notions of romance, will Hayama step in to pick up the pieces? Find out when Volume 2 of the *Kodocha* graphic novels hits the stands in July!

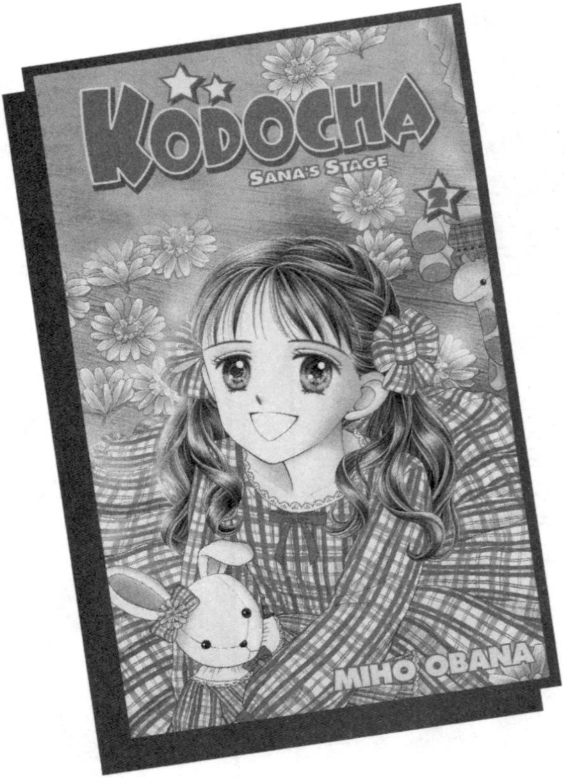
KODOCHA
SANA'S STAGE
2
MIHO OBANA

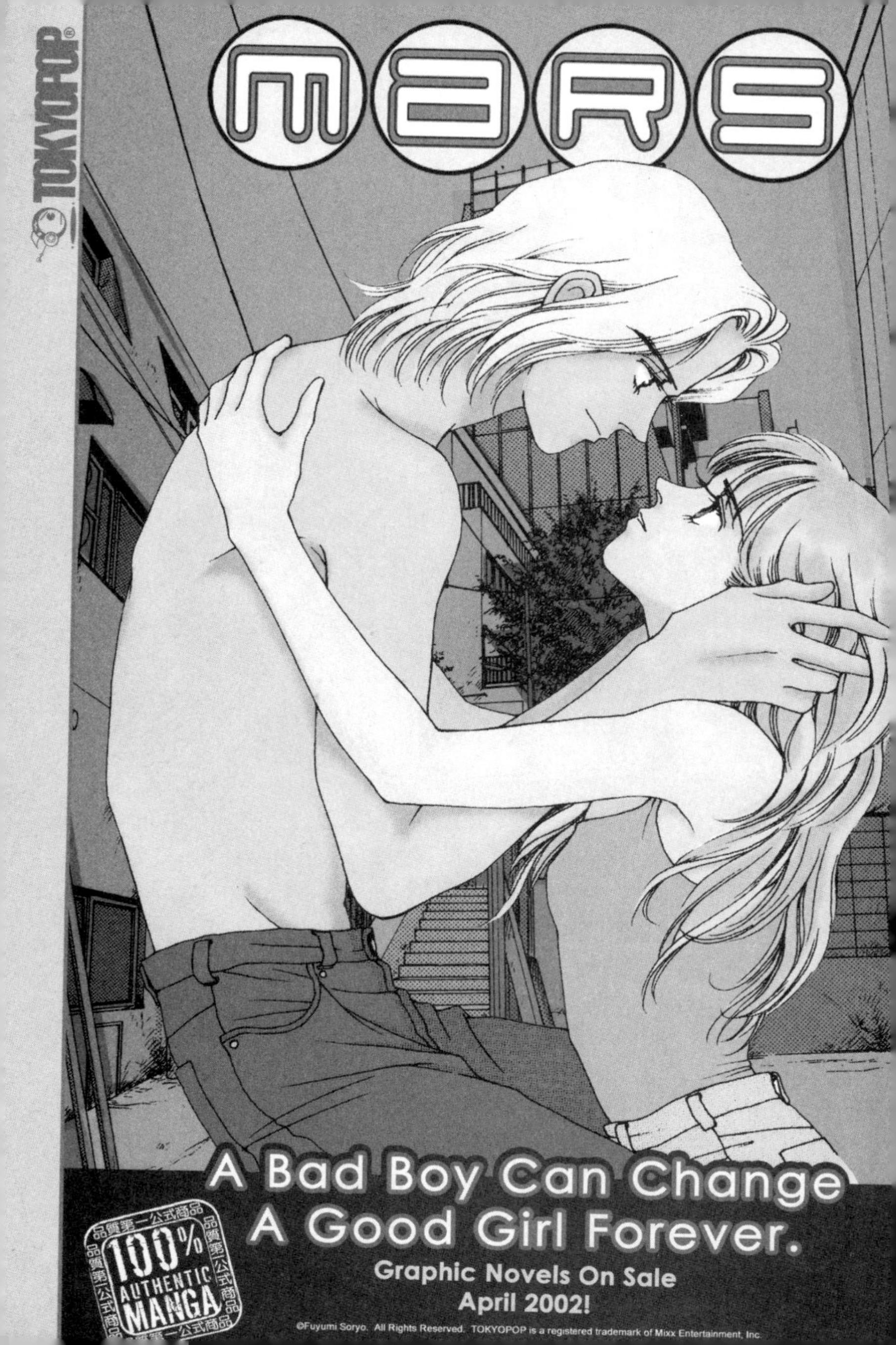
TOKYOPOP
MARS
A Bad Boy Can Change
A Good Girl Forever.
Graphic Novels On Sale
April 2002!
品質第一公式商品
100% AUTHENTIC MANGA
©Fuyumi Soryo. All Rights Reserved. TOKYOPOP is a registered trademark of Mixx Entertainment, Inc.

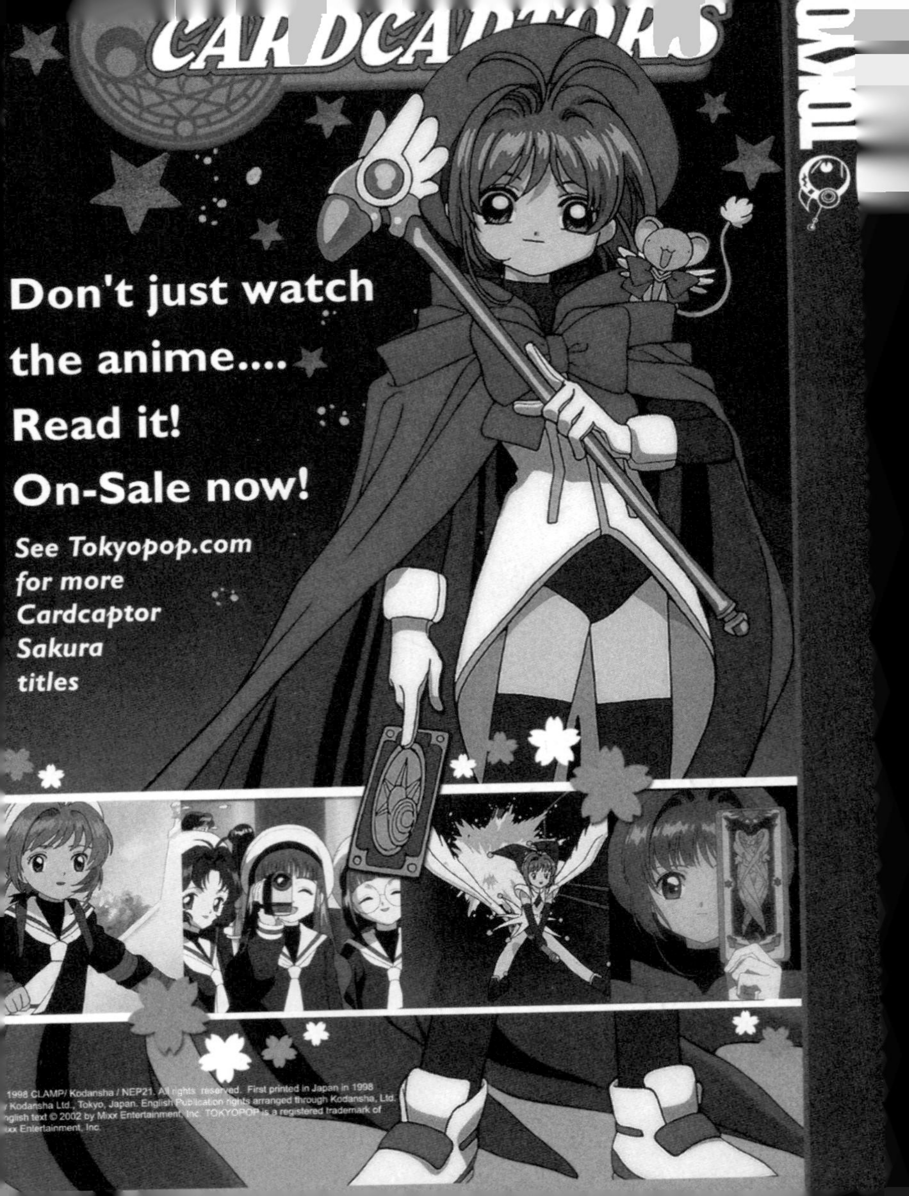

CARDCAPTORS
TOKYO
Don't just watch the anime....
Read it!
On-Sale now!
See Tokyopop.com for more Cardcaptor Sakura titles
1998 CLAMP/ Kodansha / NEP21. All rights reserved. First printed in Japan in 1998
Kodansha Ltd., Tokyo, Japan. English Publication rights arranged through Kodansha, Ltd.
nglish text © 2002 by Mixx Entertainment, Inc. TOKYOPOP is a registered trademark of
ixx Entertainment, Inc.

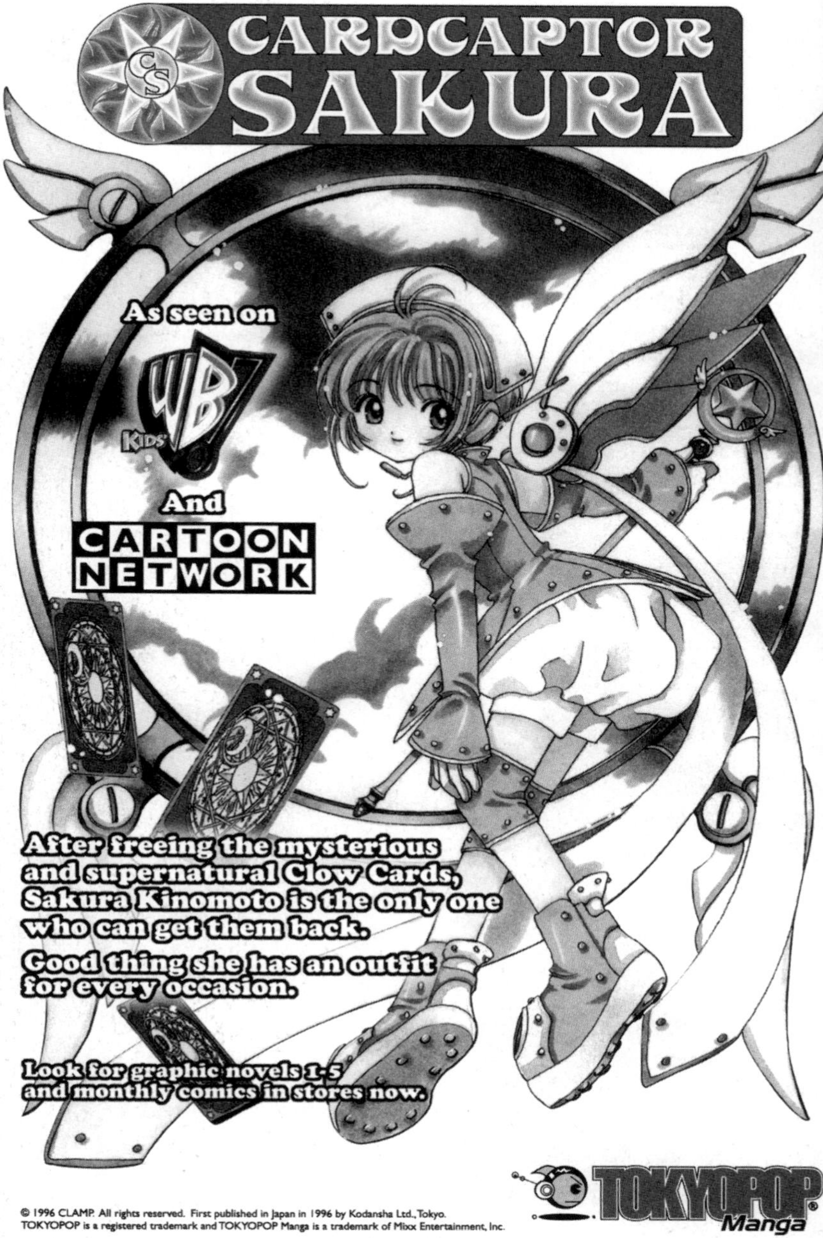
CARDCAPTOR SAKURA
As seen on
KIDS' WB
And
CARTOON NETWORK
After freeing the mysterious and supernatural Clow Cards, Sakura Kinomoto is the only one who can get them back.
Good thing she has an outfit for every occasion.
Look for graphic novels 1-5 and monthly comics in stores now.
TOKYOPOP® Manga

STOP!

This is the back of the book.
ou wouldn't want to spoil a great ending!

This book is printed "manga-style," in the authentic Japanese right-to-left format. Since none of the artwork has been flipped or altered, readers get to experience the story just as the creator intended. You've been asking for it, so TOKYOPOP® delivered: authentic, hot-off-the-press, and far more fun!

DIRECTIONS

If this is your first time reading manga-style, here's a quick guide to help you understand how it works.

It's easy... just start in the top right panel and follow the numbers. Have fun, and look for more 100% authentic manga from TOKYOPOP®!